IMMIGRATION OFFICER
★ ( ) ★
27 SEP 2001
HEATHROW (4)

IMMIGRATION DIVISION BANGKOK THAILAND
A
72
DEPARTED
- 6 FEB 1998
SIGNED

MENT OF IMMIGRAT
MITTED TO ENTER
AUSTRALIA
24 APR 1996
For stay of 12 Month
SYDNEY AIRPORT 54

IMMIGRATION & ETHNIC AFFAIRS
Person
30 OCT 1999
DEPARTED
AUSTRALIA
SYDNEY 32

人民共和国
东省公安厅

上陸許可
ADMITTED
15. FEB. 1996
Status: 4-1-   4
Duration: 90 days
NARITA(N)
Immigration Inspector
日本国

ADMITTED
20 OCT. 1998
Status: 4-1-16
Duration 180 days
Port: HANEDA
Signature

№ 011278

THE UNITED STATES
OF AMERICA
NONIMMIGRANT VISA
ISSUED AT
SED Air Port

U.S. IMMIGRATION
170 HHW 1710
JUL 20 1998

TRAVELER'S
SOUTHERN
ENGLAND
COMPANION

D1501892

The 2001–2002 Traveler's Companions
ARGENTINA • AUSTRALIA • BALI • CALIFORNIA • CANADA • CHILI • CHINA •
COSTA RICA • CUBA • EASTERN CANADA • ECUADOR • FLORIDA • HAWAII •
HONG KONG • INDIA • INDONESIA • IRELAND • JAPAN • KENYA •
MALAYSIA & SINGAPORE • MEDITERRANEAN FRANCE • MEXICO • NEPAL •
NEW ENGLAND • NEW ZEALAND • NORTHERN ITALY • PERU • PHILIPPINES •
PORTUGAL • RUSSIA • SOUTH AFRICA • SOUTHERN ENGLAND • SPAIN • THAILAND •
TURKEY • VENEZUELA • VIETNAM, LAOS AND CAMBODIA • WESTERN CANADA

Traveler's SOUTHERN ENGLAND Companion

First published 2001
The Globe Pequot Press
246 Goose Lane, PO Box 480
Guilford, CT 06437 USA
www.globe-pequot.com

© 2001 by The Globe Pequot Press, Guilford CT, USA

ISBN: 0-7267-0580-9

Distributed in the European Union by
World Leisure Marketing Ltd, Unit 11
Newmarket Court, Newmarket Drive,
Derby, DE24 8NW, United Kingdom
www.map-guides.com

Created, edited and produced by
Allan Amsel Publishing, 53, rue Beaudouin
27700 Les Andelys, France.
E-mail: Allan.Amsel@wanadoo.fr
Editor in Chief: Allan Amsel
Editor: Anne Trager
Original design concept: Hon Bing-wah
Picture editor and book designer: Roberto Rossi

Printed by Samhwa Printing Co. Ltd., Seoul, South Korea

TRAVELER'S
SOUTHERN
ENGLAND
COMPANION

by Laura Purdom

Photographed by Nik Wheeler

The
Globe
Pequot
Press

GUILFORD CONNECTICUT

Contents

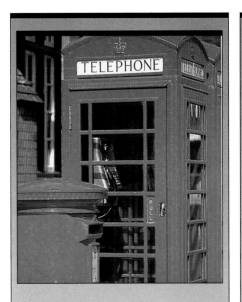

TRAVELER'S SOUTHERN ENGLAND COMPANION

SHROPSHI
Kiddermi
WOR
HEREFORDSHI
Hereford
Ross-on-Wye
Glou
G
NORTH
SOMER
Newport
Bristol
A4 Bat
Bradford-on-A
From

WALES

ATLANTIC OCEAN

Lundy Island
Ilfracombe
Dunster
Exmoor National Park
Bridgewater
Wells
SOMERSET
Bideford Bay
Barnstaple
Dulverton
Taunton
Clovelly
Bideford
Yeovil
Bude
DEVON
Honiton
M5
Okehampton
Exeter
DO
Launceston
Lydford
Lyme Regis
Dorcheste
Altarnun
Dartmoor National Park
Padstow
Tavistock
Exmouth
Isle of
Wey
CORNWALL
Bodmin
Buckfastleigh
Newton Abbot
Portland
Newquay
Liskeard
Torquay
St. Agnes
St. Austell
Darlington
Paignton
Camborne
Truro
Fowey
Looe
Totnes
St. Ives
Veryan
Polperro
Plymouth
Dartmouth
Penzance
Trescowe
St. Mawes
Kingsbridge
LAND'S END
Portleven
Falmouth
Salcombe
Lizard Peninsula
Lizard

Isles of Scilly

LEGEND

Populations

- ◉ **London** — Capital
- ○ Oxford — Cities & Large Towns
- ○ Leeds — Small Towns

Transportation

- Secondary (B) Roads
- A338 — Primary (A) Roads
- A3 — Main Routes (A) Roads
- M25 — Motorways
- Railways

Physical Features

- Bordering Countries
- National and County Boundaries
- Forests, Reserves, and National Parks
- Lakes and Rivers
- 3,030 ▲ Mountains

0 10 20 30 40 km
0 5 10 15 20 25 miles

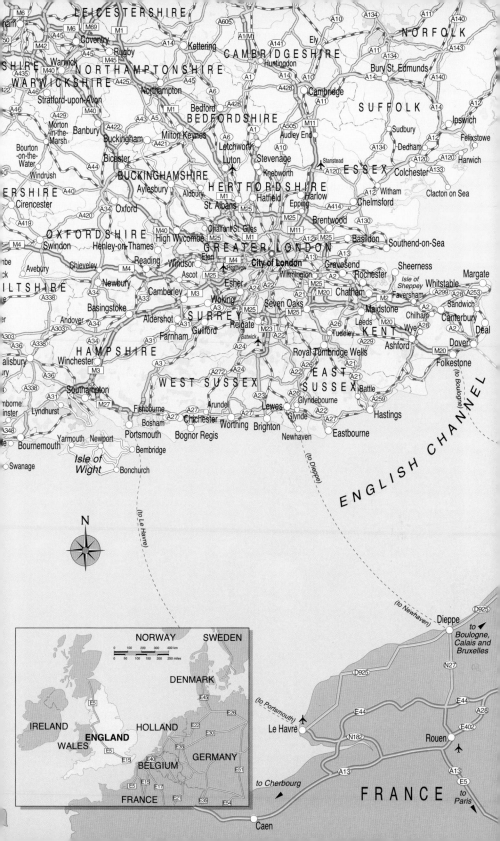

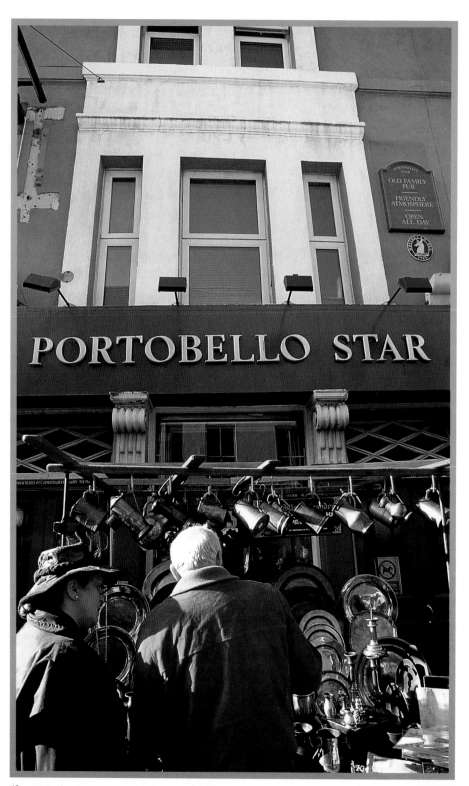

TOP SPOTS

To Market, to Market...

IF YOU WANT A SLICE OF AUTHENTIC LONDON LIFE, TAKE AN EARLY MORNING STROLL THROUGH A CITY STREET MARKET. London street markets date back to the Middle Ages, when every neighborhood had its own "cheap" (*ceap* was the Saxon word for market) overflowing with mediaeval merchandise. Today these markets represent a microcosm of this sprawling city, offering everything from high-priced antiques to bargain-basement junk, and from organic produce to kebabs and curry.

Which of London's historic markets you choose to explore will depend on your interests, but the cardinal rule at every market is: arrive early.

No one should pass up a trip to Portobello Road Market ((020) 7243-3419, from Chepstow Villas to Elgin Crescent in W11. Actually several markets in one, Portobello is at its acme on early Saturday mornings. This animated market boasts some 2,000 stalls and shopkeepers selling furniture, Victorian glassware, teddy bears, cocktail shakers, retired typewriters, ink pots, coins, paintings, silverware, gizmos and gee-gaws. Congenial crowds of shoppers mill through the streets elbow to elbow, lending the scene a festival air, but Portobello's true allure is quite simply its heaps of amazing *stuff*.

Continue down the slope of Portobello Road for the food market (Monday to Wednesday 9 AM to 5 PM; Thursday to 1 PM, and Friday and Saturday 7 AM to 6 PM), where on Thursdays (11 AM to 6 PM) there is a wonderful organic market as well.

Under the Westway flyover between Portobello Road and Ladbroke Grove the merchandise turns to clothing, crafts and oddments ((020) 7229-6898 — lots of second-hand fashions here, as well as young designers' wares, while Fridays are devoted to retro styles (Friday 7 AM to 4 PM, Saturday 8 AM to 5 PM, and Sunday 9 AM to 4 PM). At the end of the line, Golborne Road W10, between Portobello and Wornington roads, has imported fabrics, kimonos, second-hand furniture shops and Portuguese cafés (Monday to Saturday 9 AM to 5 PM). ⊖ Ladbroke Grove, Notting Hill Gate or Westbourne Park.

The oldest of the London markets is Leadenhall, on Whittington Avenue off Gracechurch and Leadenhall streets in EC3. Set in Victorian glass and iron arcades dating from 1881, trading here began as early as the fourteenth century, when poultry was the specialty. Today the gaily painted hall is a haven for delicatessens, wine bars, chocolate shops and fresh-produce stalls. It's especially lively during lunchtime. Open weekdays 7 AM to 4 PM. ⊖ Monument or ⊖/DLR Bank.

It's said that of all the London markets, the sprawling East End institution of Brick Lane comes closest to an authentic old-time market

London's Portobello Road and Camden markets draw crowds of bargain hunters and sightseers.

Hartland Road NW1, has food stalls, antiques, millennium fashions and a cyber café (Sunday 8 AM to 6 PM). Camden Lock ((020) 7284-2084 is a cobbled courtyard with handmade crafts, vegetarian food stalls and 1970s post-hippie threads (Saturday and Sunday 10 AM to 6 PM). Shop for up-to-the-minute designer clothing at Camden Canal Market, off Chalk Farm Road, south of Castle Haven Road junction NW1 (weekends 10 AM to 6 PM). Finally, the Electric Ballroom ((020) 7485-9006, Camden High Street NW1, is a nightclub that has a clothing fair on Sundays and occasional used vinyl sales on Saturdays (9 AM to 5:30 PM). ⊖ Camden Town or Chalk Farm.

Once you've had a taste of London's street markets your soul may cry out for more. If so, look for Phillip Harriss's entertaining and informative *London Markets* (Cadogan, 1999).

Make a Date with the "Daffs"

VISIT ONE OF ENGLAND'S GREAT GARDENS BEFORE THE PEAK SEASON AND UNEARTH A SECRET: THERE IS YEAR-ROUND COLOR IN THESE CULTIVATED ACRES.
To be sure, high season in the garden (variably late spring through summer), ushers in the full complement of colors, but it also brings the full complement of crowds and queues. By contrast, the only lines you'll see in March and early April are neatly clipped rows of hedges; the only crowds, bursts of early bloomers.

Besides, there is something so essentially *English* about early spring — an irresistible mix of "dodgy" weather, a spare landscape laden with good things to come, and a log glowing on the grate when you return from an afternoon of exploration. Winter's cycle of regeneration (when most gardens are closed) leads seamlessly into early spring as waxy white snowdrops decorate the woodlands — so delicate, it's difficult at times to distinguish these blossoms from the dustings of snow that can frost the landscape at this time of year. Ruby-red cascades of japonica blossoms frame garden gates and, best of all, seas of thigh-high, canary-yellow and paper-white daffodils, or "daffs" as the Brits call them, undulate in the vernal breeze.

Perhaps nowhere is the English garden's peak-off-peak seasonal contrast so apparent than at Sissinghurst Castle Garden in West Sussex. One of Southern England's most popular gardens during the high season, it is virtually ignored in early spring — and utterly lovely.

Now the property of the National Trust, Sissinghurst was created by the poet and novelist Vita Sackville-West and her husband Harold Nicholson, historian and diplomat. The couple

scene, with its down-at-heel traders offering just about everything, including the kitchen sink. It's not a tourist destination, but it's wildly popular with Londoners and thick with the cries of costermongers and the scents of the seven continents. The most interesting parts of the market are beyond Brick Lane proper, so be sure to explore further afield especially along Cheshire Street where, interspersed with trinkets and machine parts, you'll find some antiques stalls. Brick Lane Market spreads out over the streets of Brick Lane, as well as Cygnet, Sclater, Bacon, and Cheshire streets E1 and E2. Open Sunday from 6 AM to 1 PM. ⊖ Aldgate East, Bethnal Green, Shoreditch or ⊖/BR Liverpool Street.

The biggest market in London, as well as the city's fourth most popular tourist attraction, is Camden Market. Best on Sunday mornings, this vast street mart extends between Camden Town and Chalk Farm tube stations, attracting hundreds of thousands of people each week. The most concentrated part is along Camden High Street NW1. This is ripe territory for harvests of clothing and jewelry, but look out for high-priced junk. Market encampments continue on and off Chalk Farm Road (the continuation of High Street) where there are also several indoor venues: The Stables ((020) 7485-5511, off Chalk Farm Road across from

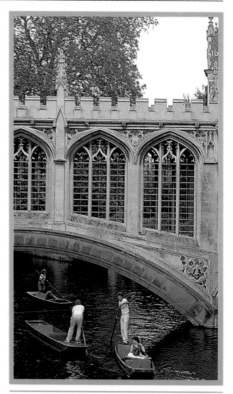

moved here in the 1930s and set to work on the ruined Elizabethan manor. Using the existing buildings and walls as a starting point, they divided the two-and-a-half-hectare (six-acre) space into a "succession of intimacies," as Harold described it: the white garden with its silvery foliage, the rose garden with scores of rare varieties, the lime walk with its pollarded lime trees and Tuscan vases brimming with impatiens, the cottage garden dressed in yellows and oranges with small beds and narrow paths and a single weathered wooden bench.

Granted some of this takes a little imagination on a damp spring day. For example, should you return in summer you'll be treated to a show of wisteria flowing over the moat walk echoing the voluptuous lines of Sir Edwin Lutyens' wooden benches along its banks. And your garden guidebook will note that while the orchard is full of daffodils in spring, later the fruit trees send out delicate blossoms and finally roses trail up through the trees giving a third burst of color in June and July.

Anyone who is game for an early tour of Sissinghurst, or any of dozens of other great Southern English gardens, will soon discover their off-season magic. For the moment these beauties are all yours — no queues, no timed tickets, no crowds. The ladies' clubs and tourist coaches are waiting for riper times.

Are You Oxford or Cambridge?

A VISIT TO BRITAIN'S TIMELESS ENCLAVES OF ACADEMIA, OXFORD AND CAMBRIDGE, IS A REQUISITE OF ANY TOUR OF THE ISLAND. But for the traveler with limited time, the similarities of these twin cities can lead to quandary: Which shall I plump for?

So strong is the resemblance between Oxford and Cambridge that tradition often lumps them under the composite name of "Oxbridge." They have comparable origins, share a common history, and organize their colleges along similar lines. In fact, Cambridge began as an off-shoot of Oxford when, in 1208, a group of scholars left Oxford to found a new center of learning. Both universities are veritable textbooks of English architectural history, with splendid buildings running from Saxon to Perpendicular Gothic to Palladian. Both offer the romance of "punting" on simple Venetian-style boats. Both cities have excellent museums, good restaurants and fun shopping.

Despite the cities' comparable merits, since the days of the first Baedeker's guide,

OPPOSITE: Elegant Eastbourne, in Sussex, blossoms with color. ABOVE LEFT: Oxford, "city of dreaming spires." RIGHT: Punting below the Bridge of Sighs, St. John's College, Cambridge.

Oxford has almost always been given the blue ribbon as a tourist destination while Cambridge has received the honorable mention: "if time allows." Today that trend continues, largely because of Oxford's central position on the tourist trail between London and the Cotswolds.

Yet it is more than their locations that set the two halves of Oxbridge apart. Those who crave a big city-buzz will likely prefer the larger, more urban, Oxford, whose famous "dreaming spires" and hilly setting contribute to its bustling skyline.

On the other hand, anyone with romantic inclinations will surely be seduced by the greener and less touristy Cambridge. Here, rather than marching along the street, colleges look wistfully down on the Backs. These green meadows spread out below the back gates of the colleges create a natural complement to the clipped lawns of the inner courtyards. Crossed by sparkling streams, the Backs seem tailor-made for picnics, promenades or impromptu games of cricket. Wrought-iron gates — sculpted with acanthus leaves and, for the richer colleges like Trinity, flashy gold leaf — further separate academia from nature and the workaday world.

Perhaps above all else, Oxford and Cambridge share a capacity to uphold the status quo with more proud tenacity than any other place in England. For the scholars and dons of Oxbridge, tradition is crystallized in a host of time-honored customs and odd-ball sporting events. For visitors, however, Oxbridge tradition is a more subtle commodity absorbed as one walks the streets in the context of the two cities' glorious architectural heritage.

The stunning seashell-shaped entrance to the Tate St. Ives overlooks the golden sands of St. Ives' Porthmeor beach. Inside, its sunny galleries and curving halls were inspired by the light and landscape of the town and its surroundings. Showing the significance of Cornwall to twentieth-century art, the heart of the Tate collection reflects the work of the St. Ives School from the 1920s onward. There are the cubist paintings of Ben Nicholson (1894–1982); Barbara Hepworth's earthy, abstract sculptures and paintings (1903–1975); and much more, including Patrick Heron's (1920–1999) vivid stained-glass window, which permanently adorns the gallery entrance.

The highlight of a St. Ives art tour is a visit to the Barbara Hepworth Museum and Garden, located in the artist's former home, Trewyn (ticketed with the Tate, but located across town). One of the many artists who migrated to West Cornwall over the last century, Barbara Hepworth arrived in St. Ives in 1939 and, with her husband Ben Nicholson, became one of the driving forces of the artists' colony in this seaside town. Hepworth moved to Trewyn Studio in 1949 and lived there until her death in 1975. Now her studio and gardens offer visitors a rare opportunity to see art in the context of the artist's own life. Some of the original furniture is in the upstairs room and photos show the studio as it looked in the 1950s, with the slight form of Hepworth alongside her monumental sculptures. In the artist's workshop, tools, half-formed chunks of marble, and a row of spattered work coats remain just as she left them. The garden was Hepworth's own creation, and she filled it with her sculptures: several large stone works and 18 bronzes stand there amid greenery and blossoms. It was at Trewyn, late in life, that Hepworth found international recognition. She is considered to have been one of the greatest sculptors of the twentieth century.

In addition to the Tate and Hepworth's studio, there are scores of galleries to explore in and around St. Ives. A handful of choices are listed in ST. IVES, page 309 in DEVON AND CORNWALL. Visitors can even roll up their sleeves and participate in classes at the St. Ives Painting School ((01736) 797180 (24-hour information) FAX (01736) 797174, Porthmeor Studios, Back Road West, St. Ives TR26 1NG. Week-long courses run from May to October, and Saturday life classes are held throughout the year.

St. Ives and the Art of Vacationing

ST. IVES HAS BEEN A MAGNET FOR ARTISTS SINCE THE EIGHTEENTH CENTURY, WHEN THE PENINSULA'S DRAMATIC LANDSCAPE BEGAN DRAWING ARTISTS TO THIS REMOTE CORNER OF ENGLAND. British landscape painter J.M.W. Turner (1775–1851) and the American painter James Whistler (1834–1903) were the first noted artists to visit the picturesque fishing village of St. Ives. From these charmed beginnings the movement grew through the twentieth century. Today St. Ives and West Cornwall harbor perhaps England's greatest concentration of sculptors and painters outside London, along with scores of galleries including the Tate St. Ives, the London gallery's exquisite West Country outpost.

A turquoise sea and golden sands frame the artists' colony of St. Ives, Cornwall, the Tate Gallery's West Country outpost.

Despite its omnipresence, not everyone comes to St. Ives for the modern art. There is plenty of artistry outside the town's galleries and studios — on the beaches and headlands, in the warren of the old fishing village, in sweeping views of the blue Atlantic. And beyond the town are the stunning uplands of the Penwith Peninsula, its cliff walks, prehistoric remains, and secret sandy beaches. It's all there for the traveler who understands the art of vacationing.

A Cotswold Ramble

THERE IS NO MORE POPULAR PLACE FOR MOTORING IN ENGLAND THAN THE COTSWOLDS — AND FOR GOOD REASON. The country lanes that connect one quaint village to another seem tailor-made for leisurely drives. Because it is so well-loved, the region can get crowded, but with a reliable map, it's easy to discover less traveled parts. The following tour takes in some of the best of the Northern Cotswolds on and off the beaten track.

Starting from the Georgian spa town of Cheltenham, drive north towards Cheltenham Racecourse, home of the National Hunt Festival, which takes place each March. From the traffic circle continue into Prestbury, then proceed in the direction of Winchcombe to begin the ascent of Cleeve Hill.

Just after passing the Hotel de la Bere, turn left onto Southam Lane entering the village of Southam. In the midst of this suburban settlement, a signpost points the way to a tiny twelfth-century church, studded with jewel-like windows, and a tithe barn opposite. Tithe barns such as this one can be seen throughout the Cotswolds. They were used in the Middle Ages to store the "tithe," 10% of each parishioner's annual crop, used by the church for upkeep and to aid the poor. The church is open summer weekends from 2 PM to 4 PM, or it's possible to visit for Sunday services at 10:30 AM.

Returning to the main road, continue to the pull-over area at the summit of Cleave Hill, at 312 m (1,040 ft), the highest point in the Cotswolds, looking out over the Severn Vale. From here a footpath leads over the rolling hills of Cleave Common, which offers some of the finest walking in the area. Continuing down the sloping road, you enter Winchcombe (page 158), an ancient wool village, that is well worth taking time to explore on foot outside the peak traveling season. A bit further along the B4632 is Hailes Abbey (page 159), founded in 1246 and laid to ruin during the

The Cotswolds — ABOVE: Motoring through Stanton. OPPOSITE: The sleepy village of Chedworth.

dissolution of the monasteries in the sixteenth century. It is open to the public.

Another one and a half kilometers (one mile) along the B4632 leads to the B4077 which you should now follow in the direction of Stow-on-the-Wold. At the junction of these routes is the entrance to the *Gloucester &Warwickshire Railway*, where a vintage steam train takes passengers on a 21-km (13-mile) round-trip excursion. After just over a kilometer (about three quarters of mile), turn left at the signs for Stanway and Stanton.

As you round the bend, the fine Jacobean gatehouse of Stanway House ((01386) 584469 comes into view. This manor house, home of Lord Neidpath, was built of golden limestone in the days of Elizabeth I. It's open for guided tours from 2 PM to 5 PM, Tuesday and Thursday from June to September. Other times by appointment.

The country lane that continues north towards Stanton dawdles through picturesque sheep pastures. Should you travel along it in early evening you're sure to see dozens of pheasants. Once in Stanton you can wet your whistle with a local brew at the Mount Inn (no phone), set atop a hill.

Returning to the B4632, head north into the handsome wool village of Broadway (page 166). There's much to explore here, including Snowshill Manor and village to the south and Broadway Hill Tower (with commanding views of the countryside). Continue on toward Chipping Campden and Hidcote Manor Garden to the northeast, or take the A429 south to Stow-on-the-Wold where the little villages of Upper and Lower Swell are islands of serenity.

The A429 continues south to Bourton-on-the-Water and The Slaughter s (pages 162 and 164). From here travel west to connect with the A40 back to Cheltenham.

A similar route, as well as other drives, is described in *The Romantic Road,* available for £3.95 from Cheltenham Tourism ((01242) 522878 FAX (01242) 255848 E-MAIL tic@cheltenham.gov.uk WEB SITE www.cheltenham.gov.uk, 77 Promenade, Cheltenham GL50 1PP. For ideas on motor touring in other parts of England, see THE OPEN ROAD, page 30 in YOUR CHOICE.

The Lions of Longleat

IN 1949, THE SIXTH MARQUESS OF BATH BECAME THE FIRST OF THE ENGLISH NOBILITY TO OPEN HIS STATELY HOME, LONGLEAT, TO THE PUBLIC. One of that rare breed of English eccentrics, the now-departed marquess was an avid collector, best known for his Churchill memorabilia, including the stub of one of the prime

minister's cigars. Then there was the Hitler collection, and a corner of his library was devoted to satire of Margaret Thatcher. All of this and more can now be viewed at Longleat House in Wiltshire, where "The Life and Times of Henry, Sixth Marquess of Bath (1905–1992)" is just one of a throng of bizarre attractions. Don't miss Hitler's dinner napkin.

When Longleat first entered the tourist market, the now Seventh Marquess worked in the car park. These days visitors may encounter the middle-aged, leonine marquess giving tours of the erotic murals that adorn the walls of the great house. A collector in his own right, Lord Bath, back in 1966, added the Safari Park to Longleat's list of attractions. It's now the crown jewel set in the midst of the old Capability Brown-designed estate.

It is a sight to behold: Lord Bath's assembly of animals from the African savanna marching through the Wiltshire downland. A drive through the grounds allows a close look at the beasts in their semi-natural habitat. Regal lions snooze under shrubs, giraffes stretch their long necks and nibble the topmost branches, zebras and deer parade across the dusty hills. The monkey enclosure is worth the price of admission if you don't mind risking some of the decorative details on your car. Here tribes of curious adult monkeys and their offspring climb atop cars, chew on radio antennae, and otherwise make adorable nuisances of themselves as your car creeps through the enclosure. (The monkey enclosure can be bypassed.)

Elsewhere on the estate there is much more to discover. The Safari Boat takes passengers on a river trip to view two silver-back gorillas (who enjoy their own satellite television), as well as hippos and pelicans and, while aboard, the opportunity to feed the California sea lions who jump and bark alongside the boat in a most diverting manner. The "world's longest hedge maze" is another crowd-pleaser. It takes about an hour to make your way through, so don't go in hungry. For the big picture, a miniature steam train takes passengers on a whirlwind tour of the grounds.

At the entrance a variety of options are offered. The Passport is a good choice for Britons who can use it for entrance to the complex for an entire year. Overseas visitors would be do best to choose from among several combinations of day entrance fees depending on their interests. For the most popular attractions, queues are likely. For information, call or write Longleat House ((01985) 844400 WEB SITE www.longleat.co.uk, Warminster BA12 7NW. Longleat is located just off the A362 between Warminster and Frome.

Dip into Georgian Bath

A CITY OF SUN-DRENCHED LIMESTONE IN COMPLETE HARMONY WITH ITS AVON VALLEY SETTING, BATH AS WE KNOW IT TODAY WAS BUILT IN THE SHORT SPACE OF 80 YEARS. Long removed from its origins as the great Roman spa Aquae Sulis, by the end of the seventeenth century Bath had become a squalid village. Then Queen Anne — most likely on doctor's advice — made two momentous visits in 1702 and 1703, and the city's modern fate was sealed. Bath had become the meeting place of fashionable eighteenth-century society. Suddenly, everyone wanted to take the waters.

"The town is taken up in raffling, gaming, visiting, and in a word, all sorts of gallantry and levity," wrote Daniel Defoe when he visited Bath in the 1720s. This "round of utmost diversion" needed a suitably elegant stage on which to be played. Into the fore came a host of entrepreneurs and designers, the most significant of whom was the architect-developer John Wood, followed by his son John Wood the Younger. This dynamic duo designed and financed the construction of a host of public spaces and buildings, all fashioned out of limestone quarried from the surrounding hills.

The Woods were great admirers of the sixteenth-century Italian architect Andrea Palladio (1518–1580), whose style was based upon classical tenets of balance and proportion. Adapting that style to modern needs, and drawing on the preferred modes of the day, the Woods also used their creations to call attention to Bath's Roman past. Their squares, avenues and buildings were designed to be uplifting to the observer, and spaces were so arranged to provide the setting for civilized life.

Enter any of the chambers at the Assembly Rooms, on Bennett Street, and you can't help but feel yourself grow a few inches. These meeting rooms provided a grand backdrop for the everlasting rounds of gaming, gossip and guzzling (of mineral water) that were the foundation of Bath society. Built in the 1770s by John Wood the Younger, their sugary interiors were designed by Josiah Wedgwood, who developed his distinctive style in Bath.

The Woods' legacy was carried on by other architects. In the later phase of Bath's eighteenth-century boom, Robert Adam

Bath — ABOVE: A sightseeing boat glides under the Palladian arches of Pulteney Bridge. BELOW: The Roman Baths below Abbey spires.

designed the Pulteney Bridge (1774), "England's Ponte Vecchio." Spanning the River Avon, the bridge still houses shops and restaurants, and passersby stop abreast it to watch the swans and narrowboats navigating Pulteney Weir. On the eastern side of the river, the circular Laura Place leads into the majestic Great Pulteney Street, held by some to be the handsomest street in Europe.

By the dawning of the nineteenth century, Bath had once again begun to lose its luster as Victorians took to the sea in their bathing machines. Still, it remained a popular vacationing spot and with the excavation of the Roman Baths gradually metamorphosed from a fashionable spa to today's richly endowed World Heritage City, and one of Britain's biggest tourist attractions.

Bath's star continues to rise. As yet another century turns, the city is on its way to becoming a living spa again with the revival of two of its historic baths, the Hot Bath and the Cross Bath. The £19-million scheme will also bring a modern spa facility with bathing and therapeutic treatments to the city by spring of 2002. Another round of utmost diversion begins.

Explore Dartmoor

A MOOR, SAYS MY DICTIONARY, IS "AN OPEN WASTE GROUND." Nothing could seem further from the truth on an August day in Dartmoor National Park. The summer light has turned the soft green banks of the River Dart fluorescent. A breeze ripples over the hills. From every point of the compass drifts the din of the moor's inhabitants: the lowing of cows, the prattling of sheep and the wild whinnying of ponies. Here and there, picnicking families dig deep into wicker hampers. In the car park an elderly couple, seated in folding chairs, pour tea from a thermos.

Despite its reputation as England's last great wilderness, many of Dartmoor's abundant gifts can be enjoyed from the comfort of a folding chair or on short hikes from roadways that traverse the park. The B3212, for example, bridges Dartmoor from southwest to northeast, making large areas accessible to all. Many of the tors (from the Celtic word for hill) — Haytor, Hound Tor, and Sharp Tor — are easily reached from the road with well-worn tracks leading up to them. A program of guided walks offered by the park authority make exploration further afield well within reach of day-trippers. There are even bus services throughout the park for those without wheels.

But far up on the high moor the words "waste ground" begin to come into focus. Ambitious hikers planning to take a walk in the moor's interior would do well to read John Hillaby's near-desperate account of his lone hike through the misty bogs of Dartmoor in the mid-1960s (Journey through Britain, Constable & Company, 1968). "Optimism vanished as I looked round for something more substantial to walk on. Couldn't see the marker when I got going again. Chose something else in what I took to be the right direction.... Mental censor asked if I wasn't feeling just a bit tired? Nonsense! Never felt better in my life. Mist is good for you. Like Guinness. But it really wasn't. I knew it wasn't."

As Hillaby so abundantly discovered, surrounding the arid tors are acres of heather, bracken and bog which act like giant sponges soaking up the moor's frequent rain and creating booby-traps for the wariest of hikers. In this no-man's-land — where it is possible to walk for miles without seeing another person — hikers meet severe conditions. There are no marked trails (compass and detailed maps are essential) and trekkers pick their way carefully around the water-soaked bogs hoping the mists don't rise before they achieve their destination.

Adding to the eerie quality of the interior are the overgrown foundations of thousands of Stone Age hut circles, standing stones, and burial mounds. Because the moor has not been plowed in the last centuries, many of these prehistoric sites have remained relatively undisturbed. Dartmoor is consequently one of Britain's most important archaeological landscapes. An archaeological wonderland, the ultimate hiker's challenge, or a lovely place for a Sunday drive — these are just three of Dartmoor's many faces. To these add the villages and hamlets that surround the moor, sheltered in lush valleys. Among other things, tourists find in these villages cozy spots for tea and scones with clotted cream served alongside shaded greens.

Whether you've come for a trek in the bog or a spot of tea, drop by for information at the High Moorland Visitor Centre ((01822) 890414 E-MAIL dnpinfo@dartnp.dartmoor-npa.gov.uk WEB SITE www.dartmoor-npa.gov.uk, Princetown, Yelverton PL20 6QF.

Wild ponies graze the vast expanse of Dartmoor National Park, Devon.

YOUR CHOICE

The Great Outdoors

Perhaps nowhere else in the world do town and country blend so seamlessly together as they do in the gentle landscapes of rural Southern England. It is the harmoniousness of village and vale, sea cliff and port, farmland and market town that makes this landscape uniquely English. Even in Dartmoor National Park, England's "last great wilderness," signs of prehistoric human habitation haunt the uplands. And from Exmoor National Park's sea cliffs one looks down on a world of snug fishing villages. The Cotswolds embody this aspect of the English countryside best, with their plump hills cradling mediaeval villages that seem as much a part of the scenery as the wooded vales.

This rapport of man and nature makes Southern England singularly beautiful. It also makes enjoying the out-of-doors a singularly civilized affair. A typical English outing, whether on heath or moor, woodland or valley, is punctuated by pots of tea, ales by the fireside, snug beds, and hearty breakfasts. Enjoying the great outdoors here also implies a good number of fellow adventurers. But, that is "getting away from it all" English style, where hearty food and good fellowship are always close at hand.

No one appreciates both the comforts and splendors of this enchanting island more than the British, who have made walking a national pastime and have seen to it that Southern England maintains a broad network of public footpaths crossing some of the most beautiful rural scenery in the world.

Resources for walkers are abundant. Take your pick from a host of excellent, and often essential, **guidebooks** and **maps** published by Ordnance Survey ((023) 8079-2773 WEB SITE www.ordsvy.gov.uk, Romsey Road, Southampton SO16 4GU; Aurum Press ((020) 7637-3225, 25 Bedford Avenue, London WC1B 3AT; or the Countryside Agency ((020) 7340-2900 FAX (020) 7340-2911 WEB SITE www.countryside.gov.uk, Dacre House, 19 Dacre Street, London SW1H 0DH. See also WEB SITES, page 336 in TRAVELERS' TIPS for web sites on the out-of-doors.

Tourist information centers in popular walking areas stock booklets detailing short walks and local day hikes. Advice is free and plentiful. Most hotels and some B&B hosts also offer maps and suggestions. For long-distance trekking, Britain has 13 **national trails**, six of which pass through Southern England. These trails are intended to be easy to get to, simple to follow (they're way-marked with an acorn symbol), and not too strenuous. Parts are open to cyclists and horse riders. Certainly the longest, and

LEFT: The silvery cliffs at Beachy Head, Sussex, shine like a beacon by day. ABOVE: The Cotswolds landscape beckons foot travelers with promises of happy trails.

perhaps the most famous, of the national trails, the **Southwest Coastal Path** runs for 982 km (614 miles) from Minehead in Somerset, rounding Land's End to finish at the Isle of Purbeck in Dorset. Even the briefest of strolls on this spectacular footpath open up cliff-top views of surf, wooded valleys, and moorland.

Another sublime national trail is the **Cotswold Way**, which rambles from Weston (a suburb of Bath) to Campden through some of England's prettiest countryside. The northern sections are the most scenic, so if you're not going the distance, head south from the trailhead at Campden. Mark Richard's *The Cotswolds Way* (Reardon Publishing, 1995) is mandatory equipment for walkers on this 162-km (100-mile) trail.

The **Ridgeway** (146 km or 90 miles) traces the country's oldest road, a Roman thoroughfare, from West Kennet (near Avebury) through the rolling downland of Wiltshire into the wooded countryside of the Chilterns in the east to finish at Ivinghoe Beacon in Buckinghamshire. Cyclists and horse riders are welcome on the western section and on some parts within the Chilterns.

The **Thames Path** (288 km or 182 miles) is unique in that it follows England's historic river from its source in the Cotswolds near Cirencester through water meadows, hamlets, ancient towns and villages, alongside castles and palaces into the heart of London, finishing at the Thames Barrier.

Said to be in part the route taken by pilgrims in the *Canterbury Tales,* the **North Downs Way** (246 km or 152 miles) meanders through the wooded hills of Surrey (starting from Farnham), the open Kent Downs, and through Canterbury, finishing dramatically at the White Cliffs of Dover. About half of this trail is open to cyclists and horse riders.

South Downs Way (160 km or 100 miles) starts at the chalk cliffs at Beachy Head running through deep valleys to the cathedral city of Winchester. Travelers can string up nights in hostels along this trail in Eastbourne, Alfriston, Telscombe, Truleigh Hill, Winchester, and Arundel. Riders and cyclists are welcome on the entire length of this path.

To learn more about Britain's national trails, contact one of the regional tourist boards (for addresses and phone numbers, see TOURIST INFORMATION, page 324 in TRAVELERS' TIPS), or visit WEB SITE www.nationaltrails.gov.uk for information on the national trails of the Southeast; or www.countryside.gov.uk for information on all the trails as well as the national parks.

Long-distance hikers don't have to carry a heavy backpack. At dusk, hikers halt along the way in pubs and B&Bs, so a daypack with a change of clothes, toiletries and trail snacks will see you through. Footpaths often run through pasture and farmland on privately held property under a time-worn system of "right-of-way." Special care should be taken to respect this symbiotic relationship. Walking guidebooks and tourist information centers provide lists of dos and don'ts for walkers. The **Ramblers Association** ((020) 7339-8500 FAX (020) 7339-8501 E-MAIL ramblers@london .ramblers.org.uk, 1–5 Wandsworth Road, London SW8 2XX, is a useful resource for questions concerning what to wear, the countryside code and more.

You'll find accommodation listed for some of the towns along the national trails in the destination sections of this book (see, for example, WHERE TO STAY headings under THE COTSWOLDS, page 147). For information on camping, refer to BACKPACKING, page 34.

Sporting Spree

ACTIVE SPORTS
There are countless ways to jump into English sports, even if it's just a friendly game of pub darts. I've focused here, however, on three of the classics: water sports, cycling, and horseback riding.

IN AND ON THE WATER
Unless you're a member of the Polar Bear Club, you may not have included a swim in the ocean on your Southern England itinerary. However, Gulf Stream currents warm many of Southern England's Atlantic beaches, which are thus not quite as cold as you might expect. Consider, if you will, the billowing palm trees of the Cornish towns of St. Ives and Newquay. These resorts have superb **swimming** beaches — Britain's best — with wide golden sands and blue Atlantic waters. So, do bring swimming togs, just in case.

The shores of north Devon are renowned for catching some of the best **surfing** waves in the United Kingdom. The breakers are at their gnarliest at resorts such as Newquay and Croyde, where it's possible to rent wetsuits and boards right at the beach. There are plenty of outfits offering lessons, too. Beginners start on foam boards so it doesn't hurt when your plank bonks you. For details, call the British Surfing Association ((01736) 360250.

If you're not getting into the water then get out on it with **sailing** lessons. Neilson ((023) 9222-2224 offers a weekend sailing course on the *Solent*, destined for the Isle of Wight, with two nights on board for £145 per person. Back in sunny Cornwall, Falmouth Harbour abounds in sheltered creeks and peaceful anchorage with magnificent scenery. These are some of the country's best sailing waters, and the Mylor Sailing School ((01326) 377633, Mylor Yacht Harbour, Falmouth TR11 5UF,

can get you under sail whether it's in a dinghy, dayboat or keel boat. All safety gear is provided; you need only bring warm clothes, deck shoes, waterproofs and a change of clothes.

CYCLING
Southern England is a superb place to explore by bicycle. It's compact, so it's possible to see a great deal even in a trip of a few days. Its landscape is a slide-show of sea cliffs, moors and woodland. As with walking, there's no need to carry heavy camping and cooking gear; while wet weather can dampen some days, cyclists, like walkers, can take advantage of tea shops and inns to make a comfortable journey of a few hours or many days.

As for the terrain, Southern England's lowlands may look like a piece of cake, but even fit cyclists are challenged by the steep road gradients in some areas, especially along the West Country coast. On the flip side, your daily mileage will perhaps be less than you might expect (if you're used to biking in North America), since towns and sightseeing attractions are so tightly packed.

Short trips are easy to arrange and bicycles are available for rent in popular cycling areas. Look for listings under

Cornwall capers — OPPOSITE: Windsurfers ready their equipment at St. Mawes, on the beautiful Roseland Peninsula. ABOVE: The rugged terrain of Bodmin Moor invites exploration on hoof and paw.

OUTDOOR ACTIVITIES, in the destination sections. Tourist information centers are an excellent resource for local information on cycling routes and rental agencies.

There are many miles of **long-distance cycling routes** in Britain, with additional mileage being added each year through the auspices of the National Cycle Network ((0117) 929-0888 E-MAIL info@sustrans.org.uk, a proposed 12,960-km (8,000-mile) cycling and walking route. The first 8,100 km (5,000 miles) were completed in 2000. Visit WEB SITE www.sustrans.org.uk/f_ncn.htm, for details, or look for the *Official Guide to the National Cycle Network* (Sustrans, 2000). See also NATIONAL TRAILS, under THE GREAT OUTDOORS, above.

You shouldn't have any problem bringing your bike to England. Most airlines will allow you to include it as part of your baggage allowance, as long as you notify the airline when you make your reservation. Ferries, also, will carry bikes, usually for free. With reservations it's possible to take bikes on the Eurotunnel Shuttle linking Calais, France, to Folkestone, Kent (see GETTING THERE, page 325 in TRAVELERS' TIPS).

The best time of year to cycle in England is between the months of May and October, when temperatures average between 8°C and 22°C (47°F to 71°F). A good map is essential. Contact **Ordnance Survey** ((023) 8079-2912, Customer Information, Romsey Road, Southampton SO1 6 4GU, to find out where to buy their touring maps. Above all, get in touch with the **Cyclists' Touring Club** ((01483) 417217 FAX (01483) 426994, 69 Meadrow, Godalming GU7 3HS, the country's largest cycling organization. They publish an annual touring directory for cyclists, as well as itineraries designed to avoid heavy traffic and to include places of interest. The British Tourist Authority publishes a useful map: "Britain for Cyclists."

HORSE-BACK RIDING

Informal riding instruction, dressage and show jumping, trail and cross-country riding, pony trekking — whatever your riding interest and level of experience, Southern England offers an ideal setting for equine activities.

Exmoor National Park, bridging the counties of Devon and Somerset, is the horse-back riding playground of England. An extensive area of open unspoiled countryside taking in coastal cliffs and inland moors is the setting for the park's 650 km (400 miles) of well maintained and signposted bridleways. Rent horses and ponies at riding centers throughout the park. Some of them are listed under EXMOOR NATIONAL PARK, beginning on page 272. A complete list of licensed and approved riding centers can be obtained from the British Horse Society ((01926) 707700 FAX (01926) 707800, Stoneleigh Deer Park Kenilworth Warwickshire CV8 2XZ.

Ordnance Survey Pathfinder maps mark public bridleways.

SPECTATOR SPORTS

American benchwarmers accustomed to watching baseball, football, basketball and ice hockey could spend a lifetime getting acquainted with the wide world of British sports, areas of which are virtually unknown in the United States. From a testosterone-drenched game of rugby to a proper cricket match on the village green, sports in the United Kingdom are a passport into a unique aspect of British culture.

Racing events are listed under FESTIVE FLINGS, page 53.

FOOTBALL

Football, known as soccer in the United States, is Britain's most popular sport, amounting at times to a national obsession. Amongst the legions of fans, team loyalties seem often to supersede national loyalties — no matter whether you're Scotch, Welsh or English, if you support Manchester or Liverpool or Arsenal, you've found your family (or your feud).

Football games take place around the country from mid-August through mid-May, usually on Saturday afternoons. The season finale is the Football Association Cup soccer tournament at North London's Wembley stadium.

Tickets are easy to get for regular league matches in the lower divisions. Buy them at the stadium or from ticket hotlines listed in local telephone directories. For the premier

clubs, tickets are in high demand. If you want to attend one of these matches you should contact the club in advance for prices and availability. Tickets for certain matches may be available through Ticketmaster ((020) 344-4444. It's almost impossible to get tickets for the FA Cup Final at Wembley as tickets are distributed among season ticket holders and officials of the league. But watching the match from a local pub can be almost as exciting as being there.

CRICKET

Even those who don't follow cricket are ready to admit that the "thwack of willow on leather" is the sound of an English summer. The English national sport, cricket is a field game of elaborately ruled play involving a leather ball and wooden bat (the "willow"), developed sometime before 1700. Matches are played on village greens on Sundays from April to September. Inquire at tourist information centers for local matches. **Cric Info** WEB SITE www.cricket.org outlines who's who and what's happening in the world of cricket, as well as the definitions of such terms as "googlies," "silly midons," and "square legs." The NatWest Trophy is the main cricket competition, with the final held at Lord's Cricket Ground in London.

LEFT: Lord's Cricket Ground, the pot of gold for the men in white. ABOVE: Wimbledon, site of the annual Lawn Tennis Championship.

If you're keen to learn the game — including the rules, known in cricket as "The Laws" — get a copy of *Wisden Cricketer's Almanack,* published annually. It's available from John Wisden and Company Limited ((01483) 570358 FAX (01483) 33153, 25 Down Road, Merrow, Guildford GU1 2PY.

RUGBY

Another very English game, rugby was invented at Rugby School in Warwickshire during a soccer match that perhaps got a little out of hand. (Gilberts, who have manufactured the standard rugby ball since 1842, have an exhibition here on the history of the game.) Rugby is similar to American football, minus the protective equipment and endless time-outs. **Rugby Union** games are the amateur version played mostly in Southern England. Games take place Saturdays in winter. **Rugby League**, the professional form of the game, is played in the north of England, with matches from March to September. Visit WEB SITE www.rleague.com for details on Rugby League or www.scrum.com for Rugby Union.

Tickets, when available, can be obtained from the event venue or from ticket hotlines listed in local telephone directories.

LAWN TENNIS

The All England Club's Lawn Tennis Championships have been played annually in the London suburb of Wimbledon since 1877. Some 30,000 spectators each day come to watch the two-week championship, which takes place in late June. Applications for the ticket lottery are available from October to December from the All-England Lawn Tennis and Croquet Club ((020) 8946-2244, Church Road, Wimbledon, London SW19 5AE. A limited number of tickets are sold each day for that day's play, on a first-come, first serve basis.

Any time of year, it's possible to visit the **Wimbledon Lawn Tennis Museum** ((020) 8946-6131, at the All-England Tennis Club, Church Road, Wimbledon, where exhibits feature the history of the sport, trophies and profiles of tennis greats. Closed Sunday morning and all day Monday; admission fee.

POLO

You can watch **polo** greats at play, often including members of the royal family, at Smith's Lawn, Great Windsor Park, in Windsor. Entrance is free of charge, or pay £10 per person for a day's club membership which gives you access to the bar and clubhouse facilities. Games are played from early May until late September, Tuesday to Friday at 3:30 PM, Saturday and Sunday at 3 PM. For additional details call the Windsor Polo Club ((01784) 434212.

The Open Road

Many unkind words have been written on the subject of motoring in Britain. Bill Bryson kvetched that "there isn't a single feature of driving in Britain that has the tiniest measure of enjoyment in it." Long before cars crowded the roads around vacation resorts, even H.V. Morton, the original English leisure motorist, spoke of the sins of the automobile.

Nevertheless, the joys of driving in Southern England, while not indisputable, are certainly legion. Despite the density of traffic, the United Kingdom enjoys the safest driving conditions in the European Union. Roads are for the most part very good, and signage is excellent. For those unused to it, the brain-bending challenge of driving on the left, shifting gears with your left hand and maneuvering "roundabouts" (traffic circles) in a clock-wise motion is a thrill for some, a nightmare for others. But the freedom a car gives you to get off the beaten track to England's most captivating scenery makes it worthwhile for many.

THE HIGH KENT WEALD

Between the North and South Downs, the High Kent Weald, though densely populated, has pockets of great charm and beauty. Running down to the coast at Hastings, this once heavily forested area is today a hilly patchwork of fields, hedges and woodlands dotted with tile-and-weatherboard houses and distinctive oasthouses — hop kilns — with their cone-shaped roofs. The route below takes you onto some of the back roads and through villages many people miss when traveling along Kent's motorways.

Start in the handsome town of **Tenterden** (page 196), which you might want to make your base for touring the Weald. Head north up the A28, joining the A262. This road takes you through **Biddenden**, home of the "Biddenden Maids." In the twelfth-century the village was the home of these Siamese twin sisters, joined at the shoulders and hip. They lived to the age of 34 and died within a day of each other, leaving the income from their property to provide food for the poor. In the green, on the corner of High Street and the A262, you'll find the village emblem which commemorates the sisters.

The limestone cliffs of Cheddar Gorge, Somerset, throw their long shadows over the roadside.

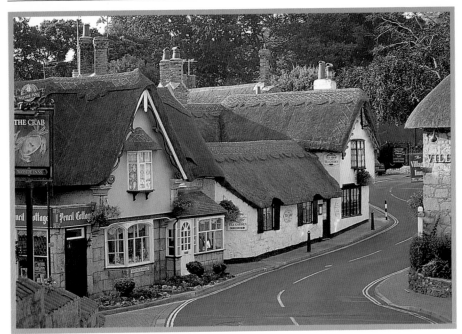

From here, follow the A274 north keeping an eye out for signs directing you to **Smarden**, a beautiful village with a fourteenth-and fifteenth-century church known as the "Barn of Kent" because of its great height of 11 m (36 ft). At this point you could choose to continue north to **Leeds Castle** (page 202), passing through the town of **Sutton Valence** on the way. This town lies just above the Weald, and the castle ruins here, home to a colony of white doves, afford panoramic views of the Wealden countryside; free. To find the castle, follow the English Heritage signs as you enter town.

Returning to Biddenden take the A262 west. On your right not far out of the village is the Three Chimneys (page 202), an excellent and atmospheric gastropub. Soon you come to the turning for **Sissinghurst Castle Garden** (page 199), one of England's most delightful gardens and not to be missed despite its popularity. From Sissinghurst, detour along the A229 for **Cranbrook** to visit the old windmill and stroll the busy streets of this market town.

Return to the A262 and head west to the high village of **Goudhurst** with its handsome church and tile-hung cottages. At 120 m (400 ft) above sea level, the church tower at Goudhurst provides outstanding views across the village and the surrounding Wealden countryside. The tower (admission fee) is open to visitors on weekends only. The Star & Eagle pub, just off the churchyard, is a good place to break your journey.

About 11 km (seven miles) west of Goudhurst, connect briefly with the busy A21 toward Tonbridge and make your way towards **Tudeley** on the B2017 just east of Tonbridge. The windows of this country church were created by Marc Chagall in the 1960s. Even on cloudy days the glass has an ethereal glow. The altar window, depicting the drowning of the young woman whom the windows commemorate, is particularly moving.

Carry on through Tonbridge to connect with the A26 south, signposted to Tunbridge Wells. In about five kilometers (three miles), take the turning towards Bidborough for the drive up to **Penshurst**. There are more good views along this ridge road leading into the prettiest part of the Weald. This is good walking territory (you'll need maps) with friendly old pubs to break the journey. Penshurst is tucked into a fold of the Weald just above Penshurst Palace (page 197) with its state rooms and Tudor gardens. There is a pub in the village, but press on through and take the third turning up Smarts Hill. At the top of the hill go left for the Spotted Dog for very good food and superb views from the terrace, or right for the Bottle House, a friendly pub with hearty fare.

From Penshurst follow the signs to **Chiddingstone** (page 197), an unspoiled village owned by the National Trust. There are a couple of tea rooms and some antiques shops here as well as a nineteenth-century mock castle and the mysterious Chiding Stone, from which the village gets its name.

YOUR CHOICE

From here you may want to go on to nearby Hever Castle (page 203) or continue along the B2169 towards Lamberhurst where you can visit romantic Scotney Castle Gardens (page 203).

Circling back toward Tenterden on the A268 you can take a short detour down to the fairytale castle of Bodiam (page 199), or return to Tenterden and have a vintage steam train ride to the castle from the town.

A similar tour and other good driving routes are detailed in the booklet "Country Tours: Circular Driving Routes in the Kent Countryside," published by Kent Tourism ((01622) 696164. Ask for it at any of the local tourist information centers.

THE PENWITH PENINSULA

Cornwall's secondary routes, a legacy of the region's mining days, make for excellent motor touring. In some areas, such as the Lizard Peninsula, these tiny thoroughfares are sunken below steep-ivy-covered walls, but this Penwith Peninsula route provides top-of-the-world views.

Starting at St. Ives, take the B3306 west. Situated between heather-filled moorland and sea cliffs, the village of **Zennor** is home to the fifteenth-century St. Senara Church with its mysterious mermaid chair. The elaborate carving depicts a local legend which tells of a mermaid who fell in love with a church chorister because of his sweet voice. The mermaid lured the hapless boy out to sea, and it's said you can still hear him singing from the

waves. From the village, a walk to Zennor Head provides spectacular scenery and a link to the Southwest Coastal Path.

Driving west along the coast, you come to **Pendeen Lighthouse** (signposted from the B3306). Dramatically perched on Cornwall's rocky coast, this turn-of-the-twentieth-century beacon boasts the largest fog horn in Britain. Be sure to look around for "Lighthouse," the black Labrador, who has an unquenchable passion for playing fetch. Guided tours of the lighthouse are offered daily from Easter to the end of September; admission fee.

The history of Cornwall mining is recounted at the **Levant Beam Engine** (NT) ((01736) 786156, one and a half kilometers (one mile) west of Pendeen at Trewellard (follow signs from the B3306). The engine was restored to working order in 1993 after 60 years of slumber. Call to inquire about "steaming days" if you'd like to see the engine in action. Open Wednesday to Friday and Sunday in June, Sunday to Friday from July to September; admission fee.

Continuing south of Pendeen is the old mining hamlet of **Botallack**, where preserved engine houses of the nineteenth century cling to the dramatic cliffs. There are excellent and rugged walks along the coast here.

At St. Just-in-Penwith, turn off the B3306 for **Cape Cornwall**, a quiet alternative to Land's End. In this craggy landscape Hottentot figs trail their succulent leaves over cliffs and hedges, while purple heather and yellow gorse blanket the hills. Birders have a ball here watching for herring gulls, shags, kittiwakes, gannets and fulmars, as well as razorbacks and guillemots, which nest off shore. A glance out to sea reveals the Brisons, two rocks rising 18 to 21 m (60 to 70 ft). These jagged islets have claimed many ships.

South of St. Just, the B3306 connects with the A30 to take you to **Land's End**. If you get there in late afternoon once the amusements are closed it's possible to take advantage of the reduced parking fee (and reduced crowds). Once past the carbuncle that is "Land's End" you've reached *land's end* where evening light bathes the spectacular cliffs.

Cliff scenery becomes a theatrical backdrop at **Porthcurno**, southeast of Land's End, where the Minack Theatre is one of the most intriguing and scenic stages in the world. Set on cliffs above the sea, the theater presents a regular season of plays. You can also stop by for a tour of the amphitheater and views from the café.

OPPOSITE: The East Wight village of Shanklin.
ABOVE: Bedazzled by Kynance Cove, Cornwall.

On your way to Penzance (page 312) you may want to visit Mousehole (page 316) and Newlyn (page 315) — two charming fishing villages with galleries and craft shops, and the fascinating Pilchard Works Museum & Factory. From Penzance take the B3111 back to St. Ives.

MORE GREAT DRIVES

Beyond the two classic journeys we've detailed above there are many more scenic byways to explore in Southern England. The B3212 through Dartmoor National Park takes motorists through the heart of this desolate landscape with views of rugged tors and herds of meandering ponies. In Hampshire, the New Forest is another haven for ponies. The forest also has carefully landscaped ornamental drives which form magnificent arcades of rare trees and plants. On the Isle of Wight, a drive along Brighstone Bay opens up stunning vistas of green downland and shining sea. Back on the mainland, the rural downland area between Marlborough and Devizes is a glorious place for road tripping, rich in prehistoric remains, chalk figures and crop circles. And don't forget to have a motorized fling in the beautiful Cotswold Hills (for route details, see A COTSWOLD RAMBLE, page 18 in TOP SPOTS).

Backpacking

All of the United Kingdom has elevated prices when compared with most of Europe and North America, and London is a budgetary jaw-dropper. Yet, backpacking travelers are drawn to England like moths to a flame. Admission fees, accommodation, food, entertainment, transportation — they're all priced in the stratosphere, but with some judicious planning it's possible to outwit the toll-takers.

GETTING THERE

There are a number of ways to take the bite out of transportation to England. Flying outside of peak season is a no-brainer.

Instead of making reservations through a standard travel agent or through the airline directly, it's sometimes possible to save a bundle by using consolidators (agencies that have discount agreements with the airlines). Some proven United States-based consolidators are: **Travac Tours & Charters** TOLL-FREE (800) 872-8800 WEB SITE www.thetravelsite.com; **Council Travel** TOLL-FREE (800) 226-8624 WEB SITE www.ciee.org; **Der Travel Services** TOLL-FREE (800) 717-4247 for air fares or TOLL-FREE (800) 782-2424 for other travel products; **STA Travel** TOLL-FREE (800) 777-0112

WEB SITE www.statravel.com. and **New Frontiers USA** TOLL-FREE (800) 366-6387 WEB SITE www .newfrontiers.com; Another good source of cheap fares are bucket shops (discount ticketing agencies that specialize in complicated itineraries). In the United States you can find bucket shop ads in the Sunday travel sections of the *San Francisco Chronicle and Examiner, Miami Herald, New York Times and Los Angeles Times*. If you want the complete story on discount airfares, refer to WEB SITE www.travel-library.com or look for Edward Hasbrouck's *The Practical Nomad: How to Travel Around the World* (Moon, 1997).

If your schedule is flexible, sign on as a freelance air courier with **Now Voyager (** (212) 431-1616 FAX (212) 219-1753 or (212) 334-5243, 74 Varick Street, Suite 307, New York, New York 01113, or another courier clearinghouse. As an air courier, you get flight discounts in exchange for the use of your check-in baggage space to provide transport for the company's own (legitimate) packages.

For a couple of years now, the Internet-only travel agency, **Go-Today** WEB SITE www .go-today.com has offered remarkably low-priced airfare and B&B packages to London during off-peak seasons. Be sure to include them in your search for the ultimate cheapie vacation. Also, if England is only a part of

your European down-market tour, check out **Europe by Air** TOLL-FREE (888) 397-2497 WEB SITE www.europebyair.com, which offers a reasonably priced city-to-city air pass.

For those traveling to the United Kingdom from continental Europe, the cheapest way to go — short of coating yourself with lard and swimming the Channel — is the **Eurolines** bus. Eurolines coaches depart six times daily from the Paris Eurolines Station, Avenue du Général de Gaulle in Bagnolet (the nearest Metro station is Bagnolet), arriving a mere 12 hours later in London. Visit their WEB SITE www.eurolines.com for branch offices throughout Europe, or contact the United Kingdom offices at: ((0990)143219 FAX (01582) 400694 E-MAIL welcome@eurolinesuk.com, 4 Cardiff Road, Luton, Bedfordshire L41 1PP.

GETTING AROUND

Because Southern England is so compact, you won't be traveling vast distances. But even short hops come at a premium. One way to save is to take a "slow coach." **National Express** ((0990) 010104, offers a pass which gives you unlimited travel on certain routes, unlimited stopovers for a period of six months, free hostel booking, transport to accommodation and trained driver-guides. Similarly, **Slow Travel Networks** ((020) 7373-7737 run coaches on a

circuit of the entire island. You can get on and off anywhere you like and for as long as you like — there's no time limit. Another slow-coach agency is **Roadtrip Overland Tours** ((0800) 056-0505 (call between 5 PM and 7:30 PM) WEB SITE www.roadtrip.co.uk, with rock-bottom-priced hop-on hop-off circuits of southwest England. Trips hit Stonehenge, Newquay, Bath, St. Michael's Mount and Dartmoor National Park. The bus comes equipped with television and videos, and mountain bikes are provided at each stop.

On its regular routes, **National Express** ((0990) 010104 offers discounts to students, seniors and families via their CoachCard program.

Finally, ride-sharing can considerably reduce the cost of getting around. Look for postings at youth hostels, or visit the ingenious **To Share** WEB SITE www.compartir.org E-MAIL toshare@compartir.org, a free, ad-supported, web site that allows you to log on and locate people planning journeys that match your own in countries all over the world, including the United Kingdom.

OPPOSITE: Staffs in hand, ramblers explore seaside Cadgwith, in West Cornwall. ABOVE: London's "exuberantly Victorian" Tower Bridge was built in 1894 to meet the needs of burgeoning traffic.

CHEAP SLEEPS

Surprisingly, youth hostels are not always the cheapest place to sleep in England. In London and other university cities you might get better value using university accommodation, provided your visit coincides with school vacation time. At the London School of Economics, for example, it's possible to stay in the heart of Bloomsbury in a private room with shared bath at **Passfield Hall** ((020) 7387-7743 FAX (020) 7387-0419, 1 Endsleigh Place, London WC1H 0PW, for £22 per person including English breakfast. If you know of better accommodation value in London, tell me! The **British Universities Accommodation Consortium** WEB SITE www.buac.co.uk has one-stop shopping for all British universities offering rooms.

Youth hostels are still a popular option, ranging in price from £16 to £22 per person per night in London, and from £7 to £12 elsewhere. If you're planning on staying in hostels much, consider joining the **Youth Hostel Association** ((01727) 845047 E-MAIL customerservices @yha.org.uk WEB SITE www.yha.org.uk, Trevelyan House, 8 St. Stephen's Hill, St. Albans, Hertfordshire AL1 2DY. You can also join at any YHA hostel by paying £2 per stay until you've paid up your membership.

With the exception of London, the hostels that are part of the Youth Hostel Association tend to attract families and scout troops, especially on weekends, making them somewhat less amenable to solo travelers. They also have curfews and all-day lock-outs. An alternative for independent and solo travelers is **Backpackers Britain** WEB SITE www.backpack.co.uk. It's possible to join at their web site or at any of 12 or so South England affiliates. While families are welcome, these hostels are geared toward individual

travelers. They often have single and double rooms (for a bit more) in addition to dorms, as well as no curfew and all day right-of-entry. Many have Internet access.

Even hard-core campers think twice about pitching a tent on this water-logged island. However, if you are well-equipped, camping gives a great deal of freedom and you can't beat the price. Rugged individualists can enjoy the cheapest sleep in London: **Tent City** ((020) 8985-7656 FAX (020) 874990-74 E-MAIL tentcity@btinternet.com WEB SITE www.btinternet.com/~tentcity (Θ Leyton), near the canal, with 200 tent pitches, profits going to charity (£5 per person). Open June to August.

Outside London, the Forestry Commission operates campgrounds in the New Forest and other forest parks. Contact them well in advance of your visit at **Forestry Commission** ((0131) 334-0303 FAX (0131) 334-3047, 231 Corstorphine Road, Edinburgh EH12 7AT. It's sometimes possible to camp rough on farmland, but always get permission from the farmer first. Some farms offer camping barns. These "stone tents" provide basic accommodation with cold showers, or at least a tap, and wooden sleeping platforms. Some have toilets, hot showers and cooking facilities. They're usually unheated, so bring warm clothing and gear. There is also a growing network of camping barns on Dartmoor and Exmoor run by the Youth Hostel Association, and some youth hostels allow campers to set up tents on the property and use hostel facilities for a reduced fee.

Many campgrounds are geared toward motor-homes (caravans) for bring-the-kitchen-sink-style camping. These "holiday parks" are usually equipped with restaurants and bars as well as a host of recreational facilities (fishing, sailing, golf, tennis, swimming). If you'd like to join the ranks of the caravanners, rent a house on wheels from **Auto Europe** TOLL-FREE (1-888) 223-5555 in the United States or (0800) 89-9893 in the United Kingdom WEB SITE www.autoeurope.com, among others.

On the other end of the spectrum, contemplative types can enjoy room and board at some Benedictine **monasteries** (sorry gals, men only) for two weeks at a time. Rupert Isaacson's *Good Retreat Guide* (Century Publishing, 1999) lists these and other low-cost retreats in Britain.

CHEAP EATS

Picnicking and self-catering can stretch your dining budget. In Cornwall and Devon pasties are a meal unto themselves, and delicious if you get them fresh. Bakeries

often serve pizza by the slice; some even have indoor seating. Keep scurvy at bay by shopping for fruit at open-air markets in towns and villages. For supermarket shopping, large chains like Tesco and Sainsbury's generally have the widest range of products and the best prices.

Fish & chips, once a staple of the British diet, have been outpaced by hamburgers and kebabs and are now relatively expensive. Even so, they remain a good choice for quick meals. In London, you'll find the best "chippies" off the beaten tourist track. In north London, for example, look for **Nautilus Fish (** (020) 7435-2532, 27 Fortune Green Road (Θ/BR West Hampstead) and **Two Brothers Fish (** (020) 8346-0469, 297 Regents Park Road N3 (Θ Finchley Central). The best places use fresh fish (not frozen) and change their frying oil daily.

Vary the menu with trips to ethnic restaurants. Buffets in Chinese restaurants can be quite sustaining. Natural food stores sometimes have hearty hot take-out food and may even have sidewalk tables. My London favorite is **Alara Wholefoods**, 58-60 Marchmont Street. Don't overlook churches where there are often quick-serve cafés in crypts or cloisters. In London, check out the **Place Below** at St. Mary-le-Bow (Θ St. Paul's), **Café-in-the-Crypt** at St. Martin-in-the-Fields (Θ/BR Charing Cross) and the **Refectory** at St. Paul's Cathedral (Θ St. Paul's). Department stores are another source for sit-down meals or picnic makings. Debenham's stores, for example, usually have budget cafés, and Marks & Spencer has a cornucopia of take-out foods.

Though not dirt cheap, British chain restaurants provide another way to beat the ultra-high prices. **All Bar One** has a flashy menu, good prices and American-style portions (i.e., you'll never eat it all). **Café Rouge**, with reliable French bistro fare, and **Pizza Express** serving superb pizzas, are found just about everywhere. For fast-food, **Prêt-à-Manger** promises "no additives" in their sandwiches and salads. **Nando's** dishes up cheap and good roast chicken with Caribbean-style sauces.

Finally, if you're ready to splash out, make it lunch rather than dinner. Some of England's top tables offer fixed-price lunches at eye-popping prices (for example, La Tante Claire and Le Gavroche; see WHERE TO EAT, page 117 under LONDON). You'll probably need to make reservations.

SIGHTSEEING AND NIGHTLIFE

Since presumably sightseeing is what you've come for, you don't want to stint your budget in this area. London, once again, takes the heaviest tolls. Happily, some of the capital city's best **museums** are free (including, the British Museum and the National Gallery),

London — OPPOSITE: Pub life spills into the street. ABOVE: St. Martin-in-the-Fields, Trafalgar Square.

and as of September 2001, adult admission prices for national museums that *do* charge (Science Museum, Natural History Museum, Victoria & Albert Museum, National Maritime Museum and the Imperial War Museum) are reduced to £1. All of Britain's national museums admit children under 16 and adults over 60 free of charge. Then there are the London museums that are free after 4:30 PM (e.g., Victoria & Albert, Imperial War Museum, Natural History Museum). Entering at this time allows you an hour or so to dive in and commune with a favorite exhibit. Some attractions offer reduced entrance fees for families. From winter to spring, lectures take place at the National Portrait Gallery, some of which are free of charge. Lecture topics and guest speakers are listed at WEB SITE www.npg .org.uk/lecindex.htm, or call ((020) 7306-0055.

Get a list of free **church concerts** and times for evensong at any tourist information center. (In London there's a handy one near St. Paul's Cathedral in the City.) By attending concerts or services, it's possible to see St. Paul's and Westminster Abbey, as well as other admission-charging cathedrals around the country, without having to pay the entrance fee (though a collection plate will be passed). You can even give the Tower of London the slip by attending Sunday morning services at the Chapel of St. Peter and Vincula here. Phone on a weekday to get the time of services, then show up 20 minutes early.

Also in the capital city, stop by the South Bank Centre and pick up a copy of the Royal Festival Hall's monthly schedule. In it you'll find a listing of **free events** that take place in the foyer: lunchtime jazz, world and folk concerts and more. There are free exhibitions here as well. There is free jazz and classical music at 6 PM on weekdays in the foyers of the Barbican and free music and plays at the Guildhall School of Music and Drama, next to the Barbican.

If you're eligible for an international student identification card (available from the Council on International Educational Exchange ((020) 7478-2000 FAX (020) 7734-7322 E-MAIL cieeuk@easynet.co.uk, 52 Poland Street, London W1V 4JQ, or 205 East 42nd Street, New York, New York 10017), it can get you **cheap theater seats**. Bring your card on a Monday evening or a weekday matinee (except at the National Theatre), an hour before curtain and pay a "rush" student price of £8 to £10.

Anyone can also take advantage of the Half-Price Ticket Booth on Leicester Square, or go directly to the theater box offices the day of the show for cut-price tickets (see PERFORMING ARTS, page 44 under CULTURAL KICKS).

Time Out magazine (available at newsstands) lists London fringe events that are often less expensive than mainstream shows. This weekly magazine, essential reading for London cruising, also lists all the free museums and galleries — so it's well worth the cover price.

Living It Up

There is a certain kind of high life we associate with England. Georgian interiors swimming in marble, butlers in coattails murmuring "as you wish, madam," a note-card on a silver salver, the rustle of silk. Old World luxuries such as these can be found throughout Southern England. Yet there are many other ways to coddle yourself; and perhaps nowhere in the world are there more varied and unusual, not to say eccentric, ways to do it.

EXCEPTIONAL HOTELS

Anyone seeking opulence in London faces an embarrassment of riches. One way of narrowing down the choices will be your preference for Old London's gilded glory or New London's chrome-plated chic. Staunchly in the former category, **Claridges** has been the choice of monarchs and heads of state since 1898. Rates for the royal suites and penthouse apartments go as high as £3,500 per night. A formal, art deco-style restaurant serves French and English cooking (and really good pastries). There is dinner and dancing on the weekends and the Hungarian Quartet entertains in the foyer each evening.

Among London's hip hotels, is newcomer **Myhotel Bloomsbury**. Conran did the interiors of this small sleek hotel; the 76 air-conditioned rooms are brilliant envelopes of comfort and

design ingenuity. It's not the least bit stiff or stuffy — staff are friendly and common areas invite relaxation rather than posing.

Outside London, Southern England's country house hotels offer genteel luxury, usually in the setting of splendid gardens and parkland. Windsor's **Oakley Court** is a Victorian country house on a spread of beautiful Thameside acres. Further north the Cotswold Hills are ideal for luxurious rural sojourns. In Oxfordshire, **Le Manoir aux Quat'Saisons**, is a gorgeous Jacobean manor set in richly cultivated gardens and parkland. The kitchen garden provides ingredients for the excellent restaurant. There are 32 deeply luxurious rooms, a heated swimming pool and cooking classes.

Less exclusive, the **Painswick Hotel**, in Painswick, Gloucestershire, gets top marks for service and its views of a classic Cotswold idyll. This former rectory has an interesting history. The wife of the rector converted to Catholicism and a chapel was built in the house for her to practice her faith. Today the chapel is a cozy bar. In the northern Cotswolds, Broadway's sixteenth-century **Lygon Arms** is perhaps unmatched in Southern England for its smooth combination

The royal treatment — OPPOSITE: Ninth-century Amberley Castle, in Sussex. ABOVE LEFT: Entering Aylesbury's Hartwell House Hotel, in the county of Buckinghamshire. RIGHT: A cool dip at the Grand Hotel, Eastbourne, Sussex.

of ancient charm and modern comforts. Period rooms with oak beams are generously proportioned, with four-poster beds and ample baths. Ancient coats of arms and tapestries decorate the superbly restored public areas. Dining is in the Great Hall with its barrel-vaulted ceiling and seventeenth-century minstrel's gallery.

Horsted Place is a 20-bedroom country hotel in East Sussex. Much of the detail in this stunning red-and-black brick Gothic Revival house was done by Augustus Pugin, the pre-eminent architect of the Houses of Parliament. When the house was privately owned, the Queen was a frequent visitor. Now the Windsor Suite is yours for the asking. A seventeenth-century castle converted to a splendid hotel, **Amberley Castle** is a small, moated country house hotel with first-class bedrooms and common areas guarded by brooding suits of armor. There is a restaurant in the twelfth-century dining room. In Berkshire, **Cliveden** is a stately home with 38 bedrooms set in lush gardens and parkland. It's in the loving hands of the National Trust now, but past owners of the palace of pomp include a prince, three dukes and the Astor family.

In the unspoiled yachting haven of St. Mawes, the **Hotel Tresanton** enjoys the temperate climate of South Cornwall. This

small seaside hotel is stylish and understated, a haven of tranquillity and good taste. There is no swimming pool, no tennis court, no fitness center — just exceptional comfort wherever you turn. The restaurant is excellent.

FOLLIES, FORTS AND FACTORIES
England not only presents a host of luxurious hotels, but also some marvelously eccentric hostelries. The Landmark Trust rents out heritage buildings — some quite grand, others charmingly humble. Bed down at **Kingswear Castle** in Devon, built around 1500 on a rocky escarpment. Or how about the engine house of **Danescombe Mine** in Cornwall, or the flamboyant **Egyptian House** in downtown Penzance?

Most Landmark Trust properties are rented by the week (maximum of three weeks), but between April and November they can be rented for shorter stays. Houses are stocked with all necessities and comforts (though not with television or telephones) as well as local walking maps, a specially selected library and housekeeping services. All properties have central heating. Contact the **Landmark Trust** ((01628) 825925 FAX (01628) 825417, Shottesbroke, Maidenhead SL6 3SW, to order a copy of the *Landmark Handbook* (£8.50 when mailed within the United Kingdom; £10.50 to Europe; £20 for the Americas; £25 to Asia). In the United States, contact The Landmark Trust ((802) 254-6868, RR1 Box 510, Brattleboro, Vermont 05301. The trust also offers a free booklet listing 23 properties on Lundy Island, including the Lighthouse and the Admiralty Lookout.

The nine members of **Homes of Architectural Distinction**, ranging in vintage from Tudor to Victorian, open their doors, or drawbridges as the case may be, to overnight guests. For details, contact the Country House Association ((01869) 812800. Prices (moderate to very expensive) include a one-time membership fee.

The National Trust owns hundreds of distinctive "holiday cottages," some of which are the stuff of dreams. Within the stunning Trellisick Estate, West Cornwall, for example, the **Water Tower** is an 1860 stone tower with Gothic windows. Four small round rooms, stacked one upon the other, are connected by a spiral staircase. Contact the National Trust Holiday Cottage Booking Office ((01225) 791199 FAX (01225) 792267, PO Box 536, Melksham, Wiltshire SN12 8SX.

BED & FERRARI
Inform your spouse that he (or she) no longer has to buy a Ferrari to assuage his (or her) mid-life crisis. The privately owned hotels that

are part of the **Pride of Britain** group ((01264) 324400 offer a three-night package that includes bed, breakfast, dinner and the keys to a Ferrari, Jaguar or Porsche for the duration of the stay. The price is £950 for two people (includes insurance). Vroom vroom.

You can also rent, *sans* accommodation, a Jaguar, Aston Martin, MG, or Morgan for a week, a weekend or a day from the following agencies: Bespokes ((020) 8421-8686; Wykehams of South Kensington ((020) 7589-6894; or AutoEurope TOLL-FREE IN THE UNITED STATES (888) 223-5555 FAX TOLL-FREE IN THE UNITED STATES (800) 235-6321 E-MAIL ae@autoeurope.com.

Family Fun

Southern England is the storybook land of Winnie-the-Pooh, *Alice's Adventures in Wonderland* and Sherlock Holmes. It's a place where it still seems possible that ghosts haunt houses and fairies flit through forests. An island where gentle waves lap the seashore. A country of woolly sheep and tumble-down hills. A land of princely castles and enchanted gardens.

In short, England is a kid's paradise. It's true that the British are not always as warmly welcoming to youngsters as many families might hope, nor do all hotels and restaurants cater to kids. Most families, however, find that the pleasures of traveling with children in England far out weigh the inconveniences.

STORYBOOK ENGLAND
The Ashdown Forest, Sussex, remains much as it was in the 1920s when **A.A. Milne**, and illustrator E.H. Shepard, set the *Winnie-the-Pooh* stories here. Young and old fans of the "bear of little brain," will find a stroll in the forest enchanting. From the Pooh car park it's a muddy but rewarding walk to Poohsticks Bridge — so don't forget your Wellingtons. The path takes you through woods and along farmland to a gurgling brook spanned by a new wooden bridge where tradition dictates a rousing game of "Poohsticks." Instructions are available at the shop at Pooh Corner, in Hartfield village, on the edge of the forest. A number of other Pooh sites can be visited along a circular walk from Gills Lap car park, including the "enchanted place" at the top of the forest, near Piglet's house, where there is a memorial to Milne (see ASHDOWN FOREST, page 209 under KENT AND SUSSEX).

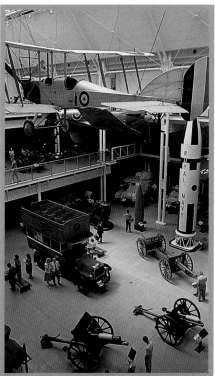

Famous Victorians — OPPOSITE: Eastbourne's Grand Hotel. ABOVE: Sherlock Holmes Museum, London. BELOW: The Imperial War Museum.

At Aylesbury, the Buckinghamshire County Museum (page 144) has a gallery dedicated to **Roald Dahl**, author of *Charlie and the Chocolate Factory* and *James and the Giant Peach*. You can see **J.R.R. Tolkien's** original map of Middle Earth at the Divinity School in the Bodleian Library at Oxford University (page 131). Oxford has scores of delights for children, many of them outlined in a sterling little booklet by Deborah Manley entitled "O is for Oxford: Over 100 Things for Families to Do in Oxford and Nearby" (Heritage Tours Publications). Pick up a copy (£2) at the Oxford Tourist Information Centre.

Way out west in Fowey, Cornwall, families can "mess about" on the river that provided inspiration for **Kenneth Grahame's** *The Wind in the Willows*. London has **Sir Arthur Conan Doyle's** Sherlock Holmes Museum, and in Kensington Gardens there is an enchanting statue dedicated to **J.M. Barrie's** *Peter Pan*.

THEME PARKS

Within day-tripping distance from London, **Legoland** ((01753) 626111, near Windsor, boasts miniature models of St. Paul's Cathedral and the Houses of Parliament, as well as roller-coasters and water slides. The park encourages picnicking, so you don't have to stick to an expensive diet of theme-park fare. As you might expect from a park dedicated to Lego blocks, there are lots of hands-on activities. The car and boat driving schools are a huge hit with older children. Overall, Legoland is probably best for kids 10 and younger.

Teens and their families might enjoy the huge **Chessington World of Adventure** ((01372) 729560, Leatherhead Road, Chessington; or the water-themed **Thorpe Park** ((01932) 569393, Staines Road, Chertsey,

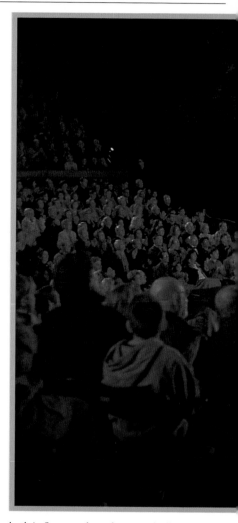

both in Surrey, where there are thrilling rides as well as more serene attractions, such as craft shops and petting farms. They're made all the more enticing by Green Line coach packages departing from London (see TOURS AND EXCURSIONS, page 86 in LONDON). At Chessington the zoo is open daily year-round, the theme park open March to October. Thorpe Park is open daily during summer months.

Further afield, **Flambards** ((01326) 564093, Helston, Cornwall, is regarded by some thrillseekers as the country's best all-round theme park. Along with rides (such as the "twist and spin hi-tech Space Orbiters, equipped with 'zapper guns' to send rival orbiters whirling out of control" or the intriguing "Junior Lifters and Shifters fork-lift trucks"), there are some one-off features including a weather-forecasting studio where you can try your hand at presenting the

weather, a Victorian Village and the Britain in the Blitz exhibition. Flambards is off the A394 on the south side of Helston. Closed November to Easter and Monday and Friday at the beginning and end of the season.

THE QUIZ

Families needn't limit themselves to kid-centric places like theme parks and petting zoos. Many grown-up attractions offer ingenious "quizzes" or activity books that open the door to learning and fun. A quiz may include anything from a scavenger hunt to mathematical problems. Some even offer a chance to win a small prize if you return the completed quiz. Adults have fun too, as they work through puzzles with their children, when, for example, searching for the giant's shrunken heart amidst the cobblestones at St. Michael's Mount, or working out the

mathematical slope of Up-along Road at Clovelly. Activity brochures can be found where you pay your entrance fee, sometimes offered for free and sometimes for a small charge.

LONDON

"London Bridge is falling down!" squeals the nursery rhyme. It may be a harsh lesson for *Mother Goose* fans, but it's a fact that London Bridge is a concrete strip. It's Tower Bridge that many people envision when they hear this nursery rhyme. Still, this post-modern London Bridge does occupy the site of the oldest bridge in the city. It was here on an ancient version of the much-heralded span that

Pageantry — OPPOSITE: A jousting festival at Warwick Castle, Warwickshire. ABOVE: Regent's Park Open-Air Theatre, London, stages Gilbert & Sullivan's *Pirates of Penzance*.

Vikings camped out, threatening war with King Ethelred the Unready and his ally King Olaf of Norway. Stumped by the Vikings' sit-down strike, Olaf and Ethelred had their troops pull down the bridge — and thereby hangs a nursery rhyme.

London is full of tales and legends. No matter how jaded adults become, it can still tickle fancies. And seeing it through kids' eyes can only help. The changing of the guards, Buckingham Palace, Tower of London, Big Ben, a ride on a double-decker bus….

Speaking of buses, at Covent Garden a triumvirate of museums leads off with the **London Transport Museum** where 15 "KidZones" offer things to pull and push, buttons to buzz, signs to spin. A punch card provided at the entrance can be added to with stamps earned from station to station. There's the Funbus for under-fives, a Tube simulator and more. Nearby, the **Theatre Museum** is brimming with fantastic displays of stage magic. There's a schedule of children's events from puppet making to theater arts to marionette shows. At the **Cabaret Mechanical Theatre**, the fun starts when you walk in the door and a wooden mechanical man stamps your ticket for you. Inside you can have your hand "cut off" by the Great Chopandoff, have your fortune told in sand on the back of your hand, or ratchet Crankenstein to life.

The **Natural History Museum** is at the top of many family museum to-do lists. This venerable museum has been recently revamped with lots of special effects and hands-on galleries. Big hits with kids are the animatronic dinosaurs, the Kyoto earthquake in the Power Within exhibit and the massive blue whale in the Mammals hall.

Across the Thames, the **London Balloon**, a tethered balloon ride, is a crowd-pleaser and much less expensive than a regular hot-air balloon ride. Next to the launch site is the unsung **Vauxhall Farm**, a free petting zoo where kids can feed the farm animals.

Dining out can be a challenge for traveling families anywhere. Fortunately, London has a number of restaurants with a family focus. At Maggiore's Classic Italian ((020) 7379-9696, 21 Tavistock Street WC2, kids eat free with an adult. R.K. Stanley's ((020) 7462-0099, 6 Little Portland Street W1, has a children's menu, as well as activity sheets and special events. Belgo Noord ((020) 7267-0718, 72 Chalk Farm Road, plunks fries on the table as soon as you sit down. The children's menu starts at £5. There's entertainment every weekday from noon to 3 PM at Smollensky's-on-the-Strand ((020) 7497-2101, 105 The Strand WC2, as well as a children's menu from £8. Bank ((020) 7379-9797, 1 Kingsway, does a children's brunch (£8.50) on weekends, served up with coloring books.

Cultural Kicks

While many vacation dreams bring up images of sunny skies and daiquiris on the deck, a trip to England, for most of us, conjures up a different vision. We go to England for culture (and good beer). We go to see great works of art and ecclesiastical architecture, to behold the achievements of a former empire, to take part in traditions that weave through

the collective unconscious from the Changing of the Guards to Christmas pudding. We go for the neon blink of London nightlife, for the Western world's most vibrant theater scene, or to walk in the footsteps of the Beatles, Virginia Woolf, or William the Conqueror.

England presents such a vast array of cultural enjoyments that it would be impossible to do it justice in this short space. But for those planning a first trip, this sampling may help you flesh out your own dreams of Albion. There are further discussions on each of these aspects of English culture throughout this book.

TOP MUSEUMS AND GALLERIES
In terms of sheer numbers of visitors, the **British Museum** stands alone. Each year some six million people enter this storehouse of antiquities, making it the second-most-visited attraction in the United Kingdom (after Blackpool Pleasure Beach in Lancashire!) A stay in London would be incomplete without a trip through the three millennia of history represented here, taking in famous finds such as the Parthenon Frieze, the Book of the Dead and the Rosetta Stone.

Almost as popular (with five million visitors each year), the **National Gallery** is Britain's state collection of Western and European painting, a repository of 2,000 masterpieces dating from the thirteenth to the nineteenth centuries. Each of the major European schools of painting is represented here, and the

museum owns masterpieces and sometimes whole bodies of work by all of the greats.

The **Tate Gallery** underwent cell division in 2000 and is now two galleries: The Tate Britain remains at Millbank; the most famous work here is probably Sir John Everett Millais' radiant vision of *Ophelia*. At a new ultra-post-modern location in Bankside, the Tate Modern continues the story of art into the twentieth and twenty-first centuries.

The **Fitzwilliam Museum** in Cambridge has been lauded as the finest small museum in Europe. Within the museum's ornate neoclassical building are Egyptian sarcophagi, Greek and Roman art, Chinese ceramics, English glass, antique furniture, illuminated manuscripts as well as the paintings of Titian, Rubens, Gainsborough, Constable, Cézanne and Picasso. Equally rich in treasures, the **Ashmolean Museum**, in Oxford, is an extraordinary collection of art and artifacts. Among its hoard is the stunning ninth-century Alfred Jewel, believed to have been a gift from the Saxon King Alfred. You can also see Guy Fawkes' lantern and a cloak once owned by the father of Pocahontas. On the upper floors is a marvelous collection of pre-Raphaelite paintings and decorative arts.

OPPOSITE TOP: The London Eye. BOTTOM: Louise Bourgeois' Abstract Expressionist spider sculpture at the Tate Modern. ABOVE: Tomb of the Black Prince, Edward Prince of Wales, Canterbury Cathedral.

THE THEATER SCENE

London's theater scene is unrivaled anywhere in the English-speaking world. Not even Broadway can boast as many star-studded productions, nor as much variety — from blockbuster musicals to cutting-edge productions. The **West End**, London's theater district, had some 50 theaters at last count, and shows run every night of the week. Best of all, when compared to New York, the London theater scene is a bargain, with ticket prices ranging from £10 to £45.

Beyond the West End's mainstream theater scene, London also bursts with fringe productions where new and cutting-edge theater is performed in intimate settings. Long-running fringe theaters in London include: the **Bush** ((020) 8743-3388 at Shepherd's Bush; **Almeida** ((020) 7359-4404 in Islington; and the **Orange Tree** ((020) 8940-3633 in Richmond.

Pub theater is another London institution. The **Gate Theatre** ((020) 7229-0706, above the Prince Albert pub, 11 Pembridge Road W11 (Θ Notting Hill Gate), has a reputation for high-quality, low-budget drama; while London's oldest pub theatre, the **King's Head** ((020) 7226-1916, 115 Upper Street N1 (Θ Angel), does small-scale musicals in the evenings and lunchtime plays. *Time Out* will list what's showing at these and other venues.

You'll also find vibrant theater happenings in towns across Southern England. At Stratford-Upon-Avon the **Royal Shakespeare Company** performs the works of the Bard

year-round, and the **Chichester Festival Theatre** has an international reputation for its stage productions and summer fringe events. Elsewhere small-scale theater performances, as in London, often take place in local pubs. Ask at tourist information centers for venues.

CATHEDRAL HIT PARADE

England's cathedrals are a reminder of a time when the Church was the very backbone of English life, as well as the keeper of vast quantities of the national wealth. The buildings and their booty went through hard times during the Dissolution, and again during the Civil War, but their glory remains, reflected in some ecstatically fine architecture. A visit to one of its great cathedrals is one of the purest pleasures England offers. If you can, time your visit to coincide with the ancient Anglican tradition of **evensong** — a sunset service featuring canticles, psalms, hymns and anthems.

Magnificent **Winchester Cathedral** is a pastiche of architectural styles from Norman (eleventh century) to Perpendicular (fourteenth century). Interior decoration includes the largest section of mediaeval floor tiles in England. Ask one of the docents to point out a "green man;" these curious fertility symbols inhabit corbels and capitals throughout the cathedral. Many kings lie buried here as well as famous figures, including the writers Jane Austen and Izaak Walton.

Praised for its unity of style, **Salisbury Cathedral** is almost pure Early English Gothic. It is unique among English cathedrals for this harmony, though two of its most splendid features — the 121-m (404-ft) spire and the chapter house — date from the fourteenth century. The West Front, with its row upon row of empty niches, was extensively renovated in 2000.

Another cathedral of singular style is the Norman **Canterbury Cathedral**, built of Caen stone imported from France. Canterbury's primary interest lies not in its heavily impressive aesthetics but in its place in English hearts as the hub of the Anglican Church.

Unlike those at Salisbury, the west front niches of **Wells Cathedral** are populated with hundreds of saints and monarchs. Inside, Wells has some particularly striking chantry chapels. Looking like miniature cathedrals, these confections of carved stone were endowed by parishioners to give priests a place to pray for the parishioners' souls. Wells's most striking feature is its stunning scissor arches.

The towers of **Exeter Cathedral** are Norman, while the rest of the building dates

from the fourteenth century. As at Wells, Exeter's west front is adorned with stone figures and the interior has magnificent rib vaulting. **Chichester Cathedral** is another Early English beauty, with an astounding collection of art, much of it modern. **Ely Cathedral** has a glorious 22-m-high (72-ft) painted wooden ceiling, and some of the finest fan vaulting and tracery in English architecture. Founded by a woman, Saint Etheldreda, Ely has a fittingly feminine feeling about it — full of light and tinted glass with an airy, gracious beauty.

LITERATURE

One of the great pleasures of traveling around England is visiting and exploring places associated with English writers and their works. To get in touch with the breadth and depth of Britain's literary history, go to the **British Library** (see WHAT TO SEE AND DO, page 105 under LONDON) where you can examine original manuscripts from Beowulf to Brontë, as well as early printed editions of the works of Shakespeare, Thomas Hardy and many others.

Once you've whet your belletristic appetite, hit the streets of **London**, steering for the homes and hang-outs of Charles Dickens, Virginia Woolf, Dr. Johnson, John Keats, Karl Marx, Robert Browning, Elizabeth Barrett Browning, and Samuel Pepys. Look for the blue oval plaques attached to houses around the city, which point out the who's-who of literary London. (Hint: Thomas and

Jane Carlyle, T.S. Eliot, George Elliot, Mrs. Gaskell and Oscar Wilde all lived in Chelsea.) A useful reference is George William's *Guide to Literary London* (Batsford, 1973). It's out of print, but you may be able to find it in one of the Charing Cross Road secondhand shops. Several of these London houses are open to the public, including Charles Dickens's house on Doughty Street (page 103). While in London, you can also visit Shakespeare's Globe Theatre Exhibition; pay a visit to the hero of J.M. Barrie's story at the Peter Pan statue in Kensington Gardens, and drop in on 221A Baker Street, the fictitious headquarters of Sherlock Holmes. Even better, take a stroll with **Original London Walks** ((020) 7624-3978 FAX (020) 7625-1932, whose guided walking tours track down Sir Arthur Conan Doyle's famous detective, Bloomsbury's literary pubs, and the London of Shakespeare, Dickens and Oscar Wilde.

Outside London, the pages keep turning. Geoffrey Chaucer (circa 1345–1400) penned *The Canterbury Tales*, a collection of yarns, sometime quite bawdy, told by a group of pilgrims on their way to the shrine for St. Thomas Becket at **Canterbury**, where you can visit the great pilgrimage cathedral yourself and see the spot where Becket was

OPPOSITE: The choir files across the lawn below the spire of Salisbury Cathedral. ABOVE: As in the Bard's day, "groundlings" stand for performances at the Globe Theatre, London.

murdered. Other writers associated with Canterbury are Charles Dickens, who set many of the scenes from *David Copperfield* here; and Christopher Marlowe, a contemporary of Shakespeare, who was born here.

Stratford-upon-Avon is perhaps England's most important literary pilgrimage center. Author of 35 plays and 154 sonnets, William Shakespeare (1564–1616) was born in Stratford, spent the latter part of his life here and is entombed in the parish church. The Royal Shakespeare Company (RSC) carries the Bard's torch, and many of the houses associated with Shakespeare and his family members are open to the public.

Jane Austen (1775–1817) wrote about the daily life of the early nineteenth century in novels such as *Emma, Pride and Prejudice, Sense and Sensibility* and *Mansfield Park*. Towns associated with Austen include **Lyme Regis**, **Winchester**, and **Bath**. Austen lived at **Chawton**, a small village 24 km (15 miles) northeast of Winchester, between 1809 and 1817. The house is now a museum devoted to her life and work, with her letters, period furnishings and a bookstore.

At **Rye** you can visit the house of Henry James. Also in Sussex, Charleston Farmhouse near **Lewes** was the countryside headquarters of the Bloomsbury Group, and Monk's House was the summer home of Virginia and Leonard Woolf. You can follow the Thomas Hardy trail through **Dorset**, visiting the sites of his imaginary Wessex as well as the writer's birthplace at Higher Bockhampton, and his residence at Max Gate. All of these houses are open to the public.

Should you thirst for more literary lore, look for Sally Varlow's *Reader's Guide to Writers' Britain* (London: Prion Books Ltd., 1997), an entertaining book full of anecdotes and illustrations of literary landscapes and shrines.

Shop till You Drop

The land described by Napoleon as "a nation of shopkeepers" boasts the largest shopping mall in Europe, Bluewater Park (near Dartford, Kent). But England is better known for its one-of-a-kind, old-fashioned, oft-eccentric shops. Some of these shops sell sought-after **English specialties** such as antiques and art, silver and pewter, teas, jams, books, linens, woolens and other fabrics. Others, like **James Smith & Sons Umbrella Warehouse and Stick Factory** (New Oxford Street, London), are simply a taste of something uniquely English. This store, for example, stocks functional to fanciful

walking sticks made of fruitwood, bamboo and horn, and a deluge of umbrellas from ultra-light collapsible numbers to Pierre Vaux fashion statements in screaming polka dots.

London continues to stoke its reputation for *haute couture* with hundreds of chic boutiques and department stores. The capital's annual January sale is an event in itself, driving bargain-hunters to queue all night outside the big departments stores. Towards the end of the month, though the choices have thinned, prices may be reduced even further. There are other, smaller, sales at the end of spring and summer.

Auction houses are another London tradition. Sotheby's ((020) 7493-8080, New Bond Street (Θ Bond Street), founded in 1744, is the oldest and largest fine-art auctioneer in the world, selling furniture, jewelry, silver, porcelain, pictures, books and more. Auctions are held regularly year-round except in August.

In general, **shopping hours** are from 9 AM to 5:30 PM Monday through Saturday. Some shops close early on Wednesday; some keep evening hours on Thursday. Shopping centers and malls are usually open from 10 AM to 4 PM on Sunday.

ART AND ANTIQUES

Britain is a superb place to buy art and antiques. Scores of unique shops, markets and fairs offer items in an array of styles and periods reflecting the long history of the commonwealth and its penchant for preservation.

You'll find antiques shops and art galleries nearly everywhere you travel in Southern England, and sometimes the off-the-beaten-path places have the best buys. There are, however, certain areas that are well known as antiques and art markets, where you'll find not only great variety but can be assured of superior quality.

London antiques markets include Antiquarius, Kings Road SW3, open Monday to Saturday; Camden Lock, Buck Street, Chalk Farm Road NW1, open weekends; Camden Passage, Angel N1, open Saturday; Greenwich Antiques Market, Greenwich High Road SE10, open weekends; and Portobello Road, Notting Hill Gate or Ladbroke Grove W10 or W11, open Saturday. While Portobello is most popular with amateurs, **Bermondsey Market**, Bermondsey Square SE1, is generally regarded as having the city's most interesting antiques market. It's frequented by dealers who start

TOP: One person's junk is another's treasure in Alfriston, Sussex. BOTTOM: In the ancient cathedral city of Wells, time seems to stand still.

When purchasing antiques look for seals bearing the "BADA" or "LAPADA" insignia to ensure authenticity.

SOUVENIRS

What to bring home for Aunt Minnie and the girls? To set your imagination spinning, I have compiled this highly subjective list of Southern England's best souvenirs.

Some of the ripest places for souvenir shopping are museum gift shops. In London, check out the handmade automata, paper cut-outs, and wooden model kits at the **Cabaret Mechanical Theatre**, Covent Garden. The shops at the **British Museum** sell replicas of many of its treasures. Intriguing and useful, Rosetta Stone mousepads (£11.99) are cut in the same broken shape as the famed linguistic puzzle-solver, and are made of basic black vinyl with white lettering.

The gift shop at the **Tower of London** is a treasure trove of interesting items. Take home Paddington Bear dressed in a Beefeater costume for £29. For something a bit more lusty, plunk down £55 for a metal-faced fiberglass replica of Henry VIII's codpiece.

In Hampstead, the **Museum Store**, 4A–5A Perrin's Court, sells art objects and oddments from museum giftshops around the world. I liked the slippers printed with a map of the London Underground (£12.50), in case you get lost while walking in your sleep?

At **Brighton**, everyone wants to take home a stick of "Brighton Rock" candy. These brightly-hued sugar sticks are sold everywhere along the beachfront, including The Brighton Rock Shop, 50 Kings Road, where you can also get pebble candy that looks convincingly like a handful of Brighton beach.

While in **Winchester**, I spotted replica mediaeval terracotta floor tiles at the cathedral gift shop (£5.95). One makes an attractive coaster; or mix and match the designs and create something grand.

I always start a trip shorn of jewelry and aim to come home with some new spangles. On a visit to **Stonehenge** (Wiltshire), I discovered some tasteful sterling-silver earrings in the shape of Stonehenge, set off by a single amber bead (Stonehenge; £11.95).

Stones Spells for Magic Feasts (Stones, Avebury; £17.95) is the second cookbook put out by Stones, the vegetarian restaurant in **Avebury** (Wiltshire). The recipes are marvelous and the illustrations make the book a joy to look at. If you don't care to tote it home, order it from your local bookseller.

There's a shop at **Standen** (Sussex) full of books and items reflecting the spirit of the Arts & Crafts Movement. There you can buy Beth

arriving at 4 AM each Friday armed with flashlights. The pros have snatched up the best stuff by 9 AM, though the market doesn't start closing until noon, so rise and shine. Θ Borough or Θ/BR London Bridge.

Outside of London, centers for art and antiques include: Cambridge, Bury St. Edmunds, the Cotswolds, Cheltenham, Gloucester, Rye, Bath, Windsor, Oxford, and The Lanes in Brighton.

Large **antiques fairs** are your chance to see a great many dealers in one spot. The BADA Fair is highly respected. For details contact the British Antique Dealers Association ((020) 7589-4128 FAX (020) 7581-9083, 20 Rutland Gate, London SW7 1BD. The largest antiques and fine art dealers association in Great Britain is the Association of Art & Antique Dealers (LAPADA) ((020) 7823-3511 FAX (020) 7823-3522 E-MAIL lapada@lapada.co.uk, 535 Kings Road, Chelsea, London SW10 0SZ. LAPADA has a useful WEB SITE www.lapada .co.uk with articles posted on every angle of purchasing antiques and art in the United Kingdom, including VAT refunds, and age certification for passing customs. For the complete picture, order their *Buying Antiques in Britain* (1999). The price is £6 for delivery within the United Kingdom, $20 for North America, and £8 for Europe.

Russell's book, *William Morris Needlepoint*, with typical Morris patterns full of peacocks, lions, tearful maidens, acanthus leaves (Crown Publishers; £30).

The decorative mushroom-shaped stones scattered about rural gardens of the southwest had me puzzled until I passed through the Cotswolds hamlet of **Lower Slaughter** and found replicas for sale at the Mill Shop. They're called staddle stones and were (and in rare instances still are) used for propping up stores of grain to keep out rodents. They go for £5 to £75, depending on the size.

Another Cotswolds treasure, the Cotswold Woolen Weavers has a wonderfully woolly shop in **Filkins** (Gloucestershire). I took home a snuggle-inducing mulberry-and-heather woolen throw to remind me of that fuzzy Cotswolds feeling. Prices start at around £25. The Woolen Weavers are the last commercial users of the wool of the original long-haired "Cotswold lion."

The well-stocked shop at the Shakespeare Centre and Birthplace, **Stratford-upon-Avon**, has piles of Shakespeare ephemera, from plume pens to Bard busts. If you have young kids with a budding interest in Shakespeare, look for the finger puppets made of dyed felt, depicting characters from *Macbeth, Romeo and Juliet, A Midsummer Night's Dream* and *The Tempest*. They're £5.50 per set of five characters — one for each finger. Lady Macbeth is particularly fetching.

In Cornwall, the land of sailing ships and secret harbors, you can dress up as pirates (or urge your kids to on pain of walking the plank) and pose for a black-and-white photo at Cast and Crew Piratical Pictures on Bunker Hill, **St. Ives**. The production values are quite good. Prices range from £12 for a one-pirate picture to four pirates for £15. Another good photo take-home is the **Land's End to John O'Groats signpost**. It's £5 if you want your hometown to appear on the signpost, but if you're not picky, you can sidle up to the post and take your own pix.

In the tiny fishing village of **Mousehole** (Cornwall), the Mousehole Craft Shop ℂ (01736) 731109, on Brook Street, has a marvelous array of jewelry, art, and automata (like those found at the Cabaret Mechanical Theatre in London). Everything in this tiny shop is tempting, but the willow lobster pots (£22.50) made by fisherman and craftsman David Harrison won my heart.

OPPOSITE: Harrods department store — "a cross between a pre-war ocean liner and an Oriental bazaar." ABOVE LEFT: Portobello Market. RIGHT: Camden market mannequins have seen it all.

Often the best souvenirs are found in the most unexpected places. My favorite English find is the sea-urchin shell I bought in **Portloe**, on the remote Roseland Peninsula in Cornwall. A reed basket near the harbor was full of freshly collected shells in pastel hues of lavender, orange and blue, and a hand-lettered sign said, "honor system, £2 each, two for £3." Unlike the shells you find in souvenir shops, these were unglazed, and for weeks mine emanated that salty scent of the sea.

Short Breaks

There are two things to keep in mind when planning a short vacation in Southern England: 1) geographically speaking, it's a small part of a tiny island; and 2) culturally speaking, it's huge. Instead of a do-it-all whirlwind trip, consider applying Susan Allen Toth's "thumbprint" method. In *My Love Affair with England* (Ballantine, 1992), Toth advises readers to settle into a cottage or hotel for a few days and explore an area "no larger than [your] thumbprint will cover on a standard folding road map of England," that is to say, about a 16–24-km (10–15-mile) radius.

A rich area for "thumbprint" travelers is the 24 km (15 miles) between Lewes and Eastbourne in East Sussex. Besides being gorgeous countryside, this area has some of the county's most interesting and varied attractions. Explore the haunts of the "**Bloomsberries**," a group of early twentieth-century artists and writers that included Virginia Woolf, at Charleston Farmhouse, Berwick Church, and Monk's House (Rodmell). Alfriston is a picture-perfect village surrounded by rolling downland and river valleys with a

December) is the ceremonial illumination of
a city tree donated each year by Norway and
lit by the Mayor of Oslo. All over Southern
England, **caroling concerts** take place during
the Christmas season. Many churches have
candlelit **midnight mass** on Christmas Eve
(December 24).

Chinese New Year (late January or early
February), celebrated in London's Chinatown,
brings the year full circle with lion dances,
processions, and firecrackers.

Galloping Gourmet

A culinary renaissance has taken root in
Great Britain, flowering most profusely in
London. English cuisine, once universally dull
and bland, is suddenly being hailed for its
versatility: Like the language, it's said, English
cooking is flexible. It's thus open to influence
and experimentation, and the chefs of Britain
are making the most of it.

It's about time. Travelers to England can
now find not only wider variety on the menu,
but some truly excellent cooking. The use of
fresh, local ingredients is the foundation
of any self-respecting "gastropub" or "Mod
Brit" café. Influences from France and the
Mediterranean are much in favor resulting in
hybrids such as roast chicken stuffed with foie
gras or grilled rabbit with pumpkin polenta.
With the advent of the good food revolution in
Britain, a host of celebrity chefs have captured
the attention of the public in a whirl of
television and radio appearances, book
signings and restaurant openings. Since the
immense success of his television cooking
show, "The Naked Chef," twenty-something
Jamie Oliver has left London's River Café and
now works as a consultant chef with buddy
and fellow River Café ex-pat **Ben O'Donohue**
at the upmarket Knightsbridge bar and
restaurant, Monte's. As this book went to
press he was preparing to launch his own
restaurant. In contrast to striplings like Oliver,
Anton Edelman has been the Maître Chef de
Cuisine at London's Savoy since 1982, where
he runs one of the busiest creative kitchens in
the world. Also in London, **Phillip Howard**
heads the kitchen at The Square, in Mayfair,
where his inventive takes on classic dishes
have earned him a second Michelin star.
Alastair Little opened his first restaurant in
1985 on Soho's Frith Street (Alastair Little),
followed by a second branch ((020) 7243-2220,
in Ladbroke Grove on Lancaster Road (W11).
A third Alastair Little enterprise, also in Soho,
L'Escargot, does modern French. Another
much-celebrated London chef-proprietor,

Gordon Ramsay, has moved on from the
hugely successful Aubergine to establish the
new Gordon Ramsay on Royal Hospital Road,
in Chelsea, which was quickly awarded two
Michelin stars.

While London sometimes seems to have a
death grip on food fashions, there are a few
bright stars in the counties. A pioneer of
Britain's good-food movement, **Rick Stein**
has a quartet of dining establishments in
the picturesque fishing village of Padstow
in Cornwall. The flagship is the Seafood
Restaurant, which for more than 20 years
has served creatively prepared fresh-off-the-
trawler fish and shellfish. **Raymond Blanc**
operates the lauded Manoir aux Quat' Saisons
in a fifteenth-century manor house in Great
Milton (Oxfordshire). The restaurant, serving
contemporary French cooking, has earned two
Michelin stars, and the hotel is a member of
the exclusive Relais & Châteaux group.

While trend-watchers lick their chops at the
latest food gossip, traditionalists still have
plenty to cheer about. Fish & chips are still a
popular take-out food in Britain. (Cod, plaice
or haddock is dipped in batter and deep fried,
accompanied by thick french fries and
wrapped in newspaper.) But, you may want
to skip lunch entirely if you've indulged in a

OPPOSITE TOP: Covent Garden *al fresco*. BOTTOM:
Oxford's Covered Market peddles upscale produce.
ABOVE: Feasting in Amberley Castle's twelfth-
century Queen's Room.

"full English breakfast" of bacon, sausage, fried eggs, and baked beans accompanied by grilled mushrooms and tomatoes, washed down with a strong cup of black tea!

Best of all, there is no shortage of homey **pubs** to tuck in to English standards like steak & kidney pudding, toad-in-the-hole (meat cooked in batter), or beef Wellington (fillet steak wrapped in puff pastry with mushroom and onion filling and port wine sauce). A pub meal, at its best, is a gastronomic event, with an ambiance that is unencumbered by notions of class.

DRINK

"There is nothing which has yet been contrived by man, by which so much happiness is produced as by a good tavern or inn," wrote Samuel Johnson. The neighborhood pub, tavern or inn is part of the social fabric of every British community. At "the local," bartenders serve up pints and half pints of golden hop-flavored bitter, as well as mild ale, stout, lager and cider. Usually an alcoholic drink in Britain, cider is often stronger than beer. The West Country version of this traditional brew is famously potent and frequently fells the unwary.

In Britain, draught beers (served from a tap) are called **real ales**. The bible for real ales — with information on varieties and where to find them — is the *Good Beer Guide* published annually by the Campaign for Real Ale ((01727) 867201 FAX (01727) 867670, 230 Hatfield Road, St. Albans Hertfordshire AL1 4LW. The book also lists breweries that offer tours.

While in London, beer lovers should take one of the **pub walks** by London Walks ((020) 7624-3978 FAX (020) 7625-1932. Paired with an experienced brew connoisseur and a group of fellow thirsties, you'll visit back alley public houses, taste some of Britain's best brews and hear your fill of pub lore.

Another beverage of passion in Britain is, of course, **tea**. While flaccid tea bags are the stuff of most English breakfasts, real (loose leaf) tea can still be found. Tea connoisseurs carefully prepare tea in the traditional way, brewing the leaves in a china pot, one spoonful of tea per person and "one for the pot." Freshly boiled water is poured onto the leaves, which are left to steep for a few minutes. Most Britons prefer their tea strong, with milk and sometimes sugar.

High tea is a meal in itself, and there are scores of atmospheric places to enjoy this English ritual, from London's Ritz to the Lygon Arms in the Cotswolds. For a laid-back version of this pinkies-up activity try the **Orangery** ((020) 7376-0239, at London's Kensington

Palace. The menu features smoked salmon, cream cheese and dill sandwiches, scones with clotted cream, Orangery sponge cake and tea or coffee (£7.75). Or if you're in an expansive mood, order the "Grand Tea," which includes all of the delights of high tea but comes with champagne and Belgian chocolate cake (£12.35).

Special Interests

The English have raised the humble hobby to the level of passion. Much respect (or at least a wide berth) is given to amateurs who throw themselves body-and-soul into their object of affection, be it lepidoptery or letter-boxing (a kind of scavenger hunt practiced on the moors). Perhaps because of the encouragement given to such eccentricities, England offers a world of special interests to explore.

GARDENS

British gardens are some of the finest in the world. County Kent claims the title of the "Garden of England," but fabulous gardens of every description abound throughout Southern England. Most gardens are open between March and October, although some, such as the Royal Botanic Gardens at Kew and Wakehurst, are open year-round.

Many great gardens are profiled throughout this book, but those thirsty for more might try the British Tourist Authority's "Britain's Gardens," a map with information on 100 British gardens open to the public; or the English Tourism Council's booklet, *A Guide to English Gardens*. See BRITISH TOURIST AUTHORITY OFFICES WORLDWIDE, page 324 in TRAVELERS' TIPS, for contact information.

For true garden connoisseurs, however, these slim volumes may not be satisfactory.

Patrick Taylor's *The Garden Lover's Guide to Britain* (Princeton Architectural Press, 1998) is an in-depth reference to 100 of Britain's most distinctive gardens, with brilliant photos. You'll find a host of other excellent guides and references in bookstores, as well as the National Trust shops, and a particularly astounding collection of books on gardens and gardening at Kew (see page 110).

If you're planning to visit several gardens, you might consider purchasing a pass or membership. The Great British Heritage Pass and National Trust membership give you free entry to scores of gardens (see MEMBERSHIPS AND DISCOUNT PASSES, page 327 in TRAVELERS' TIPS).

See TAKING A TOUR, below, for organized garden tours.

One of the many colorful gardens to be found throughout Southern England.

COOKERY CLASSES

In the wake of Britain's good food revolution has come a rising demand for recreational cookery courses. Many employ Britain's famous chefs. In London's South Bank Centre, **Butler's Wharf Chef and Restaurant School** ((020) 7357-8842 or (020) 7357-8842 puts on demonstration dinners featuring celebrity chefs as well as one-day courses where you can watch and learn.

If you want to get your hands greasy, there are plenty of obliging programs.

Chef Raymond Blanc heads up the **École de Cuisine** at Le Manoir aux Quat'Saisons ((01844) 278881 or TOLL-FREE IN THE UNITED STATES (800) 845-4274 FAX (01844) 278847, Church Road, Great Milton OX44 7PD, the distinguished Michelin-spangled restaurant and country-house hotel. Courses, including sumptuous accommodation at the hotel, are offered from September to April each year.

The world famous French cooking school, **Le Cordon Bleu** ((020) 7935-3503 FAX (020) 7935-7621 E-MAIL info@cordonbleu.net, 114 Marylebone Lane, London W1M 6HH, has a sister school in London's West End offering daily half-day demonstration classes as well as one- to five-day hands-on sessions and month-long courses. Themes include pastries, vegetarian cooking and French cuisine. There are also children's courses.

In Cornwall, the lovely seaside **Hotel Tresanton**, St. Mawes, offers three- to five-day cooking classes with master chefs during the winter months. Past themes and instructors have been Alastair Little on fish, the River Café course with Ruth Rogers and Rose Gray, Fusion with Peter Gordon, and a beginner's course with Maxine Clark. Register through Tasting Places ((020) 7460-0077 FAX (020) 7460-0029

E-MAIL ss@tastingplaces.com Unite 40, Buspace Studios, Conlan Street, London W10 5AP.

There are many more cookery courses throughout Southern England; an excellent resource for finding information on recreational cooking courses is the WEB SITE www .cookforfun.shawguides.com.

See TAKING A TOUR, below, for culinary tours.

THE ROYALS

If the brouhaha of the last few years hasn't dampened your enthusiasm for royalty, you'll probably want to take in some majestic splendor while you're in the Kingdom. A visit to Buckingham Palace, headquarters of Her Majesty Queen Elizabeth II, is a must for royalty watchers. Plan your visit carefully; the palace is only open to the public for eight weeks in August and September. Windsor Castle, Queen Elizabeth's country home, has more ample opening hours, with the State Apartments open October to March (closed some holidays during this time, so call).

The British monarchy maintains an excellent WEB SITE www.royal.gov.uk, where you can glean information about your favorite princely personalities, right up to their daily agendas. Send an e-mail from the site if you've something on your mind. Those who prefer traditional methods can get out their best stationery and write to the Queen at: Buckingham Palace, London SW1A 1AA.

If you're planning on calling on royalty, remember to address the queen as "Your Majesty" and subsequently as "Ma'am." You can learn more about royal protocol in *Whitaker's Almanack* (published annually).

WORKING VACATIONS

Seasonal, voluntary work with conservation and archaeological organizations can deepen your

understanding of English history and geography along with providing opportunities to participate in a unique aspect of English social life. And if you find manual labor relaxing, it's an inexpensive way to take a vacation.

The British Trust for Conservation Volunteers ((01491) 839766 FAX (01491) 839646 E-MAIL natural-breaks@btcv.org.uk, 36 St. Mary's Street, Wallingford, Oxfordshire OX10 0EU, has year-round working holidays ranging in duration from two to seven days. Participants might learn the art of hedge-laying in East Devon, take up coppicing in the Hambledon Hills of Dorset, or lend a hand clearing footpaths in rural Gloucestershire. Accommodation may be in tents or farmhouses. Fees, which cover room and board, start at £25. The BTCV has a useful WEB SITE www.btcv.org.

If you're interested in doing some serious digging, contact the Council for British Archaeology ((01904) 671417 FAX (01904) 671384 E-MAIL 100271.456@compuserve.com, 111 Walmgate, York Y01 2UA, for a list of sites and opportunities. They also put out *British Archaeological News*, a periodical where you'll find ads calling for volunteer help on archaeological sites in Britain. There's often a small fee charged. You can also write to the British Archaeological Association, Comway Library, Courtauld Institute, Somerset

House, The Strand, London WC2R 0RN (written inquiries only).

The National Trust has a range of 300 working vacations each year from weekend (£22) to week-long (£45 to £53) stints. Fees include meals and lodging in cottages, farmhouses and converted stables. Work might be laying out a woodland path, counting cowslips, building a drystone wall, or assisting with the running of a concert or festival. Volunteers must be over the age of 17. Call ((01891) 517751 (50p in the United Kingdom) to leave your name for a free brochure; or write National Trust Working Holidays (B), PO Box 84, Cirencester GL7 1ZP.

Students looking for short-term work can take advantage of international work exchange programs. Contact the Council on International Educational Exchange ((020) 7478-2000 FAX (020) 7734-7322 E-MAIL cieeuk @easynet.co.uk, 52 Poland Street, London W1V 4JQ, or 205 East 42nd Street, New York, New York 10017; or the British Council ((0161) 957-7755 or (020) 7930-8466 FAX (0161) 957-7762 E-MAIL general.enquiries@britcoun.org WEB SITE www.britishcouncil.org.

OPPOSITE TOP: In the candy kitchen at Cheddar Gorge, Somerset. BOTTOM: The Albert Memorial, London. ABOVE: Honor Guards, St. James's Park.

HOMESTAYS

Servas is an international network of hosts
and travelers that aims to provide person-to-
person contacts between cultures. An annual
US$65 fee gives access to host lists to find pen
pals and local contacts while on the road, or to
arrange homestays. The application process
includes an interview by a local Servas
representative. United States residents should
contact United States Servas ((212) 267-0252
FAX (212) 267-0292 E-MAIL usservas@servas.org,
11 John Street, Suite 407, New York, New
York 10038. Residents of other countries may
refer to the Servas WEB SITE www.servas.org for
contact information.

Parish Holidays ((01256) 895966 FAX (01256)
896144, 3 Winchester Street, Whitchurch,
Hampshire RG28 7AH, has been organizing
week-long homestays in the United Kingdom
for almost 20 years. Guests are placed in a host
home and taken around to see the sights.
Accommodation may be a thatched cottage, an
old rectory or a modern bungalow. Fees help to
finance repairs to local church buildings.
Southern England communities sponsoring
stays are in West Cornwall and East Kent.

Taking a Tour

"No country is easier to travel in…" writes
Paul Theroux; "the British invented public
transport." Theroux is right. There is no need to
join a coach tour to see Southern England. Still,
if your time is limited or you enjoy traveling
with a group, you have a wealth of options.

ESCORTED COACH TOURS

Globus and their low-budget partner **Cosmos**
are highly rated for offering a quality tour with
plenty of time to explore on your own. They
have scores of trips to choose from lasting from
eight to 21 days. Most of them take in not only
England but wide swathes of the British Isles,
however Cosmos's nine-day Southern England
tour is more focused, taking in London,
Stratford, Bath, Plymouth, Land's End, Looe,
Portsmouth and Canterbury. Globus's "best of
Southern England" tour is a seven-day jaunt
through London, Stratford, Bath, Stonehenge,
and Canterbury. For information visit their
WEB SITE www.globusandcosmos.com, or see
a travel agent.

Collette Tours specializes in sweeping
"European highlights" tours, some of which
include England; they also have some more
concentrated theme forays such as their Royal
Britain, which begins in London and continues
through Salisbury and Bath before heading off
to Wales. For information contact Collette

Tours in the United States at ((401) 728-3805
TOLL-FREE IN THE UNITED STATES (800) 340-5158
E-MAIL customerservice@collettetours.com.
The WEB SITE www.collettetours.com lists
offices worldwide.

Brendan Tours has a week-long circuit
that hits the highlights of London, Oxford,
Stratford, Bath, Salisbury and Stonehenge.
Like Cosmos, Brendan specializes in "value-
priced" vacations. For information see a
travel agent or visit Brendan Tours' WEB SITE
www.brendantours.com.

A small-group tour has distinct advantages
over the typical cumbersome coach tour. The
United Kingdom-based company, **Brit Tours**
((01749) 812873 FAX (01749) 813108 E-MAIL
tours@brittours.com, 8 Townsend Close,
Bruton, Somerset BA10 0HD, leads escorted
small-group (15 maximum) coach tours
though Southern England.

SPECIAL INTEREST TOURS

Adventure touring in Southern England is
not of the wild and woolly variety. Walking,
cycling and riding trips take full advantage of
England's cozy inns and gentle countryside.
Backroads ((510) 527-1555 TOLL-FREE (800)
462-2848 FAX (510) 527-1444, 801 Cedar Street,
Berkeley, California 94710-1800, specializes in
posh outdoor trips. They offer a six-day inn-to-
inn walk and a six-day cycling trip in the
Cotswolds; both include a stay and meals at
Michelin-starred Lords of the Manor in Upper
Slaughter. **Euro-Bike & Walking Tours** ((815)
758-8851 TOLL-FREE (800) 321-6060, PO Box 990,
DeKalb, Illinois 60115, organizes a one-week
walk taking in Windsor, the New Forest, the Isle
of Wight, Salisbury, and Stonehenge, and an
eight-day Cotswolds bike tour from Bath.

For birding and wildlife watching there is
Victor Emanuel Nature Tours ((512) 328-5221

TOLL-FREE (800) 328-8368 FAX (512) 328-2919
E-MAIL ventbird@aol.com, PO Box 33008
Austin, Texas 78764, with escorted tours of
Britain (as well as throughout Europe).
Maximum group size is 18. Write for their
newsletter or see WEB SITE www.ventbird.com.

Equitour ((307) 455-3363 TOLL-FREE (800)
545-0019 FAX (307) 455-2354 E-MAIL equitour
@wyoming.com, PO Box 807, Dubois,
Wyoming 82513, specialize in horse-riding
tours. They offer a three-day cross-country ride
in Dartmoor with departures from April to
September, and a five-day ride in Exmoor from
Porlock Vale with trips starting year-round.

Elderhostel TOLL-FREE (877) 426-8056,
75 Federal Street, Boston, Massachusetts
02110-1941, is a non-profit organization

The many canals that criss-cross Southern England
make barges a relaxed way to tour the countryside.

offering educational adventures to people 55 years and older. Past offerings in England have covered scores of topics from an inside look at the lives of British royalty to mediaeval pilgrimage places to classical music and opera in London. The WEB SITE www.elderhostel.org has an on-line catalog.

HF Holidays ((020) 8905-9558 FAX (020) 8205-0506 E-MAIL info@hfholidays.co.uk, Imperial House, Edgware Road, London NW9 5AL, offers a wide variety of tours including walking and hiking jaunts as well as special-interest trips featuring everything from bridge to ballroom dancing. They also do mini-coach garden tours, as well as tours of historical sights and country estates.

"A rose is a rose is a rose," said Gertrude Stein, unless it's made of sugar. **Culinary Nomads** ((541) 774-9270 TOLL-FREE (877) 946-6623 FAX (541) 773-7347 E-MAIL frm @culinarynomads.com, 820 Crater Lake Avenue, Medford, Oregon 97504, takes small groups of aspiring cooks to destinations all over the world. Their England program is Cake Gardens of England, a tour of English gardens combined with classes on cake decorating using designs inspired by the English landscape. Another culinary tour operator is **Cuisine International** ((214) 373-1161 FAX (214) 373-1162 E-MAIL cuisineintl@aol.com,

PO Box 25228, Dallas, Texas 75225, with one- to three-week spring trips to Le Manoir aux Quat'Saison for classes in French cuisine.

Smithsonian Study Tours offer a range of educational travel programs year-round. In England, choose from tours featuring the Southern England countryside, Shakespeare's England, Cornwall, Christmas in Bath, as well as a sojourn at the Oxford Seminar where you can choose from among eight subjects on English culture and history. The Smithsonian's "Ships, Trains, and Planes" tour is an intriguing survey of modes of travel and transportation from the QE II to the Eurostar. To request a catalog: ((202) 357-4700 TOLL-FREE (877) 338-8687 E-MAIL tours@tsa.si.edu WEB SITE www.si .edu.tsa/sst.

North American sister organization to the National Trust, the **Royal Oak Foundation** ((212) 966-6565 or in the United Kingdom (01989) 720-576 TOLL-FREE IN THE UNITED STATES (800) 913-6565 WEB SITE www.royal-oak.org, 285 West Broadway, New York, NY 10013, organizes study tours to Southern England, including an ultra-deluxe cruise aboard the QE II with an onboard lecture series on English gardens, accommodation in London at the Savoy and visits to private gardens, hosted by their owners.

Maupintour TOLL-FREE (800) 255-4266
E-MAIL info@maupintour.com is a major coach
tour company offering a 12-day English
Garden tour which also takes in Stonehenge,
the Cotswolds, and Warwick Castle. The tour
finishes with a tour of Parliament guided by a
member of Parliament.

It seems only fitting that London should be
the destination of a rock-and-roll travel tour.
A new outfitter, **Adventures in Rock** ((617)
696-6938 TOLL-FREE (877) 788-7625 WEB SITE
www.adventuresinrock.com, takes groups to
London to see their favorite bands followed by
a music "insider's" tour of the city. Past trips
have featured the Eurythmics, Blondie, Elvis
Costello, and Sting.

TAILOR-MADE TOURS

A new breed of web sites are offering services
once reserved for the close friends and
relatives of guidebook writers: a tour tailor-
made for your interests by *the* expert on
the territory.

Via **Guidebookwriters.com** WEB SITE
www.guidebookwriters.com, you can contact
the authors of top travel guidebooks for advice
on your trip or a personalized itinerary,
straight from the horse's mouth. Taking the
technology a step further, **12degrees** WEB SITE
www.12degrees.com offers individualized
itineraries by well-known guidebook writers
in addition to complete booking services.

DAY EXCURSIONS

Several agencies offer day excursions to places
within easy reach of London (Stratford,
Blenheim, Leeds, Stonehenge, Windsor, etc.).
Operators include London Regional Transport
((020) 7222-1234; Evan Evans ((020) 7930-2377
and Frames Rickards ((020) 7837-3111. If you'd
rather go *sans* guide, National Express ((0990)
010104 and Green Line ((020) 8688-7261
E-MAIL enquire@greenline.co.uk, offer days out
from London that include round-trip coach
fare and entrance fees to popular destinations
such as Brighton's Royal Pavilion, Flagship
Portsmouth and Leeds Castle.

Guide Friday organizes **hop-on hop-off
narrated tours** on double-decker buses in
major Southern England tourist destinations
(Bath, Cambridge, Dover, Hastings, Oxford,
Plymouth, Portsmouth, Southampton,
Stratford-upon-Avon and Windsor). If you're
planning to visit several of these cities you can
take advantage of Guide Friday's discount
book of four tickets to be used in any of these
cities. Available from BritRail or Rail Europe
TOLL-FREE (877) 274-8507; BritRail Travel Shop
(walk-in only), 551 Fifth Avenue, Seventh
Floor, New York, New York.

CRUISES

Hotel boats cruise the River Thames and its
canals between London and Oxford. Barge
Cruise Specialist offers vacations on "floating
country inns" with stops at Windsor Castle,
the country estate of Cliveden, riverside
villages and Oxford, with an optional
hot-air-balloon excursion. You can make
reservations through B&V Associates
TOLL-FREE (800) 217-4447 FAX (212) 688-3778
E-MAIL sales@europeanwaterways.com,
140 East 56th Street, Suite 4C, New York, New
York 10022. There are several other barge-
cruise companies, including **Europe Express**
((425) 487-6711 FAX (425) 487-3750 E-MAIL
barging@europeexpress.com, 1905 North Creek
Parkway, Suite 100, Bothell, Washington 98011.

The most romantic way to arrive in
England has to be by sea. The *Queen Elizabeth II*
makes frequent crossings from New York to
Southampton (five days at sea). There are also
departures from Boston and Miami. Contact
a travel agent, or Cunard TOLL-FREE (800)
728-6273 FAX (305) 463-3010, 6100 Blue Lagoon
Drive, Miami, FL 33126.

OPPOSITE: Pharaonic bust contemplates eternity in
London's British Museum. ABOVE: A costumed
character works the crowd at Hampton Court,
Outer London.

Welcome to Southern England

In travelling through England, a luxuriance of objects presents itself to our view. Where-ever we come, and which way soever we look, we see something new, something significant, something well worth the traveller's stay....

— Daniel Defoe, *A Tour Through the Whole Island of Great Britain.*

England has been a tourist destination for nearly two millennia. Hundreds of years before Daniel Defoe found so much to see and do here, citizens of the Roman Empire discovered in England a congenial home-away-from-home. Coins recently excavated from the hot springs at Bath were found to come from every corner of the Roman Empire, indicating that visitors were not just legionnaires posted to the region, but notables from all over mainland Europe.

Of the varied regions of this treasured isle, Southern England has always been the most widely traveled and well loved. Britain's lowland, the South is blessed with rich and fertile soil, a gentler climate than the northern highlands, as well as wide and verdant river valleys. In addition to two stunning national parks, Dartmoor and Exmoor, thousands of square miles of English countryside have been designated Areas of Outstanding Natural Beauty. The smallest of these "jewels of the English landscape" is the Isles of Scilly with its white quartz sand beaches, aquamarine waters, rare birds, and subtropical gardens. The largest is the Cotswolds with its mellow hills and villages.

Ever since the Romans began to suffer rheumatism here, the climate and its vagaries have been a topic of conversation in England. The old adage that "you don't come to England for the weather" may be true, but for some, the elements, foul or fair, are part of what makes this land unique. When a summer downpour turns the crowded streets of a seaside resort into an umbrella jousting fest, you know you're in England. Even on the so-called Cornish Riviera, a windbreak is a more common beach accoutrement than a parasol. For my part, I'll never forget walking out of the British Library into a thick London fog, thinking: "Now *this* is London!"

So much has been said about England that writing this guidebook seemed a daunting task. What can I say that hasn't already been said? What is there to tell about that hasn't already been discovered a hundred times over? But once my travels began, England began to take shape in my imagination, and the land, in a sense, became mine. My hope is that I've turned up a few surprises, provided a different slant, and finally charted a pleasing path through a land that offers a bewildering abundance of "objects." I trust, as did Defoe three centuries before, that though the many writers who have come this way before "may have had a harvest, yet they have always…passed over so much, that others may come and glean after them by large handfuls."

SOUTHERN ENGLAND'S REGIONS

Most visits to England start in London. The turning of the millennium has added luster to the capital city's already sparkling constellation of attractions. The London Eye is perhaps the most striking alteration to the London skyline, whirling in freewheeling contrast to the sober neo-Gothic lines of Big Ben, the Houses of Parliament, and Tower Bridge. Yet while movement and change will always define this vibrant city, the traditional pleasures that make London unique endure—a ride on a double-decker bus, an ale by the fire at Ye Olde Cheshire Cheese, a picnic at Regent's Park, a rainy day at the British Museum, and London's green heart.

While a lengthy vacation in London could be very well spent, travelers who journey into the countryside of this compact and remarkably varied land are treated to what some would call the real England. For purposes of exploring this rich field, this guide divides the South into seven areas, beginning with the Inland Shires which ring London to the north and west. Here the ancient university town of Oxford dazzles visitors with its architectural magnificence, and the Home Counties offer up treasures such as Windsor Castle, Queen Elizabeth II's private residence, and Hatfield House, the childhood home of Elizabeth I.

The Cotswolds and Shakespeare Country take in some of England's loveliest and most enduringly popular touring areas. The Cotswold Hills with their "honey-pot" villages have enchanted travelers for ages. And Stratford-upon-Avon, birthplace of the Bard, has attracted tourists since Shakespeare breathed his last.

Part of East Anglia, South Cambridgeshire and Essex stretch across the flatlands north and east of London. Cambridge is Oxford's less touristy cousin, with a wealth of glorious architecture and history to know and explore. Essex's well-preserved mediaeval villages and superb biking and birding are within easy striking distance of London.

Kent and Sussex are Britain's most densely populated areas, yet they take in many magnificent open spaces, as well as miles of coastline including the celebrated white cliffs of Dover. Nicknamed the "Garden of England," this region is known for its stately manor houses, castles, and glorious gardens. The area is home, as well, to the ancient pilgrimage town of Canterbury, bucket-and-shovel seaside resorts from Ramsgate to Brighton, and "1066 country," where the Battle of Hastings changed the course of Britain's history.

The handsome cathedral city of Winchester is the heart of Hampshire and Dorset. Along the coast, Portsmouth boasts a fascinating maritime heritage, and Dorset is studded with both twinkling resorts and a wild, sandy seashore.

Somerset and Wiltshire excel in prehistoric remains, with Stonehenge the chart-topper in Somerset. The friendly cathedral city of Wells offers contrast in the form of inspiring mediaeval architecture. One of England's most popular destinations is found at the heart of this varied region: the Georgian spa town of Bath with its magnificent abbey and a history that dates back to the Roman era.

Devon and Cornwall are favored by the British for seaside vacations. From Devon's fertile pastures to the cliffs at Lands' End, this area, often called the West Country, boasts England's most dramatic natural scenery. Cornwall's remote peninsulas and golden beaches make the "far west" an ideal destination for outdoor adventurers, from ramblers to surfers. Devon is home to the wilds of Dartmoor National Park, while the county's prized dairies produce clotted cream, a staple of English tea time.

OPPOSITE: Thames riverboaters get an eyeful of the 135-m (450-ft) London Eye. ABOVE: A black "brolly," more than a fashion statement.

England
and Its
People

This fortress built by Nature for herself
Against infection and the hand of war,
...This precious stone set in the silver sea,
Which serves it in the office of a wall
Or as a moat defensive to a house
Against the envy of less happier lands....

— William Shakespeare, *Richard III*

Britain's history has been shaped by its island geography. Separate, inviolate, remote — at times viewed as the very edge of the world, this kingdom with its watery defenses has only been conquered twice: in AD 43 by the Romans and in 1066 by the Normans. Both of these invasions profoundly influenced the course of English history.

While the twentieth century saw the breaching of this silver sea by plane and then by tunnel, the island of Great Britain, of which England is a part, remains in many senses distinct from the rest of Europe in both geography and sensibility.

CELTS AND ROMANS

Some 300,000 years ago, the island that we know as Britain gradually separated from the continent as the tremendous funneling force of the ocean running through what is now the English Channel broke through and eventually stranded the inhabitants. Later the islanders' ranks were swollen by Stone Age immigrants who arrived in 4,000 BC, settling the fertile Salisbury Plain, farming the land, and eventually erecting over centuries the monuments at Stonehenge, Avebury and other sites around the country.

Around 700 BC, Celts from the Rhine Valley flooded western Europe and the British Isles, overwhelming the indigenous races. The artifacts these settlers left behind show that they were an advanced society. They grew corn which they kept in underground storage areas, they mined lead, which was carried to St. Michael's Mount and sold to merchants from overseas; and when they rode into battle, they did so in chariots.

In 55 and 54 BC the Romans came calling, but Celtic warriors repelled these early advances. Following unsuccessful invasions by Julius Caesar's armies, nearly 100 years lapsed before the Roman conquest of Britain began in earnest. In AD 43, Claudius invaded the island, landing 40,000 Roman soldiers at Richborough, Kent, and conquering Southeast England. Years of fighting followed, including the famous uprising led by Boudicca, the Queen of the Iceni, who burned London and several other important Roman administrative centers before she was captured.

Once the Romans had things well in hand, there followed a period of relative peace and plenty on the island. The Romans imported their Mediterranean know-how and their language, transforming yet never fully erasing Celtic society. They introduced Classical architecture and built roads. The romanization of Britain also meant the rise of cities and towns, most of which contained public baths, and markets where goods from the continent were traded. London was the most important in terms of trade and commerce, becoming the capital of the province, and the most romanized.

In 337, Emperor Constantine died and the security of the island rapidly disintegrated as a series of military rebellions and invasions from Scotland weakened the Roman hold on their island outpost. The Romans retreated in 409. For decades following their retreat, Britons continued to plead with Rome to rescue them, but their calls went unheeded.

ANGLO-SAXONS, DANES AND VIKINGS

With the Romans gone, the Celts fell to hiring Germanic mercenaries to defend them against invading Northern European tribes of Angles, Saxons and Jutes. But the Celts and their hired armies fought to no avail. From the mid-fifth century onward, the conquering tribes gradually established themselves in small fiefdoms throughout the former Roman colony. These new settlers, in turn, contended with Danish raiders, vying for control of Eastern England from the eighth through the eleventh century.

While the Danes overran eastern England, it was the Viking threat, beginning in the latter part of the eighth century, that created a common cause amongst the Anglo-Saxon tribes of the island, bringing portions of them together under Alfred the Great, who became king in 871. During his 28-year reign, the Anglo-Saxons called themselves "Angelcynn" (kin of the Angles) and called their land "Engla-lond" (land of the Angles), and their language, "Englisc" (now called Old English). Their story is told in the Old English *Anglo-Saxon Chronicle*, the first important prose work in English literature.

THE NORMANS AND THE PLANTAGENETS

In 1042, the Saxon kingdoms were united under Alfred's descendant, the pious Edward the Confessor. So devout was Edward, he appears to have taken a vow of celibacy, thus leaving the kingdom without an heir. When he died, four men laid claim to the English throne: the King of Norway, the Duke of Normandy, and two of Edward's brothers, Tostig and Harold.

Harold quickly took the upper hand and had himself crowned at Westminster Abbey, after which he successfully fought off attacks by Tostig

survey of English land holdings completed in 1086 provides rich pickings for historians even to this day.

Henry II's crowning in 1154 began an era that would last for 300 years: the reign of the Plantagenets. Henry ruled a vast empire taking in not only Britain and Normandy but Anjou, Brittany and Aquitaine, representing most of modern France. He is remembered as a wise and just ruler having instituted reforms of the courts and introduced a system of common law which not only operates in modified form in England, but eventually influenced the American legal system. Despite his accomplishments, Henry is primarily remembered for his association with Thomas

and the King of Norway. He then brought his exhausted troops to Sussex to face the army of the Norman Duke William, who had landed at Pevensey. Troops clashed at Hastings and Battle, and Harold was killed, shot through the eye by an arrow. The Duke was crowned William I, later known as William the Conqueror.

Norman rule brought immense changes to English society. French became the language of court as William rapidly replaced English aristocrats with French-speaking Normans. The invaders built "motte-and-bailey" castles and imposed a feudal system. With their cathedrals they introduced a monumental architecture to the island with solid features and rounded arches. One of William's greatest accomplishments was the *Domesday Book*, so called because its information was said to be as unassailable as the Day of Judgment, or Doomsday. This massive

Becket, Archbishop of Canterbury. The king had pinned high hopes on his friend and ally as a conduit to smooth relations between Church and State, but Becket had his own notions. Finally Henry, in one of his famous rages, declared, "Who will rid me of this turbulent priest?" His knights, taking the king at his word, slunk away to Canterbury where they murdered Becket in the cathedral.

The fall-out from the murder of Becket, as well as turbulence within the royal family as his sons and wife fought over their legacies, caused Henry's reign to end in discord. Eventually the kingdom was split, with Henry's son Richard taking Normandy, Anjou and England, while Brittany and Aquitaine went to two other sons.

OPPOSITE: The sun has shone on Stonehenge for five millennia. ABOVE LEFT: The tomb of a Roman official, at Colchester, Essex. RIGHT: Warwick Castle's Great Hall, Warwickshire.

Richard, dubbed *Coeur de Lion,* or the "Lionheart" for his brave exploits as a knight, only visited England twice, being taken up by crusading throughout his rule. When he died in battle, the throne was passed to Henry II's son, John, remembered for his role in another significant moment in English history. It was King John who, under pressure from a group of his barons, signed the Magna Carta in 1215 at Runnymede. Not the document of human rights that it is now often supposed to be, the barons' charter was essentially meant to protect feudal rights against royal abuse. But more importantly, the document established the principle that the king is not above the law.

the sporadic wars with France, however, was the catastrophic outbreak of bubonic plague. During 1348–49 the Black Death wiped out a third of England's population.

By the late fourteenth century, things were changing due to the effects of the Black Death. The resulting decline in population had caused a labor shortage, and repressive measures were instituted to keep the peasantry from demanding more wages. Widespread resentment against the government as well as the riches and corruption of the clergy led to the Peasants' Revolt in 1381. Rioters sacked the archbishop's house at Southwark, burned the lawyers' rolls at the Temple, stormed the Tower of London and

King John died the following year and his son was crowned Henry III. Growing discontent amongst the nobility, added to Henry's excesses and his failure to command respect, lead to a battle at Lewes backed by Simon de Montfort, where Henry was defeated and imprisoned. De Montfort summoned the Great Council to meet at Westminster, along with representatives from each shire and most of the larger towns. This meeting is seen as the forerunner to Britain's Parliament.

THE HUNDRED YEARS WAR AND THE BLACK DEATH

Toward the close of the Plantagenet rule, Edward III claimed the French throne through his mother Isabella, setting off the Hundred Years War (1337 to 1475) with France. More devastating than

beheaded the Lord Treasurer and the Archbishop of Canterbury on Tower Hill. The rebellion was finally put down by the 14-year-old King Richard who met the rebels at Smithfield and killed the ringleader, Wat Tyler.

It was many years before the economic decline set off by the Black Death began to be reversed. During this period, the wool industry developed, farmland was cleared for pasture and rich wool farmers and merchants used their wealth to create the buildings which are still seen in many parts of the English landscape, especially the Cotswolds. Churches were being built throughout the country in Perpendicular style, the last stage of English Gothic architecture, with large windows, vertical lines and fan vaulting.

Meanwhile back at the royal castle Henry Bolingbroke, the first of the Lancastrian kings, had

Key industries were nationalized, social services were expanded, and the National Health Service was created, offering free medical treatment and care. All of this was taking place during a time of terrible economic hardship.

By the time Elizabeth II ascended the throne in 1953, Britons were enjoying a much improved standard of living. By 1957, Prime Minister Harold MacMillan could claim that British people "had never had it so good."

In the 1960s, the post-war baby boom and rising prosperity brought youth culture to the fore and London was "swinging" with the music of the Beatles, the Rolling Stones, the Who, and the Kinks. The 1970s saw the United Kingdom's reluctant entrance into the European Union. Prime Minister Margaret Thatcher began her tenancy at No. 10 Downing Street in 1979. Thatcher's years as prime minister saw the dismantling of the welfare state, massive unemployment, continuing mistrust of the European Union, and the Falklands War in 1982.

Violence marred the 1980s with the miners' strike in 1984, IRA bombings, and riots in inner-city Liverpool and London. Economic stratification gripped the country during these years. While more people had a higher standard of living than ever before, there were also more people living below the poverty line than there had been before Conservative rule, and homelessness was on the rise.

Thatcher's 11-year incumbency was brought to an abrupt end by her own party in 1990. She was succeeded by the Conservative John Major who presided over the connection of the English and French sides of the Channel Tunnel. Regular rail service started in 1995, and with it, Britain and the Continent were physically joined for the first time in 10,000 years.

A drawn-out recession had set in by the end of the decade as unemployment increased and thousands of companies went bankrupt. The royal family experienced what the Queen described as her *annus horribilis* in 1992. Three of her married children were divorced or separated, she agreed to pay taxes for the first time, and a disastrous fire struck at her private residence, Windsor Castle.

John Major remained in office until the 1997 general election, when the Labour Party's Tony Blair was swept into power with its largest-ever parliamentary majority. Within months of the victory, Diana, Princess of Wales, was killed in a car crash in Paris. Yet with the establishment in 1999 of governing bodies in Scotland, Wales and Northern Ireland, and with the telegenic Blair at the helm, the late 1990s brought a rising sense of better times ahead.

Faces of Britain —LEFT to RIGHT: Girl Guide at your service; feeding pigeons in Trafalgar Square; Notting Hill Carnival couture; a bobby shows off his handlebar mustache.

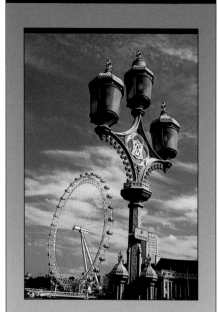

London

London is chaos...without any plan or logic; an omnipotenwt, slightly melancholy, insatiable chaos. A dark tropical forest whose sole architect, Time, is fussy, contradictory, charmingly naive, full of irrational appendages.

— Nikos Kazantzakis, *England*

From the banks of the snaking River Thames, London extends its chaotic magic over more than 1,570 sq km (600 sq miles). The population of Britain's sprawling capital city is seven million, making it one of the word's largest metropolises. An international center of government and finance, it is also one of the great cultural centers of the world.

With its vibrant blend of ancient and modern, Britain's capital city attracts more than 23 million visitors each year. The most popular tourist spots can test the nerves with noise, queues and detritus, but these areas are concentrated — a few yards away and you're back in a real city again.

The building and renovating boom that led up to the millennium celebrations created more to see than ever. London pulled out all the stops for the millennium, spending more than £6 billion on construction and renovation projects. Preparations also saw the addition of new wings at the Science Museum and the National Portrait Gallery, new galleries for the Wallace Collection, a Great Court at the British Museum, and the grand

London isn't built along a New-York-style grid, but as mile after mile of stitched-together villages, each with their high-street shops and corner stores: Chinatown's twinkling arches and open-air massage doctors, Camden Town's lost-in-the-sixties street fairs, Soho's bohemian chic, Mayfair's dignified glow. In some areas, blocks of multi-story buildings mar the skyline. But the traces of what London was — a group of mediaeval and Tudor villages joined by seventeenth-, eighteenth- and nineteenth-century housing schemes — has not been entirely erased.

Cradled in this eclectic atmosphere is London's greatest miracle: its green heart. Hyde Park, with its Serpentine Lake, is the refuge of boaters, bathers and people-watchers. Queen's Garden within Regent's Park is a miracle of roses, while the smaller Green Park has a wild woods feel, and St. James's has its placid natural lakes and bird life.

re-opening of the renovated Royal Opera House at Covent Garden.

No matter when you visit London, there is bound to be a festival or special event on tap. Major happenings are described under FESTIVE FLINGS, page 53 in YOUR CHOICE. A complete listing is available from the British Tourist Authority ((020) 8846-9000 WEB SITE www.bta.org.uk, Thames Tower, Black's Road, London W6 9EL.

BACKGROUND

Starting with Roman Londinium right up to the marking of the new millennium, London's history has been that of rapid growth and expansion followed by destruction and rebirth.

In AD 60, already an important Roman administrative center, London was attacked and destroyed when Queen Boudicca led the Celtic Iceni tribe of East Anglia in revolt against Roman rule. (You can visit Boudicca's statue at Westminster Pier.) Some 65 years later, *circa* 125, London was laid waste again, this time by a massive fire. Each time, the Romans rebuilt, fortifying and enlarging the city.

After the Roman retreat at the beginning of the fifth century, London declined as the Dark Ages drew a mantle over the island. Danish invasions heated up in the 800s, and London, now part of the Saxon Kingdom of Mercia, came under repeated attack until peace was brokered by Alfred the Great in 886, making London the capital of England. Christianity arrived eventually, and Edward the Confessor built Westminster Abbey and his palace. When 1066 rolled around, William the Conqueror took the city, building the Tower of London to subdue its inhabitants as much as to protect it from invasion.

During the Middle Ages, London flourished again, reveling in its role as the seat of the court and government at Westminster. London also prospered as the hub of the country's road system and as the major port for trade with the continent.

The golden age ended in the year 1348 when the Black Death, bubonic plague, arrived in London and the rest of the island, wiping out one third of the population. But, by 1600, London's population had not only rebounded but burgeoned to 200,000, spilling beyond the city walls and into Southwark. By now London had emerged as a major financial center with the establishment of the Royal Exchange.

Life, and trade, went on — unprepared as always for the next disaster. In 1666 the Great Fire broke out, destroying two-thirds of London — a toll of 10,500 houses, 89 stone churches, most of the Guildhall, and St. Paul's Cathedral. Surprisingly, however, the fire took only eight lives. It's said that within a week of the conflagration, Sir Christopher Wren, then a professor of astronomy at Oxford, submitted his plans for a new cathedral. He spent the rest of his life overseeing the construction of his masterpiece. Most of London's houses were rebuilt in a flurry by 1682, this time of less flammable materials.

By 1720 there were 750,000 people living in London, which was by now the hub of a growing empire, and the last remnants of mediaeval London disappeared as Georgian architects built London's Palladian residential squares.

By the mid 1800s, London, with a population of half a million, was the largest city in Western Europe. The city continued to expand dramatically through the nineteenth century, creating vast tracts of Victorian suburbs. With the rest of the country, Londoners suffered from and enjoyed the technological advances of the ensuing years. World War II arrived and with it another tale of devastation. During the Blitz of 1940, German air raids destroyed large areas of Georgian and Victorian

London, yet, miraculously, Sir Christopher Wren's St. Paul's Cathedral, by now one of the city's greatest architectural treasures, survived.

The years following the war created the London we see today, with a not-always-palatable backdrop of stark concrete planes against which spires and gables of surviving parts of old London throw their delicate shadows. The London Docks, heavily damaged in the war, never recovered, and shipping eventually moved out to Tilbury. After years of decline, the old docks were discovered by developers in the 1980s and Docklands was born.

Today, rapid redevelopment of urban wasteland continues in London with the revitalization of the Greenwich peninsula and ongoing reclamation along the South Bank. New architectural masterpieces have forever altered the city's skyline, from the new Tate to Waterloo station and the London Eye. Culturally, London has perhaps never been more diverse nor more dominant, rivaling New York for art and nightlife, and Paris for fashion and streetlife.

Meanwhile, ever mounting numbers of visitors continue to arrive in Britain's capital city — whether headed for the British Museum or Madame Tussaud's, the opera or the latest techno dance floor, the street markets or Harrod's department store. London welcomes them all with open arms.

GENERAL INFORMATION

The **Britain Visitor Centre** is located at 1 Regent Street in Piccadilly Circus, London SW1Y 4XT. You'll find an exchange bureau, a Britrail representative, a National Express coach representative, and assistance with accommodation. Open weekdays from 9 AM to 6:30 PM, weekends from 10 AM to 4 PM. The center does not take phone calls.

Information is also available through the **London Tourist Board** ((0839) 123456 (50p per minute), or (020) 7932-2020 (lodging) FAX (020) 7931-7768, 9 AM to 5:30 PM Monday to Friday.

There are **point-of-arrival information services** (all of which will make accommodation reservations) at Heathrow Terminals 1, 2, 3, and at the Underground Station Concourse, Heathrow Airport as well as Liverpool Street Underground Station, Victoria Station Fourcourt, and Waterloo International Arrivals Hall.

London has a growing number of **cybercafés** where you can download e-mail and surf the web for an hourly fee. Among many others, look for Cyberia, 39 Whitfield Street W1; Dillons Bookshop, Gower Street WC1; Cyberspy Restaurant Café, 15 Golden Square W1; Café Internet, 22-24 Buckingham Palace Road, Victoria SW1; and the Internet Exchange at 125–127 Baker Street NW1; as well as at 37 The Market, Covent Garden WC2; and the First Floor, Trocadero Centre, Piccadilly W1.

The *Cutty Sark* moored at Greenwich Pier.

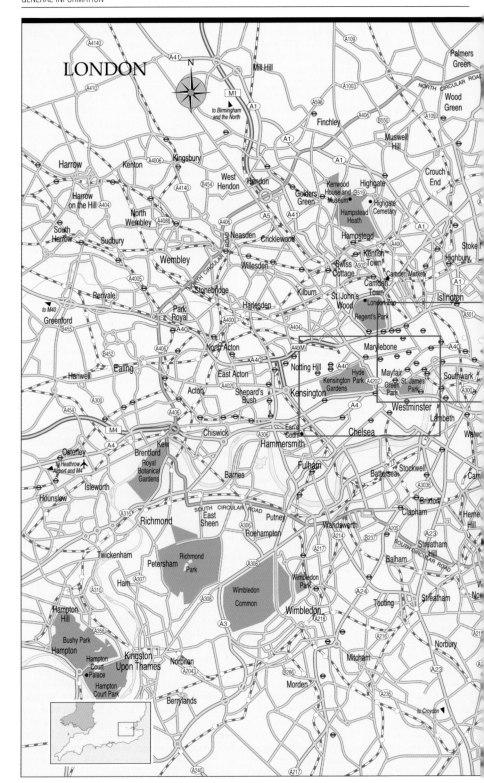

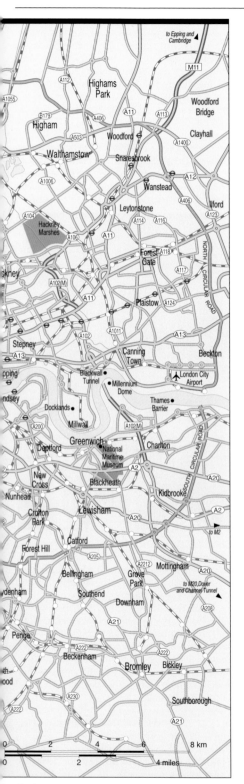

GETTING AROUND

Dense traffic, one-way systems, and scarce and expensive parking make London a driver's nightmare. Fortunately, there is no need to have a car in London. Public transportation is plentiful and pervasive. If you prefer not to ride the subway and buses, cabs are everywhere, though not cheap. See below for London taxi information.

Most visitors take advantage of the London Transport's excellent Underground and bus network. Purchasing a **TravelCard** can save money and time, since you avoid having to stand in line to buy a ticket each time you travel. TravelCards are available in one- or seven-day versions (you'll need a photo for the seven-day card). They give you access to London buses, the Underground, Docklands Light Railway and parts of the mainline rail system. Cards can be purchased at Underground stations, London Transport Travel Information Centres (below), mainline railway stations and London Tourist Board Information Centres. The **Visitor TravelCard** must be purchased before you arrive in the United Kingdom. It gives unlimited rides on all six zones of the London Underground (including transit to and from Heathrow Airport on the Piccadilly line) and bus rides. This card can only be used after 9:30 AM. Contact BritRail Travel International ((212) 575-2667 TOLL-FREE IN THE UNITED STATES (800) 677-8585.

If you're only going to be traveling in Zone 1, which takes in most of what's covered in this guide, it may be just as convenient to buy a **carnet**, a booklet of 10 single Underground tickets.

The Underground and buses run until approximately 12:30 PM, after which there are **night buses** (marked with an "N") operating out of Trafalgar Square, about one per hour, until early morning when the tube starts up again. You can get a timetable at one of the London Travel Information Centres or at major Tube stations. At the time of research there were noises about new ordinances allowing pubs to stay open past 11 PM. It would follow that London Transport might make some changes to its nighttime schedule, so night owls should check with London Transport or the Tourist Information Centre for the latest details.

Riding **double-decker buses** is more scenic than the tube, and sometimes quicker, depending on your route. In any case, these wheeled icons are an essential part of the London experience and not difficult to master. Large stations such as Victoria have helpful staff to show you the ropes and you can pick up a map detailing the central routes. The $64,000 question is, of course: How will I know when to get off? Ask the conductor to alert you when your stop comes up; he (or she) will be happy to help.

For more information on bus or subway services in Greater London, call **London Travel Information** ℂ (020) 7222-1234 (24-hours) WEB SITE www.london transport.co.uk. If you'd like to receive information on services and route maps in advance of your visit, write to London Regional Transport, 55 Broadway, Westminster SW1. There are Travel Information Centres at King's Cross, Oxford Circus, Piccadilly Circus, St. James's Park, Heathrow Terminals 1, 2, and 3, and at Euston and Victoria mainline railway stations. London Transport also operates a French language telephone inquiry service ℂ (020) 7233-0101, daily from 9 AM to 9 PM.

Taxis are ubiquitous in London. Hotels and major tourist areas have "black cab" (not always black these days) stands, or you can hail a cab from the street. If the yellow "for hire" sign above the windshield is lit, the taxi is available. It's possible to book a cab by calling ℂ (020) 7272-0272 or (020) 7253-5000. Mini-cabs are unlicensed taxis that provide a cheaper fare than the black cabs; they're not permitted to pick people up on the street, at rail stations or at airports. To use one, book by telephone and agree on a fare when you call. They're listed locally and in the phone book.

Riverboats operate between most of the central London piers. There are services year-round to Greenwich and the Thames Barrier in the east, and summer-only services as far as Hampton Court in the west (see EXCURSIONS, following, and FURTHER AFIELD, page 106).

EXCURSIONS

The best way to get to know London's neighborhoods is to explore them on foot. Several companies offer **guided walks**. The best is generally acknowledged to be Original London Walks ℂ (020) 7624-3978 FAX (020) 7625-1932, with an extensive roster of themed walks, from the Beatles to beer to the Bloomsbury Group. Good walking tours are also offered by City Walks ℂ (020) 7700-6931, Streets of London ℂ (020) 8346-9255, and Citisights ℂ (020) 8806-4325.

There are scores of books and pamphlets detailing **self-guided walks** in and around London. Andrew Duncan's *Walking London* (Passport Books, 1999) takes you to many places you might otherwise miss. The same author has done *Secret London*, which visits way-off-the-beaten-track places, throwing in little-known trivia. There are also resources of this nature at the British Visitor Centre (under GENERAL INFORMATION, above) and at London bookstores on the tourist trail.

Even if you're in London for only a few days, you'll need an *A–Z* ("A to Zed") **street atlas** (A-Z Map Company Limited), easily found at bookstores, newsstands and Tube stations near tourist attractions. If you plan to stick to the city center, you can make do with one of the pocket-sized versions.

If you want a sweeping view of the highlights, open-top **double-decker bus tours** will oblige. You can hop off at any of 20 or so stops (Trafalgar Square, Piccadilly Circus, St. Paul's, Westminster Abbey, etc.), and then get back on at any time during the day. Tickets can be bought all over the city. The major bus tour operators are: The Big Bus Company ℂ (020) 8944-7810; London Pride ℂ (01708) 631122; and The Original London Sightseeing Tour ℂ (020) 8877-1722.

Double-decker **city buses** are a cheaper way to see the sights, though you don't have the tin-can commentary (no great loss). For the price of a ride on the tube, the No. 10 bus, for example, takes you from Hyde Park past Albert Hall, down Oxford

Street to Leicester Square. The No. 24 goes from Hampstead through Camden to Leicester Square and Trafalgar Square. If you buy a TravelCard, you can hop on and off all day. For additional routes visit WEB SITE www.londontransport.co.uk.

Black Taxi Tours ℂ (020) 7289-4371 FAX (020) 7224-2833 will pick you up at your hotel and take you on a two-hour daytime or nighttime whirl around the city, stopping for photographs along the way at all the major sights. Heavy traffic and buses can, however, limit visibility and slow the pace. Two-hour tours are £65 per cab with a five person maximum.

It's possible to **cruise the Thames** from April to October. Vessels leave from Westminster Pier ℂ (020) 7930-4097; Charing Cross Pier ℂ (020) 7839-3572, Victoria Embankment; and Tower Pier ℂ (020) 7488-0344. Downstream trips visit the Tower of London, Greenwich, and the Thames Barrier;

upstream routes take in Kew Gardens, Richmond, and Hampton Court. For a shorter float there is the **Pool of London Ferry** which stops at the Tower of London, Butler's Wharf, London Bridge, the HMS *Belfast*, and St. Katherine's Dock. The ferry departs April to October every 30 minutes; November to March Saturday and Sunday only.

In summer months barges and narrow boats cruise London's two canals, the Grand Union and Regent's. Jason's Trip ((020) 7286-3428 E-MAIL enquiries@jason.co.uk, does one-way and return **narrow-boat trips** on Regent's Canal, which flows between Little Venice (Θ Warwick Avenue) and Camden Lock (Θ Camden Town). A round-trip tour lasts about 90 minutes. From March to September

coach tours for the full scoop. The possibilities are virtually limitless. See BRITISH TOURIST AUTHORITY OFFICES WORLDWIDE, page 324 in TRAVELERS' TIPS, for contact information. See also DAY EXCURSIONS, page 62, under TAKING A TOUR in YOUR CHOICE.

WHAT TO SEE AND DO

With some 300 museums and attractions to choose from, a lifetime of visits to Britain's capital city would barely scratch the surface. In addition to world-class storehouses of art and history, there are specialized museums to appeal to every whim, from caffeine addictions (the Brahma Tea & Coffee Museum) to celebrity fanaticism (Madame Tussaud's).

and on winter weekends, the London Waterbus Company ((020) 7482-2550 makes round-trip **canal cruises** from the London Zoo to Camden Lock (combination zoo and waterbus tickets are available). Canal Cruises ((020) 7485-4433 offers trips from March to October on the *Jenny Wren*, and year-round from Tuesday to Saturday their **floating restaurant** *My Fair Lady* offers dinner and entertainment or Sunday lunch.

Many people use London as a base for **day trips** to provincial points of interest. At the Coach Travel Centre, London Victoria Coach Station, Buckingham Palace Road SW1, it's possible to arrange day trips out of London with National Express ((0990) 010104 and Green Line ((020) 8688-7261. Daily departures take in Canterbury, Brighton, Leeds Castle, Bath, and Stratford-Upon-Avon. Visitors might also like to ask the British Tourist Authority for a copy of their fact sheet on

With such a cornucopia, anyone with limited cash-flow could go broke in a hurry in London. However, with careful planning it's possible to protect your bottom line. Most importantly, take advantage of free and reduced admissions. The following museums are free of charge, though most ask for donations: Bank of England Museum, Bethnal Green Museum of Childhood, British Museum, British Library, Sir John Soane's Museum, and the Geffrye Museum. Major galleries offering free admission include: the Tate Modern, the Tate Britain, the National Portrait Gallery, the National Gallery, the Photographer's Gallery, the Wallace Collection and the Museum Of. Several museums are free after 4:30 PM, including the Victoria & Albert Museum, the Imperial War Museum and

OPPOSITE: London street life. ABOVE: The curves and angles of Albert Bridge.

the Museum of London. The Courtauld Gallery offers free admission on Monday mornings. The Science Museum, Natural History Museum, Victoria & Albert Museum, National Maritime Museum and the Imperial War Museum offer free admission to children under 16 and adults over 60, and as of September 2001, a regular adult entrance fee of only £1.

For the rest, discount cards can help you do London without losing too many pounds. The **GoSee Card**, for example, gives you unlimited admission to 15 London museums. It's available for individuals or for families (defined as two adults and up to four children), in three- or seven-day packages. Purchase the card from a British Tourist Authority foreign office (see TOURIST INFORMATION, page 324 in TRAVELERS' TIPS) or from Edwards & Edwards ((020) 7839-3952, 12 Lower Regent Street, London SW1Y 4NR. For more information on sightseeing discounts, including those for sights outside of London, see MEMBERSHIPS AND DISCOUNT PASSES, page 327 in TRAVELERS' TIPS.

Points of interest are arranged on the following pages in six geographical chunks: the City of London and South Bank; West End and Soho; Westminster, Lambeth and Pimlico; Kensington, Chelsea, Hyde Park and Knightsbridge; Bloomsbury, Holborn and Regent's Park; and Further Afield. Under these headings, sights are listed under the nearest tube station, indicated by the Θ symbol, while British Rail mainline train stations are marked with a "BR."

THE CITY OF LONDON AND SOUTH BANK

While Greater London occupies some 1,570 sq km (600 sq miles), the area called the City of London is just a single square mile. This is the oldest part of London, lying within the ancient walls. Here are concentrated the city's financial and business institutions: the Bank of England, the Stock Exchange, Lloyd's of London, as well as major sights such as the Museum of London, St. Paul's Cathedral, and the Tower of London.

Across the Thames is South Bank, a redeveloped area of modern architecture packed with cultural venues, galleries, boutiques, craft shops, vendors, cafés and museums.

Θ Monument

A logical place to start a tour of London is at the **Monument** ((020) 7626-2717, Fish Street Hill. This generically-named 62-m-high (202-ft) Doric column topped by a golden flame was designed by Sir Christopher Wren and built in 1677. It commemorates the 1666 Great Fire which was set off by Charles II's Pudding Lane baker. Climbing the 311 steps to the caged-in observation platform might help you get your bearings. Open daily, closed Sundays in winter; admission fee.

Immortalized by T.S. Eliot as "inexplicable splendour of Ionian white and gold," **St. Magnus the Martyr** stands just south of the Monument, on Lower Thames Street. It's worth a visit for that very ivory and gold interior as well as its Wren-designed pulpit. Open Tuesday to Friday from 10 AM to 4 PM.

A couple of blocks north stands the **Lloyd's Building**, 1 Lime Street, designed by Richard Rogers in 1986 for the international insurance company. It's one of London's more interesting modern structures — an inside-out building, not unlike Rogers's (and Renzo Piano's) Pompidou Center in Paris. Not open to the public.

Θ St. Paul's

The City of London **Tourist Information Centre** (no phone) is found along St. Paul's Churchyard.

The largest church building in England, St. Paul's Cathedral, Ludgate Hill, was built between 1675 and 1710 to the designs of Sir Christopher Wren, who introduced new forms to English architecture. The cathedral is viewed as an "encyclopedia" of all that the architect had gleaned on his travels on the continent. The façade with its two tiers of Corinthian columns resembles those of the Louvre; the towers are thought to be inspired by those of Borromini's church of St. Agnes in Rome; and, rising above a two-story base, the 110-m-high (365-ft) dome is a salute to Bramante's Tempietto of 1502. It is the second-largest unsupported dome in the world (after St. Peter's in Rome). In the **crypt** are buried Admiral Lord Nelson, Sir Christopher Wren and other English notables.

St. Paul's is open to visitors daily except Sunday, subject to restrictions during services and ceremonies; admission fee. Open on Sundays for services only. **Evensong** takes place weekdays at 5 PM when the celebrated choir sings. The licensed **Refectory** is an agreeable place for morning or afternoon cream tea (scones, preserves and clotted cream) or a glass of (non-sacramental) wine.

Some say that the cathedral should be loved from a distance, for it is the massive dome that *is* St. Paul's. One of the best views of St. Paul's cathedral is from Cardinal Cap's Alley, on Bankside by the Globe Theatre (see under SOUTH LONDON, page 92) where the massive dome rises high above the City.

Northeast of St. Paul's, the **Guildhall** ((020) 7606-3030, off Gresham Street, dates partly from 1411, though all but the porch and crypt, with its fine vaulting, were destroyed in the Great Fire of 1666. In the library, the Clockmaker's Company Museum tells the 500-year history of timekeeping. The Guildhall is open daily in summer, closed Sunday in winter; free.

Built by Sir Christopher Wren between 1675 and 1710, St. Paul's Cathedral is one of London's greatest architectural treasures.

⊖ Tower Hill

England's best example of a mediaeval castle, the **Tower of London** ((020) 7709-0765, Tower Hill EC3, has served over the eons as fortress, palace, prison, mint and arsenal. Though it's called "The Tower", it comprises not one but 20 turrets, the oldest of which is the White Tower, dating to the time of William the Conqueror, who ordered its construction in 1078 as a fortress to guard the river approach to London. Today the Tower of London is a World Heritage Site, museum, and guardian of the Crown Jewels.

There's much to see here, so plan your assault on the Tower carefully. You'll want to go to Waterloo Block to see the **Crown Jewels**. The visit starts with a rousing video of the Queen's fan club, after which a moving sidewalk whisks you in the direction of the vault to the accompaniment of ethereal music. You'll see St. Edward's Crown, which is used for coronations; the Queen Mother's crown with its famous Koh-i-noor ("mountain of light") diamond; and other confections of ermine, gemstone and gold. Interestingly, because they're priceless, the jewels are uninsured.

The eleventh-century **White Tower**, London's oldest building, has been a tourist attraction since the sixteenth century. The "Line of Kings," now in the Spanish Armory, was one of the first exhibits when it opened 300 years ago. Another highlight here is the Norman Chapel of St. John.

Yeoman Warders (often called Beefeaters) can be seen standing about in Tudor-style costumes, or feeding the ravens. Legend says that if the ravens leave the Tower, Britain will fall. There are free Beefeater-guided tours, as well as an audio tour which can be rented at the entrance. The Tower of London is open daily year-round; admission fee.

Just east of the Tower of London, **St. Katharine Dock** is a delightful area to explore. See DOCKLANDS, under OUTER LONDON, page 107.

"Exuberantly Victorian," said V.S. Pritchett of **Tower Bridge** ((020) 7403-3761 or (020) 7378-1928. Built in 1894 to meet the needs of burgeoning river and road traffic, Tower Bridge is one of London's most recognizable landmarks. In the early 1980s, the bridge was transformed into a tourist attraction and dubbed the Tower Bridge Experience. There is consensus in the guest-book here: interesting and a good time for all, but *too expensive*. However, if you have been in London for more than 24 hours you've gone numb at the mention of admission fees, so press on and join the queue to see how this masterpiece of Victorian engineering works. Ask the staff when the next bridge opening will be. Good viewing points are the gift shop and from Tower Bridge Park in Southwark. The high-level walkways were included in the design because it was thought that the bascules would remain up for long periods of time. That didn't turn out to be the case, and pedestrians

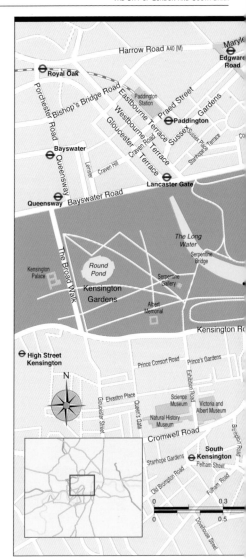

elected to wait rather than climb the stairs. The walkways were closed in 1910 and only opened again in 1982 as part of the "experience." The visit ends in the engine rooms where you can learn about the hydraulic engines that operated the bascules; some hands-on exhibits teach a few fundaments of physics. Stop in the gift shop for an interesting view of the underbelly of the bridge. Open daily year-round.

⊖ Barbican

Note: The Barbican tube station is closed on Sundays; use St. Paul's.

The Barbican is a large area that was redeveloped after World War II with the aim of bringing residential and cultural life to the City. Parts of the Roman and mediaeval city wall are incorporated

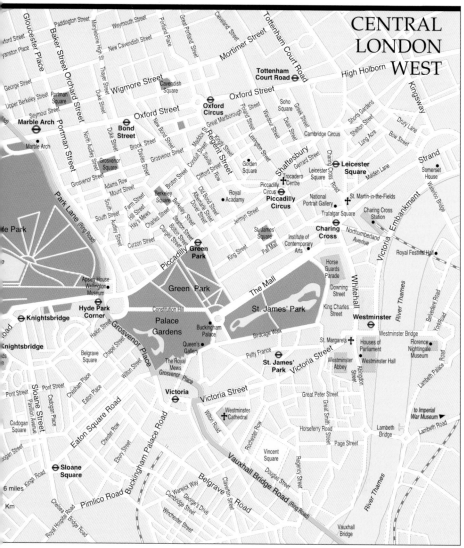

CENTRAL
LONDON
WEST

into a series of serpentine elevated walkways. A one-kilometer (one-and-three-quarter-mile) **wall walk** follows the lines of the original walls of the city. Within this mercilessly ugly and confusing complex are the Museum of London and the Barbican Arts Centre, incorporating a concert hall and theater for the Royal Shakespeare Company. The **Barbican Art Gallery** ((020) 7382-7105, Barbican Centre, Silk Street EC2, is renowned primarily for its photographic shows. Open daily year-round; admission fee.

The best reason to visit the Barbican is the **Museum of London** ((020) 7600-3699 or (020) 7600-0807 (24-hour recorded information), London Wall EC2, which traces the 2,000-year evolution of Britain's capital. Dioramas construct vivid pictures of life from pre-historic times

through the Roman era with emphasis on daily routines. One of the star exhibits is the furiously ornate seventeenth-century Lord Mayor's state coach, which leaves the museum once each year (and for coronations) for the Lord Mayor's Procession. There is a shop and café. The museum is closed Mondays and all of January and February; admission fee (free after 4:30 PM).

Θ/BR Waterloo

Visitors arriving or departing on the Eurostar get a chance to view the gorgeous interior of the new Waterloo International station, designed by Nicolas Grimshaw. Very near it, another impressive piece of architecture is the **BFI London IMAX Cinema** ((020) 7902-1234, 1 Charlie Chaplin Walk SE1. The cylindrical glass building is the setting for a mural as well as a movie screen "the height of five double-decker buses." Open daily with daytime and evening screenings.

The **South Bank Centre**, Europe's largest arts complex, is bursting with cultural activities. Despite its dreary concrete face, the area is alive with color, from *bouquinistes* by the Thames to buskers. The **Royal Festival Hall** ((020) 7921-0682 (recorded events information), along with two smaller concert halls, has excellent productions as well as star-studded literature and talks programs. In the foyer, look for free exhibitions, lunchtime music most days and "commuter jazz" on Fridays, as well as cafés and shops to browse in. The foyer is open daily; free. See NIGHTLIFE, page 121, for information on performances.

Also in the South Bank Centre, the three halls of the **Royal National Theatre** ((020) 7452-3400 are said to have the best acoustics in Europe. Here, too, the foyer is abuzz with restaurants and shops. The terrace is a superb place to watch free performances in Theatre Square. Tours of the building are offered daily except Sunday. The **Hayward Gallery** ((020) 7928-3144 can be distinguished from the other concrete cubes of the South Bank Centre by its multi-hued neon tower; the flashing lights are influenced by the direction and strength of the wind. Inside, four blockbuster exhibitions a year are supplemented by gallery talks and a commendable art bookstore. Open daily during exhibitions; admission fee. The **National Film Theatre** ((020) 7928-3232 has an exciting program of theme screenings as well as a trendy riverside café. The Museum of the Moving Image (MOMI) ((020) 7928-3535, South Bank SE1, is closed for renovations until 2003.

East along Thameside, Queen's Walk is the villagey **Gabriel's Wharf** with dozens of tiny craft shops and gift boutiques, notably Henrietta Park ((020) 7928-2019 for knitwear. Interspersed among the shops are a beer garden, a crêperie and a couple of real restaurants. In summer there's outdoor entertainment.

Climbing way upscale is the landmark **Oxo Tower Wharf** ((020) 7401-2255, where you can tread metal gangplanks to the designer galleries and studios on the second story, showing one-of-a-kind silver jewelry, textiles and handmade papers. On the eighth floor, Oxo Tower restaurant has stunning views of the city and an observatory. It's all very *very*. If you've emptied your wallet upstairs, Eat is a cheap café on the ground floor with basic fare, cappuccino and the award-winning "fruit slice" (a nutty, grainy snack bar; very filling).

Behind the Oxo Tower, the **Museum Of** ((020) 7401-2255, The Barge House, Oxo Tower Wharf, Barge House Street, is a free, ever-morphing museum exhibition. See *Time Out* or ask at a visitor center for details on the latest show. Open Wednesday to Sunday afternoons.

Θ/BR London Bridge

Between London Bridge and Blackfriars Bridge is another buzzing cultural area in what was a few years ago an industrial wasteland.

The earliest crossing point on the Thames, five bridges have stood where **London Bridge** now spans the river, the first dating to around AD 60. The present London Bridge was built in 1967, a flying design by city engineer Harold Knox King; the previous 1831 stone bridge was purchased for £1 million by the McCullock Oil Company who intended to use it for a theme park. Today the old bridge spans the Colorado River near Lake Havesu, Arizona, surrounded by desert scenery.

The focal point of redeveloped Bankside is the new **Tate Modern** ((020) 7887-8000, which houses the celebrated gallery's international, contemporary holdings dating from 1900 to the present. Works by Vincent van Gogh, Paul Cézanne, Pablo Picasso, Henri Matisse, Henry Moore, David Hockney and Andy Warhol hang in the reconstructed turbine and boiler halls of what was formerly the Bankside Power Station. There are two entrances, one by the chimney stack, reached via the river walkway, and a second on Holland Street. Open daily year-round, until 10 PM on Friday and Saturdays; free (except for special exhibitions).

Connecting the Tate Modern with the quay in front of St. Paul's Cathedral is the new Millennium Bridge. This ultra-high-tech footbridge closed shortly after its grand opening due to "wobbling." By the time you read this, the bridge may be reopened.

Medieval Bankside was wiped out by the German *Luftwaffe*, and redevelopment since the 1950s has not always been sympathetic. One priceless exception is **Shakespeare's Globe Theatre Exhibition** ((020) 7401-9919, New Globe Walk, Bankside SE1, a faithful reconstruction of the 1599 Globe Theatre, and the first thatched building to be constructed in London since the Great Fire of 1666. It's the centerpiece of the Shakespeare Centre, which when completed will include a second, indoor theater from the the 1617 designs of Inigo Jones. Entertaining tours are offered during the day, and there is an exhibition on the original Globe and its descendant. The exhibition is open daily year-round, May to September from 9 AM to noon, October to April from 10 AM to 5 PM; admission fee. See NIGHTLIFE, page 121, for information on performances.

The thirteenth-century Gothic **Southwark Cathedral**, Borough High Street, at the foot of London Bridge, was originally the church of an Augustine Priory, founded by Henry I. It was inaugurated as a cathedral in 1905. The church is said to have been founded in AD 860 by St. Swithun — that latter-day rain god. It is also said that if it rains on St. Swithun's Day, July 15, it will continue to do so for the next 40 days. There's a memorial to Shakespeare who was a regular here, as well as one to John Harvard (founder of Harvard University in Cambridge, Massachusetts), who was christened here and whose family owned an inn near the cathedral. Open daily year-round; admission fee.

The *Golden Hinde* ((0870) 011-8700 is docked along Cathedral Street, just west of the church. This floating museum is a scale model of Sir Francis Drake's legendary galleon. Open daily; admission fee.

The new **Vinopolis City of Wine** ((020) 7645-3700, Park Street, Bankside SE1, takes visitors, equipped with audio guides, on a "wine odyssey" through the world's major wine regions, followed

by wine tasting (five samples included with price of admission). Open daily year-round. It's located just off Thames Path between the Globe Theatre and Southwark Cathedral, entrance at the corner of Bank End and Clink Street.

Moving east of London Bridge, **Hays Galleria**, off Tooley Street, is an old dock that has been beautifully converted to a shopping arcade with restaurants, centered around a delightfully eccentric sculpture of a pirate ship by David Kemp, called *The Navigators*.

Newly refitted and painted, the **HMS** *Belfast* ((020) 7407-6434 or 7940-6328, Morgan's Lane, Tooley Street SE1, was England's flagship during the Korean War, and is now the last of the World War II era "big gun" warships. Climb aboard to explore the decks and gun turrets, and find out about daily life below decks. Open daily year-round; admission fee.

Continuing east, **Shad Thames** SE1 is an unusual street with iron breezeways connecting the former warehouses, now a revitalized shopping and dining area. Two contrasting museums are found here. The **Design Museum** ((020) 7378-6055, Butlers Wharf, 28 Shad Thames SE1, focuses on the history and practice of mass-produced objects from the 1950s onward, with changing exhibitions. Open daily; admission fee. The museum's Blue Print Café on the first floor looks out on the wharves and river (moderate). Around the corner, but a world away, is the **Bramah Tea & Coffee Museum** ((020) 7378-0222, Maguire Street, harking back to the coffee and tea shipping heyday of Butler's Wharf. The museum recounts tales of those uplifting beverages through displays of ceramics, silver objects and poster graphics. Freshly ground coffees and British teas are served in the café. Open daily; admission fee.

WEST END AND SOHO

London's nocturnal center of gravity is the West End, where the streets heat up as the stars come out. While the West End proper reaches from Tottenham Court Road in the east to Park Lane in the west, in its broader sense, and for purposes of this guide, the West End also takes in Covent Garden, Mayfair, and Soho. Though not the geographical heart of London, the West End is in many senses its core; you'll find such familiar places here as Trafalgar Square, Piccadilly Circus and Leicester Square, as well as the West End theaters and cinemas, and the shopping land of Oxford and Regent Streets.

Θ/BR Charing Cross

So very British in its grave gray style, **Trafalgar Square** was designed by John Nash and completed in 1841. This confluence of pigeons, pedestrians, and (on some weekends) protesters, links four of London's main thoroughfares: the Strand, Charing Cross Road, Whitehall, and the Mall. Admiral Horatio Nelson, hero of the 1805 Battle of Trafalgar, commands the square from atop the 51-m-high (170-ft) Nelson's Column. (Why so high? So he can have a view of the sea, naturally.) The lions at the base of the column are by Edwin Landseer.

Brooding over the square is the **National Gallery** ((020) 7747-2885, Trafalgar Square, Britain's treasure house of art containing some 2,000 works of art dating from 1260 to 1900. The viewing rooms are arranged by period in four wings: the Sainsbury Wing (1260 to 1510), the West Wing (1510 to 1600), the North Wing (1600 to 1700), and

---

Shakespeare's Globe, Bankside, stands on the site of the Bard's original Globe; built in the final years of the sixteenth century.

the East Wing (1700 to 1900). There are free one-hour guided tours in English only Monday to Friday at 11:30 AM and 2:30 PM, Saturday at 2 PM and 3:30 PM, Wednesday at 6:30 PM. Look also for listings of lunchtime lectures and film events. There is a free audio guide with commentary on just about every painting on the main floor — available at the main entrance and Sainsbury Wing entrance. A "highlights" tour of 30 paintings is available in French, Italian, Spanish, German, Japanese and English. The National Gallery is open daily year-round from 10 AM to 6 PM, Wednesday until 9 PM; free admission. Temporary exhibitions and exhibitions in the Sainsbury Wing usually stay open until 9:55 PM on Wednesdays. When you get hungry, there is a brasserie in the Sainsbury Wing with table service from 10 AM to 5 PM, Wednesday to 9 PM; there is also a sandwich shop in the main building.

Painted and photographic portraits of famous English men and women hang in three floors of the **National Portrait Gallery** ((020) 7306-0055, St. Martin's Place. Works span the ages, from the Tudor period through to the present. The Portrait Café provides lunch and teas. Open daily; free (except special exhibitions).

With its graceful portico and towering spire, **St. Martin-in-the-Fields** flanks the east side of Trafalgar Square. Built in the early 1700s by James Gibbs, it took much damage during the Blitz, but extensive restorations of this Grecian-style church have given it new life. In the crypt you'll find a gift shop and the Café-in-the-Crypt as well as the London Brass Rubbing Centre (/FAX (020) 7930-9306, where you can create impressive brass rubbings by running silver or gold wax crayons over replica memorials onto black paper. The world-famous Academy of St. Martin-in-the-Fields has frequent lunchtime and evening chamber concerts (see NIGHTLIFE, page 122). All of their recordings are available in the crypt shop.

⊖ Covent Garden

The inspiration for George Bernard Shaw's *Pygmalion* and its Broadway adaptation, *My Fair Lady,* Covent Garden was the old fruit and flower market of central London. The markets are long gone, replaced by a shopping and entertainment area usually stuffed to the brim with tourists. Add to the crowds of shoppers and hangers-about a host of jugglers and mimes and you have a chaotic mix. Despite the frenetic atmosphere, Convent Garden has some quiet pockets and some very good museums.

The **London Transport Museum** ((020) 7379-6344, Covent Garden Piazza WC2, is a resting place for the vehicles of bygone days. Under the museum's lofty glass and cast-iron roof (the former market) are steam and electric locomotives, horse-drawn buses, tram cars and trolleys.

Just about everything can be handled and crawled about on, so this is a particularly fun place for children. The Transport Café serves snacks and sandwiches overlooking the piazza. Open daily year-round, last admission 5:15 PM; admission fee.

Tucked away on the lower level of the piazza, the **Cabaret Mechanical Theatre** ((020) 7379-7961 is a tribute to human ingenuity, imagination and humor. Jammed with hundreds of captivating "automata" art that moves, this mini-museum gives visitors the opportunity to play with dozens of machines. The shop has a score of coin-operated machines, or buy a ticket and enter the museum to see and work 64 more automata, which are operated at the push of a button. The gift shop sells handmade automata and more. Open daily; admission fee.

Four hundred years of British theater, from the Elizabethan era to the present, are celebrated at the **Theatre Museum** ((020) 7836-7891, Russell Street WC2. Everything is here, from the life stories of great actors to Victorian marionettes, costumes spanning the ages, scene sets, photos and reminiscences. Daily scheduled demonstrations give visitors a chance to try on costumes and learn about theatrical make-up techniques. The best exhibitions are the temporary ones, which often feature hands-on exhibits and sometimes live performances. There are guided tours daily at 11:30 AM, 2 PM, and 4 PM. Closed Monday; admission fee.

Known as the actors' church, **St. Paul's**, Covent Garden, is an oasis of calm. George Bernard Shaw's *Pygmalion* opens under the portico of St. Paul's, and a plaque on the wall records that Punch's puppet show was first performed here in 1662.

⊖ Leicester Square

London's Time Square, Leicester Square is a pedestrian precinct packed with multiplex cinemas and cut-price ticket kiosks (see NIGHTLIFE, page 122). The latest technoblast in this chaotic acre is a four-story-high **video screen**, billed as "the world's largest digital arts platform." Tuned in and turned on 24 hours a day, it's a kind of giant canvas which passersby can interact with via phone or Internet. Leicester Square was laid out in quieter times, between 1635 and 1670, and named after the Earl of Leicester, whose home was on the square's north side. Portraitists William Hogarth and Sir Joshua Reynolds also lived here.

Along **Charing Cross Road**, book lovers can feast their eyes on the written word — new, used and antique. Scores of specialist genres are catered to in shops from large to small, including stores dedicated to cinema, mystery, science fiction and cookery. There are several major chains here as well.

Gerrard Street, a pedestrian-only street bounded by ornamental gates, is the heart of **Chinatown**, a fascinating area of markets, pungent-smelling restaurants and sidewalk massage "doctors."

⊖ Piccadilly Circus

The statue of **Eros**, erected to commemorate Lord Shaftsbury, stands serenely above the frenetic fray of Piccadilly Circus. This whirlpool of neon lights above and earth-toned slackers below is one of the hubs of young London. Teenagers can have a rip-roaring time here at Trocadero Centre; for the rest, Piccadilly Circus is an avoidable tourist trap.

On the east side of Piccadilly, the **Trocadero Centre** is a vast, clanking entertainment complex where teens can lose their lunch on the Max Drop indoor ride or play computer and VR games until their eyes begin to resemble Ren and Stympie's. Also within Trocadero is **Segaword** ((0990) 505040, with 400 more video games, including virtual

⊖ Tottenham Court Road

Stores on Tottenham Court Road, otherwise known as "Electric Avenue", offer good prices on computers, stereos and other Info Age gadgets. It's another of London's sensory overload zones. The tube station, however, can deliver visitors to the delightfully human scale of **Soho**. All summer long, Soho Square attracts flocks of people-in-black to its seared lawn, lazing under the eyes of a distempered Charles II. At night the area is a sea of colorful humanity, promenading from one trendy restaurant, pub or club to another with the center at Old Compton Street, also London's gay Shangri-La. Soho can also be reached from ⊖ Leicester Square and Piccadilly Circus.

bobsled and simulated roller coaster-rides. Finally there is the **Rock Circus** ((020) 7734-7203, a wax exhibition of rock-and-roll history, which pales in comparison to Madame Tussaud's exhibition in Marylebone, though parts are intriguing. **IMAX 3D** is a new seven-story cinema at the Trocadero in Piccadilly Circus with 11 daily screenings where viewers don headsets for surround-sound listening. The Trocadero Centre is open until midnight daily and until 1 AM on Fridays and Saturdays; admission charged for some attractions.

On a different note, the venerable **Royal Academy of Arts** ((020) 7439-7438, Burlington House, Piccadilly W1, founded by George III in 1768, holds special exhibitions throughout the year. The opening of the annual summer exhibition of works by living artists here marks the beginning of the London arts season. Open daily year-round; admission fee.

⊖ Oxford Circus

Running from Marble Arch to Holborn, **Oxford Street** is London's "high street," the place where all the moderately-priced chain stores sell their wares. More on that under SHOPPING, page 110.

About four blocks north of the Oxford Circus tube station, mediaholics can find out how Britain's national broadcasting service works at the **BBC Experience** ((0870) 603-0304, Portland Place, W1. Exhibitions document 75 years of broadcasting history, from the dawn of radio to the open-ended present. Visitors can try their hand at directing a soap opera, sports commentary or creating film sound effects. Open daily year-round by timed ticket; admission fee.

The fountain at teaming Piccadilly Circus, topped by the Eros statue, is a hangout for young Londoners and backpackers.

⊖ Bond Street

London's Fifth Avenue, **New Bond Street**, runs from Oxford Street to Piccadilly. This **Mayfair** neighborhood, was made for window-shopping. See SHOPPING, page 110.

At Manchester Square, four generations of collectors, some of whom were rather brilliant at it, others rather not (lots of Canalettos) form the **Wallace Collection** ✆ (020) 7935-0687, Hertford House. Housed here is the fine collection of French rococo and English painting formed by the third and fourth Marquesses of Hertford and the latter's son, Richard Wallace. The collection features works by Rembrandt, Peter Paul Rubens, Reynolds, Thomas Gainsborough, Van Dyck, Velasquez and Titian. The

collection used to have "lots of Rembrandts," but with the uproar of verification that took place a few years ago, the Wallace is down to one (a portrait of Titus, the artist's son). The rest are believed to be from Rembrandt's studio. At the time of research new galleries and a glass-roofed restaurant were under construction. Closed Sunday; free.

⊖ Marble Arch

In the northeast corner of Hyde Park is **Marble Arch**, which lends its name to the tube station. Designed by John Nash, the arch was intended to form the main entrance to Buckingham Palace, but it was constructed too narrow to admit the State Coach. It has occupied its present site since 1851. Hard by the arch is **Speaker's Corner** where every Sunday morning people with a bee in their bonnets preach to an audience if they can gather one; if not, the pigeons will do. Speaker's Corner

has been a London tradition since 1872 when Parliament designated this spot as an area for public oratory. More interesting usually than the speakers themselves is the lively exchange of questions from the crowds.

For the rest of Hyde Park, see ⊖ Hyde Park Corner, page 103.

WESTMINSTER, LAMBETH AND PIMLICO

This city-within-a-city dates back to the eleventh century when King Edward the Confessor built his original cathedral (or "minster") west of the City. Westminster is a pleasant area to stroll around, with lots of green space. It's chock-a-block with British political institutions: the Houses of Parliament, Whitehall, and Downing Street, as well as the home of Her Majesty the Queen and the splendid Westminster Abbey.

⊖ Westminster

A World Heritage Site along with the remnants of the Palace of Westminster and St. Margaret's Church, the neo-Byzantine **Westminster Abbey**, Parliament Square, is one of the masterpieces of the Middle Ages. The abbey was founded *circa* AD 800, and the present structure was built in the thirteenth century, planned as a mausoleum by Henry III in memory of Edward the Confessor. Until George III, most of the Kings of England were buried here. The abbey has also been the coronation site of all but two British monarchs. (Edward V was murdered before he could be crowned, and the Duke of Windsor, Edward VIII, abdicated before his coronation); the Coronation Chair is in Edward the Confessor's Chapel. Not only kings, but poets are commemorated here. Poets' Corner is crowded with graves and tablets memorializing the country's literary giants, from Geoffrey Chaucer to Dylan Thomas. The Abbey Museum, in the Norman undercroft, relates the history of the abbey and features a collection of royal effigies and death masks. Services are held daily. Tours are offered weekdays from 10 AM to 3 PM. The nave is closed during Sunday services, and other parts of the abbey are closed all day Sunday, but the Chapter House and museum are open daily; admission fee.

In the shadow of the abbey, **St. Margaret's Church**, Parliament Square, is the official church of the House of Commons. Sir Walter Raleigh is buried here. Just south stands one of only two surviving buildings from the original Palace of Westminster. The **Jewel Tower** (EH) ✆ (020) 7222-2219, Abingdon Street, was King Edward III's fourteenth-century treasure house. Today it houses an exhibition on the history of Parliament. Open daily year-round; admission fee.

A stone's throw from Westminster Abbey are the neo-Gothic **Houses of Parliament**, SW1, built in 1840 on the site of the Old Palace of Westminster, which was destroyed by fire in 1834. When Parliament is in session, a flag flies from Victoria Tower. Political junkies can get their fix at the Strangers' Gallery at the House of Commons ((020) 7219-4272, by observing the houses in session. Queue at St. Stephen's entrance for admission (free); call for times and dates. You can't miss catching sight of "London's grandfather clock," as V.S. Pritchett called the capital's most recognizable landmark. Most people identify this 96-m-high (320-ft) clock tower as **Big Ben**; however Ben's actually the bell inside. It was named after Sir Benjamin Hall, Chief Commissioner of Works when the bell was installed in 1858. The clock is

Whitehall, the wide avenue extending from Parliament Square northward to Trafalgar Square, was once part of the Palace of Whitehall. Today it's synonymous with British government. A walk from Parliament Square north reveals Old Scotland Yard to the right. Near the Cenotaph monument stands the gated entrance to **Downing Street**, site of the official residence of the Prime Minister (No. 10). The **Banqueting House** ((020) 7930-4179, designed by Inigo Jones and built from 1619 to 1622, is the only surviving building of Whitehall Palace, which was destroyed by fire in the 1600s. Among other adornments, the house is famous for its splendid painted ceiling by Sir Peter Paul Rubens. Open Monday to Saturday;

no less impressive. Its hands measure seven and four meters (24 and 14 ft).

Westminster Hall, Parliament Square, is the main surviving fragment from the old Palace of Westminster, built in 1097 by William Rufus and rebuilt in 1394–99 under Richard II, who added the magnificent oak ceiling. Once used for State trails (Charles I, Sir Thomas More, Guy Fawkes and Warren Hastings), it is today the site of important functions and "lying in state." Westminster Hall is not open to the public.

Moving toward St. James's Park, the **Cabinet War Rooms** ((020) 7839-6961, Clive Steps, King Charles Street SW1, was one of the bunkers used by Sir Winston Churchill and his cabinet during the air raids of World War II. Displays include the map room, Churchill's office, bedroom and the transatlantic telephone room. Open daily year-round; admission fee.

admission fee. Further north along Whitehall mounted sentries stand duty in the **Horse Guards' Parade**, the former palace jousting yard. Less crowded but just as fascinating as the Changing of the Guards, the horse guards change two mounted sentries each morning; 11 AM weekdays, 10 AM on Sunday.

Across the Thames along Westminster Bridge stands the old County Hall, which now houses the **London Aquarium** ((020) 7967-8000, South Bank SE1, one of Europe's largest. There are exhibits of marine life from around the world, including a touch pool for curious kids to discover the world of starfish and rays. The three-story Pacific and Atlantic tanks hold some two million liters (half a million gallons) of water between them, and are home to several sharks. Open daily; admission fee.

OPPOSITE: Getting a rubdown in Leicester Square.
ABOVE: Marble Arch, Hyde Park.

From just about any place in central London, it's hard to miss the new **London Eye** ((0870) 500-0600, on Belvedere Road next to the aquarium. This giant, 135-m (450-ft) Ferris wheel — the largest in the world, with cars enclosed in clear perspex bubbles — went up in late 1999 and started rides in early 2000. Call for opening hours or visit WEB SITE www.ba-londoneye.com. It takes 45 minutes for the Eye to complete a single turn, and visibility spans a 40-kilometer (25-mile) radius, as far as Windsor Castle on a clear day. Try to time your climb to the top with sunset for a peak experience.

Θ St. James's Park

St. James's Park ((020) 7930-1793, London's oldest royal enclosure, was laid out in 1531 as a deer park for the hunting appetite of Henry VIII, being convenient to his palace at Whitehall. Later, the French landscape gardener Le Notre redesigned the park along the lines of Versailles for Charles II. It was re-vamped again by John Nash for the tastes of George IV. Today the 37-hectare (93-acre) park is the habitat of a variety of waterfowl — famous for its pelicans — as well as flocks of lunching office workers. During the summer you can rent deck chairs ((020) 8401-0155, and there is a café called the Cake House. There's a marvelous view atop the bridge that crosses the lake: to the west you can see Buckingham Palace and to the east the government offices at Whitehall. In summer, brass bands give concerts in the park. St. James's is also convenient to Θ/BR Charing Cross.

The **Mall** runs along St. James's northern edge, a one-kilometer-long (half-a-mile) ceremonial approach to Buckingham Palace with the triumphal **Admiralty Arch** anchoring the other end. In addition to the government buildings that line the Mall, there are some picture galleries, most notably the **Institute of Contemporary Arts (ICA)** ((020) 7930-3647 with several galleries, cinemas, a theater and a bookstore. Closed mornings; admission fee.

Buckingham Palace ((020) 7839-1377, The Mall, residence of Her Majesty Queen Elizabeth II, was opened to the public for the first time in 1993 to raise money for repairs to Windsor Castle. When the Queen is in residence, the royal standard flies from the mast. At other times, the Union Jack is raised. The palace dates to 1703 when it was built by the Duke of Buckingham. George III bought it in 1761, and it was again rebuilt by George IV. In 2000, the palace ballroom, built in 1856 to celebrate the end of the Crimean war, was opened to the public for the first time. Remodeled in the twentieth century, this grand room was the setting of the Prince of Wales's 50th-birthday bash. Tours of Buckingham Palace draw some 400,000 visitors a year during the eight weeks that they

occur. Tickets are sold from a booth opposite the palace by the entrance to Green Park, or by phone ((020) 7839-1377 (ask for the Visitor Office). Open August to September by timed ticket.

When the palace is closed, you can still get that royal feeling at several peripheral palace attractions. The **Queen's Gallery**, Buckingham Palace SW1, holds changing exhibitions of masterpieces from the royal art treasury. Open daily during expositions; admission fee. A working stable, the **Royal Mews** ((020) 7839-1377, Buckingham Palace SW1, houses the state carriages and coaches and the fine steeds that power them. Open Monday to Thursday afternoon; admission fee. Finally, the ever-popular **Changing of the Guard** takes place daily from April to July, every other day the rest of the year. Call the London Tourist Board's Changing of the Guard Hotline ((0839) 123411 (49p per minute) for details.

Θ Green Park

Green Park is a 21-hectare (53-acre) expanse of lush lawns, forming a miles-long emerald necklace with St. James's Park to the east and Hyde park to the west. In March, the park is awash with daffodils. On its edge stands **Spencer House** ((020) 7499-8620, 27 St. James's Place SW1, built in 1756 for the First Earl of Spencer, ancestor of Diana, Princess of Wales. The state rooms, decorated in neoclassical style, have been restored to their original splendor. Open by guided tour only, Sundays only (closed in August and January); admission fee.

Θ/BR Victoria

A transportation axis with massive Victoria station handling coach, bus, train and subway traffic, this area is also a popular stop-over for anyone wanting low-budget lodging.

Just east of the station are the headquarters of Britain's Catholic Church. **Westminster Cathedral**, Ashley Place, opened in 1903. Architect John Francis Bentley built the cathedral in the Christian-Byzantine style of St. Sophia at Istanbul. There's an elevator ride to the 85-m-high (284-ft) camponile. The cathedral is open daily year-round; free entrance. The elevator to the viewing gallery is open daily from April to November, Thursday to Sunday only from December to March; admission fee.

Θ Lambeth North

In South London, the out-of-the-way **Imperial War Museum** ((020) 7416-5000, Lambeth Road SE1, documents and illustrates every war that Britain has been involved in since August 1914.

"Liquid 'istory"— The River Thames flows past the Houses of Parliament and Big Ben.

Despite the name, the museum does not glorify war. Rather, it presents stories in art, photos, film archives and text exhibitions as well as through dramatic re-creations of life in the trenches during World War I, and the Blitz of World War II — with sounds, smells and special effects. Open daily; admission fee (free after 4:30 PM).

Toward the Thames, on Lambeth Palace Road are three more points of interest. **Lambeth Palace** ((020) 7665-1540 or (020) 7898-1198 (bookings) is the 700-year-old London residence of the Archbishops of Canterbury (open by appointment). The **Florence Nightingale Museum** ((020) 7620-0374, in St. Thomas's Hospital, tells the story of the nurse and health reformer of the 1800s, includ-

ing a reconstruction of a Crimean War hospital ward. Closed Monday; admission fee. And in the restored St. Mary-at-Lambeth Church, there is the **Museum of Garden History** ((020) 7261-1891, with a permanent exhibition of garden lore as well as a recreated seventeenth-century garden. Open daily year-round; free.

Θ/BR Vauxhall

Across from Vauxhall Bridge bobs the **London Balloon** ((020) 7587-1111 (24-hour information) WEB SITE www.londonballoon.co.uk, Spring Gardens. A 15-minute, 120-m-high (400-ft) ride in this tethered, helium-filled balloon offers ample time to take in the sweeping views of Greenwich, the Thames, and sights of London. Rides take place from 10 AM to dusk. Closed November to March and in questionable weather (call to confirm).

After going aloft, linger in Spring Gardens long enough to visit the charming **Vauxhall City Farm** (no phone), Tyers Street, one of London's best-kept secrets: a petting farm with ponies, a red poll heifer, sheep, goats, guinea pigs, rabbits, ferrets and various feathered creatures. Kids can bring their own animal feed (apples and carrots, for example) or buy a bucket for 50p from the farm. Closed Monday; free.

Θ Pimlico

The Tate Gallery, Millbank, renamed with the opening of the extension at Bankside (see under THE CITY OF LONDON, AND SOUTH BANK, above), is now the **Tate Britain** ((020) 7887-8000 or (020) 7887-8008 (recorded information) E-MAIL information@tate.org.uk, featuring British art from 1500 to the present, from Elizabethan portraits to the avant-garde. Collections also include works by Millais, Hogarth, William Blake and Constable. The Turner collection is housed in the Clore Gallery extension. Open daily; free (but there is a charge for special exhibitions).

KENSINGTON, CHELSEA, HYDE PARK AND KNIGHTSBRIDGE

Kensington is another well-stocked touring area, with the Victoria & Albert Museum, the Science Museum, the Natural History Museum and Kensington Palace. Chelsea and Pimlico, home to many famous literary figures, spread out along the Thames south of Westminster. The Tate Britain Gallery is in Pimlico, and Chelsea has scores of upscale fashion and antique shops. Hyde Park is London's outdoor recreational center, and Knightsbridge is another upscale shopping area, home of Harrods department store.

Θ High Street Kensington

The Jacobean **Kensington Palace** ((020) 7937-9561, Kensington Gardens, was designed by Christopher Wren for William III. Purchased in 1689 by William and Mary, it was to be the residence of many a monarch, including Queen Victoria, who lived here until she was 18. Now it is remembered chiefly as the London home of Diana, Princess of Wales, until her death in 1997. Two areas are open to the public, the state apartments and the Royal Ceremonial Dress Collection. Open daily year-round; admission fee. Outside the palace, explore the Sunken Gardens and enjoy tea in the sunny Orangery.

Kensington Gardens, formerly the palace's private grounds, is now a wooded parkland adjoining Hyde Park. At the Round Pond, children sail miniature boats, and there is an enchanting statue of Peter Pan, by the Long Water, a continuation of Hyde Park's Serpentine Lake. The **Serpentine Gallery** ((020) 7402-6075, just south of the Serpentine Bridge, has changing exhibitions of modern art. Open daily year-round; free.

⊖ South Kensington

Three daunting and delightful museums cluster around this tube stop, which also gives its name to a lively neighborhood of cafés, art dealers and antiques shops. Also worth seeing in this area is the Italian Renaissance-style **Oratory**, on Brompton Road. This nineteenth-century edifice is known for its fine musical services. Open daily; free admission.

Housed in splendid mid-nineteenth-century Alfred Waterhouse building, the **Natural History Museum** ((020) 7938-9123, Cromwell Road SW7, recounts the history of the Earth from the Big Bang to present-day quakes and tremors. In addition to the traditional displays — row on

portions of Darwin's collection of 12 million specimens, many of them brought back from his voyage aboard the *Beagle*. For up-to-date information, visit WEB SITE www.nhm.ac.uk/darwincentre.

Topped by four domes and a stonework crown, the massive **Victoria & Albert Museum** ((020) 7938-8500, Cromwell Road SW7, is one of the world's great museums of decorative arts with works of art, craft and design from every continent and spanning 15 centuries. To make the most of a visit, keep in mind that there are two types of galleries at the V&A. The "Art and Design Galleries" arrange objects by place or date, while "Material and Techniques Galleries" present objects of a single material or type. The new Canon

row of rock, mineral, and fossil specimens — there are a host of new super-stimulating exhibitions taking in subjects as diverse as human biology, evolution, and dinosaurs and their living relatives. The museum does a good job of showing the influence that humans exert as consumers on the planet. The blue whale in the Mammals Gallery is a stunning sight, and the Kyoto earthquake is literally moving. Open daily year-round; admission fee (free for children under age 17; free for everyone after 4:30 PM weekdays, 5 PM, weekends).

A multi-million-pound project slated to be open to the public by 2002, the **Darwin Centre**, to be built alongside the Natural History Museum's Waterhouse building, will enable visitors to watch hundreds of museum experts at work, and to learn about their research on guided laboratory tours. The center will also showcase

Photography Gallery is the national collection of the art of photography. Included in the collection are some of the world's earliest photographs. The V&A is open daily year-round; admission fee (free after 4:30 PM).

The **Science Museum** ((020) 7938-8000, Exhibition Road SW7, presents scientific, engineering and industrial feats and flights of imagination. With 40 galleries on seven floors, this is a huge and hugely popular museum. Many exhibitions allow younger children to learn by touching, poking, pulling and playing games. The Space Gallery with its Apollo 10 command module is quite popular. The exhibit on time unwinds the story of clocks. Another intriguing exhibition is the world's first computer — Charles Babbage's

OPPOSITE: Westminster Abbey. ABOVE: A man with a message at Speaker's Corner.

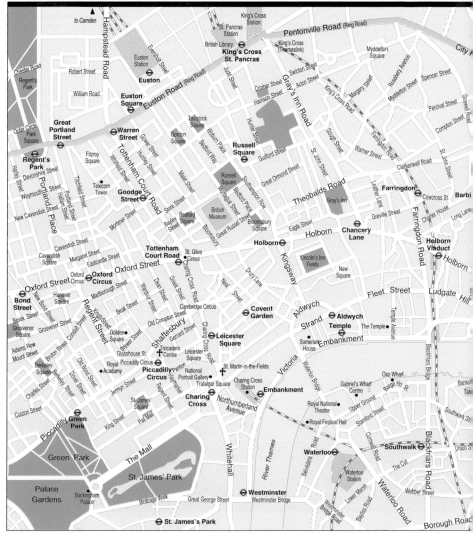

calculating engine. Open daily year-round; admission fee (free for children under age 17). Book tickets for the Science Museum's new IMAX theater on ((0870) 870-4868.

In the southwest corner of Kensington Gardens (see above), the glittering **Albert Memorial** ((020) 7495-0916, Alexandra Gate, depicts Queen Victoria's consort, who died in 1861. Built at a cost of £120,000, it took 20 years to construct. The recently completed restoration has spiffed up the monument considerably. There are guided tours on Sunday at 10 AM and 11 AM; admission fee. Across Kensington High Street, **Royal Albert Hall** is home to the BBC "Proms" concert series. It's London's largest concert hall with a capacity of 8,000, and was completed in 1871. See FESTIVE FLINGS, page 53 in YOUR CHOICE; and NIGHTLIFE, page 121.)

⊖ Knightsbridge
Someone once described **Harrods** department store as a "cross between a pre-war ocean liner and an Oriental bazaar." Founded in 1849 as a grocery store, this legendary purveyor of gourmet foods and high-priced clothing occupies two hectares (four and a half acres) of Knightsbridge real estate. Owner Mohammed Al Fayed is often in the news over feuds with politicians, but Harrods remains one of London's icons, with its green-liveried doormen, gourmet treats and wonderful bookstore. The marble-pillared food halls are really the main attraction, with servers dishing out exotic items from chocolates dusted with gold to English specialty foods. Or take a stool at one of the bars and sample raw oysters, beef sandwiches or sushi. When lunch is through, take a slow trip up the "Egyptian escalator." Viva Las Vegas.

TRAL LONDON EAST

The residence of the first Duke of Wellington, **Apsley House** is now open to the public as the **Wellington Museum (Apsley House)** ((020) 7499-5676 or (020) 7495-8525, Hyde Park Corner. On display are paintings by Velasquez, Goya and Rubens, as well as the works of Dutch and Flemish masters and collections of sculpture, porcelain, silver and furniture. Part of the palace is dedicated to the memory of the "the Iron Duke," including a video narrated by the Eighth Duke of Wellington, who lives here along with his family in private apartments. Open Tuesday to Sunday; admission fee.

BLOOMSBURY, HOLBORN AND REGENT'S PARK

A walk around Bloomsbury reveals the former homes and hangouts of the free-thinking Bloomsbury Group. Today it's known for its university life as well as throngs of moderately-priced hotels. Sightseeing highlights here are the British Museum and Madame Tussaud's. Holborn is London's leafy, legal heart, while Regent's Park has the London Zoo, Shakespeare under the stars, and acres of greenery and color.

⊖ Russell Square

With the opening of its new Great Court, the world's oldest museum now boasts Europe's largest covered public square. Designed by Norman Foster & Partners, the two-acre square, glass-roofed courtyard has transformed the main entrance to the British Museum. At its center is the refurbished Reading Room, along with new galleries, a restaurant, and educational facilities. In addition to the transmogrified Great Russell Street entrance, the Montague Place entrance has also undergone something of a facelift. Inside the 1857 building lies one of the world's greatest collections, with treasures spanning several millennia and encompassing celebrated finds such as the Rosetta Stone and the Parthenon frieze, manuscripts from the Magna Carta to Beatles lyrics, as well as mummies, amulets and the Book of the Dead.

Guided 90-minute tours take in highlights of museum collections, while 60-minute "focus" tours zero in on specific themes. For information on tours, films, and lectures, call ((020) 7323-8920 or WEB SITE www.thebritishmuseum.ac.uk. The museum is open daily with evening hours on Thursday and Friday; free (but certain exhibits charge a fee). The Great Court is also open daily with extended evening hours.

About six blocks from the British Museum is **Charles Dickens's House** ((020) 7405-2127, 48 Doughty Street, WC1, the home of the well-known writer for two productive years (1837 to 1839) during which he wrote *Oliver Twist* and *Nicholas Nickelby*, and completed *The Pickwick Papers*. The house is now a museum of Dickens memorabilia. Closed Sunday; admission fee.

⊖ Hyde Park Corner
The 136-hectare (340-acre) Hyde Park is London's recreational hub, with facilities for rollerblading, cycling, horse riding, boating and swimming. On Sundays the park brims with activity from the soap box oration at Speakers Corner (see under MARBLE ARCH, above) to sunbathing on the Serpentine Lido. Hyde Park is also accessible from ⊖ Knightsbridge, Lancaster Gate and Marble Arch.

At the Serpentine, a large lake in the center of the park, there are paddle boats for rent by the hour. The Serpentine Lido is open for swimming from June to September. A lakeside cafeteria at the Lido is open year-round. For horse riding, contact Richard Briggs Stables ((020) 7723-2813 or Ross Nye Stables ((020) 7262-3791. There is in-line skate rental at the London Skate Centre ((020) 7727-4669, the Queensway.

⊖ Holborn

The core of London's legal district, this area of tranquil courtyards, leafy gardens and historic buildings of the Inns of Court is great for walks. One of four inns of Court, housing barristers chambers, **Lincoln's Inn (** (020) 7405-1393, Chancery Lane, contains a 70,000-volume law library and an 1623 Inigo Jones-designed chapel. The inn is open upon application and the chapel can be seen by attending Sunday service at 11:30 AM. Across from the inn, **Lincoln's Inn Fields** is a green and pleasant open space surrounded by distinguished houses, one of which is **Sir John Soane's Museum (** (020) 7405-2107, 13 Lincoln's Inn Fields WC2, full of art and antiques collected

by the enigmatic architect, Sir John Soane, in a house he designed in 1812. Closed Sunday and Monday; free.

⊖ Temple

Note: Temple station is closed on Sunday; use Holborn or Covent Garden station.

Fleet Street was once synonymous with London journalism, but all the major newspapers have now moved out to Docklands. The **Temple**, Fleet Street, was named after the mediaeval Knights Templar, whose mission it was to protect pilgrims traveling to the Holy Land. This complex of quiet squares, with the feel of old London, is now the site of two more Inns of Court, Inner Temple and Middle Temple. The Tudor **Middle Temple Hall** with hammerbeam roof and stained-glass windows is open Monday to Friday (closed midday and all of August).

Set in the Palladian-style Somerset House, The Strand, the **Courtauld Gallery (** (020) 7848-2526 houses Britain's finest collection of Impressionist works, displayed in gorgeous eighteenth-century rooms, formerly the palace of the Duke of Somerset. It's often compared to New York's Frick for its "jewel-like setting." Closed Sunday morning; admission fee; free to all Monday from 10 AM to 2 PM).

⊖ Baker Street

Off Marylebone is Baker Street, the fictitious stomping ground of Sir Author Conan Doyle's larger-than-life detective. The **Sherlock Holmes Museum (** (020) 7738-1269, 221B Baker Street, details the life times of legendary sleuth and his sidekick Dr. Watson. Open daily year-round; admission fee.

While 221B Baker Street may be one of the world's most famous address, these days Marylebone is better known for **Madame Tussaud's (** (020) 7935-6861, Marylebone Road NW1. With no interactive computer stations, no video loops, not even a quiz for the kids, this is a museum in the Victorian pattern. Its exhibits need no introduction: hundreds of life-sized wax figures of famous, near-famous and once-famous people from Hollywood stars to heads of state. Many of the celebrities have posed for Madame Tussaud's sculptors, and some of have even donated personal objects or clothing to adorn their doppelganger. Sophie Rhys-Jones's dress designer furnished the museum with an exact replica of Princess Sophie's wedding dress. Queen Elizabeth has been modeled 17 times. The tour leads through a series of theme rooms including the Hall of Horrors (followed by the cafeteria. Hamburger, medium rare, anyone?). The visit ends with a nod to twentieth-century museum technology with a Disneyesque tribute to 400 years of London history on the *Spirit of London* ride.

But there's more. From Hollywood stars to celestial bodies, Madame Tussaud's shepherds visitors next into the **Planetarium** (separate admission fee) where a series of interactive displays and scale models tell the story of the galaxy, ending with the sound and light show, narrated in English, French, German, and Spanish. Madame Tussaud's and the Planetarium are open daily year-round (last admission 5:30 PM). It's possible to book in advance with a credit card (** (020) 7935-6861 and go directly to the ticket-holders line; which may avoid the frightfully long queues.

⊖/BR King's Cross–St. Pancras

The British Library sits back from Euston Road in its new warm-red brick building. Just a few short blocks north is a secret and quiet alternative to the London Zoo: **Camley Street Natural Park (** (020) 7261-0447, 12 Camley Street NW1, backed by the Grand Union Canal. Closed Friday; free admission.

The enormous **British Library** ((020) 7412-7332 is the repository of some 150 million items relating to the written word. Three exhibition rooms presenting a host of awe-inspiring written and printed matter are open to the public. See Shakespeare's First Folio (published in 1623, seven years after his death); a Gutenberg Bible that was printed around 1455; and the Magna Carta (1215). Other exhibits examine the *Anglo-Saxon Chronicles* and Admiral Nelson's log books, while Commander Robert Scott's journals bring his ill-fated polar expedition to life when you read that his crew is "...on the verge of serious frostbites" (sic).

Among the exhibitions is the library's new computer-based display that simulates the experience of turning the pages of, for example, the eighth-century Lindisfarne Gospels, or unrolling a ninth-century Buddhist scroll, or the pages of Leonardo da Vinci's notebook.

The library is also a major repository for sound recordings, and the galleries offer samplings from the songs of Kalahari Bushmen to James Joyce reading from *Ulysses* or the first-known recording of a song bird. On the lower level is an exhibit that explains the processes of bookmaking with a schedule of live craft demonstrations of printing, calligraphy, wood engraving, and more.

Guided tours of the public areas of the library are offered on Monday, Wednesday and Friday at 3 PM and on Saturday at 10:30 AM and 3 PM (admission fee). Tours that additionally take in reading rooms happen each Tuesday at 6:30 PM and Sunday at 11:30 AM and 3 PM (admission fee). For information on events call ((020) 7412-7332 or visit library's WEB SITE www.bl.uk. The exhibition galleries are open daily; free admission.

The British Library bookstore is really superb. There's a café on the lower level, and the upstairs restaurant is the prettiest casual lunch spot in the city (hot main dishes £5). It's a gorgeous setting with a balcony view of the "King's Library," a six-story glass tower built to house the 65,000-volume collection of George III. A blossom decorates each table, and modern light fixtures pour down light from high above all in a perfect library hush.

Θ Regent's Park

Practically deserted on a weekday morning, Regent's Park is a green oasis where frazzled urbanites can shake off city jitters, breath clean air and revel in Nature. Once a part of the vast Middlesex Forest and a favorite hunting ground of Henry VIII, the trees were cut down in the seventeenth century to pay off the cavalry, and the land came into use as a dairy farm. In 1811 John Nash proposed a park here for the "wealthy and the good" of London, and in 1836 the eastern part of the park was opened to the rest of us.

In the center of Regent's Park, **Queen Mary's Gardens** is a sea of roses. Hundreds of varieties are represented here, many labeled with evocative names such as "Ingrid Bergman," or "Ice Cream." Nearby, grebe, moorhens and ducks dabble in the ponds, and there are rowboat trips on the boating lake.

Regent's Park Open-air Theatre (see NIGHTLIFE, page 121) is a wonderful spot to see the works of Shakespeare, as well as musical revivals and children's productions. An elaborate picnic — crystal goblets, champagne, etc. — before the show is a tradition.

In the northeast corner of the park, some 600 different species of animals, from black rhinos

to giant African snails, inhabit the **London Zoo**. A number of new exhibits aim to bring this antique zoo into the new millennium while "celebrating bio-diversity and its conservation." The zoo has an active program of breeding endangered species including rare snails (the mind boggles), Sumatra tigers, and Gila monsters. The Web of Life examines animals and ecosystems. There is a new bug zoo called the Micrarium. Daily scheduled events include the elephant weigh-in and bath, penguin feeding and pony rides. The London Zoo ((020) 7722-333, on the northern edge of Regent's Park (main entrance on Albert Road) NW1, is open daily (last entry at 3 PM); admission fee.

See EXCURSIONS (page 86) for details on narrowboat trips from Regent's Park along **Grand Union**

OPPOSITE: All is "elementary, my dear Watson" at the Sherlock Holmes Museum. ABOVE: John Nash's Cumberland Terrace, Regent's Park.

Canal. It's an adventure to follow the canal on foot all the way to **Little Venice** (Θ Warwick Avenue), the "floating city" of Maida Vale. It's not always easy to keep to the towpath because of obstructions — and some areas are a bit seedy — but you really get to see canal life. It's a world away from work-a-day London.

FURTHER AFIELD

While the sights of central London seem inexhaustible, there are some wonderful areas to explore further afield — all easily reached by tube (Θ), mainline train (BR), or the new Docklands Light Railway (DLR).

for its blocks of vintage clothing stores and outdoor markets. For more on that, see TO MARKET, TO MARKET…, page 13 in TOP SPOTS. Islington's center of gravity is at Θ Angel.

Hampstead and Highgate

Once an eighteenth-century spa and fashionable health resort, Hampstead still has the charm of a village. Centered around the Hampstead tube station are warrens of winding streets and Georgian terraces, while boutiques and airy restaurants line sloping Hampstead High Street. **Guided walks** of the historic village start from the tube. See the *Hampstead & Highgate Express* for details on these and other events. Θ Hampstead.

Notting Hill and Portobello Road

In August, Notting Hill erupts into Europe's best street carnival, but any time of year is fine for visiting this kaleidoscopic neighborhood of restaurants and funky shops selling everything from kidney-shaped coffee tables to second-hand books. The area is also known for its antiques, clothes, organic produce and bric-a-brac markets on Portobello Road (see TO MARKET, TO MARKET…, page 13 in TOP SPOTS). Θ Ladbroke Grove or Notting Hill Gate.

Camden and Islington

Camden and Islington are rediscovered neighborhoods that have blossomed into eclectic, trendy residential areas with vast resources for shopaholics, partyers and diners. Camden (Θ Camden Town or Chalk Farm) is the closest to the heart of London and really can't be passed over by fashionistas

The houses of two of Hampstead's famous residents can be visited. The home of Erno Goldfinger along with his artist wife Ursula Blackwell, **Two Willow Road** (NT) ((020) 7435-6166, 2 Willow Road, Hampstead NW3, was designed and built by the architect. The house contains the couple's art collection as well as furniture designed by Goldfinger. Closed Mondays and some Saturdays; admission fee. Θ Hampstead. The **Freud Museum** ((020) 7435-2002, 20 Maresfield Gardens, Hampstead NW3, is the house where Sigmund Freud, the father of psychoanalysis, worked and died. His study is arranged exactly as it was during his lifetime, including his library and the famous couch. Open Wednesday to Sunday afternoon; admission fee. Θ Finchley Road or Swiss Cottage.

It's only natural to combine a stroll around Hampstead village with a walk through the wild and enchanting **Hampstead Heath**, 320 hectares

(800 acres) of varied countryside with holly forests, vast tracts of undulating grasses, ancient woodlands with secluded walking paths, lovely ponds for swimming and fishing, and Parliament Hill, where there are panoramic views of London and scores of weekend kite flyers. Θ Hampstead.

Overlooking Hampstead Heath, the magnificent estate, **Kenwood House** (EH) ((020) 8348-1286, Hampstead Lane NW3, was remodeled by Robert Adam in neoclassical style in 1767 for the Earl of Mansfield. Ornately decorated rooms provide a backdrop for the fine collection of Old Dutch Masters (including Vermeer's *Guitar Player*) as well as works by Thomas Gainsborough, J.M.W. Turner, Sandro Botticelli, and Joshua

Reynolds. There is a café, and picnicking is permitted on the grounds. The house is open daily year-round; admission fee. Attending the Kenwood House summer weekend **lakeside concerts** ((020) 7413-1443 is as sweet as it gets. Θ Golders Green or Archway, then #210 bus.

Originally a mediaeval tollgate (hence the name), Highgate (just east of Hampstead Heath) is home to **Highgate Cemetery** ((020) 8340-1834, Swain's Lane N6, the final resting place of Karl Marx as well as scores of poets, thinkers, politicians and actors. Guided tours of the spooky west cemetery take place Saturday and Sunday from 11 AM to 6 PM; admission fee (permission to carry a camera costs extra). Θ Highgate or Archway.

The East End

Adjoining the City of London, the East End, home of the Cockney, is a culturally diverse area at its best during weekend markets (see SHOPPING, page 110). Not far from St. Paul's Cathedral, **St. Mary-le-Bow Church**, Cheapside, has a special significance for East Enders. True Cockneys, it's said, must be born within earshot of the "Bow bells."

Though the East End is off the beaten tourist trail, a pair of delightful (and free) museums here draw visitors in the know. The interesting **Geffrye Museum** ((020) 7739-9893, on Kingsland Road E2, is housed in a row of converted eighteenth-century almshouses. The museum displays are consecrated to the British living room. A series of period rooms are fitted with typical domestic scenes, furniture and furnishings, household equipment and musical instruments of middle-class households from the Elizabethan period to the 1950s. Closed Mondays; free admission. On Thursday evenings, classical music performances are held at the Geffrye; call for details (Θ/BR Old Street). **Bethnal Green Museum of Childhood** ((020) 7983-5200 or (020) 8980-2415 (recorded information), Cambridge Heath Road E2, a branch of the Victoria & Albert, boasts the largest collection of toys in the world, taking in doll houses, early toys from the seventeenth century onward, and Victorian games. A star attraction is the eighteenth-century Venetian puppet theater that inspired Punch & Judy. Closed Friday; free admission. Θ Bethnal Green.

Docklands

During the eighteenth and nineteenth centuries, the Thames, from London Bridge east to Greenwich, peppered with warehouses and wharves, formed the world's largest port. Bombing during World War II and the need for deeper waters put the docks out of business mid-century, but the region has been undergoing stop-and-start redevelopment since the 1980s, and Docklands is finally becoming something of an attraction, with points of interest accessible via Docklands Light Railway (DLR).

The best of Docklands, however, is right next to the Tower of London. **St. Katherine Docks**, built in 1827, were used to stored cargoes from around the world. The massive warehouse buildings have been restored and incorporated into a shopping and dining precinct with cobbled walks and more than 200 moorings for pleasure boats. The eighteenth-century British warship *Grand Turk*, docked here, is open for inspection year-round; admission fee. There are several **restaurants** to choose from at the docks: The Aquarium ((020) 7480-6116 is an upscale Scandinavian seafood place with a pretty terrace. Dickens Inn ((020) 7488-2208, is a flower-decked pub, and the Mala ((020) 7480-6356 dishes up Indian cuisine. Catamaran Cruisers ((020) 7987-1185 operates

A light snowfall blankets Hampstead Heath.

and more than 200 moorings for pleasure boats. The eighteenth-century British warship *Grand Turk*, docked here, is open for inspection year-round; admission fee. There are several **restaurants** to choose from at the docks: The Aquarium ((020) 7480-6116 is an upscale Scandinavian seafood place with a pretty terrace. Dickens Inn ((020) 7488-2208, is a flower-decked pub, and the Mala ((020) 7480-6356 dishes up Indian cuisine. Catamaran Cruisers ((020) 7987-1185 operates **boat tours** between Embankment Pier, Tower of London and Greenwich, with regular departures from St. Katharine Docks. During the summer a varied line-up of **entertainers** perform at St. Katherine Docks' Marble Quay on Fridays and Saturdays (mid-July to mid-August), and there are free **walking tours** Saturday afternoon from 1 PM to 3 PM, departing from the East Gate of the Tower of London, guided by a "London Docker and his wife." Tours last one hour.

The former West India docks are today an area of modern skyscrapers dominated by the tallest building in the United Kingdom: **Canary Wharf Tower** ((020) 7418-2000. A financial and residential center, the complex has a shopping center, a Marco Pierre White restaurant called the Big Chef, high-street shops and a couple of Starbucks cafés. The Canary Wharf **Tourist Information Centre** ((020) 7512-9800 is at Canary Wharf Station, Docklands Light Railway Ticket Office. DLR Canary Wharf.

Greenwich

If it looks like a flying saucer has landed along the Thames, you've sighted the **Millennium Dome**. A massive big-top with 12 canary yellow masts supporting a fiberglass bubble large enough to house 10 St. Paul's Cathedrals. The dome was set up with huge amounts of public money to celebrate the new century, but high ticket prices and a sturdy refusal, by the British, to be awed put the dome in dire financial straits. The Dome closed as a tourist attraction early in 2001. Negotiations to sell the big bubble to the highest bidder for transformation into an "urban entertainment resort" or concert venue were stalled at press time. Check locally to see what's up with the Dome.

Meanwhile, the World Heritage Site of **Maritime Greenwich** remains the enduring attraction in this historic section of Greater London. There's much to see here, from Greenwich village to antique tall ships and the prime meridian, where it's possible to straddle the Eastern and Western hemispheres. When you've had enough sightseeing, Greenwich Park is a prime place for a breather with its acres of green lawn, landscaped gardens, boating lake, and deer enclosure. In the village, Greenwich Antiques Market, High Road, stocks vintage clothing on weekends. During the week

it's a fruit and vegetable market, a good place to stock up for a picnic in the park.

The **Tourist Information Centre** ((0870) 608-2000 FAX (020) 8853-4607, at 46 Greenwich Church Street, is open daily year-round; closed Sunday in the off-season. **Guided walks** of Greenwich are offered from the center. There's a **covered market**, off Turnpin Lane, with art, crafts and antiques on sale, Wednesday to Sunday. The shops that line the market are open daily.

Two tall ships grace Greenwich Pier. The *Cutty Sark* ((020) 8858-3445, King William Walk, is England's last surviving tea clipper. Launched in 1869 for the China tea run, it's been brilliantly restored. Inside is one of the world's largest collections of carved ship's figureheads. Next to the great tea clipper is the little *Gipsy Moth IV*, in which Sir Francis Chichester sailed solo around the world. Open daily year-round; admission fee.

The focal point of Maritime Greenwich is the **National Maritime Museum** ((020) 8858-4422 or (020) 8312-6565 (recorded information), on Romney Road, reopened after a £20 million renovation. The museum encompasses a 20-gallery main site as well as the Queen's House and the Old Royal Observatory. Open daily year-round; admission fee.

The principal exhibit at the National Maritime Museum features Admiral Lord Nelson, icluding comments on battle strategies recorded in his diaries. Elsewhere in the museum are more state-of-the-art galleries. The Passengers' Galley puts visitors below the decks of a luxury liner. In the central glass-roofed courtyard, explore the dragon boat, marvelous ships' figureheads, an exhibition on uniform styles over the years, and displays on Franklin's Arctic voyage and the British Navy.

Part of the seventeenth-century Royal Naval College, the **Queen's House** was built in 1638 for Anne of Denmark and finished for Queen Henrietta Maria, wife of Charles I. With the Banqueting House at Whitehall (see page 97), this Inigo Jones masterpiece marked the introduction of Palladian architecture into England. It reopened in 2000 after extensive refurbishment. Opening hours are as the National Maritime Museum; an audio tour is available.

Atop Greenwich Hill, the **Old Royal Observatory** is the original home of Greenwich Mean Time. Today it's a museum of space and time. Get a feel for the nature of both by taking a look at the prime meridian, longitude $0°$, the starting point for the measurement of time and distance on Earth. Exhibitions trace the fascinating history of the search for reliable navigational tools, from the "powder of sympathy" right up to modern satellite technol-

Canary Wharf, Docklands, reflects modern London.

Beyond Greenwich, the **Thames Barrier** is the world's largest movable flood defense. The Visitor Centre ((020) 8854-1373, Unity Way, Woolwich SE18, offers insights on how it functions. Call to find out when the barrier will lift. This impressive event takes place three times a year. Open daily; admission fee. BR Charlton.

Hampton Court
Mirroring the magnificence of Henry VIII's Tudor realm, Hampton Court Palace and Gardens ((020) 8781-9500, Hampton, Middlesex, is a lavish palace of pomp set in 248 magnificent hectares (620 acres) of parks and gardens. The palace was built by Cardinal Wolsey in 1515. As the grandest palace of its day, Hampton Court soon aroused the envy of Henry VIII, and within a decade of its construction it was presented to the covetous monarch. From then until George II, it remained a Royal residence. The palace contains a host of fine sixteenth- to eighteenth-century Italian art. The grounds and gardens, with the Orangery by Wren and the famous Maze, were laid out in the late seventeenth century. Guides wear period costumes. Hampton Court Palace and Gardens is open daily year-round; admission fee.

To get to Hampton Court take the mainline train from Waterloo to BR Hampton Court Station. Green Line ((020) 8688-7261 coaches depart from Bulleid Way (Victoria station) at 10 AM Monday to Friday from the last week in May through September, returning from Hampton Court at 4 PM. Journey time is around an hour. In summer, take a boat from Westminster Pier.

Richmond and Kew Gardens
The pretty village of Richmond is a short ride on the District Underground line from central London. In addition to the must-see Kew Gardens, the **towpath walks** at Strand-on-the-Green, by Kew Bridge, provide a worlds-away feeling with their eighteenth- and nineteenth-century wisteria-covered cottages. Scenes from the Beatles' *Help!* were filmed here.

The **Royal Botanic Gardens at Kew** ((020) 8332-5000, Kew Road, Richmond, Surrey, are the world's most celebrated gardens; a beautifully cultivated 120-hectare (300-acre) parkland and conservation center situated along the Thames. Within the grounds are seven glass conservatories, including Decimus Burton and Richard Turner's Palm House, completed in 1848, where a jungle of palms and ferns as well as cocoa, rubber, banana and coffee-bean plants and tropical fruits thrive. A Kew landmark is the Chinese Pagoda. Ask nicely and you may be allowed to climb the 10-story tower. The Princess of Wales Conservatory comprises 10 climactic zones from rainforest to desert. From February to March it's the setting for a glorious display of orchids. Another good time to visit Kew is in May when the Bluebell

Woods, a legacy of Queen Victoria, blossom. Kew is open daily year-round (last entry varies with the season from 6:30 PM to 3:30 PM), guided tours available; admission fee. ⊖ Kew Gardens.

In July there is an open air **swing jazz festival** ((020) 8332-5655 (recorded information) in the botanic gardens, followed by fireworks. Tickets can be purchased from Ticketmaster ((020) 7316-4710. Another tradition is Sunday **cream teas** on Kew Green, when you can watch the weekly cricket match as you sip. In the churchyard look for the **tomb of Thomas Gainsborough**. Another place for a bite is the **Maids of Honour Tea Room** ((020) 8940-2752, 288 Kew Road, Richmond, a timeless spot for a warming drink. Try a "maid of honour," a sweet-and-sour curd cake made with puffed pastry. Richmond's best gastropub is the **White Horse** ((020) 8940-2418, behind the Red Cow, at 14 Worple Way.

Nearby are the vast expanses of **Richmond Park** ((020) 8948-3209, Richmond, Surrey, with its herd of 700 tame miniature deer. The centerpiece of this 1,000-hectare (2,500-acre) wilderness of rolling hills and forest is the fabulous Isabella Plantation, a woodland garden dotted with majestic oaks and crossed by gurgling streams. It's at its best in spring, when the magnolias, rhododendrons and azaleas come into color. Open daily year round, dawn to dusk; free. ⊖/BR Richmond.

Across the Thames is **Syon House** ((020) 8560-0881, London Road, Brentford, summer home of the Duke of Northumberland. The highlight here is the neoclassical interior created by Robert Adams in the 1760s, some say his best work. In addition to confections of plaster and pillar, the house contains a fine collection of paintings, including portraits by Joshua Reynolds and Thomas Gainsborough. The gardens were laid out by Lancelot "Capability" Brown, and at the London Butterfly House, exotic insects fly free in a tropical greenhouse. Open Easter to September Wednesday to Sunday and Sundays in October; admission fee. Gardens open daily year-round. BR Syon Lane.

SHOPPING

Some people see London as a center of world culture, others as the clubbing capital of the known universe. But diehard shoppers will perhaps be forgiven for viewing London as a vast concourse of capitalism to be pillaged at will, credit card in hand. Major shopping areas are detailed below. Keep in mind that some of the best buys in London are at the **street markets**. See TO MARKET TO MARKET, page 13 in TOP SPOTS, for an orientation to this essential part of London life. For information on Value Added Tax refunds for foreigners, see ARRIVING (AND LEAVING), page 323 in TRAVELERS' TIPS.

7828-6812 FAX (020) 7828-6814 E-MAIL elizabeth @argyllhotels.com, 37 Eccleston Square SW1V 1PB, faces a leafy private garden with tennis court to which guests have access. The 40 rooms (35 with bath) are smallish, as are the baths, but they're nicely lit and decorated in soothing colors. Triple rooms have garden views. Θ/BR Victoria.

Fabulous bird prints decorate the common areas of the **Edward Lear Hotel** ((020) 7402-5401 FAX (020) 7706-3766 E-MAIL edwardlear@aol.com, 28–30 Seymour Street, London W1H 5WD. The prints are by the illustrator Edward Lear, also known as the author of "The Owl and the Pussycat." Rooms are well-equipped and spacious, beds are firm, and amenities include television with a free film channel. Baths in the doubles are large, with nice touches like built-in dressing tables. Children aged three to 13 sharing with parents stay free on weekends and for £9.50

other nights (no charge for children under three). Θ Marble Arch.

Situated in an eighteenth-century terrace, the **Morgan Hotel** ((020) 7636-3735 FAX (020) 7636-3045, 24 Bloomsbury Street, London WC1B 3QJ, lies in the heart of Bloomsbury, right around the corner from the British Museum. You'll need to book ahead as this small, family-run hotel has many loyal customers. The bedrooms with bath are decorated with period furnishings and suites are suitable for longer stays. Θ Tottenham Court Road or Russell Square.

Function prevails over form at the homey and comfortable **St. Margaret Hotel** ((020) 7636-4277 or (020) 7580-2352 FAX (020) 7323-3066, 26 Bedford Place, WC1B 5JL. With 68 rooms (10 with bath), it's larger than some of the area's hotels, but the staff treat

Somerset House, home of the Courtauld Gallery, Britain's finest collection of Impressionist works.

guests like family. The crowning touch is the hotel's access to one of London's wonderful secret gardens: a long green space shaded by ancient elms, property of the Duke of Bedford. Guests need only ask for the key. The most popular room is the ground floor suite with sauna and solarium, and a view of the duke's garden. ⊖ Holborn or Russell Square.

For cost-conscious families, the **County Hall Travel Inn Capital Hotel** ((020) 7902-1600 FAX (020) 7902-1619, Belvedere Road SE1, may be attractive. Set in the old County Hall which was from 1922 to 1986 the home of London government, the much-renovated rooms sleep up to two adults and two children. Don't expect English charm. This is very much a chain hotel of the American model, but you couldn't get much more central, just over the bridge from Big Ben and right next to the Aquarium, the London Eye and South Bank Centre. It's also handy for people coming in on the Eurostar, as it's only steps from Waterloo. ⊖ Westminster or ⊖/BR Waterloo.

The **Swiss House Hotel** ((020) 7373-2769 FAX (020) 7373-4983 E-MAIL recep@swiss-hh .demon.co.uk, 171 Old Brompton Road SW5 0AN, with its ivy-clad façade, is one of London's best value, small hotels. The 16 bedrooms (15 with bath) and public areas are charmingly decorated in bright gingham. Gracious hosts ensure that all is to your liking. The room rate includes continental breakfast. English breakfast is available for an additional fee. ⊖ Gloucester Road.

Situated in a Georgian house near Victoria Station, **Morgan Guest House** ((020) 7730-2384 FAX (020) 7730-8442, 120 Ebury Street SW1W 9QQ, is a welcoming place with 11 bedrooms (three with bath). Though bedrooms are small, the huge many-paned windows bring in lots of light. Bathrooms are closet-like, but tidy. ⊖/BR Victoria.

In northwest London, the **Anchor Hotel** ((020) 8458-8764, 10 West Heath Drive, Golders Green, London NW11 7QH, is a small, family-run guest house within walking distance of the tube, which gets you to central London in 15 minutes. It's located on the northwestern edge of Hampstead Heath; moderate. ⊖ Golders Green.

INEXPENSIVE

The popular **Cherry Court Hotel** ((020) 7828-2840 FAX (020) 7828-0393 E-MAIL info@cherrycourthotel .co.uk, 23 Hugh Street, London SW1V 1QJ, is a kindly hotel in a row of doll-like houses near Victoria Station. Rooms are small but clean and they have large windows looking out on the quiet street. Beds are equipped with cozy duvets. In summer, you must book at least two weeks in advance for this known hotel. On the same street, the **Oak House Hotel** ((020) 7834-7151, 29 Hugh Street SW1, offers cheap rooms for five or more consecutive days.

You could do worse than settle in the leafy suburb of Kew. **Melbury** ((020) 8876-3930, 33 Marksbury Avenue, Kew, Richmond, Surrey TW9 4JE, offers comfortable bed and breakfast within walking distance of Kew Garden tube.

Other inexpensive hostelries include: **Driscoll House Hotel** ((020) 7703-4175 FAX (020) 7703-8013, 172 New Kent Road SE1, where breakfast and dinner are included (⊖/BR Elephant and Castle); **Aaron House** ((020) 7370-3991 FAX (020) 7373-2303, 17 Courtfield Gardens, London SW5, in the popular Earl's Court neighborhood (⊖ Gloucester Road); and the **Garden Court Hotel** ((020) 7229-2553 FAX (020) 7727-2749, 30-31 Kensington Gardens Square, W2 4BG (⊖ Bayswater or ⊖ Queensway).

HOSTELS

There are seven YHA hostels in London as well as several independents, all in the inexpensive price range. I've offered a mere sampling of London's world of dormitory lodging. See BACK-PACKING, page 34 in YOUR CHOICE, for more on hostels and other cheap lodging choices.

The **Generator** ((020) 7388-7666 FAX (020) 7388-7644 E-MAIL generator@lhdr.demon.co.uk, Mac-Naughten House, Compton Place, London WC1H 9SD, bills itself as a "hard-edged," "futuristic" urban refuge. This vast hostel has 810 beds in 200 rooms of one to eight (no private baths). A bar and licensed café fuel inmates, and there's Internet access in the Talking Heads room. Despite its girth, the hostel can be difficult to locate. Look for it off Tavistock Place between Judd Street and Woburn Place. ⊖ Russell Square or ⊖/BR King's Cross–St. Pancras.

If you want that bright-lights-big-city feel, the **Oxford Street Youth Hostel** ((020) 7734-1618 FAX (020) 7734-1657 E-MAIL oxfordst@yha.org.uk, 14 Noel Street, London W1V 3PD, may be a good choice. In the middle of Soho and London's frenetic shopping district, this rather basic hostel also puts you close to the nightlife action. The hostel has 75 beds in two- to four-bed rooms, a lounge with television, a kitchen, laundry and showers. Θ Oxford Street.

The well-organized **Earl's Court Youth Hostel** ((020) 7373-7083 FAX (020) 7835-2034 E-MAIL earls court@yha.org.uk, 38 Bolton Gardens, London SW5 0AQ, is also right in the action, bordering Earl's Court. Internet access and cable television

VERY EXPENSIVE

Refer to EATING OUT, page 328 in TRAVELERS' TIPS for a description of price categories.

Befitting its status as one of London's most affluent neighborhoods, Mayfair is home to some of the city's top French tables. Chef Michel Roux creates a classic menu at the elegant **Le Gavroche** ((020) 7408-0881, 43 Upper Brook Street W1 (Θ Marble Arch). The set lunch menu here is excellent value, making it an ideal place to splash out. Jacket and tie required; closed weekends. A Mayfair upstart, the **Square** ((020) 7495-7100, 6 Bruton Street W1 (Θ Bond Street or Green Park),

are available in the lounge, and there is a self-catering kitchen, luggage and cycle storage, laundry, a garden, currency exchange. All accommodations are in single-sex dormitory rooms of six to 10 beds each.

WHERE TO EAT

While NIGHTLIFE (below) offers a peek at the city after dark, in many Londoners' minds, dining out *is* entertainment. It's been that way since London found its foodie soul some years ago and began blossoming as one of the world's great good-food cities.

Popular London restaurants can be booked up to days or even weeks in advance. To avoid disappointment, reserve early. For more helpful morsels on the London dining scene, see GALLOPING GOURMETS, page 57 in YOUR CHOICE.

boasts the modern French preparations of Chef Philip Howard in a grand contemporary setting. Smart casual dress required; closed Saturday lunch and Sunday.

Having moved from Chelsea to its new Knightsbridge digs, **La Tante Claire** ((020) 7493-5699, Berkeley Hotel, Wilton Place SW1, boasts Pierre Koffman's French *haute cuisine*, long viewed as London's best. The set lunch menu is your chance to try this swanky restaurant without the swooninducing cost; closed weekends. Jacket required at dinner. Θ Knightsbridge or Hyde Park Corner.

Appropriately close to Belgravia's Pakistan embassy, **Salloos** ((020) 7235-4444, 62-64 Kinnerton Street, has a distinguished reputation for fine, authentic Pakistani food, served in a setting worthy of the Raj. Open until 11:15 PM; closed Sunday.

The controversial Millennium Dome.

Smart casual dress required. Θ Knightsbridge or Hyde Park Corner.

A change in staff has not dampened enthusiasm for South Kensington's **Aubergine** ((020) 7352-3449, 11 Park Walk SW10, where new Chef William Drabble's classic French *haute cuisine* has been getting favorable reviews; closed Saturday lunch and Sunday. The restaurant is a longish walk from Θ South Kensington or Gloucester Road.

Across the Thames in Bermondsey (South Bank) overlooking Tower Bridge, **Le Pont de la Tour** ((020) 7403-8403, Butler's Wharf Building, 36D Shad Thames SE1, does seafood with French-Mediterranean influences. Outdoor Thameside tables are available on fine days. Θ Tower Hill.

Despite its primary function as London's business district, the City has a few excellent places to dine. **Tatsuso** ((020) 7638-5863, 32 Broadgate Circle, is one of the select, serving superb Japanese food. Closed weekends. Θ/BR Liverpool Street.

EXPENSIVE

Legal London is the home of **Bank** ((020) 7379-9797, 1 Kingsway, WC2, where Mod Brit fare and brasserie classics are served in an oh-so-modern open-plan setting. Θ Holborn.

In Theatreland, a doorman in a top hat stands guard outside the **Ivy** ((020) 7836-4751, 1 West Street, WC2, the West End's star-studded Modern British spot. The menu might include delicacies such as cold veal and ox tongue with baby beets and balsamic vinegar. Reservations are essential (and notoriously difficult to obtain). Θ Leicester Square.

London's oldest restaurant is found at Covent Garden. **Rules** ((020) 7836-5314, 35 Maiden Lane WC2, has been serving good quality British traditional fare since 1798. Open until 11:30 PM. Θ Covent Garden.

Go to Soho for **L'Escargot** ((020) 7437-2679, 48 Greek Street W1, celeb Chef Alastair Little's modern French brasserie. Θ Tottenham Court Road.

In Belgravia's embassy land, **Zafferano** ((020) 7235-5800, 16 Lowndes Street SW1, has earned the title of "London's top Italian restaurant" from at least one reviewer. It makes the grade for its marvelous, authentic cooking and Continental atmosphere. Open until 11 PM; closed Sunday. Θ Knightsbridge or Sloane Square.

While no one claims that the Modern British fare is the main attraction at **Pharmacy** ((020) 7221-2442, 150 Notting Hill Gate W11, the megatrendy restaurant is a hit for its sheer audacity. Waiters in the downstairs bar dress in Prada-designed surgeon's coats, and Damien Hirst's medicine cabinets filled with boxes of pills line the walls. There is a decently-priced set two-course lunch. Θ Notting Hill Gate.

Le Pont de la Tour Bar & Grill shares the same blissful Thameside location and terrace dining as Le Pont de la Tour (see VERY EXPENSIVE, above), but at much better value. The *plateau de fruits de mer* with a glass of champagne is especially easy on the wallet. Open until 11:30 PM; no booking. Θ Tower Hill.

MODERATE

Some Londoners swear **Fung Shing** ((020) 7437-1539, 15 Lisle Street WC2, is the best in Chinatown, especially when it comes to seafood. Order exotics like crispy spicy eel or cold herbboiled chicken with jelly fish. One goes here for the food, not the atmosphere or the service, either of which you may doubt the existence of. Θ Leicester Square.

An animated venue tucked away in a Covent Garden cellar, **Joe Allen's** ((020) 7836-0651, 13 Exeter Street WC2, is known more for star-spotting than fine food. Almost identical to the original in New York, the burgers (not listed on the menu) are recommended. Θ Covent Garden. **Belgo Centraal** ((020) 7813-2233, 50 Earlham Street WC2, corner Neal and Shelton, serves up Belgian *moules–frites* and beer. Take advantage of the early specials; it can be loud and cramped at peak hours. Open until 11:30 PM. Θ Covent Garden.

A Soho institution for over 20 years, **Vasco and Piero's Pavilion** ((020) 7437-8774, 15 Poland Street W1 (Θ Oxford Circus), is an Italian restaurant where the set menus offer good value. There's not much atmosphere, but the food's enchanting. Open until 11 PM; closed Saturday and Sunday except for one Saturday dinner each month. Smart casual dress expected. Also in Soho, **Andrew Edmunds** ((020) 7437-5708, 46 Lexington Street, is one of the city's most romantic spots, serving good-value Modern British and interesting wines. Θ Piccadilly Circus. **Melati** ((020) 7437-2745, 21 Great Windmill Street W1, has been going strong for many years, serving well prepared Malaysian cuisine in this convenient location. Θ Piccadilly Circus.

In the same area, Britain's oldest Indian restaurant, **Veeraswamy** ((020) 7734-1401, Mezzanine, Victory House, 99 Regent Street W1 (enter on Swallow Street), has been recently renovated and proclaimed "best Indian restaurant" by *Time Out*. Authentic fare from both the northern and southern sub-continent are served in the contemporary dining room; moderate. Θ Piccadilly Circus.

In Camden there's another branch of the Belgo Group, **Belgo Noord** ((020) 7267-0718, at 72 Chalk Farm Road NW1; see Belgo Centraal (above). Θ Chalk Farm.

Hampstead's, the **House** ((020) 7435-8037, 34A Rosslyn Hill NW3, mixes French and Modern British cooking in a sleek café setting. Veal

dishes and mussels catalan are among the specialties; moderate. On the same street, the **Bar Room** ((020) 7435-0808, 48 Rosslyn Hill NW3, serves wood-oven-fired pizzas under a lofty ceiling. Also on the menu are fine wines and delicious bar snacks; inexpensive.

On the South Bank, **Tentazioni** ((020) 7237-1100, 2 Mill Street SE1, near Tower Bridge, is another contender for the title of best Italian restaurant in London. Open until 11 PM. Closed Saturday and Sunday. Θ/BR London Bridge.

While service isn't terribly smooth, the food is superb and great value at the chef's school restaurant, the **Apprentice** ((020) 7234-0254, 31 Shad Thames SE1. Θ/BR London Bridge.

Traditionalists won't go hungry in the City where **Sweetings** ((020) 7248-3062, 39 Queen Victoria Street EC4, does fresh fish and more. Θ Mansion House, Bank or Blackfriars.

INEXPENSIVE

Oh, so Soho: Piled into a room reminiscent of a primary school cafeteria, diners at **Mildreds** ((020) 7494-1634, 58 Greek Street, happily munch on veggie burgers and fries or a sandwich of *masa harina* cakes. For dessert, there are gooey items along with lighter choices like Greek yogurt drizzled with honey. Certain items are available for take out at lower prices. Service is fast and friendly. There's often a queue to get in, but you can leave your name and have a drink in the Pillars of Hercules across the street. Beverages run from organic gin to blue-green algae infusions. Θ Tottenham Court Road.

At the futuristic **Yo! Sushi** ((020) 7287-0443, 52 Poland Street, a 60-m-long (197-ft) conveyor belt delivers plates of sushi to diners, while cold beer and warm sake are served up by robotic trolleys wandering around the restaurant, and sparkling water is piped to dispensers at every seat. Downstairs at **Yo! Below** ((020) 7439-3660, the wait-staff double as masseurs and drinks are served at low Japanese tables with built-in smoke-extracting ash trays and personal beer taps — no waiting at the bar (that might stress you out). Open midday to midnight. Yo! is two blocks south of Oxford Street; Θ Oxford Circus.

Above one of Soho's most famous pubs, the **French House Dining Room** ((020) 7437-2477, 49 Dean Street W1, does good value Modern British; reservations advised. Θ Tottenham Court Road.

The smell of garlic leads theater-goers to **Pollo** ((020) 7734-5917, 20 Old Compton Street W1, a tiny Italian with crammed together booths and a vast menu. Θ Leicester Square. **Stockpot** ((020) 7287-1066, 18 Old Compton Street W1, is famous as one of London's best dining deals. English fare is supplemented by choices from the Continent, and there are always several vegetarian choices. Θ Leicester Square.

Behind Gray's Inn in London's legal heart **Fryer's Delight** ((020) 7405-4114, 19 Theobald's Road, may be "best chippy". Open until 10 PM. Θ Holborn.

In London's Chinatown, **Mr. Wu** ((020) 7287-3885, 28 Wardour Street W1, a very few pounds entitle you to unlimited servings from a small buffet featuring three meat dishes, two veg dishes, soup, spring rolls, rice and noodles. Because they do a brisk business, the food stays fresh. Service is incredibly efficient, and there's no temptation to blow your budget on alcohol or dessert because they're not on the menu. Θ Oxford Circus.

One of Bloomsbury's best-kept secrets is **Alara Wholefoods** ((020) 7837-1172, 58-60 Marchmont Street WC1, serving tasty hot dishes like vegetarian shepherd's pie and hearty veg, cheese and bean

Cheap eats — OPPOSITE: A neighborhood "chippie." ABOVE: Pub grub, *al fresco*.

casseroles sold by the pound for take out. On fine days you can eat at the sidewalk tables out front. Θ Russell Square.

In Knightsbridge, just steps from Harrods, **Gloriette** ((020) 7589-4750, 128 Brompton Road, corner Montpellier Street SW7, is part Viennese café, part American soda fountain. Delightfully Old World with orchids on tables and gas heaters warming sidewalk diners, the menu offers all-day dining starting with breakfast. For lunch there is a combination of standby salads and dishes along with some imaginative combinations. The chicken club is stacked high with chicken, avocado, bacon, lettuce and tomato. Everything is freshly prepared. Θ Knightsbridge.

salmon with a tapenade crust, served with pesto potatoes and followed by organic chocolate cake. Θ Notting Hill Gate.

Khan's ((020) 7727-5420, 13-15 Westbourne Grove W2, has been serving superb Indian food for 20 years. You'll probably have to wait for a table, but the food is abundant and cheap, and the atmosphere is as close to India as you'll come without a plane ticket; Θ Bayswater, Queensway or Royal Oak.

A tiny kiosk that serves delicious pancakes while you wait, at **La Crêperie de Hampstead** (no phone) 77 High Street, corner Perrin's Lane, fillings run the gamut from ratatouille or tandoori chicken to more traditional combinations such as

A Mayfair cheapie, **Café Ripaille** ((020) 7495-5509, Shepherd Market, Mayfair, has adorable crêpes (and raffish French waiters). Try to claim one of the few terrace tables or order for take-out. Θ Green Park.

Wagamama ((020) 7409-0111, 101 Wigmore Street W1, is a no-frills noodles refectory in Piccadilly. Go early to avoid the lines. Open until 11 PM; no smoking; no booking. Θ Piccadilly Circus. There are two other branches: ((020) 7292-0990, 10A Lexington Street W1 Θ Piccadilly Circus; and ((020) 7323-9223, 4A Streatham Street WC1. Θ Tottenham Court Road.

In Notting Hill, you can eat in or take out co-conut curry and rice at **Makan MalaysianTake-Away** ((020) 8960-5169, 270 Portobello Road W11, a storefront in Ladbroke Grove. Θ Ladbroke Grove. The **Organic Restaurant** ((020) 7727-9620, 35 Pembridge Road W11, does baked filet of

jambon et fromage (ham and cheese). The dessert crêpes are good, too.

Camden has the family-run **Marine Ices** ((020) 7485-3132, 8 Haverstock Hill NW3, providing authentic Italian for unbelievable prices. Choose from a list of pastas and match your choice with one of the dozen or so sauces. Service is super-efficient. Θ Chalk Farm.

Within walking distance of Tower Hill, **Lahore Kebab House** ((020) 7488-2551, 2 Umberston Street, is a basic but excellent place for a tasty low-cost meal.

PUBS

The **Eagle** ((020) 7837-1353, 159 Farringdon Road EC1, has long been one of London's best good-food pubs. The Mediterranean fare is prepared with the freshest and finest ingredients. While the pub takes a page from some of London's stylish restaurants, with open kitchen and modern art on the walls, it retains a pubby, casual atmosphere. ⊖ Farringdon/Old Street.

In South London, convenient to the Imperial War Museum and the Old Vic, **Fire Station** ((020) 7620-2226, 150 Waterloo Road SE1, is a converted fire house serving creative fare in a lively, sociable atmosphere. Mismatched furniture and contemporary art decorate the dining room. In addition to ales, there is a good selection of wines. The menu changes daily.

An East End institution, the **Prospect of Whitby** ((020) 7481-1095, 57 Wapping Wall (⊖ Wapping), is a good example of an authentic old-style English pub. It's London's oldest riverside pub,

dating from the reign of Henry VIII. Inside, the floors are still paved with flagstones and the bar is a long expanse of pewter balanced on barrels. It's a much-loved coach-tour pit stop, but a great place to visit, nevertheless.

Situated on a sunny corner in Brook Green, the **Havelock Tavern** ((020) 7603-5374, 57 Masbro Road W14 (⊖ Kensington/Olympia), was one of the first gastropubs and continues to serve some of the best pub food in London. The menu changes daily.

With a sublime location overlooking Hampstead Heath, **Freemason's Arms** ((020) 7433-6811, 32 Downshire Hill NW3, is a nineteenth-century pub boasting a spacious garden and a Pell Mell pitch (similar to English bowls). Inside, the beamed bar has an open fire on chilly days.

In Hampstead village, the **Flask** ((020) 7435-4580, 14 Flask Walk NW3 is another recommended pub, specializing in "flask pie" (mince

with cheese, leek and potato topping). Families with children of all ages are made welcome here, as are dogs. An open fire cheers the bar.

NIGHTLIFE

London presents a sublime abundance of nocturnal adventures. *Time Out* magazine, found at newsstands, is essential for any in-depth exploration of the capital city after dark. There is also the monthly *Best Read Guide*, full of useful information on mainstream events and attractions.

Festivals and annual events figure prominently in London's rich cultural life. See FESTIVE FLINGS, page 53, for details.

Most London restaurants and bars close before midnight, but there are still plenty of places to sate the midnight munchies. Refer to your dog-eared copy of *Time Out* for listings of late-night and all-night eateries and bars.

Tube stations are indicated here, but partyers should get in touch with London Transport for a schedule of night buses, as the tube closes at 12:30 PM. See GETTING AROUND, page 85. Taxis get hard to find in the West End after the tube stations have shut. It is best to ring for a minicab to pick you up, and then be prepared to wait. Private cars do cruise the crowds offering unlicensed lifts. Those who choose this option should have a vague idea how much to pay and a clear idea of where they're going.

THEATRE AND CINEMA

London is the undisputed champion of Western theater. There are more than 150 venues hosting more than 200 shows any night of the week in London, a quarter of which are found in the **West End**, London's Theatreland. Expect anything from *Cats* to *Richard III* to oddball events like singalong *Sound of Music* to street theater in Covent Garden.

Outside the West End, the works of the Bard are performed *al fresco* at **Shakespeare's Globe Theatre** ((020) 7401-9919, New Globe Walk, Bankside SE1 (⊖/BR London Bridge), an O-shaped theater with shows from mid-May through the third week in September. Productions take place much as they did in Shakespeare's day, with no spotlights, recorded music or elaborate sets and plenty of audience participation. The theater seats 1,500 in three tiers of wooden benches (bring a cushion or rent one at the theater) and a further 500 "groundlings."

On the same side of the Thames, the **Royal National Theatre** ((020) 7452-3000 is one of the word's great stage companies, presenting an eclectic range of productions from classics to comedy to new works. The company is based at the Thameside **South Bank Centre** ((020)

London nocturne.

7921-0600, Belvedere Road SE1 (Θ Waterloo), with its three auditoriums — the large open-staged *Olivier*, the proscenium-arched *Lyttleton*, and the small studio space of *Cottesloe*. Locked in healthy competition is Britain's other major theater company, the **Royal Shakespeare Theatre**, playing at their London home, the **Barbican** ((020) 7638-8891, Silk Street EC2 (Θ Barbican or Moorgate), during the winter months. In summer, the company tours throughout England and abroad.

At the **Open-air Theatre** ((020) 7486-2431 or (020) 7486-1933, Regent's Park (Θ Regent's Park), the season runs from late May to early September with Shakespeare, musical revivals, and children's productions. The top row of seats are cheapest by far (around £10) and the views are fine. Wear a sun hat for the matinee.

Those eager to see a specific London performance should purchase tickets well ahead, since popular shows sell out days or even weeks in advance. Ask at your local British Tourist Authority office (see TOURIST INFORMATION, page 324 in TRAVELERS' TIPS). Once in London it's easy to book tickets direct with theaters or at theater booking agencies. When using an agency, check the original price of the ticket. You'll be charged a booking fee, but it shouldn't exceed 30% of the original ticket price. Also, check the seating plan carefully to make sure you're not getting an obstructed view. If the agent refuses to show you a seating plan, buy your tickets elsewhere.

For West End shows, if you're not terribly choosy, join the queue at the **Half-Price Ticket Booth** for a chance at deeply discounted seats. The booth, run by the Society of London Theaters, is located on the south side of the Leicester Square in a large freestanding kiosk near the corner of St. Martin's Street, across from Hampshire House. Open Monday to Saturday from noon for matinee performances and 2:30 PM to 6:30 PM for evening show. Tickets are sold in person only and are limited to four per person; cash only. It's unwise to buy tickets from scalpers outside the booth or theaters.

See CULTURAL KICKS, page 44 in YOUR CHOICE, for a note on **fringe** and **pub theater**, vital elements of the London theater scene.

London is a feast of films with more than 400 **cinema** screens, many in the West End, including a host of genre theaters showing vintage, avant-garde or foreign language films, most notably the National Film Theatre ((020) 7928-3232, at the South Bank Centre.

COMEDY

Even if English is your first language, the rapid-fire delivery and borough accents of London comics might leave you dazed. A better bet for kids is

to look for physical comedy acts such as the **Circus Space** ((020) 7613-4141, Coronet Street N1, set in a splendid Victorian-era power station where shows every other Saturday at 8 PM feature derring-do and circus comedy. Θ/BR Old Street.

To get a taste of that renowned British humor, head for a stand-up comedy venue such as **Jongleurs Camden Lock** ((020) 7924-2766, Dingwalls Building, Middle Yard, Camden Lock NW1 (Θ Camden Town), a large space with top-notch line-ups followed by a disco; the **Comedy Store** ((01426) 914433, Haymarket House, 1 Oxendon Street SW1 (Θ Piccadilly Circus), London's most celebrated comedy spot with shows six nights a week; or **Comedy at Soho Ho** ((020) 8348-2085, The Crown & Two Chairmen, Dean Street W1 (Θ Leicester Square or Tottenham Court Road), a small, lively pub venue.

CLASSICAL MUSIC, OPERA AND DANCE

London has scores of excellent classical music and chamber groups, as well as some 600 dance troupes performing in dozens of venues from acoustically-engineered modern stages to ornate music halls.

The Barbican (above) is home to the world-famous **London Symphony Orchestra** and the **London Classical Orchestra**. Top musicians also come to the South Bank Centre's (above) three auditoriums. London's classical music season reaches its peak with the "Proms" at **Royal Albert Hall** ((020) 7589-8212, Kensington Gore SW7 (Θ South Kensington). The restored **Wigmore Hall** ((020) 7935-2141, Wigmore Street W1 (Θ Bond Street), is an intimate concert space where quartets or pianists perform every night of the week with an additional Sunday matinee, as well as lunchtime performances every Monday.

Nearly every day of the week there are musical events in London churches. **St. Martin-in-the-Field** ((020) 7930-0089, Trafalgar Square (Θ/BR Charing Cross), has an excellent program of chamber music, as does **St. John's, Smith Square** ((020) 7222-1061, Smith Square SW1 (Θ Westminster).

It's nearly impossible to get tickets for the elaborate productions of the newly re-opened **Royal Opera House** ((020) 7304-4000, Floral Street WC2 (Θ Covent Garden), since only 67 seats are sold to the general public. The **English National Opera**, based at the **London Coliseum** ((020) 7632-8300, St. Martin's Lane WC2 (Θ Leicester Square), is probably more fun anyway, with its daring English-language productions.

The Royal Opera House (above) is home to the **Royal Ballet**, and the London Coliseum (above) houses the **English National Ballet**, while the historic **Sadler's Wells** ((020) 7314-8800 reopened in 1999, is one of the city's pre-eminent venues for both ballet and modern dance. More of London's extraordinary contemporary dance scene takes place at the **Institute of Contemporary Art** ℂ (020) 7930-3647, The Mall SW1 (Θ/BR Charing Cross); the **Place Theatre** ℂ (020) 7380-1268, 17 Duke's Road WC1 (Θ/BR Euston); and the **Royalty Theatre** ℂ (020) 7484-5090, Portugal Street WC2 (Θ Holborn).

POP, FOLK AND JAZZ

No matter what your musical inclination, you're sure to find something up your alley any night of the week in the capital city.

Mega-venues like **Wembley Arena and Stadium** ℂ (020) 8900-1234 (Θ Wembley Park or BR

174 Camden High Street NW1 (Θ Camden Town), below the World's End pub, has a standing-room-only basement featuring established bands like the Cranberries and Radiohead. Also in Camden, **Falcon** ℂ (020) 7482-4884, 234 Royal College Street, Camden NW1 (Θ Camden Town), is the place to catch future pop stars.

Folk and world music also thrive in London. **Jamaica Blue** (no phone), 18 Maddox Street, off Regent Street W1, hosts the godfathers of ska, calypso jazz and other Caribbean genres from Thursday to Saturday nights. Shows generally start at 7 PM. Leading African bands play the **Africa Centre** ℂ (020) 7836-2206, 38 King Street WC2 (Θ Covent Garden or Leicester Square). Traditional

Wembley Central), with 12,000 and 70,000 seats respectively, host the likes of Michael Jackson and Madonna. These places are so huge that most of the audience has to be content with viewing the performance on wide screens. You'll probably get more satisfaction at **Shepherd's Bush Empire** ℂ (020) 7771-2000, Shepherd's Bush Green W12 (Θ Shepherd's Bush), former BBC studios converted into a modern theater presenting a wide variety of bands.

There are scores of dance clubs that headline live bands. The **Borderline** ℂ (020) 7734-2095, Orange Yard, Manette Street WC2 (Θ Tottenham Court Road), is a laid-back place with bands on weekend nights. The **Rock Garden** ℂ (020) 7836-4052, Covent Garden Piazza WC2 (Θ Covent Garden), has a basement stage featuring new bands as well as scheduled indie, blues, funk and pop nights. **Camden Underworld** ℂ (020) 7267-3939,

English music jiggles **Cecil Sharpe House** ℂ (020) 7485-2206, 2 Regent's Park Road NW1 (Θ Camden Town). And the **Swan** ℂ (020) 7978-9778, 215 Clapham Road SW9 (Θ Stockwell), hosts traditional Irish ensembles.

Soho has a good number of clubs and bars offering jazz combos, but London's vibrant jazz scene stretches far beyond the West End. The **Jazz Café** ℂ (020) 8963-0940, 5 Parkway NW1, Camden (Θ Camden Town), has a Sunday afternoon jam session every week from noon to 4 PM. There's a balcony restaurant here with good views of the performing area where there's standing room for about 400. A diverse range of acts perform on regular nights. Another superb place for jazz is **Ronnie Scott's** ℂ (020) 7439-0747, 47 Frith Street (Θ Leicester Square, Tottenham Court Road

Hyde Park's Serpentine Lake in summer.

or Piccadilly Circus), run by the British saxophonist. If you want a view of the stage, book a table early. Another Soho swinger, **Pizza Express** ((020) 7437-9595, 10 Dean Street W1 (Θ Tottenham Court Road), has a basement stage with a varied line-up, from American jazz stars to local up-and-comers.

CLUBS

Since the 1980s, when the House and rave scene stormed across Europe, London has been at the heart of this youth genre. I've listed a few clubs, but always call ahead as London's dance club scene is in constant flux.

Arguably London's most famous House and Garage space (it even has its own record label and apparel line) is the **Ministry of Sound** ((020) 7378-6528, 103 Gaunt Street SE1 (Θ Elephant & Castle), with its hallmark big-name guest DJs and thumping sound system. In addition to several dance floors, there are lounge rooms, video game stations, and a vodka-shot bar.

Along the same lines, two vast new supertrendy multi-dance-floor clubs opened in 1999. **Fabric** ((020) 7490-0444, 77A Charterhouse Street EC1 (Θ Farringdon) in the heart of the East End, has 24-hour music and dance from Thursday to Sunday. **Home** ((020) 8964-1999, 1 Leicester Square (Θ Piccadilly Circus or Leicester Square), boasts a "multimedia café" and a restaurant with a view of the city in addition to a line-up of top DJs. Sunday is gay night.

Dedicating most nights to a gay crowd are **Heaven** ((020) 7839-3852 or (020) 839-5210, Under the Arches, Craven Street WC2 (Θ/BR Charing Cross); and **Fridge** ((020) 7326-5100, Town Hall Parade, Brixton Hill SW2 (Θ Brixton).

Outside the House scene, there are glitzy discotheques such as the **Equinox** ((020) 7437-1446, Leicester Square WC2 (Θ Leicester Square); and the **Hippodrome** ((020) 7437-4311, Charing Cross Road WC2 (Θ/BR Charing Cross), pulling in a largely tourist crowd. Latin beats cause spontaneous dancing at clubs like **Salsa!** ((020) 7379-3277, 96 Charing Cross Road WC2 (Θ Leicester Square); and **Havana Central** ((020) 7629-2552, 17 Hanover Square W1 (Θ Oxford Circus).

Then there are the glitzy dress-up dinner-and-dancing clubs such as **Browns**, 4 Great Queen Street, WC2 (Θ Holborn); and **Stringfellows** ((020) 7240-5534, 16–19 Upper St. Martin's Lane WC2 (Θ Charing Cross). These two are popular with people of all ages, while thirty-somethings (and beyond) drift toward the stylings of **Limelight** ((020) 7434-0572, 136 Shaftsbury Avenue WC2 (Θ Piccadilly Circus or Leicester Square); the **Wag** ((020) 7437-5534, 35 Wardour Street W1 (Θ Piccadilly Circus); and in Mayfair, the **Iceni** ((020) 7495-5333, 11 White Horse Street, off Curzon Street W1 (Θ Green Park).

HOW TO GET THERE

Getting to London, the transportation hub of Western Europe, is roughly the same proposition as getting to Southern England. You'll find advice on that subject under GETTING THERE, page 322 in TRAVELERS' TIPS.

If you are flying into Heathrow or Gatwick, you'll find a number of options for ground transportation into London. From Heathrow, the easiest is **Heathrow Express** ((0845) 600-1515, a train that runs direct to Paddington tube station, departing every 15 to 20 minutes (£10 single /£20 round trip). Alternatively, the **Piccadilly Underground line** serves Terminals 1 to 4, so if you're traveling light you can take the subway into town (one-way £3.40; 50 minutes) and save a bundle. **Airbuses** ((020) 7222-1234 (£6 single/£10 return) run every 15 to 20 minutes to Victoria Station with limited stops in between. They are more expensive than the Underground, and usually slower as well, but they can be an attractive alternative if you're carrying a lot of luggage. An Airbus Direct service runs to a number of hotels. **Taxis** from Heathrow to central London cost £30 to £35 and take approximately one hour.

From Gatwick, there are three main ground transportation services to London by rail. All depart from the same station at Gatwick and run every 15 minutes or so for much of the day, every 30 minutes at night. **Connex South Central** ((0870) 603-0405, and **Gatwick Express** ((020) 7973-5000 rail services run direct to Victoria station (30 to 35 minutes). The former is somewhat faster, while the latter offers more suburban connections. The **Thameslink** ((020) 7620-5760 runs across London, stopping at Blackfriars, Farringdon, King's Cross, and at City Thameslink station in Central London before continuing on to Luton or Bedford. Night service on this line is limited. **Flightline** ((020) 8668-7261 coaches operate hourly every day to Victoria Coach station ((020) 7730-3466 or (booking) 730-3499, 164 Buckingham Palace Road, as does **National Express** ((0990) 808080 or (0990) 010104. A **taxi** ride from Gatwick runs to £55 and takes an hour and a half.

A city landmark, the "inside-out" Lloyd's Building was designed for the international insurance company by Richard Rogers in 1986.

Inland
Shires

ALTHOUGH NOT KNOWN FOR DRAMATIC SCENERY, THE landlocked counties Bedfordshire, Berkshire, Buckinghamshire, Hertfordshire, and Oxfordshire boast some stellar points of interest, from royal castles to duke's palaces and academic melting pots.

While East Berkshire has been swallowed by London, Windsor and its Great Park still embody the rich character of the region. In addition to the royal country residence, there is Eton, which educated Orwell, Huxley and Shelley as well as most of Britain's princes and lords. At its western edges, Berkshire is wilder and has many good places to walk.

Cradle of Britain's oldest university, the city of Oxford has splendid architecture and tranquil flotillas of punts navigating the River Isis, as the Thames is called here. Off the river, and sometimes even on it, "tranquillity" rarely describes Oxford. It's a popular destination, so you may want to choose your dates carefully. The county of Oxfordshire is also home to grand and glorious Blenheim Palace, charming south Cotswold villages, and Henley-on-Thames, where the Royal Regatta is an annual tradition.

Buckinghamshire, Bedfordshire and Hertfordshire form a compact touring area just north of London, with several worthwhile stately homes and the fabulous landscape garden at Stowe. Bedfordshire is the place for village-to-village walks, and the Chiltern Hills of Buckinghamshire offer gorgeous wooded scenery. The stands of beech here are especially stunning in autumn. Cyclists can choose from the easy, flat country of Bedfordshire to the more challenging countryside of the Chiltern Hills.

WINDSOR AND ETON

BERKSHIRE — Situated along the River Thames, just 32 km (20 miles) west of London, the town of Windsor is dominated by its castle, the weekend retreat of Her Majesty Queen Elizabeth II. Windsor Castle, the largest inhabited castle in the world, covers over one hectare (three acres) of land. The town, though dwarfed in scale and importance by the castle (which it evolved to serve), is attractive, with many half-timbered and Georgian buildings.

Neighboring Eton, with its famous public (private) school, is steeped in historic and literary connections. To the south, the royal park contains acres of woods and magnificent gardens. Just outside town is Legoland, an amusement park where 20 million Lego bricks recreate Amsterdam, Brussels, Paris and London in miniature.

Windsor's **Tourist Information Centre** ((01753) 852010 or (01753) 841746 (lodging) FAX (01753) 833450 is located at 24 High Street.

Saturday is **market** day in Windsor.

WHAT TO SEE AND DO

Windsor Castle

The royal castle stands on the outcrop of chalk upon which William the Conqueror built his original fortress in 1070, a wood-and-earth citadel whose purpose was to guard the western flank of London. He chose the spot because of its elevation high above the Thames, its location on the edge of a Saxon hunting ground, and its distance from the capital — one day's march from his Tower of London HQ. Over the years, successive monarchs left their mark on this motte-and-bailey castle. Henry II erected the first stone buildings, including the Round Tower, Henry III put up most of the defenses, and Edward III, who was born here, extended the state rooms and founded the Order of the Knights of the Garter. The castle was extensively remodeled under George IV in 1823, giving it the outlines that it has today.

If your time at Windsor Castle is short, go straight to **St. George's Chapel**. This sumptuous Perpendicular Gothic edifice was begun in 1478 by Edward IV as a private chapel for the Knights of the Garter, whose arms and flags deck the stalls. It's a dazzling monument with its richly carved choir stalls, elaborate fan vaulting, paintings, chantries and ironwork. Closed to visitors on Sundays. Check in advance as it can be closed at other times on short notice.

The 16 **state rooms** — decorated with Grinling Gibbons carvings and lavishly painted ceilings by Antonio Verrio — contain remarkable collections of porcelain and armor. The apartments are richly furnished and hung with works of art from the vast Royal Collection, including notable works by Rembrandt and Van Dyck. A devastating fire badly damaged the state rooms in 1992, but they've been flawlessly restored (thanks to money flowing in from the establishment of limited public visiting hours at Buckingham Palace). Open October to March only; the castle may be closed when the Queen is in residence.

Also included in the price of admission is a visit to **Queen Mary's Doll's House**, a miniature twentieth-century house in 1:12 scale, designed for Queen Mary by Sir Edwin Lutyens in 1924, with exquisite detailed furniture and decorations. There are even tiny bottles of vintage wine in the wine cellar.

Windsor Castle ((01753) 868286, (020) 7839-1377 or (01753) 831118 (24-hour recorded information) or (01753) 743900 (Royal Windsor Information Centre) is open daily year-round except April 2, June 14, and December 25 and 26; admission fee. Opening schedules vary in certain sections of the

Etonians on the march.

Mill Street, is dedicated to the preacher and author of *The Pilgrim's Progress*, John Bunyan (1628–1688), who was born in Bedford. There is a good **Tourist Information Centre (** (01234) 215226, at 10 St. Paul's Square.

John Bunyan fans can make pilgrim-like progress to the appealing village of **Elstow**, the actual birthplace of the itinerant preacher on the outskirts of Bedford. Timbered houses surround the green. Bunyan was baptized in the parish church, where you can view the Pilgrim's Progress window. The fine sixteenth-century Moot Hall has Bunyan memorabilia and a shop. Open Tuesday to Thursday and weekend afternoons from April to October; admission fee.

Southwest of Bedford, **Woburn Abbey (** (01525) 290666 is the grand residence of the Duke of Bedford, and perhaps one of the most delightfully endowed of all the stately homes. It's one of the country's most popular attractions, partly due to the **safari park** with its lions and tigers and monkeys roaming free within a 142-hectare (350-acre) enclosure. The house was built on the foundations of a twelfth-century Cistercian monastery and reflects a range of styles, with the south side having been designed by Henry Holland. Inside are collections of eighteenth-century furniture, silver, and paintings by Rembrandt, Van Dyck, Reynolds and Gainsborough. The house is surrounded by 1,200 ha (3,000 acres) of parkland landscaped by Humphrey Repton. Several species of deer forage here and there are ducks and other waterfowl on the lake, as well as a new aviary aflutter with the duke's green-yellow-blue pet budgerigars (Australian parakeets). Open daily from March to October and weekends only in January and February; admission fee.

Continuing the wildlife theme is **Whipsnade Wild Animal Park (** (01582) 872171, Whipsnade, about 16 km (10 miles) from Woburn, high in the Chilterns. Set in lovely countryside, this branch of the London Zoo was a pioneer in using natural, spacious enclosures. The park spreads out over a vast 240 ha (600 acres) with some 2,000 animals in residence. It's possible to drive through some areas, or take the little steam train that crosses the park. Open daily year-round; admission fee.

WHERE TO STAY AND EAT

At Woburn, the **Bell (** (01525) 290280, Woburn MK17 9QD, is a beautiful old inn with attractive bedrooms and good food; moderate.

If you need to stay in Bedford, there is **Jays End Guest house (** (01234) 406813, 13 Putnoe Heights, Bedford MK41 8EB, with two bedrooms, within walking distance of the center; inexpensive.

You'll find the county's best dining around Woburn. **Paris House (** (01525) 290692 is a timbered building in Woburn Abbey's deer park,

serving English and French food (expensive). Northwest of Woburn, just over the county line, **Spooners (** (01908) 584385, 61 High Street, Woburn Sands, is a friendly restaurant set in a Victorian terrace, good for lunch or dinner. Steaks are a specialty; moderate to inexpensive. The **Red Lion (** (01525) 210044, in Milton Bryan (just southeast of Woburn), is a cozy pub with beamed bar and good food; moderate to inexpensive.

HOW TO GET THERE

Bedford is 81 km (50 miles) north of London and 49 km (30 miles) west of Cambridge. There are frequent **trains** from London Farringdon (one hour)

and St. Pancras (40 minutes) to Bedford. National Express **coaches** run from London Victoria via Milton Keynes; the ride takes two to three hours. During the summer, Green Line runs a coach service from its Buckingham Palace Road station to Whipsnade. Bedford's bus station is about half a mile (one and a half kilometers) from the center.

HERTFORDSHIRE

Bordering Greater London, Hertfordshire's south is commuter country, while the north of the county runs to farmland. The shire's main attraction is Hatfield House, the Jacobean manor associated with the childhood of Elizabeth I, as well as the superb Roman museum at St. Albans.

ST. ALBANS

St. Albans is the ancient city of Verulamium, one of the earliest established and most important Roman administrative centers in Britain. Such was its stature that by the middle of the first century, Verulamium was elevated to the status of *municipium*, the only British city to be designated as such, which gave the city's inhabitants the right of Roman citizenship.

OPPOSITE: Henley-on-Thames riverfront. ABOVE: Rhinos roam the safari park at Woburn Abbey.

That didn't keep the city from being sacked in AD 61 by Boudicca, but Verulamium was rebuilt and continued to thrive. Today St. Albans — with its narrow, hilly streets — flourishes as a bedroom community of London. You'll find the **Tourist Information Centre** ((01727) 864511 FAX (01727) 863533 at the Town Hall in Market Place.

The excellent **Verulamium Museum** ((01727) 819339, St. Michael's, has a wealth of Roman artifacts, including some stunning mosaics. A highlight is the meticulously recreated Roman room, based on local excavations of plaster fragments. Open daily year-round; admission fee.

St. Albans' **cathedral** ((01727) 860780 was founded in AD 793 to commemorate Alban, the first

St. Albans was much battled over during the Wars of the Roses, so it's perhaps appropriate to find here the **Gardens of the Rose** ((01727) 850461, Chiswell Green, the flamboyant showground for the National Rose Society. Eight hectares (20 acres) with some 30,000 plants and 1,700 varieties of Britain's national flower grow here, at their peak in June. Open daily from mid-June to mid-October; admission fee.

Where to Stay and Eat

Near the city center in a residential area, **Ardmore House** ((01727) 859313 FAX (01727) 859313, 54 Lemsford Road, St. Albans AL1 3PR, is an Edwardian building with modern bedrooms decorated with

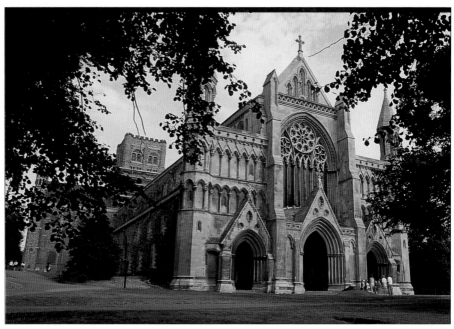

British Christian martyr who was put to death by the Romans in the fourth century for helping a priest to escape. Constructed for the most part from brick and flint taken from Roman ruins, the oldest parts of the cathedral are the rounded Norman arches and windows which form part of the 84-m (276-ft) nave. Elsewhere in the building the works of other ages are evident, such as the Early English Gothic pointed arches (thirteenth century) and Decorated arches (fourteenth century) that were added when some of the Norman arches caved in. The remnants of St. Alban's shrine form a marble stand composed of thousands of tiny fragments. A copy of the Magna Carta is ensconced on the cathedral wall. It is here that the barons gathered to draw up this document before taking it to Runnymede for King John's unwilling signature. The Abbey Refectory serves tea and inexpensive hot dishes.

comfort in mind. There is a bar and a dining room where snacks and meals are available, and breakfast is served overlooking the gardens; moderate.

For a B&B convenient to the train station there is **No.76 Clarence Road** (/FAX (01727) 864880, St. Albans AL1 4NG, another Edwardian abode. The two bedrooms share a bath; inexpensive.

Along the River Ver, at a working sixteenth-century water mill (also a museum), the **Waffle House** ((01727) 853502, Kingsbury Watermill, St. Michael's Street, is a scenic riverside setting for sweet and savory waffles; inexpensive.

Ye Olde Fighting Cocks ((01727) 865830 is set in a converted fifteenth-century pigeon house at end of Abbey Mill Lane. This octagonal inn serves inexpensive pub fare.

Only slightly less ancient, the **Rose & Crown** ((01727) 851903, 10 St. Michael Street, is a sixteenth-century pub across from Verulamium Park and the Roman Museum. The beamed bar has a large inglenook fireplace, and the terrace is pleasant in fine weather; inexpensive.

How to Get There

St. Albans is 44 km (27 miles) northwest of London, and 65 km (40 miles) southwest of Cambridge. **Trains** leave London Euston for St. Albans every 40 minutes on weekdays and hourly on Sunday for the 25-minute trip. Green Line ((020) 8688-7261 **coaches** serve St. Albans with frequent departures from London Victoria.

AROUND ST. ALBANS

Stately homes and gardens with rich historical and literary connections make for interesting touring around St. Albans.

The superb Jacobean-style **Hatfield House**, Hatfield, was built between 1608 and 1612 by the statesman Robert Cecil. The Cecil family still lives here, but this illustrious mansion is best known for its associations with Queen Elizabeth I, who spent much of her childhood at the Tudor Hatfield Palace. One wing of the original palace survives. It contains mementos of the Virgin Queen, including her silk stockings.

The **park** surrounding Hatfield House is the largest in the country. Within it, the remains of the oak tree under which Princess Elizabeth was seated when she received the news of her accession to the throne are still preserved. The rare seventeenth-century garden was laid out by Robert Cecil with the help of John Tradescant (founder of the Ashmolean Museum in Oxford). There are local buses from St. Albans City Station to Hatfield Station, directly across from Hatfield House. Open Tuesday to Sunday from mid-April to mid-October; admission fee.

About eight kilometers (five miles) north, **Knebworth House** ((01438) 812661 is a Tudor mansion with a Gothic exterior and a vast and lovely park. Though the original house dates from 1492, what you see today was built mostly in the nineteenth century by Sir Edward Bulwer-Lytton, the First Lord Lytton, statesman and author of *The Last Days of Pompeii*. The house contains some of Lord Lytton's manuscripts and some fine furnishings. The splendid, mostly-Jacobean banqueting hall with plastered ceiling and detailed screen is a highlight. Open Tuesday to Sunday from June to August, and weekends only from Easter to May and in September; admission fee. There are frequent trains from London King's Cross to Stevenage, one and a half kilometers (five miles) north of Knebworth, as well as local bus service direct to Knebworth from St. Albans.

Just south of Knebworth, **Shaw's Corner** (NT) (/FAX (01438) 820307, Ayot St. Lawrence, was the home of George Bernard Shaw from 1906 until his death in 1950. The rooms and gardens of this Edwardian villa remain just as he left them, with many of the dramatist's possessions remaining. In the garden is a revolving writing shed designed to maximize the sunlight. Open Wednesday to Sunday afternoon from April to October; admission fee.

BUCKINGHAMSHIRE

The valleys and secluded villages of Buckinghamshire's Chiltern Hills are ideal for walking and cycling. A scenic section of the River Thames meanders along the county's southern borders. To the north, the county museum in Aylesbury has the Roald Dahl Gallery and the fabulous landscape gardens at Stowe.

WHAT TO SEE AND DO

Southwest of St. Albans, the attractive village of **Chalfont St. Giles** is known for its connections with the poet John Milton, who brought his family to live here in 1665 to escape the plague that was sweeping London. **Milton's Cottage** ((01494) 872313 was the family's brief homestead. When Milton arrived at this "pretty box" in Chalfont he was blind and in the midst of work on his epic poem *Paradise Lost*. He only lived here for a year before returning to London, but this small Tudor cottage is the only surviving home of the poet. A museum here is dedicated to his life and work, and surrounded by a garden of herbs and flowers mentioned in Milton's poetry. Open Tuesday to Sunday from March to October (closed from 1 to 2 PM); admission fee.

Practically on London's doorstep, the **Chiltern Hills**, a designated Area of Outstanding Natural Beauty, offer prime outdoor scenery and recreation, despite their commuter-country aspects. Extending from Reading (Berkshire) 65 km (40 miles) northeast across southern Buckinghamshire, these heavily wooded, plump, hills embrace Britain's most extensive beech woodlands, encompassing prehistoric pathways and the Ridgeway national trail, an ancient Roman route.

Several Chiltern villages make good bases for walking. **Bradenham** has a seventeenth-century church and manor house (not open to the public), a sloping village green, and a network of paths to explore the surrounding hilly countryside of farmland and beechwood groves. **Wendover**, a small town on the Ridgeway, is another good base for rambling. You'll find a Tourist Information Centre ((01296) 696759 here at the Clock Tower on High Street. There is frequent train service to Wendover from London Marylebone, a trip of about 45 minutes; as well as buses from Aylesbury.

St. Albans Cathedral, where the Magna Carta was composed.

In **Jordans** you can visit the grave of William Penn, founder of Pennsylvania, and the Mayflower Barn, said to have been constructed from the wood of the Pilgrim's returned sailing ship.

Hughenden Manor (NT) ((01494) 440718, High Wycombe, was the home of statesman and writer Benjamin Disraeli (1804–1881). The manor is now a museum dedicated to the life of Disraeli, and many of his books and pictures remain. There are beautiful walks in the surrounding parkland. Open Wednesday to Sunday from April to October, and weekends only in March; admission fee (separate admission fee for the garden).

is a small visitor center and a nature trail. Open year-round from dawn to dusk.

WHERE TO STAY AND EAT

Near Milton's Cottage, the **White Hart** ((01494) 872441, Three Households, Chalfont St. Giles HP8 4LP, is a century-old pub with imaginative fare served in the bar or restaurant. The inn has four bedrooms (moderate).

Over the county line in Oxfordshire is the **Walnut Tree** ((01491) 638360, Fawley, near Henley-on-Thames, Oxfordshire RG9 6JE, another superbly set dining pub with rooms (with shower); moderate.

OUTDOOR ACTIVITIES

Two national trails traverse the Chilterns. The Ridgeway runs from **Ivinghoe Beacon** (230 m or 754 ft above sea level) to the River Thames and on to the North Wessex Downs. Ivinghoe Beacon, also the starting point of Icknield Way running across Bedfordshire to Suffolk, can be intensely crowded on summer weekends. The **Thames Path** crosses the southern section of the Chilterns on its way from London to the Cotswolds.

The Chilterns's highest point (260 m or 853 ft), **Combe Hill** (NT) has good, if not dramatic, views over three counties. It's one and a half kilometers (a mile and a half) west of Wendover.

The **Warburg Reserve** protects a slice of Chiltern Valley woodland, downland and wildlife at Bix Bottom in southeast Oxfordshire. There

There are two handy youth hostels in the area, both at rock-bottom prices. **Ivinghoe Youth Hostel** ((01296) 668251 FAX (01296) 662903 E-MAIL ivinghoe@yha.org.uk, High Street, Ivinghoe LU7 9EP, is a Georgian manor with 50 beds, located in the village center. **Jordans Youth Hostel** ((01494) 873135, Welders Lane, Jordans, Beaconsfield HP9 2SN, is a small hostel with 22 beds, just under a kilometer (half mile) out of Jordans.

AYLESBURY

BUCKINGHAMSHIRE — A study in contrasts, Aylesbury's modern office buildings tower over the cobbled Market Square with its Victorian Gothic clock tower. Despite its busy modern ambiance, this ancient town has retained much charm and many interesting features. In Market Square, the fourteenth-century King's Head (NT) is typical of the coaching inns of the Middle Ages that once flourished here. A window in the bar has 20 remaining panes of fifteenth-century stained glass. This is just one among many interesting buildings that a stroll around Aylesbury will reveal.

GENERAL INFORMATION

The **Tourist Information Centre** ((01296) 330559 is located at 8 Bourbon Street.

A **flea market** takes place on Tuesday, and regular **market** days are Wednesday, Friday, and Saturday.

WHAT TO SEE AND DO

The **Buckinghamshire County Museum** ((01296) 331441, St. Mary's Square, Church Street, is set in an eighteenth-century building that once housed a grade school. A new addition is the Roald Dahl Gallery, packed with hands-on activities that link science learning with characters and situations from Dahl's oft-surreal stories. There are interesting interactive displays in other galleries as well, describing the culture and history of the county. Closed Sunday morning. Dahl gallery closed until 3 PM weekdays during term-time; admission fee.

Ten kilometers (six miles) northwest of town is the French Renaissance-style **Waddesdon Manor** (NT) ((01296) 653211, Waddesdon. This chateau was built by Baron Ferdinand de Rothschild in the 1870s as a place to throw his lavish parties. Rooms are filled with unusual collections and portraits, and the landscaped gardens are much prized for their views and exotic plantings. Garden open Wednesday to Sunday from March to December; house open Thursday to Sunday from April to October with additional summer hours. Red Rover buses from Aylesbury drop off passengers in Waddesdon village.

The **Vale of Aylesbury** to the northeast of Aylesbury is dotted with unspoiled villages, such as **Wing** with its Saxon church and sixteenth- and seventeenth-century buildings and **Whitchurch**, with its many half-timbered and thatched cottages. **Aldbury** (Hertfordshire) is a most attractive village, set in good walking country on the edge of the Chilterns. In the large triangular village green is a pond overlooked by the parish church and many thatched cottages. For refreshment the village has tea rooms and pubs. Aldbury is also within easy reach of St. Albans.

WHERE TO STAY AND EAT

Aylesbury has the grand **Hartwell House** ((01296) 747444 FAX (01296) 747450 E-MAIL info @hartwell-house.com, Oxford Road, Aylesbury

HP17 8NL, thee kilometers (two miles) southwest of town. Set in 36 hectares (90 acres) of parkland, this restored eighteenth-century stately home has style, polish, splendor and obliging staff. The bedrooms are vast and sumptuous; luxury (breakfast is not included; special breaks available). The health center is equipped with heated swimming pool, tennis courts, sauna, gym and Jacuzzi, as well as a café. Finally, the elegant restaurant (expensive) has a fixe-price menu. Children age eight and over are welcome.

Not far from Aylesbury, **La Chouette** ((01296) 747422, Westlington Green, Dinton, is a Belgian restaurant set in an attractive sixteenth-century building; moderate.

HOW TO GET THERE

Aylesbury is 75 km (46 miles) northwest of London and 36 km (22 miles) east of Oxford. **Trains** depart London Marylebone for the one-hour trip to Aylesbury.

STOWE

BUCKINGHAMSHIRE — **Stowe Gardens** (NT) ((01280) 822850 is five kilometers (three miles) north of Buckingham. Laid out in the Georgian era, this superb garden was planned on an immense scale. The National Trust likes to refer to it as "Britain's largest work of art...an epic garden" and at 320 hectares (800 acres) it certainly is grand. Dotted throughout the parkland — the work of Capability Brown and William Kent — are c.lassical buildings, arches, temples and a Palladian bridge designed by Vanbrugh, Gibbs and Kent. Stowe House (a school and not open to the public) and the deer park are being restored. Opening hours vary; call for details. Admission fee.

The Cotswolds and Shakespeare Country

FROM THE RIVER THAMES, THE COTSWOLD HILLS RISE gently to their highest point over the Severn Valley, taking in parts of the counties of Gloucestershire, Oxfordshire, Hereford and Worcester, and Warwickshire. This designated Area of Outstanding Natural Beauty, with its gentle landscape and "honey-pot" villages, has been praised and marveled at by travelers for centuries. In the 1930s J.B. Priestley, in his classic touring book *English Journey*, wrote:

"Even when the sun is obscured and the light is cold…these walls are still faintly warm and luminous, as if they knew the trick of keeping the lost sunlight of centuries glimmering about them. This lovely trick is at the very heart of the Cotswold mystery."

the demands of the tourist that keep the Cotswold economy spinning.

Some visitors reproach the Cotswolds for being "twee" — a word that derives from the childish pronunciation of "sweet." You'll be warned about avoiding "charming olde worlde" villages, steering clear of "Cotswolds kitsch," and "Ye Olde game" as J.B. Priestley called the Cotswolds' self-promotional bent back in 1934. If in your travels you discover truth in this admonition, remember that these ancient villages are the original item — they invented "twee," and are therefore entitled, perhaps, to some excesses.

A superabundance of commercial zeal is also evident in England's most visited literary shrine,

It was the wool trade that made the Cotswolds' architecturally distinctive towns possible. During the Middle Ages the area was famed across Europe for its native sheep, the "Cotswold lion." In market centers like Cirencester, Chipping Campden, Northleach and Stow-on-the-Wold, prosperous wool merchants built sumptuous houses and lavished money on the construction of elaborate "wool churches." The early 1600s saw a sharp drop in the Cotswold woolen industry, and by the mid-1800s the area had fallen into decline, its wool trade captured by Australia and New Zealand. Through the Industrial Revolution, the Cotswolds slept, to be revived in the late nineteenth century as an artists' haven, and in the twentieth century as a tourist destination.

The lands hereabouts are still dotted with sheep, and Cotswold's wool production continues, though in a limited way. Today it is largely

Stratford-upon-Avon, which lies about 16 km (10 miles) beyond the Cotswolds' northern reaches. Stratford, you may recall, was the home of William Shakespeare — poet, playwright, actor, and one of the giants of world literature — who was born there in 1564 and returned three years before his death in 1616. Literary pilgrims have been coming to Stratford ever since.

If you come as far as Stratford into what could arguably be deemed beyond "Southern England," you really should stretch your itinerary just a few miles further north to visit Warwick Castle, England's finest original mediaeval castle, where Madame Tussaud's has created a fascinating waxworks spectacle.

A hiker's dream, the Cotswolds boast some 4,860 km (3,000 miles) of public footpaths. The most famous is the 162-km (100-mile) **Cotswold Way** from Bath to Chipping Campden. Warden's

The Cotswolds and Shakespeare Country

and Windrush Way, each around 23 km (14 miles) in length, link up in Winchcombe and Bourton-on-the-Water. **Warden's Way** takes in the Slaughters, Naunton, and Guiting Power; **Windrush Way** runs into the hills surrounding Winchcombe to the Windrush River and Bourton. The 105-km-long (65-mile) **Oxfordshire Way** starts from Bourton-on-the-Water and ends in Henley-on-Thames.

To obtain informational materials in advance of your trip, write or call the **Cotswold District Council (** (01285) 657280 FAX (01285) 641345 E-MAIL cotswold.tourism@star.co.uk, Trinity Road, Cirencester GL7 1PX; or the **West Oxfordshire District Council (** (01993) 702941 FAX (01993) 770238 E-MAIL tourism@westoxon.gov.uk, Woodgreen, Witney, Oxfordshire OX8 6NB.

BURFORD

OXFORDSHIRE — The ancient wool town of Burford is the eastern gateway to the Cotswolds, and a center for antiques, art and crafts. Mediaeval houses and inns flank the wide, sloping High Street, and a packhorse bridge, built in 1323, spans the River Windrush at the town's northern end.

Bucolic Burford has a bloody history. It was here in 1649, at the Church of St. John the Baptist, that Oliver Cromwell captured and executed 340 Levellers, mutineers of the Parliamentary Army. The fate of the Levellers, who had taken refuge in the church, is commemorated here each May.

The countryside around Burford is ideal for **walks** (see AROUND BURFORD, below). The town also makes a fine base for visiting Blenheim (see AROUND OXFORD, page 137).

The well-stocked **Tourist Information Centre (** (01993) 823558 FAX (01993) 823590 is at The Brewery, Sheep Street; open year-round. **Parking** in Burford is free, but limited.

WHAT TO SEE AND DO

Pick up the "Burford Trail" brochure at the Tourist Information Centre. This **self-guided walk** through town takes you through the village's winding streets to reveal many handsome Tudor and Georgian buildings, starting at the **Tolsey Museum**, High Street, set in the sixteenth-century Guildhall, where a diverse collection of oddments and artifacts spills out onto the pavement.

On the opposite end of town is the wool church of **St. John the Baptist**, on Lawrence Lane, with its "bale" tombs in the yard. The arched tops represent bundles of wool. Curiously, the design only came into fashion long after the demise of the wool industry. The church was begun in 1170 and gradually enlarged up to the sixteenth century. Note the carved and painted mediaeval pulpit, the traces of filled-in arches in the nave, and the unusual raised chapel commemorating Thomas Becket. The

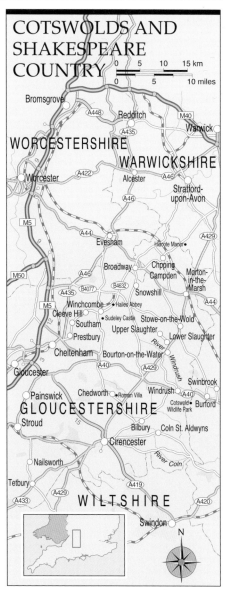

tiny painted-wood chapel of St. Peter's became the Lord Mayor's pew after the Reformation; today it's used as an altar. The Spicer Brass is the church's only surviving mediaeval brass; you'll have to make a special request to view it. By the churchyard are the **Warwick Almshouses** founded in 1457. The Earl of Warwick gave the parish permission for the building of these almshouses on the condition that residents regularly pray for the souls of the Earl and his wife. A brochure at the church notes that "the almshouses still fulfill their original purpose, but the Warwick souls have to

The sloping High Street of mediaeval Burford, eastern gateway to the Cotswolds.

fend for themselves." The church hosts **concerts** by the Cotswolds Chamber Orchestra ((01993) 822305.

WHERE TO STAY AND EAT

The **Lamb Inn** ((01993) 823155 FAX (01993) 822288, Sheep Street, Burford OX18 4LR, is an elegant place with a superb restaurant. Parts of the inn date from the fifteenth century, and much of its ancient character remains intact, with flagged floors, a walled garden, low beamed ceiling, and log fires. Wing-back chairs and Persian rugs add latter-day comforts. The attractively decorated bedrooms have bath; moderate. Even if you're not staying at the Lamb, make sure to dine here at least once during

your visit. A three-course menu (moderate) might include a starter such as tartlet of avocado and Parma ham on tomato salsa, followed by a main of fillet of cod with parsley and sun-dried tomato crust with a lobster champagne sauce. For dessert, consider the Bailey's Irish Cream parfait.

Burford House ((01993) 823155, Sheep Street, Burford OX18 4LR, is a 500-year-old inn with 15 bedrooms. Common areas are warmed by log fires in winter, and antiques add character. The restaurant serves good food and there is a walled garden; expensive.

The last remaining coaching inn in a town that once boasted 20 of them, the **Old Bull** ((01993) 833330 FAX (01993) 823243, 105 High Street, Burford OX18 4RG, has 14 bedrooms with bath, some with four-poster beds; moderate. At street level, the pub serves real ales and a good selection of wines. Sandwiches and snacks are available in the bar and English cooking in the restaurant. The brick and stone façade dates from the seventeenth century, but the interior was destroyed by fire in 1982 and completely refurbished the following decade.

HOW TO GET THERE

Burford is 122 km (75 miles) northwest of London, and 32 km (20 miles) west of Oxford. From Oxford there is **bus** service to Burford (four departures per day). National Express operates **coach** service to Burford from London Victoria, but there are many stops en route.

AROUND BURFORD

OXFORDSHIRE, GLOUCESTERSHIRE — One and a half kilometers (one mile) east of Burford, you can visit the grave of writer Nancy Mitford (1904–1973) in the pretty little hamlet of **Swinbrook**, as well as admire the unusual seventeenth-century effigies of the Fettiplace family lounging in "bunkbeds" beside the altar. A one-kilometer (three-quarter-mile) riverside walk from here leads to the hamlet of **Widford**, where the little church has fragments of Roman mosaics.

West of Burford, the church at **Windrush** has a splendid Norman doorway and interesting eighteenth-century table tombs in the churchyard. In nearby Great Barrington, the **Fox Inn** ((01451) 844385 is a rural food pub with lamp heaters on the terrace for chilly days. Tables are set right up to the willowy water's edge where diners watch swans grazing.

About eight kilometers (five miles) south of Burford, the compact village of Filkins is home to **Cotswold Woolen Weavers** ((01367) 860491, where you can shop for locally-made woolen items (see SHOP TILL YOU DROP, page 48 in YOUR CHOICE) from knitwear to throws and accessories. Next to the shop is a **museum** housing a working weaving mill in an eighteenth-century barn, where visitors can wander amongst the monstrous black looms dressed in bolts of delicate plaid, and plunge their hands into wicker baskets stuffed with raw, lanolin-soaked wool. Outside a mobile shepherd's hut is set up for a winter's sojourn. Closed Sunday morning. Filkins also has a local history **museum** ((01367) 860334, with a collection of nineteenth-century craft tools (limited opening hours), as well as a gallery selling the work of local artisans and a mid-nineteenth-century **church**.

BIBURY

GLOUCESTERSHIRE — Built around the nature preserve of Rack Isle and watered by the sparkling River Coln, Bibury is the jewel of the Cotswolds. William Morris loved Bibury, calling it "the most beautiful village in all of England." Tourists love it too; get there early, before the cars and coaches mar the views.

Rack Isle is actually a meadow bounded on three sides by water. It is so-named because in the Middle Ages, woolen cloth was hung there on racks to dry.

WHAT TO SEE AND DO

Early in the morning it's a joy to walk along the **Street**, which parallels the River Coln, where trout feed on the mossy river bottom. The Swan (below) holds fishing rights to Rack Isle, but you can fish, feed the fish or buy trout at **Bibury Trout Farm** ((01285) 740215. The shop here also carries delicacies such as smoked fillet of trout, chutneys and

The **Parish Church of St. Mary's** is a pastiche of architectural styles. Treasures include a cast of an Anglo-Saxon tombstone dating to AD 1000 (the original is in the British Museum), a Norman doorway in the north wall, and what is believed to be an early Saxon tombstone built into the north wall of the chancel.

There's a lovely riverside **walk** from Bibury to Coln St. Aldwyns. Ask locally for directions.

WHERE TO STAY AND EAT

The **Swan** ((01285) 740695 FAX (01285) 740473 E-MAIL swanhot1@swanhotel-cotswolds.co.uk, Bibury GL7 5NW, is an elegant inn decorated with

fish pâtés. Tea is served on the leafy terrace by the mill falls (below) amid the quacking of ducks.

Next door is **Arlington Mill** ((01285) 740368, a restored seventeenth-century water mill where machinery demonstrations take place daily. The museum here houses antiquated farm machinery and tools. Hours vary; admission fee.

At the opposite end of Rack Isle, the much photographed **Arlington Row** (not open to the public) is a mediaeval agricultural building converted to a wool storehouse in around 1380. In the seventeenth century it was converted again to house the weavers who supplied the cloth for "fulling" (degreasing) at the mill. So enchanting is this row of vernacular buildings that Henry Ford tried to buy it and transport it to America. A local architectural trust prevented him. Arlington Row is now owned by the National Trust, which leases it as private housing.

etched glass, painted wood paneling and fresh flowers. The bedrooms are individually decorated, some with four-poster beds, each with ample and luxurious bath. Choose from half-board or B&B rates; luxury. The **restaurant** features grilled Bibury trout; moderate.

An impressive Tudor mansion, **Bibury Court Hotel** ((01285) 740337 FAX (01285) 740660 is surrounded by magnificent gardens and grounds. Public areas and the bedrooms are furnished somewhat sparsely but with interesting antiques, and some of the bedrooms have wood paneling and four-posters. There's trout fishing in the River Coln which crosses the property. The elegant **dining room** offers inventive cooking. Breakfast is served in the conservatory; expensive. Two-day breaks are available.

OPPOSITE: Burford antiques. ABOVE: Bibury's famous Arlington Row was built in 1380.

The **William Morris** ((01285) 740555 FAX (01285) 850648 E-MAIL alex@ndra2000.freeserve.co.uk, 11 The Street, Bibury Gloucestershire GL7 5NP, is a licensed brasserie, tea room (formerly the Jenny Wren) and B&B. In the tea room, bright white walls with low beams and window seats create a cozy setting. The menu features light meals and sandwiches, afternoon teas, rich sweets and beverages from Coke floats to elderflower tea. The cheese scones are mouthwatering. In summer you can dine in the garden; in winter an open fire warms the interior. Bedrooms are decorated with fabrics and wall coverings inspired by the works of the great designer; inexpensive.

Between Bibury and Chedworth Roman Villa (see page 164), the **Bathurst Arms** ((01285) 831281, North Cerney, Cirencester GL7 7BZ, is a great little inn for a meal and an overnight. The beamed bedrooms have mullioned windows that look out over the garden, river and wooded hills. They're furnished with unpretentious antiques and comfy touches such as a cushioned window seat and soft carpet; inexpensive. The food is also very good. The pub closes at 11 PM, after which a hush descends on the verdant countryside.

HOW TO GET THERE

The nearest train station is at Kemble, 21 km (13 miles) southwest of Bibury. There are several trains each day from London Paddington to Kemble. National Express operates **coach** service to Cirencester, 11 km (seven miles) southwest of Bibury, but there are no local buses from either of these towns to Bibury.

CIRENCESTER

GLOUCESTERSHIRE — The spirited market town of Cirencester (pronounced *sir*-en-sester) is refreshingly low on pretense. A superb museum of Roman artifacts is the main attraction, and not to be missed. Accommodation and dining are low key for the most part, and less expensive than some other Cotswold population centers. Artisans and craftspeople show their wares at various venues around town and several ancient market places have been converted into fashion emporia.

GENERAL INFORMATION

The biweekly **Cotswold Craft Market** in Corn Hall features regional products. From mid-June to early July, the annual **Festival of Music & Arts** comes to town.

You'll find the **Tourist Information Centre** ((01285) 654180 FAX (01285) 641182, at Corn Hall, Market Place. The staff here are particularly knowledgeable. Weekly guided **historical walks** depart each Sunday at 3 PM from the Church of St. John

the Baptist; fee charged. The Cirencester Ramblers ((01285) 712692 welcome visitors to join their **guided hikes** to a variety of destinations, such as their 11-km (seven-mile) jaunt to Toddington, returning via the vintage *Gloucester & Warwickshire* Railway. Call for prices and times.

WHAT TO SEE AND DO

A five-minute walk from the Tourist Information Centre at Market Place brings you to the **Corinium Museum** ((01285) 655611, Park Street, which presents the treasures of decades of archaeological research that have revealed Cirencester's Roman origins. Exhibits take you from the city's Roman

foundation through to mediaeval Cotswolds and Cirencester in the Civil War. A series of authentic fourth-century mosaics kicks off the Roman history section. Especially impressive is the second-century "Seasons" mosaic which was found under Dyer Street in 1849. Shop and café. Open year-round; admission fee.

The pleasingly decrepit **Parish Church of St. John Baptist** is often mistaken for a cathedral. With its liberal dimensions and multiple side chapels, it's one of the largest parish churches in the country. This wool church is notable for its Lady Chapel in the northeast corner, where the effigy of Thomas Master looks like he's enjoying a day at the beach. St. Catherine's chapel has 350-year-old fan vaulting and wall painting remains dating from 1150. The delicately carved Jacobean wine-glass pulpit is a beauty, and the Boleyn Cup is a rare Tudor silver gilt chalice set behind glass on the east wall. The church's three-level porch was the town hall until the turn of the last century.

OUTDOOR ACTIVITIES

The green lawns of **St. Michael's Park** are ideal for lounging and strolling. You can rent croquet mallets or golf clubs here. Cirencester is the **polo** capital of England. Fans can watch the spirited matches at Cirencester Park ((01285) 653225; call for details.

The Thames and Severn Way long-distance **footpath** passes close to Cirencester, meandering through open countryside before it descends into the Thames Valley through a series of locks along the Thames and Severn canal. Details and maps at the Tourist Information Centre.

SHOPPING

Contemporary art and crafts are on show at the **Brewery Arts Centre** ((01285) 657181, Brewery Court, which houses the workshops of 17 artisans working in media from reeds to precious metals to clay. Open year-round; free admission to studios. Swan Yard Woolmarket and Bishop's Walk are for **fashion**-hunters. A regular **craft** market is held at the Corn Hall and the Brewery Arts Centre, Brewery Court, has craft workshops, a craft shop and gallery. Closed Sunday.

WHERE TO STAY

Victoria Road, within easy walking distance of the center, is the place to browse for B&Bs. Among many others, there is **Wimborne House** ((01285) 643653 FAX (01285) 653890 E-MAIL wimborneho @aol.com, 91 Victoria Road, Cirencester GL7 1ES, a large stone residence with six spacious bedrooms. Breakfast is served in the dining room at separate tables. Children eight years and older welcome; high end of inexpensive range.

The **Bungalow** ((01285) 654179 FAX (01285) 656159 E-MAIL cbeard7@compuserve.com, 93 Victoria Road, Cirencester GL7 1ES, also has six bedrooms, including some family rooms, and a lounge. Dinner is served by prior arrangement; low end of inexpensive range.

There is also the **Ivy** ((01285) 656626, 2 Victoria Road, Cirencester, GL7 1EN, an attractive house on the corner; inexpensive. And, the **Leauses** ((01285) 653643, 101 Victoria Road, Cirencester, GL7 1EU, with five bedrooms, is surrounded by a symphony of marigolds; inexpensive.

For hostel-goers, there is **Duntisbourne Abbots Youth Hostel** ((01285) 821682, eight kilometers (five miles) northwest of Cirencester, situated in a rambling former vicarage. It's been scheduled to close for a couple of years, but has so far risen from the ashes each season; be sure to call

before making the long trek out. It's a wonderful rural location and the starting point for a network of footpaths. Open Monday to Saturday, April to October; rock-bottom. Because it's on the brink of oblivion, it's rarely full.

WHERE TO EAT

Harry Hare's Restaurant & Brasserie ((01285) 652375, 3 Gosditch Street, across from the church, looks like a pub from the outside but inside is a warm, busy restaurant serving Modern British fare in mellow decor; moderate.

Another place with both good food and a pleasant atmosphere is the **Swan Yard** ((01285)

641300, 5 Swan Yard, where vegetarian lasagna is served in a conservatory setting. On fine days you can dine on the terrace amid designer-clothing mavens.

The **Brewery Arts Centre** ((01285) 657181, Brewery Court, has a wonderful little coffee shop with a wide choice of sweets from a folksy poppyseed cake topped with raspberry jam to rich cappuccino squares. From 11 AM to 3 PM they serve toasted sandwiches filled with inventive combinations such as brie and cranberry, stilton and apple or ham and cheddar for the purist; inexpensive.

Next to the church, **Jeraboams** is a sandwich and picnic supply central. English cheeses, scrumpy, and baked goods such as sun-dried-tomato bread and olive bread are some of the temptations.

Roman Britain — OPPOSITE: Tile mosaic.
ABOVE: Centurion and mascot.

HOW TO GET THERE

Cirencester is 146 km (90 miles) west of London. You can take one of the frequent **trains** from London Paddington to Kemble, to connect with local **bus** service for the six-kilometer (four-mile) ride to Cirencester. National Express operates frequent direct **coach** services to Cirencester.

TETBURY

GLOUCESTERSHIRE — Tetbury grew rich in the Middle Ages as one of the major wool towns. Today it's known as the hub of some royal resi-

dences. You're unlikely to catch sight of any royalty here, as they keep a low profile, but about two and a half kilometers (a mile and a half) southwest of town is Highgrove, the country home of Charles, Prince of Wales. Gatcombe Park is the home of Anne, the Princess Royal, six and a half kilometers (four miles) north of town. Slightly further on is Nether Lypiatt, home of Prince and Princess Michael of Kent.

Look for the small **Tourist Information Centre** ((01666) 503552 at 33 Church Street; open year-round, services limited during winter months.

The seventeenth-century Market House, with its bulging Tuscan pillars, is the venue for the **antiques market**, held each Wednesday.

WHAT TO SEE AND DO

Built between 1777 to 1787, the **Parish Church of St. Mary** has undergone extensive renovation recently. Victorian tampering has been largely done away with and the church, restored to its Georgian lines, now enjoys a reputation as one of the country's best Georgian Gothic structures. Its slender wood columns and large windows with Victorian stained glass have given it the nickname of the "lantern church." The unusual box pews were once individually owned by the lords of the parish manors.

In mediaeval times, **Chipping Steps** ("chipping" is Saxon for market) was the site of the Mop Fair, where farmhands and housemaids came to seek work. The steps lead to the foot of **Gumstool Hill**, famed for the Woolsack Races. Dating from the 1500s, the games still take place annually, with Prince Charles looking on as teams of men and women race up and down the steep hill with 65-pound wool sacks slung over their backs. The hill got its name from the "gumstool," or dunking stool, which once stood at the bottom of the hill and was used to punish knaves and rogues.

May and October are the best times to visit the wooded, 240-hectare (600-acre) **Westonbirt Arboretum** ((01666) 880220. In spring there are magnolias, rhododendrons and carpets of bluebells to delight the eye, and in autumn foliage turns to shades of gold and vermilion. If you visit during peak seasons, you'll enjoy more tranquillity on a weekday visit. There are 28 km (17 miles) of waymarked trails, and exhibits on the area's flora and fauna at the visitor center. Open daily year-round; admission fee. The arboretum is located five kilometers (three miles) south of Tetbury on the A433.

Three kilometers (two miles) north of Tetbury, **Chavenage** ((01666) 502329 is an Elizabethan manor house decorated with tapestries and furniture from the Cromwell period. Family members conduct tours telling of the house's history, from the latest filming (it's a popular set location for television programs) to the resident ghosts. Open Thursday and Sunday from May to September; admission fee.

WHERE TO STAY

About eight kilometers (five miles) northwest of Tetbury in the town of Nailsworth, **Egypt Mill** ((01453) 833449 FAX (01453) 836098, Nailsworth, Stroud GL6 0AE, occupies a sixteenth-century corn mill and miller's house along the River Frome. The mill, later a clothing factory, was converted in the 1980s to a hotel. In the common areas, gilt-framed portraits look down from rough stone walls, and furniture made from mill implements lend character. Rooms don't match the finish of the lobby and lounge, but are comfortable, all with bath and many extras. Room 8, a double, is probably the best, with its view of the weir and swans. Rates are in the high end of the inexpensive range. Two-night breaks are available. A brasserie on the lower level is softly lit and cozy with sunny terrace seating along the river on fine days.

Out near the Westonbirt Arboretum **Tavern House** ((01666) 880444 FAX (01666) 880254, Willesley GL8 8QU, is a seventeenth-century former coaching inn offering bedrooms with bath. It's six kilometers (four miles) from Tetbury and one and a half kilometers (a mile) from Westonbirt; moderate.

In the town center, the **Crown Inn** ((01666) 502469, Gumstool Hill, Tetbury GL8 8DG, is the traditional starting point of the Woolsack Races. This historic roadhouse has copper-topped tables in the bar and a conservatory restaurant. Up the inn's original Jacobean staircase are four bedrooms with shared bath; inexpensive.

WHERE TO EAT

The glistening **Close Brasserie** ((01666) 505852, 7–9 Church Street, serves mussel paella and roast cod with pesto parmesan crust, accompanied, if you like, by a swimming-pool-sized glass of wine; moderate.

Settle in at the **Welcome Chair** ((01666) 503337, 3 Long Street, for sandwiches and cream teas in big wicker armchairs. Take a bay window seat, if you can, to watch town life pass by; inexpensive.

Edges ((01666) 505660, 25A Church Street, is a sweet little tea room a couple of doors down from the Tourist Information Centre; inexpensive.

HOW TO GET THERE

Tetbury is 181 km (112 miles) west of London. The closest **train** station is 11 km (seven miles) away at Kemble for which there are frequent departures from London Paddington. You can also take a National Express **coach** from London Victoria to Cirencester and connect with local bus service there for the 16-km (10-mile) ride to Tetbury.

PAINSWICK

GLOUCESTERSHIRE — A beautiful wool town of mediaeval cottages interspersed with staid seventeenth- to nineteenth-century merchants' and millers' houses, Painswick's written history dates to the Domesday Book: William the Conqueror's census of his realm 20 years after the Norman Conquest. Peering even further back into the past, Painswick Beacon was an ancient earthworks built to protect tribes from wolves and invading clans. You can walk there from the golf course for a view of the Severn Valley and, on a clear day, Brecon Beacon in Wales.

The **Tourist Information Centre** ((01452) 832532 is in the library on Stroud Road; open Tuesday to Saturday.

WHAT TO SEE AND DO

The needle of **Parish Church of St. Mary** mounts to the sky above the town. Massed around the churchyard, as if for prayer, 99 rotund yew trees have been pruned into arches and tunnels. Look also for the "spectacle" **stocks** behind the wall in the northeast corner of the churchyard (often obscured by parked cars); they resemble a pair of

eyeglasses. There is an interesting carved **lych-gate** at the entrance to the churchyard.

The **Fiery Beacon Gallery** ((01452) 814068, New Street, has spring, summer and Christmas exhibitions of contemporary crafts. Also on New Street, the workshop of **Dennis French** produces fine woodcrafts in the tradition of the Arts & Crafts movement. Open Tuesday to Saturday.

Nearby, you can visit the **Painswick Rococo Garden** ((01452) 813204, a restored eighteenth-century garden with trimmed hedges, winding paths, a maze and an outlandish collection of garden architecture. Open Wednesday to Sunday from mid-January through November. Open daily in July and August; admission fee.

Painswick Beacon makes a good **walking** objective. At the summit are the remains of some ancient earthworks, probably used by the Celts as a protection from wolves. There are wonderful views from here of the Malvern Hills.

WHERE TO STAY

Built in 1790 in Palladian style, the **Painswick Hotel** ((01452) 812160 FAX (01452) 814059 E-MAIL reservations@painswickhotel.com, Kemps Lane, Painswick GL6 6YB, is deeply comfortable. Choose a room in the old house or one in the new wing. Both have mullioned windows and are decorated in a similar fashion. Rooms in the house are larger and mellower, while the new wing offers garden views and a more standard feel, and smaller dimensions. Graceful common areas are adorned with baskets of fresh fruit and art objects. The restaurant serves Cotswold meats, Severn salmon, and Vale of Evesham veggies. Rates vary from expensive (garden room) to very expensive (luxury and four-poster rooms). Two-night breaks are available.

For B&B accommodation, **Hambutts Mynd** ((01452) 812352, Edge Road, Painswick GL6 6UP, is popular. Two blocks from the village center, this eighteenth-century former mill has pleasant countryside views from each of the bedrooms, and electric blankets to take the chill off. There is an 11 PM curfew and greetings at each return by two friendly Dobermans. Your pets are welcome, too; inexpensive.

WHERE TO EAT

At the **Painswick Hotel** (above), the wood-paneled dining room features seasonal game and local produce such as a starter of warm salad of Cotswold lamb with rosemary dressing and, for the main course, saddle of venison with white beans and wild mushroom ragout. Lunch on the terrace is delightful and won't bend your budget, with sandwiches and salads as well as a moderately-priced set menu.

Parish Church of St. Mary's, Tetbury.

The **Royal Oak** (no phone) is a dignified pub with homemade fishcakes and vegetarian lasagna on the varied menu; inexpensive.

HOW TO GET THERE

Painswick is 173 km (107 miles) west of London and five kilometers (three miles) north of Stroud. The nearest **train** station is at Stroud with a direct link to London Paddington (some routes require a change at Swindon). From Stroud, local **buses** run throughout the day to Painswick.

CHELTENHAM

GLOUCESTERSHIRE — Cheltenham is another of England's Regency spa towns — not as harmoniously laid out as Bath, but very pretty in parts with graceful, tree-lined avenues, green gardens, and floral displays. Neptune's Fountain, modeled after Rome's Trevi Fountain, spurts dramatically at one end of The Promenade. Montpellier Gardens is framed by lime trees, fashionable shops, and buxom caryatids supporting white pillars. Pittville Park is the city's largest green space, with paved walkways around the lake.

Cheltenham's origins as a spa date to 1716, when a salt spring was discovered here and news of its purported healing powers spread. With the rising popularity of spas in the eighteenth and nineteenth centuries, the town enjoyed some golden years. Following a visit by King George In 1788, a building boom gained momentum through the early 1800s — when the population rose from 3,000 to 13,000. Though Cheltenham eventually declined as a fashionable resort, today the population has burgeoned to 100,000.

GENERAL INFORMATION

The **Tourist Information Centre** ((01242) 522878 FAX (01242) 255848 or 515535 E-MAIL tourism @cheltenham.gov.uk, 77 The Promenade, is staffed by knowledgeable personnel. Closed Sunday from September to June. In summer the Tourist Information Centre organizes **coach tours** of the Cotswolds and regular **guided walking tours** of the historic town.

Cheltenham has a hopping calendar of **festivals**. In February there is the Folk Festival, while March brings the National Hunt Racing Festival and April the Jazz Festival. The International Festival of Music with its Fringe Festival happens in July. Each October brings the town's distinguished Festival of Literature, a two-week extravaganza of lectures, readings and workshops featuring well-known writers from around the world. In November the Festival of Christmas Lights closes out the year with a street party. For more information see WEB SITE www.cheltenhamfestivals.co.uk.

There is **Internet access** at Netscafé, 9 Bennington Street; or at Rendezvous, a charity shop on Portland Street.

Rent **cycles** from Compass Holidays ((01242) 250642 E-MAIL compass.holidays@dial.pipex.com, 48 Shurdington Road, Cheltenham GL53 0JE, who also do guided trips; or Crabtrees ((01242) 515291.

WHAT TO SEE AND DO

The **Pittville Pump Room** ((01242) 523852 is a copper-domed Regency pile at the north end of Pittville Park. Opened in 1830, it quickly became the focal point of Cheltenham's fashionable society, who paid a shilling a day to "take the water" to the accompaniment of a band. The hall with its graceful rotunda is used for concerts, but during the day a spike-haired youth lets visitors into the hall to sample the salty waters (free of charge) at the original marble pump. Pumpside comments range from "It's not repulsive" to "Yuck!." While the waters were once used to cure everything from gout to worms, today they've proven to be a mild antacid, much like drinking a glass of water sprinkled with baking soda. A small **museum of costumes** offers a glimpse at society life in Cheltenham's golden days. Closed on Tuesday; admission fee (for the museum only).

The **Cheltenham Art Gallery & Museum** ((01242) 237431, Clarence Street, has three floors dedicated to art, architecture and history. Its collection of Arts & Crafts movement furniture and metalwork, inspired by native son William Morris, is internationally celebrated. There is also Chinese and English pottery, as well as 300 years of Dutch and British paintings, local archaeological treasures and a social history of Cheltenham. Finally, the story of a local explorer who perished on the 1912 Scott Antarctic expedition is told in the Edward Wilson gallery. Open Monday to Saturday; free admission. There is a café and shop.

At 4 Clarence Road, the **Gustave Holst Birthplace Museum** ((01242) 524846 is a Regency terrace house where the life of the composer of *The Planets* is commemorated. Open year-round; admission fee.

The **Cheltenham Racecourse** ((02142) 513014, at nearby Prestbury Park, is the home of National Hunt racing, 15 days of horse racing from October to April, culminating in the National Hunt Festival in March when worthies compete for the Cheltenham Gold Cup. Throughout the year you can visit the **Racecourse Hall of Fame** ((01242) 513014 for a glimpse at racing history.

SHOPPING

The **Promenade** is lined with fashion boutiques and bookstores, and plenty of cafés to rest up between bouts of retail madness. **High Street** and its tributaries have the chains (Marks & Spencer, Debenhams, etc.), as well as a bubble-blowing clock that performs on the half hour. In the **Montpellier** quarter, boutiques, gift shops and antiques dealers are interspersed with yet more sidewalk cafés and trendy wine bars. Antiques hunters should inquire at the Tourist Information Centre for a guide to Cheltenham's many dealers.

WHERE TO STAY

A sixteenth-century Elizabethan manor house, the **Greenway** ((01242) 862352 FAX (01242) 862780 TOLL-FREE IN THE UNITED STATES (800) 543-4135 E-MAIL relax@greenway-hotel.demon.co.uk,

with half-board. The restaurant offers a seasonal menu. The summer menu may feature chilled fruit soups, *foie gras* parfait with apple and grape chutney, and caramelized monkfish. Desserts run from *crème brulée* to cheese and chutney; moderate.

Guests receive a warm welcome at **Lypiatt House** ((01242) 224994 FAX (01242) 224996, Lypiatt Road, Cheltenham GL50 2QW, a beautiful Victorian tucked away in a close of tall trees in the leafy Montpellier neighborhood. The house is elegantly decorated throughout with a graceful drawing room, a conservatory with wicker furniture and a bar. The bedrooms (all with bath) are well laid out. There is plenty of off-street parking; moderate to expensive.

Shurdington, Cheltenham GL51 5UG, is a gracious luxury hotel a few miles south of Cheltenham. The bedrooms are handsomely decorated and have bath, terry robes and views of the extensive gardens; luxury rates (a two-night package, including breakfast and dinner, is available). The dining room is quite popular locally; dinner reservations are recommended. If you're staying in Shurdington, there's nightlife at the **Bell** ((01242) 862245, Main Road, which hosts live jazz on the first Monday of every month starting at 8 PM.

Overlooking serene Pittville Park, the **Hotel on the Park** ((01242) 518898 FAX (01242) 51526, Evesham Road, Cheltenham GL52 2AH, is a townhouse furnished in polished Regency style with a cozy lounge and a predilection for teddy bears. The bedrooms are furnished with antiques; expensive. English or continental breakfast is available for additional charge. Two-night breaks available

The **Lawn House** ((01242) 578486, 11 London Road, Cheltenham GL52 6EX, is a family-run Regency house, three minutes' walk from the center with private gardens; inexpensive.

Not to be confused with the above, **Lawn Hotel** ((01242) 526638, 5 Pittville Lane, Cheltenham GL52 2BE, is a Regency building in a tree-lined cul-de-sac close to Pittville Park; inexpensive.

WHERE TO EAT

Set in a seventeenth-century building, **Kingshead House** ((01452) 862299, Birdlip, Gloucester, is one of the best restaurants in the area, serving fine British country cuisine. Sample menu items include medallions of pork with tapenade and roast pepper, baked monkfish with saffron, a starter of *rillettes*

A caryatid holds court alongside a Cheltenham promenade.

of duck with onion and apple compote and toasted brioche. The dessert card has homemade fruit ice cream as well as richer choices; expensive. The restaurant is about a 15-minute drive south of Cheltenham. Accommodation is also available; call for rates.

In town, Cheltenham has much to offer hungry travelers. The Queen's Hotel, on The Promenade, has two restaurants: **Le Petit Blanc** ((01242) 266800 provides regional French cuisine with strong hints of the Mediterranean and Orient; moderate. **Blanc Vite** offers "fast-food" such as roasted red pepper soup and *moules–frites* (inexpensive). There is a children's menu.

The **Daffodil** ((01242) 700055, 18–20 Suffolk Parade, serves lunch, dinner and afternoon teas in a converted Art Deco cinema. The fare is English with Mediterranean accents, and you can watch the chefs at work in the upstairs bar, or dine in the downstairs brasserie; moderate.

The **Orange Tree** ((01242) 234232, 317 Lower High Street, has very good vegetarian food, including organic beers and wines; moderate.

Tiffin's ((01242) 222492, 4 Montpellier Walk, is good for sandwiches, but get there before the office workers close in at lunchtime; inexpensive.

NIGHTLIFE

What's On, distributed monthly in the *Echo*, is available at the Tourist Information Centre (above) and at newsstands. It lists **events** throughout Gloucestershire as well as in Bristol, Bath, Oxford and Stratford-upon-Avon.

The **Everyman Theatre** ((01242) 572573, Regent Street, presents classics and new works as well as touring West End productions. The **Pittville Pump Room** ((01242) 227979 (box office) is a superb setting to enjoy classical music; concerts are held throughout the year, and every Sunday from May to September brings cream tea and live music. More classical music — as well as comedy, dance, exhibitions, and antiques fairs — take place at the Cheltenham's baroque **Town Hall** ((01242) 227979 (box office). The **Axiom Centre for the Arts** ((01242) 253183, Winchcombe Street, programs alternative music.

There are a couple of colossal nightclubs on Regent Street. The **Attic** ((01242) 516645, High Street; and **Axiom** ((01242) 253183, Winchcombe Street, are popular rock venues. **Subtone** ((01242) 575925, on The Promenade, offers live jazz in the piano bar on Thursday night from 9 PM to 2 AM, and big name jazz on Sundays from 12:30 PM to midnight.

HOW TO GET THERE

Cheltenham is 160 km (100 miles) northwest of London. There is frequent **train** service to Cheltenham from London Paddington (12 per day;

some routes require a change at Bristol or Swindon). From the train station it's a 20-minute walk to the center or a short ride on the shuttle bus. National Express has frequent **coach** service from London Victoria to Cheltenham's bus station near the town center on Royal Crescent.

WINCHCOMBE

GLOUCESTERSHIRE — Noted for its grotesque-studded church, tea shops, and castle, the village of Winchcombe is well worth a visit outside of the high-season bedlam. This ancient village was first settled by the King of Mercia, who founded a Benedictine Abbey here in the eighth century.

The compelling ruins of Hailes Abbey are just up the road.

By the seasonal **Tourist Information Centre** ((01242) 602925, High Street, are the **seven-hole stocks**. Speculation abounds about the stocks' uneven number of leg holes — built for a one-legged offender, or by an absent-minded carpenter?

Winchcombe lies along the River Isbourne in hilly country. It's a stop along the Cotswold Way as well as the Warden's Way, making it a superb walking base.

WHAT TO SEE AND DO

A chestnut-lined section of the Warden's Way wanders prettily south from Winchcombe to **Sudeley Castle** ((01242) 602308, former home of Katherine Parr, sixth and final wife of Henry VIII. There is not much left of the mediaeval castle, but parts of the fifteenth-century structure were incorporated into the nineteenth-century reconstruction. There are some fine pictures, tapestries and furniture to see. The formal gardens are particularly enjoyable. There is a restaurant, shop, plant center, and playground. Open daily March through October; admission fee.

In the village, the **Parish Church of St. Peter's**, built in the Perpendicular style, is famous for its outrageous gargoyles, some of which are thought to be caricatures of local worthies. Look for announcements of **choral concerts** that take place periodically at the church.

Six potters share studio space and produce stoneware for sale at the **Winchcombe Pottery**, on

farmhouse with beautiful views of the valley and village. It's about one and a half kilometers (a mile) from Winchcombe. There are three comfortable bedrooms; inexpensive.

The **Olde Bakery & Tea Shoppe** ((01242) 602469, Main Street, is a friendly place for a hot drink or a hearty lunch. Exposed stone walls and small rooms make the inside cozy, or you can eat in the conservatory; inexpensive.

A couple of good dining spots for families with young children are found in nearby villages. In Greet, **Harvest House** ((01242) 602430 has a wide-ranging menu with daily blackboard specials. Eat in the bar or in the airy dining room. The **Pheasant Inn** ((01242) 621271, Toddington (not to be

the road to Broadway, north of the center of Winchcombe; closed Sunday.

WHERE TO STAY AND EAT

Dating from 1435, the half-timbered **Wesley House** ((01242) 602366 FAX (01242) 609046 E-MAIL reservations@wesleyhouse.idps.co.uk, High Street, Winchcombe GL54 5LJ, once welcomed the founder of Methodism into its cozy halls and tipsy floors. The five small bedrooms all have shared bath (the "terrace room" has the best views); moderate. The lounge is warmed by a log fire. The dining room is quite good, drawing on English regional specialties from Cotswold lamb to Cornish sea bass. The early menu, offered from 6:45 PM to 7:45 PM on weekdays, is good value.

Sudeley Hill Farm (/FAX (01242) 602344, Winchcombe GL54 5JB, is a fifteenth-century listed

confused with nearby Teddington and Taddington!), is a chain-operated pub run like a restaurant (table service). The fare is nicely seasoned and well-cooked. It's on the Toddington round-about.

HOW TO GET THERE

Winchcombe is 11 km (seven miles) northeast of Cheltenham and 13 km (eight miles) south of Broadway. Local **buses** run to Winchcombe from both of these towns.

AROUND WINCHCOMBE

GLOUCESTERSHIRE — Three kilometers (two miles) northeast of Winchcombe (off the B4632) **Hailes Abbey** (EH and NT) ((01242) 602379 lies in

Sudeley Castle, childhood home of Katherine Parr, sixth wife of Henry VIII.

resplendent ruin. It was built in 1246 by Richard, Earl of Cornwall, following a pledge he made after he had narrowly escaped drowning at sea in 1242. Once one of Southern England's principal Cistercian monasteries, the original abbey was demolished soon after the Dissolution. A small museum offers a close-up look at ecclesiastic architectural bits that are normally leagues above the eye, including six beautifully detailed bosses found in the floor of the chapter house in 1899. Open daily from April to October, weekends only from November to March; admission fee. Audio tours can be rented at the admissions window. There is a music festival at Hailes Abbey each July; call for details.

Belas Knap Long Barrow (EH) is a restored Stone Age burial mound to the south of the Winchcombe. Dated at around 3000 BC, the tomb is unusual for its false entrance at the northern end, set there, perhaps, to deter malevolent spirits or grave robbers. The actual entrances are at either side. It's just over three kilometers (two miles) south of Winchcombe, near Charlton Abbots. You can visit any time; free admission.

CHIPPING CAMPDEN

GLOUCESTERSHIRE — The fourteenth and fifteen centuries were Chipping Campden's golden age, when the wool merchants of this market town dispensed their wealth to build St. James Church and the intriguing stone houses that still line High Street. Today Campden attracts large numbers of visitors for its fine buildings and craft shops.

Above the village, Dover's Hill is the sight of the **Cotswold Olympicks**. Begun in the 1600s, this annual competition features, among other festivities, the traditional sport of shin-kicking. The games are held each year on the Friday following Spring Bank Holiday.

WHAT TO SEE AND DO

Campden's **Market Hall** was built in 1627 for the trading of butter, poultry and cheese. Today it's a good place to dodge the ubiquitous Cotswold rain shower.

Church Street, with its 36-m (120-ft) tower, is an avenue of lime trees leading to the south porch of the **Parish Church of St. James** and **almshouses**. Inside, note the life-sized memorial brasses, especially the fine likeness of a wool merchant and his wife embedded in the chancel floor.

A remnant of another golden age in Campden, the **Guild of Handicrafts Trust** ((01386) 841100, at the Old Silk Mill, Sheep Street, is the only continuously operated Arts & Crafts movement workshop left in the country. At the beginning of the twentieth century, architect C.R. Ashbee, attracted by the Campden's low rents and faded beauty,

founded the Guild of Handicrafts here. Inside the eighteenth-century building there's a small exhibit on the history of the Arts & Crafts Movement in the Cotswolds (an admission fee is charged). Upstairs you can watch the artisans of D.T. Hart at work by the light of Bunsen burners, fashioning sterling-silver tableware. Hart is a descendant of George Hart, who was an original member of the Guild. The workshop makes and sells domestic silverware (cutlery, bowls, jugs). Open Monday to Saturday.

Silverware and **jewelry** are also produced and sold at several other places in town, including the studio shops of Robert Welch on Lower High Street; Ann Smith, Peacock House; and Martin Gotrel, The Square. Inquire at the Tourist Information Centre for hours.

Hidcote Manor Garden (NT) ((01386) 438333, Hidcote Bartrim, is considered one of the country's greatest gardens. It consists of a series of outdoor "rooms," each with its unique personality and color palette, separated by walls of hedges. The garden is noted for its rare shrubs and trees, as well as its antique rose varieties. There is a restaurant, tea room, shop and plant center. Hidcote is six and a half kilometers (four miles) northeast of Chipping Campden. Open March to October; closed Tuesday and Friday; admission fee.

OUTDOOR ACTIVITIES

Chipping Campden is the start of the 160-km-long (100-mile) **Cotswold Way** which ends near Bath (see THE GREAT OUTDOORS, page 25 in YOUR CHOICE).

Because of the beauty of the countryside and the plenitude of accommodation, the Northern Cotswolds are ideal **cycling** country. Bicycles are available for rent, year-round, from Cotswold Country Cycles ((01386) 438706 FAX (01386) 438442 E-MAIL cotscy@premier.co.uk, Longlands Farm Cottage, Chipping Campden GL55 6LJ. They also arrange complete cycling vacations with route maps and accommodation. See TAKING A TOUR, page 62 in YOUR CHOICE, for more companies offering cycling tours in the Cotswolds.

WHERE TO STAY AND EAT

The **Noel Arms** ((01386) 840317 FAX (01386) 841136, High Street, Chipping Campden GL55 6AT, has 26 bedrooms, spread throughout new and old wings, with larger, beamed rooms in the old wing. Some of the bedrooms look out on the busy, noisy street. All bedrooms have baths. Fresh flowers adorn the wood-paneled lobby hung with tapestries and Civil War armory; expensive. The **restaurant** provides a changing menu of Modern British fare; moderate. Dining reservations are strongly advised.

The mediaeval **Eight Bells** ((01386) 840371, Church Street, Chipping Campden GL55 6JG, is so named because it once housed the church bells while work proceeded on St. James's. This "pub of pubs" has great character, with heavy oak beams throughout and log fires at both ends of the dining room. There are two bedrooms (inexpensive). In the **restaurant**, choose from daily blackboard specials and finish with a heavenly dessert.

In nearby Broad Campden, **Wyldlands** ((01386) 840478, Broad Campden, Chipping Campden GL55 6UR, is a Cotswold stone house with garden and pretty views; inexpensive.

Badger's Tea Room, on High Street, is a sociable place serving luscious layer cakes and other "puddings" as well as good homemade soup, salads and sandwiches; inexpensive.

demonstrations with a chance to handle some of the birds. Open March to November; admission fee.

Moreton is a handy and economical base for those using public transportation. Centrally located, the **Townend Cottage & Coach House** ((01608) 650846, High Street, Moreton-in-Marsh GL56 0AD, is a laid-back B&B with four small bedrooms, garden and free parking. It's at the top end of High Street next to the police station; inexpensive.

Ditchford Farmhouse ((01608) 663307, Stretton on Fosse, Moreton-in-Marsh GL56 9RD, is a four-hectare (10-acre) farm and Georgian farmhouse with a large garden and a log fire in winter. There are home-cooked meals in the evening,

MORETON-IN-MARSH

GLOUCESTERSHIRE — A market town straddling the ancient Fosse Way (the Roman road known now as the A429), Moreton-in-Marsh is a transportation center of the region. It's not a Cotswolds beauty spot, but it does have some interesting points of interest as well as boasting the Cotswolds' largest street **market**, which attracts crowds of shoppers every Tuesday.

There is a limited-service **Tourist Information Centre** ((01608) 650881 at the Cotswold District Council Offices; open year-round.

Northwest of town, **Batsford Arboretum** ((01608) 650722, Batsford Park, is a 20-hectare (50-acre), private collection of rare tree species. Also within Batsford Park, the **Cotswold Falconry Centre** ((01386) 701043 is a flyway for eagles, hawks, owls, falcons and other birds of prey. There are daily falconry

using farm produce. The six bedrooms with bath are at the upper end of the inexpensive price range.

Roosters ((01608) 650645, Todenham, Moreton-in-Marsh GL56 9PA, is a seventeenth-century Cotswold stone house with oak beams and an inglenook fireplace in the dining room. Meals are provided on request. There are three bedrooms with bath; inexpensive.

For fine dining, **Marsh Goose** ((01608) 652111, High Street, is a cozy, sophisticated place serving creative English cooking, such as lamb's liver with red onion compote and mustard *jus*. Allow plenty of time as service can be slow; expensive.

The **Bell Inn** ((01608) 651688, High Street, Moreton-in-Marsh GL56 0AF, serves bar meals and cask ales — on the spacious patio in summer months. It also has five bedrooms with bath (call for rates), three of them in the converted stables.

Ruins of thirteenth-century Hailes Abbey.

HOW TO GET THERE

Moreton-in-Marsh is 133 km (82 miles) northwest of London. There is daily **train** service to Moreton from London Paddington, and National Express operates one **coach** daily to Moreton.

STOW-ON-THE-WOLD

GLOUCESTERSHIRE — Shops selling vintage treasures line the streets of Stow-on-the-Wold, the **antiques** capital of the region. For **crafts**, Traffords, on Digbeth Street, has the best selection (open daily). The annual Cotswold Antique and Fine Arts Fes-

tival takes place here during the first week in February. Morris dancers take to the streets on Stow's **Day of Dance** in September. The **Cotswold Tourist Information Centre** ((01451) 831082 is at Hollis House, The Square; open year-round.

Stow is an excellent base for exploring the Northern Cotswolds and Shakespeare Country (see below) with a range of interesting accommodation. The seventeenth-century **Old Stocks Hotel** ((01451) 830666 FAX (01451) 870014, The Square, Stow-on-the-Wold GL54 1AF, is right on the Green, where the eponymous stocks still stand. The comfortable bedrooms (including one single) have bath. Ask about their "budget breaks"; moderate.

An exceptionally comfy seventeenth-century cottage B&B, **Cross Keys Cottage** ((01451) 831128, Park Street, Stow-on-Wold, GL54 1AQ, has three well-equipped bedrooms, including one with king-sized bed. All bedrooms have bath; inexpensive.

Just outside the village, **Little Broom** ((01451) 830510, Maugersbury, Stow-on-the-Wold GL54 1HP, is a country cottage with three bedrooms, a log fire in the den, and a heated pool. There is one comfortable, nest-like single room. It's a five-minute walk to town through pretty woods. Extraordinary breakfasts are cooked to order featuring traditional English breakfast dishes and French toast; inexpensive.

The Rolls Royce of YHA hostels, **Stow-on-the-Wold Youth Hostel** ((01451) 830497 is situated right on Market Square, in a restored sixteenth-century brew house. Beds in the lofty dormitory rooms are equipped with duvets, and some of the rooms have skylights. It's open April to early September (sometimes longer); rock-bottom.

HOW TO GET THERE

Stow is six kilometers (four miles) south of Moreton-in-Marsh and 26 km (16 miles) northeast of Cheltenham. The nearest **train** station is at Moreton-in-the-Marsh. Local buses run from there to Stow. National Express operates **coach** services from London Victoria, Oxford and Cambridge to Cheltenham where you can also connect with local buses to Stow.

BOURTON-ON-THE-WATER

GLOUCESTERSHIRE — At Bourton-on-the-Water, pretty houses of locally quarried stone line the Windrush River, which is spanned by a series of eighteenth-century mill bridges. This market town is the Cotswolds' most popular destination, a conspicuous example of Cotswolds commercialism run amuck. If you're looking for lots of things to do, then Bourton-on-the-Water may be your answer. On the other hand, if you're after quiet Cotswolds charm, try elsewhere.

Despite its popularity, Bourton has no formal tourist information center; however, you can find the village on the Internet at WEB SITE www.bourton-on-the-water.co.uk, or write to the **Bourton-on-the-Water Chamber of Commerce**, PO Box 5, Bourton-on-the-Water, Cheltenham GL54 2YJ, in advance of your visit.

WHAT TO SEE AND DO

Tread like Gulliver through the one-ninth scale **Model Village** ((01451) 820467, High Street, constructed of Cotswold stone in the 1930s. The Lilliputian village is complete with working waterwheel, music emanating from the church, and a glimmering River Windrush with each of its unique bridges. Open year-round; admission fee.

At the **Perfumery** ((01451) 820698, Victoria Street, there is an exhibition on the process of mixing scents. You can sample some of the essential oils used in the perfumes next door in the shop. Open year-round; admission fee.

Set along the broad River Windrush, **Birdland** ((01451) 820480, Rissington Road, is an aviary of rare and exotic birds including penguins, parrots, and flamingos. There is a coffee house and playground here. Open year-round; admission fee.

The **Cotswold Motor Museum and Toy Museum** ((01451) 821255, Sherborne Street, is housed inside an old water mill. On display are vintage cars from the early years of motoring through to the 1950s, along with a toy collection. Closed December to January and occasional winter weekdays.

Of the many tea rooms in Bourton, **Small Talk** ((01451) 821596, The Old Forge, High Street, is particularly genial, serving tea with clotted cream and homemade cakes seven days a week from 10 AM.

The **Coach & Horses** ((01451) 820664, Stow Road, is a Cotswold-stone pub just outside the village serving meals and ales.

HOW TO GET THERE

Bourton is 16 km (eight miles) south of Moreton-in-Marsh, 21 km (13 miles) east of Cheltenham, and about five kilometers (three miles) south of Stow-on-the-Wold. Moreton has the nearest **train** station with **bus** connections to Bourton. National Express

WHERE TO STAY AND EAT

Rooftrees Guest house ((01451) 821943 FAX (01451) 810614, Rissington Road, Bourton-on-the-Water, Cheltenham GL54 2DX, is a Cotswold-stone house within 10 minutes' walking distance of Bourton. There are three bedrooms with bath, two of which have four-poster beds; inexpensive. Evening meals are served and a half-board option is available.

The **Cotswold House** ((01451) 822373, Landsdowne, Bourton-on-the-Water, Cheltenham GL54 2AR, is a stone house offering homey bedrooms (with bath) both overlooking the garden; moderate.

For lunch or dinner you might try the solid English fare at **Old New Inn** ((01451) 820467, High Street (moderate to expensive); or English-Continental cooking at the **Old Well** ((01451) 820286, in the Chester House Hotel and Motel, Victoria Street (inexpensive).

operates **coach** service to Cheltenham and Stow-on-the-Wold, where there are several local buses per day to Bourton.

NORTHLEACH

GLOUCESTERSHIRE — Another handsome wool town, Northleach has several interesting attractions, but its main appeal is its uncomplicated Cotswolds charm. In 1984 the A40 bypass diverted heavy traffic off Northleach's ancient main street. Now quiet and prospering, it's one of the most delightful and authentic villages in the region.

There is a seasonal **Tourist Information Centre** ((01451) 860715 at the Cotswold Heritage Centre (below), just outside the village center; open April through to the end of October.

OPPOSITE: The Square, Stow-on-the-Wold.
ABOVE: Bourton-on-the-Water.

WHAT TO SEE AND DO

Mediaeval wool merchants endowed the magnificent **Church of St. Peter & St. Paul**, called the "Cathedral of the Cotswolds." It is considered one England's finest examples of the Perpendicular Gothic style. Rubbings from the memorial brasses of the fifteenth-century wool merchants — with sheep and bundles of wool at their feet — line the floor. You can do brass rubbings on the genuine article in its original resting place here — a rarity nowadays. Inquire at the Post Office ((01451) 860205 in Market Place (closed Sunday).

Keith Harding's World of Mechanical Music ((01451) 860181, High Street, is a collection spanning 300 years of automated musical instruments, from barrel organs to juke boxes to minstrel bands, music boxes and antique juke boxes. Exhibitions are constantly changing as new gadgets are added. The tour lasts from 30 to 90 minutes, depending on which guide you get. Open daily (but call for tour times); admission fee.

Outside the center, on Fosseway, the House of Correction, built in the eighteenth century, is now the **Cotswolds Heritage Centre Museum of Rural Life** ((01451) 860715. The old prison dates from 1791. The collection is composed mostly of agricultural tools and vehicles dating from the nineteenth century, detailing rural life in the Cotswolds. Open April to October, other times by arrangement; admission fee. There's a tea room here.

In a remote valley west of Northleach, **Chedworth Roman Villa** (NT) ((01242) 890256 is the well-preserved ruins of a Roman country estate. Dating from AD 120, the remains paint a picture of a modest villa containing mosaic floors, an under-floor heating system, baths, and a water shrine still filled by an ancient spring. A minuscule museum presents artifacts found during excavations. The tranquil woodland setting adds much to the experience. Open March to November Tuesday to Sunday; admission fee. Chedworth is located 13 km (eight miles) southeast of Cheltenham; follow the A40 then A429 towards Cirencester, signposted from Yanworth on right.

WHERE TO STAY AND EAT

In Northleach's West End, the **Wheatsheaf Hotel** ((01451) 860244 FAX (01451) 861037 E-MAIL whtshfhtl@aol.com, Northleach GL54 3EZ, is an old coaching inn with nine bedrooms with bathrooms, a good restaurant and bar; moderate.

Once the home of an Elizabethan wool merchant, **Cotteswold House** ((01451) 860493 FAX (01451) 860493 E-MAIL cotteswoldhouse@talk21.com, Market Place, Northleach GL54 3EG, is a lovely
164

old residence with some original features. The bedrooms are comfortable and spacious, and all have bath; moderate. Children age 15 and over are welcome.

A couple of less expensive choices include the **Sherborne Arms** ((01451) 860241, in Market Place, Northleach GL54 3EE, which has recently refurbished bedrooms with bath; inexpensive. Pub fare is served in the bar with its inglenook fireplace and in the restaurant, a converted blacksmiths forge. The 400-year-old **Market House** ((01451) 860557, Market Square, Northleach GL54 3EJ, is a stone building with steps leading from the main street down into the house; inexpensive.

HOW TO GET THERE

Northleach is 19 km (12 miles) east of Cheltenham and 49 km (30 miles) northwest of Oxford. There are several local **buses** per day operating between Oxford and Cheltenham via Northleach.

THE SLAUGHTERS

GLOUCESTERSHIRE — The charms of two of England's prettiest villages are no secret. Upper and Lower Slaughter get masses of visitors in summer, but have so far avoided the perils to which neighboring Bourton has fallen. At Upper Slaughter, there's a picturesque, duck-filled ford over the River Eye, also called Slaughter Brook, a favored painter's tableau.

The same brook, a tributary of the River Windrush, parallels the main street at Lower Slaughter. Crossed by several bridges, some of stone and some of oak planks, the brook runs on through the waterwheel of the eighteenth-century **Old Mill** ((01451) 820052, before tumbling on into the countryside. At the mill there is an interesting gift shop, a small museum (an admission fee is charged) and tea room. Open daily; phone for winter hours.

The well-signposted **Warden's Way** long-distance footpath begins at Upper Slaughter's central car park, kicking off with a scenic riverside walk to Lower Slaughter, about one and a half kilometers (a mile) away.

WHERE TO STAY AND EAT

The Slaughters have some high-brow hostelries. **Lower Slaughter Manor** ((01451) 820456 FAX (01451) 822150 E-MAIL lowsmanor@aol.com, Lower Slaughter GL54 2HP, is a gorgeous seventeenth-century manor house surrounded by two colorful hectares (four acres) of gardens, parkland, and clipped green lawns. Though the interior is rather stiff, there's no question that the bedrooms are more than comfortable. There is a tennis court, croquet, and an attractive indoor pool for relaxing. The **restaurant** prepares excellent Modern

English meals. Public areas are adorned with fresh flowers, antiques and paintings, and log fires add a touch of warmth; very expensive to luxury.

A former rectory dating from the 1600s, **Lords of the Manor** ((01451) 820243 TOLL-FREE IN THE UNITED STATES (800) 872-4564 FAX (01451) 820696, Upper Slaughter GL54 2JD, is set in several acres of gardens and parkland. The bedrooms (most with bath) are decorated in fine style with period antiques and rich fabrics. The **restaurant** (expensive) provides modern English cooking in a candlelit room overlooking the gardens; prices range from very expensive to luxury.

Floating down to earth in both price and pretension, the **Old Farmhouse Hotel** ((01451) 830232,

stone buildings. Chippy's more of a lived-in town than in some Cotswold tourist shrines, with all the fixtures of a typical English community from butcher to baker to a fish-and-chips shop. The **Visitor Information Centre** (/FAX (01608) 644379, is at the sixteenth-century Guildhall, in Goddards Lane; open year-round. Wednesday is **market** day.

WHAT TO SEE AND DO

Chipping Norton's wool trade lasted well into the last century, and the town's main landmark remains the Victorian **Bliss Tweed Mill**, now converted into residences. Within the lovely fourteenth- and fifteenth-century **Parish Church of St. Mary's** are a

Lower Swell, Cheltenham GL54 1LF, offers good value in a placid setting. There are 13 shared-bath or en-suite bedrooms. The bedrooms are fairly spacious, with ruffles-and-checks decor. Room 1, with a view of the lovely little garden, is best. The Malt Bar with log fire and restaurant, also with fireplace, make for cozy lounging and dining. Service is efficient and professional. The hotel reception has maps detailing walks around the scenic countryside. Rates vary widely depending on the rooms, from inexpensive to expensive. Prices are higher on weekends. Half-board rates are available.

CHIPPING NORTON

OXFORDSHIRE — Another pleasant old Cotswolds town, Chipping Norton, or "Chippy" as the locals call it, has a broad marketplace and numerous graceful, sixteenth- and seventeen-century

series of unusual bosses (at the cross-sections of the vaulting) depicting fantastic creatures. Much of the church's mediaeval stonework has been restored, and the Perpendicular clerestory, with its high glass windows, fills the church with light. In summer the town history **museum** in the Co-op Hall is open Tuesday to Sunday afternoons. The beautiful 100-seat, Victorian **theatre** ((01608) 642350, presents a wide-ranging program of touring productions throughout the year. In addition to a dozen or so good **antique shops**, the **Oxfordshire Craft Guild Shop** ((01608) 641525 in Goddards Lane (open Tuesday to Saturday), and the **Mason House Gallery** ((01608) 642620, West Street, show the works of contemporary British artists.

Five kilometers (three miles) north of Chipping Norton (between the A44 and A3400), are

The River Eye meanders through Upper Slaughter.

the **Rollright Stones**, the Cotswolds' most important prehistoric remains. This late Neolithic stone circle, dating from around 2000 BC, is composed of a broad circle of standing stones, some of which reach two meters in height (seven feet). Across the road a single standing stone, The King Stone, is believed to date from the Bronze Age. To the east is another group of stones are known as the Whispering Knights. The area is steeped in legend, and the superstitious claim that no one can accurately count the stones. Whether you can count the stones or not, this is a wonderfully quiet and enigmatic place to visit. Any time of year is fine, but if you're fortunate enough, your visit may coincide with on of the occasional evenings

through the summer when a traveling **theater** group performs Shakespeare amongst the stones. Call the Visitor Information Centre (above) for details.

A number of other worthwhile spots surround Chipping Norton. **Chastleton House** (NT) ((01608) 674284, Chastleton, west toward Moreton-in-Marsh, is a fine Jacobean house with beautiful gardens. Tickets must be purchased in advance. To the east of Chipping Norton, Great, Little and Duns Tew form **The Tews**, a group of picture-perfect villages with thatched cottages. Great Tew, a planned village of the Tudor era, is the most captivating of the lot. Just south of the Tews, **Sandford St. Martin** has a thirteenth-century church and manor house, and further east, **Rousham House** ((01869) 347110, Rousham, is a stately seventeenth-century country house set in a splendid eight-hectare (20-acre) ornamental garden.

WHERE TO STAY AND EAT

A restored seventeenth-century flour mill, the **Mill House** ((01608) 658188, Station Road, Kingham, Chipping Norton OX7 6UH, offers rooms with views of the rural Cotswold landscape; expensive. The cozy restaurant serves good food.

There are three moderately-priced accomodation options in Shipton-under-Wychwood, 13 km (eight miles) south of Chipping Norton. The **Shaven Crown** ((01993) 830330, Shipton-under-Wychwood OX7 6BA, is a comfortable beamed hostelry built around a courtyard with an impressive mediaeval hall, old stone walls and a winding staircase. There's a log fire in the bar and candlelight in the restaurant, which boasts a good wine list. The **Lamb** ((01993) 830465, Shipton-under-Wychwood OX7 6DQ, is an ancient stone pub with five snug rooms, an open log fire in the beamed bar, and good food in the restaurant. Somewhat less expensive is **Shipton Grange House** ((01993) 831298, Shipton-under-Wychwood OX7 6DG, a converted coach house and stables offering three attractively-furnished rooms and a walled garden.

The pretty village of Church Enstone, just east of Chipping Norton, is home to the **Crown** ((01608) 677262, Mill Lane, Church Enstone, Chipping Norton OX7 4NN, an inexpensive Cotswold stone inn serving good food in the restaurant and bar.

Michelin-starred **Chavingnol** ((01608) 644490, 7 Horsefair, is an outstanding French restaurant ensconced in a charming Cotswold cottage with beams and open fires; expensive.

HOW TO GET THERE

Chipping Norton is 32 km (20 miles) northwest of Oxford and 32 km (20 miles) southeast of Stratford-upon-Avon. Connections can be made from nearby Charlbury, which is a one-hour **train** ride from London Paddington.

BROADWAY

WORCESTERSHIRE — One of the finest of the Cotswold villages, Broadway has gained a great measure of peace and quiet since a bypass road opened in 1998. Broadway's High Street is flanked by mellowed buildings of carved masonry. The high street, with bay windows brimming with antique treasures, rises through town, punctuated by a sheep pasture at one point.

An important staging post until the advent of the railway, Broadway became a haven for artists in the years that followed.

There is a tiny, volunteer-staffed **Tourist Information Centre** ((01386) 852937 at 1 Cotswold Court, The Green, which links Church Close car park and High Street.

WHAT TO SEE AND DO

The chief activity in Broadway is meandering along **High Street**. Contemporary crafts, including ceramics, wood, and metalwork, are on sale at the Anderson Gallery, at No. 96. Bang in the center of town, the venerable **Lygon Arms** is a trip in a time machine. Step inside to the scent of wood smoke, the glistening sheen of gilded coats of arms and halls muffled by tapestries. High tea at the Lygon is sublime.

On Church Road, **St. Michael's** is the attractive "new" parish church (built in the nineteenth century), which replaced the ancient **Church of**

beamed five-star inns. Most of the village B&Bs are located on Upper High Street just below the trailhead for the Cotswold Way, making convenient stopovers for walkers.

An inn since 1532, the splendid **Lygon Arms** ((01386) 852255 FAX (01386) 858611 E-MAIL info @the-lygon-arms.co.uk, High Street, Broadway WR12 7DU, offers luxury accommodation in an authentically mediaeval setting. The sumptuous bedrooms are decorated in period style but have all modern conveniences right up to voicemail, fax and modem jacks. Continental breakfast is included (but VAT is not included in the rate); very expensive to luxury. Ask about special deals. The restaurant here is excellent. For informal meals

St. **Eadburgha**, located about one and a half kilometers (a mile) out of town. You can get to St. Eadburgha along Church Road — a pretty walk with thatched cottages and sheep folds lining the way, or take the one-and-a-half-kilometer (milelong) **footpath** (can be muddy) from High Street. Another footpath across from the churchyard leads up to Broadway Tower.

You may wonder why the old church is so far from the village. Legend says that while it was being built, the Devil threw three stones at the church, but missed. The local people decided to move the building further away just in case Beelzebub should persist.

WHERE TO STAY

Accommodation in Broadway ranges from honey-colored Cotswold stone farmhouses to broad-

there is a brasserie. Guests have the use of the Lygon Arms Country Club with its indoor pool, fitness center, and health and beauty treatments.

Built as an abbot's retreat in the fifteenth century, **Broadway Hotel** ((01386) 852401 FAX (01386) 853879, The Green, Broadway, Hereford & Worcester WR12 7AA, is a fascinating pastiche of ancient stairs (some leading nowhere at all), carved mahogany paneling, and eclectic antiques. A minstrels' gallery looks down on the restaurant (reservations recommended). Racing memorabilia in the Jockey Bar is a reminder that the hotel sponsors two race horses. The bedrooms are spread between the old structure and a new wing. The nicest rooms overlook the courtyard; expensive.

The **Olive Branch** ((01386) 853440 FAX (01386) 859070 E-MAIL olive@theolivebranch.u-net.com,

OPPOSITE: The prehistoric Rollright Stones.
ABOVE: Broadway's wide High Street.

78 High Street, Broadway WR12 7AJ, is a listed sixteenth-century house with ruffles-and-bows bedrooms with lots of thoughtful extras. Breakfast, served in the Cotswold stone dining room, includes a vegetarian choice. There is a car park and garden; inexpensive. Nearby is the seventeenth-century **Milestone House** (/FAX (01386) 853432 E-MAIL milestone.house@talk21.com, 122 Upper High Street, Broadway WR12 7AJ, with four bedrooms, one of which overlooks the garden. There are sitting rooms to relax in and breakfast is served in the conservatory overlooking the garden. Children over 15 are welcome. Outside the house stands its namesake, a restored milestone noting that Broadway lies 90 miles (146 km) from London.

For farmhouse accommodation there is **Leasow House** ((01386) 584526, Laverton Meadows, Broadway WR12 7NA, a farm manor house full of charm and creature comforts. Rooms have phones and cuddly chenille bedspreads. The usual complement of in-room tea and coffee is supplemented by cookies and hot cocoa. A library lined with leather-bound books offers a place to convene, with sherry on the table; moderate.

WHERE TO EAT

The restaurant at the **Lygon Arms** ((01386) 852255, High Street, is a five-star affair. In the barrel-vaulted dining room, under the gaze of a dozen stag heads, the menu offers roasted monkfish wrapped in chorizo with caramelized apple, or miniature rack of Cotswold lamb with olive and herb crust; expensive. Its also a fine setting for afternoon tea. For casual dining the Lygon has **Olivers Wine Bar** serving creative fare in a bistro setting. The pepper steak is a good choice; moderate.

The local Indian restaurant is **Sheikh's** ((01386) 858546, The Green, serving Bangladeshi fare in a pleasant setting. Service can be slow; inexpensive.

The **Swan Inn** ((01386) 852278, High Street, is a steak house with a children's menu. Reservations are advisable during the high season; moderate to inexpensive.

For snacks and picnic supplies go to **Hampers**, in Cotswold Court, where you can pick up fresh sandwiches, as well as wine and champagne.

HOW TO GET THERE

As the milestone reports, Broadway is 90 miles (146 km) northwest of London. The nearest **train** stations are at Moreton-in-Marsh, 11 km (seven miles) to the southeast, and at Evesham (eight kilometers or five miles). There are local bus connections from Evesham to Broadway, but not from Moreton. National Express offers daily **coach** services to Broadway from London Victoria.

AROUND BROADWAY

WORCESTERSHIRE, GLOUCESTERSHIRE — From the center of Broadway, travel five kilometers (three miles) down Church Road to reach **Snowshill Manor** (NT) ((01386) 852410. This Tudor manor house (with a seventeenth-century façade) houses the extraordinary collection of Charles Paget Wade, "one of the last of a famous company, the eccentric English country gentry," as J.B. Priestley wrote when he visited Snowshill in the 1930s. Rooms brim with oddities and treasures, the best known of which are probably the 26 suits of Japanese samurai armor. There are also large collections of toys, tapestries, dolls and clocks. Outside there is an organic garden, and the parkland surrounding the manor is managed to encourage wildlife; kestrels thrive there as well as red and fallow deer. Open afternoons from April to October, daily except Tuesday; admission fee. Further down the road is the upland village of **Snowshill**, with its pretty houses nestled in a crescent around the church close. The Snowshill Arms serves local ales.

It's possible to walk or drive to **Broadway Tower Country Park** ((01386) 852390, following the signs from Snowshill village. Built by the sixth Earl of Coventry, this eighteenth-century folly was later a country retreat for William Morris and his Pre-Raphaelite pal, Dante Gabrielle Rossetti. There's a small exhibition on past inhabitants of this unusual structure. Climb to the top for views over 12 counties. Around the open parkland you can see red deer, sheep and llama in enclosures. There is a café and shop. Open April to October; admission fee.

STRATFORD-UPON-AVON

WARWICKSHIRE — Stratford-upon-Avon, birthplace of William Shakespeare, has been a tourist destination since shortly after the Bard's death in 1616. In fact, six years after his death visitors so plagued the inhabitants that actors in his old company were paid *not* to play the town. In the eighteenth century the owner-occupant of New Place, Shakespeare's home for the last years of his life, deliberately destroyed the house in an attempt to stem the tide of pilgrims. It didn't work. Fans of the Bard continued to come in droves and still do today.

Despite the crowds and commercialism of Stratford, it is a worthwhile destination. Visiting out-of-season is strongly recommended, though it's not especially deserted even then. When the hustle and bustle begin to unravel your nerves there are fetching gardens and parks to retreat to; the canal and surrounding park are also good for a breather.

Broadway Tower, an eighteenth-century folly.

Not that travelers need any additional incentive to visit Stratford, but in October, the English Music Festival adds to the general merriment with nine days of concerts in and around town. Shakespeare's birthday is celebrated in April, the Stratford Festival takes place in July, and the Mop Fair in October.

GENERAL INFORMATION

The **Tourist Information Centre** ((01789) 293127, (01789) 415061 (lodging), or (01789) 267522 (24-hour brochure requests) FAX (01789) 295262 is at Bridge Foot; closed Sundays in winter. It's a large, full-service center, and almost always packed.

Actors from the Royal Shakespeare Company ((01789) 412602 take **guided two-hour walks** telling the Bard's story within the context of historic Stratford. Walks depart at 10:30 AM from the Royal Shakespeare Company, Waterside, Thursday and Saturday year-round, and on Sundays from July to September.

Double-decker bus tours take in the highlights of Stratford and environs, including all five of the Shakespeare houses. Tickets (£8/£2.50) are valid all day for hop-on hop-off touring; available at the Tourist Information Centre. Or you can stay put for the hour's ride. If you want something more rustic, look for the Shakespearean ((01676) 532222, a **horse-drawn omnibus** that carts visitors around town on fine afternoons.

Avon Cruises ((01789) 267073, Swans Nest Lane, offers half-hour and one-hour cruises along the River Avon in restored narrowboats. Trips run from Easter through October. They also rent **rowboats** by the hour. Cruises leave also from Bancroft Gardens daily from Easter to November.

WHAT TO SEE AND DO

The Shakespeare Trail

Among other notable sites, there are three Shakespeare family houses to visit within Stratford and two in nearby Shottery and Wilmcote. You can purchase a combined ticket for all five houses; all are open the same hours. There is also a joint ticket for the three Stratford houses. A hop-on hop-off tour bus (an admission fee is charged) links all five the sites (see GENERAL INFORMATION, above), though you don't need transportation for the in-town sites as they are all within walking distance of each other.

Shakespeare's Birthplace ((01789) 204069 is on Henley Street. A visit to this large half-timbered house starts with an interesting exhibition on the life and times of the Shakespeare family. Once you enter the recently refurbished rooms, docents can answer any questions that come to mind as you meander over the teetering floors. The visit finishes in the garden, which blooms with flowers mentioned in Shakespeare's works.

There are two combined properties to visit on Chapel Street, **Nash's House & New Place** ((01789) 292325. New Place is the site of William Shakespeare's Stratford home from the age of 37, bought the year after his son, Hamnet, died. Shakespeare only lived there for the last five years of his life. The house was destroyed by its owner in the eighteenth century, but the Elizabethan knot garden remains. Next door, **Nash House**, where Shakespeare's granddaughter lived with her husband, has a good collection of period furniture. Behind these two properties is the **Great Garden** (free entry), planted with topiaries and flowering shrubs.

The most impressive of the Shakespeare houses, gabled Tudor **Halls Croft** ((01789) 292107, Old Town, was the home of Shakespeare's daughter Susanna and her doctor husband, John Hall. In each of the rooms burnished wood floors glow, and interesting objects await discovery as you move from salon to apothecary to kitchen. You may even gain some

insights into Tudor medicine, perusing the good doctor's instruments and letters from his patients.

Also in Old Town, pay your respects to Shakespeare's dust at The **Holy Trinity Church**, a graceful building set amongst shady trees. There is a small fee to approach Shakespeare's grave in the chancel.

Anne Hathaway's Cottage ((01789) 292100 is in Shottery, on the western outskirts of Stratford. This thatched Tudor farmhouse was the home of Shakespeare's wife, to whom he famously bequeathed his "second best bed." Inside is an exhibition of Elizabethan-era domestic life. Open daily; admission fee.

A timbered farmhouse, **Mary Arden's House** ((01789) 293455 is believed to have been the home of Shakespeare's mother before she married John Shakespeare and moved to Stratford. In the barn there is a large collection of farm gadgets and displays detailing country life and work from Shakespeare's day to the present. Open daily; admission fee.

More Points of interest

The ornate **Harvard House** ((01789) 204016, High Street, a fine Elizabethan townhouse, was the home of Katherine Rogers, mother of John Harvard who founded Harvard University. Closed Monday and all of mid-October to April; fee charged.

Bancroft Gardens is a pretty place to idle along the Avon Canal, watch the narrowboats and enjoy the floral displays. The statues of the Bard amongst some of his better-known characters — Lady Macbeth, Falstaff, Hamlet, and Prince Hal — make good photo backdrops.

Tours of the **Royal Shakespeare Theatre** ((01789) 412602, Waterside, with lively commentary and a chance to dress up in costumes, depart from the Swan Theatre at 1:30 PM and 5:30 PM daily (except for Thursday and Saturday), and four times every Sunday afternoon; fee charged.

Birthplace of the Bard.

Finally, there is the **Ragdoll Shop** ((01789) 404111, 11 Chapel Street, where kids can talk to their favorite television characters on play telephones, see themselves on a video screen, take a ride on Brum the magical car, and frolic in the Teletubbies play area. Open daily year-round (closed Sunday mornings); free admission.

OUTDOOR ACTIVITIES

For **self-guided walks** into the countryside surrounding Stratford, pick up a copy of the Ramblers Association *Stratford Walks*, available at the Tourist Information Centre (above) and in shops around town.

Bicycles can be rented at Clarke's Stratford Cycle Shop ((01789) 205057; or from Off the Beaten Track ((01926) 817380 or (0468) 477740 which also offers guided bicycle tours.

WHERE TO STAY

Stratford has heaps of accommodation. For B&Bs try around Evesham Place, Grove Road, Broad Walk, Banbury Road, and Alcester Road.

In the center, the **Shakespeare Hotel** ((0870) 400-8182 FAX (01789) 415411, Chapel Street, Stratford-upon-Avon CV37 6ER, has had some famous visitors, including Margaret Thatcher and Liz Taylor. The 74 rooms, named for Shakespeare's characters and plays, are corporate in style, but top-notch nevertheless. Baths are large. Many of the bedrooms look out on the garden. The beamed public rooms are cozy, with open fires and flowers; very expensive to luxury. The restaurant serves traditional English fare, and there is also a bistro, a bar, and a lounge.

One of my favorite places in Stratford is the **Payton Hotel** (/FAX (01789) 266442, 6 John Street, Stratford-upon-Avon CV37 6UB, a listed Georgian townhouse located in a quiet restored neighborhood. This corner house has sun streaming in from all sides, and a warm welcome from the host. Bedrooms and common areas are tastefully decorated in Regency style with pink and white tones predominating. All rooms have bath. You do have to cross a busy Guild Street to get to the hotel from the town center, but it's only a three-minute walk; moderate (discounts of up to 30% are available on Sunday to Thursday nights depending on availability and season).

Also in the center, **Caterham House** ((01789) 297070, 58 Rother Street, Stratford-upon-Avon CV37 6LT, has 10 comfortable, individually decorated rooms with brass beds and antiques. There is a hotel bar, and free parking; moderate.

A stand-out amidst the many B&Bs of Stratford, **Melita Private Hotel** ((01789) 292432 FAX (01789) 204867 E-MAIL melita37@E-MAIL.msn.com, 37 Shipston Road, Stratford-upon-Avon CV37 7LN, is a flower-decked, blue-and-white Victorian with

12 bedrooms, lounge with open fire, and good breakfasts; moderate.

Walcote Farm (/FAX (01789) 488264 E-MAIL john-finnemore@compuserve.com, Walcote, Haselor, Alcester B49 6LY, is about six and a half kilometers (four miles) west of Stratford. Bedrooms are spacious and comfortable with lovely garden views and the sound of birds chirping in the morning. Downstairs the sitting room has a large inglenook fireplace; inexpensive.

The **Stratford-upon-Avon Youth Hostel** ((01789) 297093 FAX (01789) 205513 E-MAIL stratford @yha.org.uk, Hemmingford House, Alveston, Stratford-upon-Avon CV37 7RG, is situated in a Georgian mansion, three kilometers (two miles)

from the center. Unusual for a YHA hostel, it has 24-hour access and some rooms have private bath; rock-bottom.

WHERE TO EAT

There are three wine bars to choose from on Sheep Street, all in the moderate price range. **Opposition** ((01789) 269980, 13 Sheep Street, does pasta, fish, chicken and vegetarian dishes in a pleasant, casual setting. **Lambs** ((01789) 292554, 12 Sheep Street, is a bit more refined, and a bit more expensive. Fresh flowers decorate the dining room which is warmed by a log fire in winter. On the menu are pastas and salads, and imaginative twists on English fare, such as the lamb-and-apricot pie. A set menu is available from noon to 2 PM and 5 PM to 7 PM. Reservations required Saturday night. Finally, **Vintner Wine Bar** ((01789) 297359, 5 Sheep

Street, with its Elizabethan decor, specializes in Continental fare. Daily specials supplement the menu which may offer roulade of smoked salmon, or lemon sole on a red pepper *coulis*. Desserts are traditional diet destroyers such as double chocolate sponge cake with hot chocolate sauce.

At **Glory Hole** ((01789) 293546, 21–23 Sheep Street, snack on sandwiches, fish & chips, *moules–frites*, and pastas in comfy upholstered chairs set by bay windows along bustling Sheep Street; inexpensive.

For tea, sweets and inexpensive meals, there is the **Hathaway Tea Rooms** ((01789) 292404, 19 High Street, with a fudge shop and bakery in front and sit-down dining in back. Pasties, sausage rolls and other savories are on the menu.

Waterside, where the Royal Shakespeare Company performs the works of the Bard. Reservations for this 1,500-seat theater can be made by mail in the United Kingdom: The Box Office, Royal Shakespeare Theatre, Stratford-upon-Avon CV37 6BB (include a stamped self-addressed envelope). For ticket reservations contact Edwards & Edwards ((020) 7839-3952 TOLL-FREE IN THE UNITED STATES (800) 223-6108 WEB SITE www.globaltickets.com, 12 Lower Regent Street, London SW1Y 4NR.

Two other theaters share a box office with the RSC. The 430-seat **Swan** is a theater-in-the-round, designed in the manner of an Elizabethan playhouse. This intimate stage is a setting for plays by Shakespeare and his contemporaries as well as

The **Shakespeare Hotel** (above) also does pleasant afternoon teas.

By the riverside, the **Dirty (a.k.a. Black Swan)** ((01789) 297312, Waterside, is where RSC players hang out. The **Slug & Lettuce** ((01789) 299700, Guild Street, part of a large chain, does good food. The half-timbered **Falcon** ((01789) 279953, Chapel Street, is the oldest inn in town. The **White Swan** ((01789) 293276, Rother Street, hosts well-known jazz musicians on Sunday nights, and there is usually no cover charge.

NIGHTLIFE

Theater
The **Royal Shakespeare Theatres** ((01789) 295623 or (01789) 412666 (24-hour booking) FAX (01789) 261974 (booking), offer something for everyone. The main stage is the Royal Shakespeare Theatre,

unsung classics. The newest stage in Stratford is the **Other Place**, an experimental theater. It's located a few blocks from the RSC and Swan on Southern Lane.

HOW TO GET THERE

Stratford-upon-Avon is 163 km (100 miles) from London. **Trains** leave London Paddington six times a day for the trip to Stratford. There is also frequent train service from Oxford. For information call ((01203) 555211. National Express **coaches** arrive three times daily from London Victoria. The coach station is on Warwick Road. There is also regular bus service from Bath, Oxford and Cheltenham. For bus information call ((0121) 622-4373.

OPPOSITE: A narrowboat works the River Avon. ABOVE: Wax tableaux bring Warwick Castle history to life.

WARWICK

WARWICKSHIRE — Distinguished by its mighty mediaeval castle, Warwick is a market town of about 20,000 inhabitants. As it's just a 20-minute drive from Stratford, you could easily include it in your visit to the area. Allow the better part of a day to explore the castle.

The area was first fortified in the late tenth century. In 1086, William I ordered the hill fort enlarged and a "motte-and-bailey" castle arose over the earthworks. The present structure dates mainly from the fourteenth and fifteenth centuries. In 1604 the castle was converted from a fortress into a dwelling.

There is a **Tourist Information Centre** ((01926) 492212 FAX (01926) 494837 in Jury Street.

Warwick's weekly **market** is held on Saturday at Market Place.

WHAT TO SEE AND DO

The Castle

The august towers and ramparts of Warwick Castle ((01926) 406600 rise dramatically between the town center and the River Avon. One of Britain's most visited tourist attractions, the castle is owned and operated by Madame Tussaud's, who know a thing or two about entertainment. The waxwork exhibitions are superb, even to the point of stealing the show at times from the marvelous old castle itself.

Inside the **Great Hall,** docents describe the scene as it was in the earliest days of the castle, when everyone ate and slept together on an earthen floor. Later the lords of the manor had drawing rooms added — a word derived from "withdrawing" — so that they might remove themselves from the muddy masses in the hall.

Throughout the rest of the castle there's little need for knowledgeable guides or even an ounce of imagination. In the fourteenth-century **Ghost Tower** with its spookily creaky door you'll find out how the castle's owner, Sir Fulke Greville, was murdered here in 1628 by a servant for stinting him in his will. The gripping **"Kingmaker"** exhibition is a series of waxwork tableaux complete with sounds and even the smells (fresh herbs, manure) of the era. It tells the story of Richard Neville, Earl of Warwick, an important figure in the War of the Roses. He imprisoned King Edward IV and helped restore Henry VI to the throne, thus earning his moniker, Kingmaker. Neville died fighting the deposed Edward's troops in 1471. At the **"Royal Weekend Party"** another series of tableaux shows the Victorians at play. The star of this exhibition is "Daisy," Countess of Warwick, famed hostess and beauty, who welcomed future kings and statesmen to her castle

home during the eighteenth century. The exhibition takes you through a series of 12 rooms of what were once private apartments.

Outside you can ramble around on the ramparts and descend the lofty towers and fortifications, or peer down from the drawbridge and portcullis to the "Killing Ground" and "Murder Holes" where unsuspecting invaders got their just desserts.

On the grounds you'll find a café as well as two restaurants and a picnic area. Special events take place throughout the year, including several exhilarating "jousting weekends" during the summer months. The castle is open daily year-round; admission fee.

Beyond the Wall

Beyond the castle walls, the town of Warwick has some notable buildings, such as the delightful timbered **Lord Leycester Hospital**, High Street, established in the fourteenth century as an old soldier's home, and **Market Hall** (1670). At Lord Leycester Hospital you can visit the regimental museum and garden. The **County Museum** ((01926) 412500, at Market Place, tells about Warwick's natural and human history (free admission).

WHERE TO STAY AND EAT

Across from the entrance to Warwick Castle, the **Tudor House** ((01926) 495447 FAX (01926) 492948, 90–92 West Street, Warwick CV34 6AW, is a 1472 inn with a black-and-white timbered façade. Suits of armor decorate the beamed interior. English and Continental cooking are served in the bar and dining room. The simply furnished bedrooms have private bath; moderate.

Brethren's Kitchen, in the Lord Leycester Hospital, High Street, is a relaxing place for an old-fashioned lunch or relaxing cup of tea.

HOW TO GET THERE

Warwick is 160 km (100 miles) northwest of London and 13 km (eight miles) northeast of Stratford-upon-Avon. **Trains** operate direct to Warwick from London Marylebone; Chiltern Railways ((08705) 165165 offers combined rail and castle entrance packages. National Express has **coach** services three times daily from London Victoria to Warwick, stopping at Puckerings Lane. The ride takes about three hours. There is hourly local bus service to Warwick from Stratford; schedules are available from the Stratford Tourist Information Centre. There are also numerous **coach tours** to Warwick from London with Evans Evans ((020) 7950-1777, Frames Rickards ((020) 7837-3111 and Golden Tours ((020) 7233-7030; and from Stratford with Guide Friday ((01789) 299866.

The River Avon skirts Warwick Castle.

South Cambridge- shire and Essex

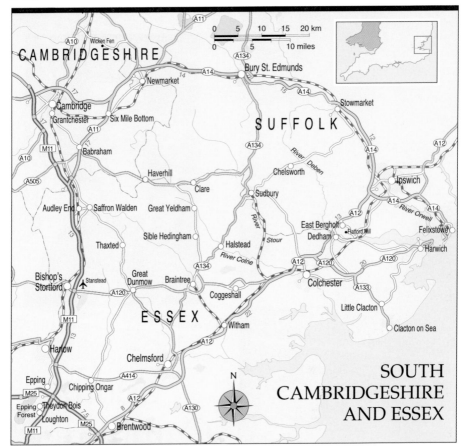

CAMBRIDGESHIRE

Wicken Fen
Newmarket
Bury St. Edmunds
Cambridge
Grantchester   Six Mile Bottom
Stowmarket
SUFFOLK
Babraham
River Deben
Haverhill   Chelsworth
Ipswich
Clare
Sudbury   River Orwell
Audley End   Saffron Walden   Great Yeldham
East Bergholt
Dedham   Flatford Mill   Felixstowe
Sible Hedingham
Thaxted   Halstead   Stour   Harwich
River Colne
Bishop's   Stansted   Great   Colchester
Stortford   Dunmow   Braintree
Little Clacton
Coggeshall
ESSEX   Witham   Clacton on Sea
Harlow
Chelmsford
Epping
Chipping Ongar
Epping   Theydon Bois
Forest   Loughton   Brentwood

N

SOUTH
CAMBRIDGESHIRE
AND ESSEX

THE UNIVERSITY TOWN OF CAMBRIDGE, LIKE OXFORD, has a wealth of splendid architecture and a lively cultural life. But Cambridge's lower status on the coach tour cavalcade makes it a better choice for independent travelers. Smaller crowds as well as lush green spaces make Cambridge one of the treasures of Southern England.

To the northeast of Cambridge, Ely's cathedral is a must-see. It's a short trip from Cambridge (24 km or 15 miles) through the stark beauty of the flat, low-lying, Cambridgeshire landscape. Here at Wicken Fen, and along the corrugated coast in neighboring Essex, there is great scope for birding.

Tourists don't exactly flock to Essex, which borders London to the south and extends along the North Sea at its eastern edge. Despite its proximity to the capital, much of the county is surprisingly rural and agricultural. In the northwest corner of the county, the small towns of Saffron Walden and Thaxted are rich in well-preserved mediaeval buildings.

Essex's Dedham Vale is "Constable Country" where the landscape painter John Constable painted some of his most memorable works. It's much-favored walking country. Cycling is easy in the low-country landscape of South Cambridgeshire and

Essex. Bob Shingleton's *Cycle East Anglia* (Sigma Leisure, 1999) is a handy guide detailing a number of routes. Finally, Essex has some of the best off-road cycling terrain in the country at Epping Forest.

CAMBRIDGE

CAMBRIDGESHIRE — Home to one of Britain's great universities, the city of Cambridge is a seductive blend of magnificent architecture, youthful energy and time-honored tradition. There are frequent reminders that this ancient university town was once chock-a-block with monks and priors, not only in the architecture but in intriguing place names like Jesus Green and Christ Pieces, just two of the town's many attractive green spaces.

Cambridge had its beginnings as a university in 1208, when student riots in Oxford prompted 100 scholars to move to Cambridge, where they established an academic community the following year. Like Oxford, the University of Cambridge is set up as a federation of colleges, the oldest being Peterhouse, founded in 1284. The population of Cambridge, 116,000, includes around 16,000 students.

Festivals in Cambridge celebrate university as well as local folk traditions. Trinity College Choir ((01223) 338400 sings from the college towers at noon and from lamp-lit punts at nightfall, one day in May each year. The third week in June brings the Cambridge Midsummer Fair. A week later the Grassroots Festival delivers new works to the Cambridge Drama Centre for a month. The Cambridge Folk Festival ((01223) 457000, at the end of July, is one of Europe's most important folk events.

GENERAL INFORMATION

The **Tourist Information Centre** ((01223) 322640 FAX (01223) 457588 is on Wheeler Street. Excel-

Tourist Information Centre for details. Don't miss a stroll through the Backs — the water meadows that border several of the colleges (see OUTDOOR ACTIVITIES, below).

Colleges
One of the six colleges bordering the Backs, **King's College** was founded in 1141 by Henry VIII. The iron-fisted monarch destroyed nearly one-quarter of the mediaeval town to begin construction of the college and, adding insult to injury, it stood empty for 300 years during the Wars of the Roses. When things got going again, the magnificent English Perpendicular **King's College Chapel** rose up. It was started in 1446 and took 90 years to complete. The

lent **walking tours** depart from here five times daily in summer. It's best to buy your ticket in advance as group size is limited. There are also **hop-on hop-off bus tours** operating daily year-round; fee charged. Details at the Tourist Information Centre.

Internet access is centrally located at the Internet Exchange, 2 St. Mary's Passage, off King's Parade.

WHAT TO SEE AND DO

Originally for the education of clerics, each of Cambridge's 31 colleges has the architectural ingredients of a monastery — a chapel, a library, a master's lodge, a dining hall and refectory and students' rooms. Many of the colleges are open to the public. Few charge admission. Opening hours vary from college to college; contact the

Flemish and Dutch Renaissance windows are the largest collection of sixteenth-century stained glass in the world. At the altar is Peter Paul Rubens's "Adoration of the Magi," painted in 1634. Most of the rest of the King's College was built in the mid-1800s to match the chapel.

More of Cambridge's 31 colleges spread their architectural tentacles throughout the center of town. Though it's the second-oldest of the colleges, the buildings of **Clare** date from the seventeenth century and are of classical Renaissance style. **Corpus Christi**, founded by the town merchants in 1352, has been restored and added to but maintains much of its original fourteenth-century appearance. Grandly impressive **Jesus** has a notable chapel with Norman portions and decorations by Augustus Pugin, William Morris and Edward

King's College Chapel, Cambridge.

Burne-Jones. Founded by Henry VIII in 1546, **Trinity** is the largest of the colleges, alma mater to Newton and Shakespeare. The Wren Library, built at the end of the seventeenth century, is open to the public from noon to 2 PM. See the dining hall here if you can; it's the largest and most richly decorated in the university. **St. John's** has the famous "Bridge of Sighs" (named after the original in Venice), best viewed from Kitchen Bridge. **Queen's** is noted for its half-timbered courtyard and elaborately painted hall.

More Points of Interest
The **Fitzwilliam Museum** ((01223) 332900, housed in an ornate classical structure on Trumpington

of fossils as well as objects collected by Charles Darwin on his adventures aboard the *Beagle*. Along the same street are the **Museum of Archaeology and Anthropology** and the **Museum of Zoology**. The **Museum of Classical Archaeology**, Tennis Court Road, has Greek and Roman sculpture; and the **Whipple Museum of Science**, Free School Lane, displays a fine assortment of antique scientific equipment.

Several churches merit exploration. The eleventh-century **St. Benet's Church**, Benet Street, with its square Saxon tower, is the oldest building in Cambridge. At the **Holy Sepulchre**, Bridge Street, a rare round church, you can do brass rubbings ((01223) 871621. **Great St. Mary's Church**, King's

Street, is one of England's oldest and most important public museums. Its eclectic collections take in Egyptian, Greek and Roman antiquities; mediaeval works; and drawings, paintings and sculpture representing every artistic school, including masterpieces by Titian, Veronese, Rubens, Van Dyck, Hals, Gainsborough, Constable, Monet, Degas, Renoir, Cézanne and Picasso. In short, it's breathtaking. Closed Monday; free. There are **guided tours** (fee charged) Sunday at 2:30 PM.

The 16-hectare (40-acre) **University Botanic Garden** ((01223) 336265, Bateman Street, is an agreeable spot for a walk. As well as stands of adult trees, there are several theme areas including a rock garden, a water garden, and winter garden as well as scores of rare plants. Open weekdays. Other university museums take in a range of academic interests. The **Sedgwick Geology Museum**, Downing Street, has a great collection

Parade, is a fifteenth-century university church in the Perpendicular style where it's possible to climb the tower (admission fee) for a view of the city. Across from the church is the gracefully classical **Senate House** where graduation ceremonies are held.

Set in a sixteenth-century former inn, the **Cambridge & County Folk Museum** ((01223) 355159, 2–3 Castle Street, takes a fascinating look at local life and customs. Open daily from April to September with reduced hours other months; admission fee.

Kettle's Yard ((01233) 352124, Castle Street, is a superb avant-garde arts center and gallery, with permanent displays in the adjoining house, once the home of an assistant keeper at the Tate Gallery. The house contains his early twentieth-century art collection donated to the university along with the adjoining gallery in 1966. Closed mornings and all day Monday; free.

Outdoor Activities

Part of the Cambridge experience is **punting**, along the Backs. If you like you can go as far as the delightful village of Grantchester, where the Orchard Tea Gardens makes a nice break. There are also several pubs here. Rent punts from Scudamores ((01223) 359750, Mill Lane; or other stations along the water.

The **Backs** is a swath of parkland and water meadow adjoining "the backs" of seven of the colleges. The River Cam flows here crossed by a series of unique bridges which connect this wild green space with the crew-cut lawns of the college yards. The most famous of these bridges

Shopping

Cambridge is a great place to shop for **clothing** and accessories, whether you're looking for charity shop hand-me-downs or one-of-a-kind fashions. For previously owned stuff, head for the pedestrian-only area leading up to the Grafton Shopping Centre just east of Christ's Pieces. There are upscale and down-market boutiques throughout the town center.

Not surprisingly in this university town, there are dozens of **bookstores** (27 at last count). In the center are the chains, Heffers on Trinity Street and Waterstones on Bridge Street. Heffers has a broader

is the Mathematical Bridge at Queen's College, a wooden construction that's said to have been built without and bolts are fasteners.

The river towpaths are ideal for **walking and cycling**. Follow the River Cam to Grantchester, just under five kilometers (three miles) south of the city. Ambitious walkers can go as far as Ely (27.5 km or 17 miles) along the Fen Rivers Way; the Tourist Information Centre sells a map of the way. The Gog Magog Hills just outside town are also popular for walking. The Tourist Information Centre stocks booklets and brochures on area walks. Ask, for example, about *Walks in South Cambridgeshire*.

Rent cycles at Geoff's Bike Hire ((01223) 365629, 65 Devonshire Road, located next to the Youth Hostel (see WHERE TO STAY, below) and convenient to the railway station. They also offer **guided cycle tours** in town and country. Open daily except Sundays from October to March.

selection, but Waterstones has the added attraction of a coffee bar. Cambridge University Press has a vast bookstore opposite the Senate House, on King's Parade. Second-hand books are found, among other places, at Browne's, on Mill Road.

Ryder and Ames, in King's Parade, is the **university store**, selling scarves, T-shirts, sweats, cuff links and more, emblazoned with college insignia.

The **high street shops** are mostly along the pedestrian-only Sidney Street, which changes names several times.

Where to Stay

The best lodging in Cambridge is found along the river. Within easy walking distance of the center, **Cambridge Garden House** ((01223) 363421

OPPOSITE: Cambridge's open-air market.
ABOVE: Punting on the River Cam.

FAX (01223) 300483 E-MAIL revgh@queensmoat.co.uk, Granta Place, Mill Lane, Cambridge CB2 1RT, is a thoroughly modern hotel that takes full advantage of its tranquil setting. Not all of the well-appointed bedrooms (some recently refurbished) have river views, but the bar, lounge and stylish restaurant (moderate) do; very expensive (rate does not include breakfast; special breaks available). If you need a break from a grueling round of sightseeing, head for the hotel's indoor heated swimming pool, sauna, solarium, gymnasium or Jacuzzi.

Much less expensive, but out of the center, **Arundel House** ((01223) 367701 FAX (01223) 367721, 53 Chesterton Road, Cambridge CB4 3AN, also has a prime situation overlooking the River Cam and surrounding parkland with well-equipped bedrooms, six with shared bath; moderate (includes continental breakfast). Public areas give you a wealth of choices. Have a snack in the conservatory, a drink in the smart bar, or dinner in the gracious **restaurant** (moderate) where there is garden seating in fine weather.

Closer to the center, **Lensfield Hotel** ((01223) 355017 FAX (01223) 312022, 53 Lensfield Road, Cambridge CB2 1EN, is a small, family-run hotel done up in a sea of valances and ruffles. Rooms are small (baths very small), but thoughtfully decorated. Staff is friendly and obliging; moderate. A spiral staircase leads to a cellar restaurant (moderate) and cozy lounge with curved banquettes.

For inexpensive accommodation there is **Number 136** (/FAX (01223) 461142, 136 Huntingdon Road, Cambridge CB3 0HL; **Belle Vue Guest House** ((01223) 351859, 33 Chesterton Road, Cambridge CB4 3AN; and **Fairways Guest House** ((01223) 246063 FAX (01223) 212093, 143 Cherry Hinton Road, Cambridge CB1 4BX.

Cambridge Youth Hostel ((01223) 354601 FAX (01223) 312780 E-MAIL cambridge@yha.org.uk, 97 Tenison Road, Cambridge CB1 2DN, is located a 15-minute walk from the center of town and a few minutes from the train station. There is 24-hour access; rock-bottom.

WHERE TO EAT

You must book several weeks in advance for the popular **Midsummer House** ((01223) 369299, Midsummer Common. This sophisticated French-Mediterranean restaurant has an upper dining room where in summer you can watch the punts float by on the River Cam; expensive. Closed Monday, Saturday lunch and Sunday dinner.

No. 1 King's Parade ((01223) 359506, The Cellars, 1 King's Parade, is situated in a 350-year-old vaulted cellar. Candlelit dinners feature Scottish fare such as whiskey cured-salmon gravlax; moderate.

In a whitewashed cottage across from Peterhouse College, **Loch Fyne Oyster Bar** ((01223) 362433, 37 Trumpington Street, offers daily fish specials including nicely done salmon and trout, served in the attractive dining room with rough pine walls and log fire; expensive to moderate. The adjoining shop sells smoked and fresh fish.

Dojo ((01223) 363471, 1–2 Millers Yard, is a noodle bar promising "noodlessence." If that means delicious, large, steaming bowls served quickly in the small bright space, they deliver. Flavors span the East from Japan to China, Vietnam and Thailand. Lunch and dinner are served; inexpensive.

Also inexpensive, **Clowns** ((01223) 355711 or (01223) 460453, 54 King Street, is a hole-in-the-wall serving food all day, including a wide choice of casseroles. It's a popular student hang-out where the walls are decked with clown pictures. **Rainbow Vegetarian Café** ((01223) 321551, 9A Kings Parade, has decent eats such as Latvian potato bake and a variety of homemade soups, served in a brightly painted cellar.

Hot beverages are the province of **Grinders** ((01223) 301689, Lion Yard, which makes good coffee any way you want it without the Starbucks storm-trooper attitude. This is a good place to check out local happenings at the bulletin board.

The **Eagle** ((01223) 505020, Benet Street, is a sixteenth-century pub decorated with World War II memorabilia, left here by United States airmen who frequented the pub during the war. The food's cheap and good and there's a studious atmosphere. The **Anchor** ((01223) 353554, Silver Street, has waterside tables just below Scudamore's and the weir. The **Mill** ((01223) 357026, Mill Lane, is a pretty, old pub with food service, overlooking the water.

NIGHTLIFE

For a list of what's happening, look for *Ad Hoc* ((01223) 568960, a weekly entertainment guide for Cambridge and region.

Concerts at **King's College Chapel** ((01223) 331232, King's Parade, are always inspirational. The world-renowned choir performs evensong Tuesday to Saturday at 5:30 PM and at 3.30 PM on Sunday during term time, and on 24 and 25 December.

Among the clubs and bars hosting live music, the **Corn Exchange** ((01223) 357851, Wheeler Street, is the place for headliners. **Boat Race** ((01223) 508533, 170 East Road, does blues, retro rock, and folk music. If you just want some space to gyrate, there are DJs at **Po Na Na** ((01223) 323880, 7B Jesus Lane; **Fez** ((01223) 519224, 15 Market Passage; and **Kambar** ((01223) 357503, 1 Wheeler Street. Wednesday and Friday at Kambar you can take a salsa lesson and dance the rest of the night to Latin grooves. For jazz, check what's playing at the **Elm Tree** ((01223) 363005,

42 Orchard Street; and **La Mimosa (** (01223) 362525, 4 Rose Crescent (cellar).

There is university and amateur theater at the **ADC Theatre (** (01223) 359547, Park Street (off Sidney and Bridge Street); and opera, concerts and drama (average entry £8) at the **Cambridge Arts Theatre (** (01223) 503333, 6 St. Edward's Passage.

How to Get There

Cambridge is 97 km (60 miles) north of London. There is frequent **train** service throughout the day from London Liverpool Street and King's Cross stations. The trip takes 50 minutes. National Express has hourly **coach** service to the bus station

The **Tourist Information Centre (** (01353) 662062 FAX (01353) 668518 occupies the front rooms of **Oliver Cromwell's House**, 29 St. Mary's Street. The fourteenth-century half-timbered building was Cromwell's home from 1636–1646 when he was the local tithe collector. It's possible to view an audiovisual presentation and tour the house. Closed Sunday in winter; admission fee.

Ely Cathedral ((01353) 667735 was founded by Etheldreda, a queen of Northumbria who turned away from the court (and her second husband) to become a nun. After her death and canonization the abbey became a pilgrimage site, eventually prompting the construction of the cathedral, which was completed in 1189, a fine

on Drummer Street (along Christ's Pieces) from London Victoria. It's a ride of about two hours.

ELY

This sudden high hill crowned with its towered cathedral seen above the white mist of late summer is one of the most beautiful things in the whole of England. It is a spellbound hill....

— H. V. Morton, *In Search of England*

CAMBRIDGESHIRE — Perched above the River Ouse on a rise that once formed "Eel Island," Ely (pronounced *ee*-lee) is a lively market town. Until the fens were drained in the seventeenth and eighteenth centuries, it was accessible only by boat or causeways. Though the city itself is not extraordinary, the cathedral, founded in 673 by Saint Etheldreda, is a must-see.

example of Norman Romanesque architecture. When the central tower collapsed in the fourteenth century, Alan of Walsingham, one of the great architects of the Middle Ages, built the octagonal tower and lantern for which the cathedral is famous. The 164-m-long (537-ft) nave with its rows of Norman columns is one of the longest in England. The Lady Chapel, added in the fourteenth century, is the largest in the country. There is a **stained glass museum** (admission fee charged) in the triforium, and **guided tours** of the cathedral as well as a separate tour of the octagon and roof. Open daily; admission fee.

Between Cambridge and Ely, **Wicken Fen National Nature Reserve** (NT) **(** (01353) 720274 WEB SITE www.wicken.org, Lode Lane, Wicken, is the country's oldest nature preserve and one of the

Ely was once accessible only by boat.

area's last remaining wetlands, a haven for water-fowl. A boardwalk nature trail leads to several hides. There's a visitor center here with information on the natural history of the area. Open daily dawn to dusk; admission fee. Visitor center open weekdays only.

WHERE TO STAY AND EAT

If you decide to lodge in Ely, you might try the **Lamb Hotel** ((01353) 663574 FAX (01353) 662023, 2 Lynn Road, Ely CB7 4EJ, is a fifteenth-century former coaching inn near the cathedral with two bars and a restaurant (expensive) serving Modern British fare. Some of the bedrooms have four-poster beds; expensive (special breaks available).

There is a comfortable B&B at **Hill House Farm** ((01353) 778369, 9 Main Street, Coveney, Ely CB6 2DJ, five kilometers (three miles) west of Ely. On this 96-hectare (240-acre) working farm, the Victorian house has three rooms with views of the surrounding fenlands; inexpensive.

The **Old Fire Engine House** ((01353) 663582, 25 St. Mary's Street, across from St. Mary's Church, dishes up very good food in a casual, comfortable atmosphere; moderate.

For snacks and light meals there is the **cathedral refectory**.

HOW TO GET THERE

Ely is 113 km (70 miles) northeast of London and 24 km (15 miles) northeast of Cambridge. There is an express **train** service from Cambridge as well as frequent direct trains to Ely from London's Liverpool Street and Kings Cross stations. There are frequent local **buses** between Cambridge and Ely.

EPPING FOREST

ESSEX — In the northeast corner of Greater London, just 20 km (12 miles) from Marble Arch, Epping Forest is a rare surviving 2,400-hectare (6,000-acre) wedge of old forest. Famous for its coppices of 400-year-old oaks and beeches, the forest is also a popular place for outdoor activities from cycling to horse riding (there are several stables in the area), fishing and walking. **Tourist Information** is available form the Epping Forest District Council ((01992) 564000, or at the **Visitor Information Centre** ((020) 8508-0028, High Beech, in Loughton.

Off-road cycling daredevils love Epping Forest for its obstacle-laden trails. Every Sunday at 9 AM groups of mountain bikers depart from Heales Cycles ((020) 8527-1592, 477 Hale End Road, London E4, for a wild ride in the forest. Riders of all ability levels are welcome to join them. If you're going it alone, contact Heales for trail maps and rentals.

Walkers can set out in any direction on the extensive trail network. If you're concerned about getting lost, take the well-signposted Forest Way.

At Chingford, **Queen Elizabeth's Hunting Lodge**, Rangers Road, is a renovated, timbered sixteenth-century building with an exhibition on its own history (Elizabeth I, an avid hunter, often used the lodge) and that of the forest.

Inexpensive **B&B** in the area is kindly offered by Mrs. Bayliss ((01992) 575424 and Mrs. Stacey ((01992) 573733. There is also the **Epping Forest Youth Hostel** (/FAX (020) 8508-5161, Wellington Hall, High Beach, Loughton, Essex IG10 4AG, self-catering only; rock-bottom.

Epping Forest is 20 km (12 miles) from the heart of London. Mainline **trains** run from Liverpool Street station to Chingford, or you can take the **tube** to Θ Theydon Bois or Θ Loughton.

COLCHESTER

ESSEX — Britain's oldest recorded town, Colchester was Roman Britain's original administrative center before London grabbed the spotlight. Besides its longevity, Colchester is also renowned for its oysters and roses. Situated on the River Coln, Colchester has a number of historical buildings, some ancient remains of interest, and a sprinkling of charming local museums. The **Tourist Information Centre** ((01206) 282920 FAX (01206) 282924 is at 1 Queen Street. Guided **walking tours** give a good overview of Colchester's rich history; from June to September daily at 2 PM, 11 PM on Sunday (fee charged).

There is **Internet** access at Webs Netcafé, 2A Queen Street.

Market days are Friday and Saturday in Pelhams Lane.

WHAT TO SEE AND DO

After Boudicca and her armies burned Roman Colchester in AD 60, a three-meter-thick, nine-meter-high (10-ft by 33-ft) wall was thrown up

ABOVE: An ancient beech in Epping Forest.
RIGHT: Ely's famous tower.

round the city to protect it from further attacks by marauding Iceni. Parts of these **Roman walls and gates** remain, best seen at Balkerne Way and Priory Street.

More traces of Rome can be found at **Colchester Castle** ((01206) 282931. Twice the size of the Tower of London, it is the largest and oldest Norman keep still standing in England. The castle was built in 1076 on the foundations of a Roman temple using stones and tiles from surrounding Roman buildings. A collection of Roman-British artifacts can be viewed in the museum, which also has exhibitions relating the history of the town from its earliest days through to the Civil War. Open daily from March to November; Monday to Saturday from December to February; admission fee.

West of the castle, and just north of High Street, the steep lanes of the **Dutch Quarter** still have some of the original tall houses built by in the sixteenth century by Protestant refugees from Holland.

On High Street, the delightful **Hollytrees Museum** ((01206) 282931, features antique toys and costumes; and the **Natural History Museum** (same phone), takes a look at local flora and fauna. Nearby on Trinity Street, in a fifteenth-century half-timbered mansion, **Tymperleys** ((01206) 282943 ticks and tocks in a celebration of the craft of clock-making. Outside is a formal Tudor garden. Open Tuesday to Saturday from April to October; free.

One and a half kilometers (a mile) south of the town center, **Bourne Mill** (NT) ((01206) 572422, Bourne Road, was built as a fishing lodge in the sixteenth century and later converted into a mill. The machinery is still in tact and the large mill pond makes a tranquil setting for a stroll. Open Tuesday to Sunday afternoons in July and August; admission fee.

In the small town of **Coggeshall**, about 11 km (seven miles) west of Colchester, there are antique shops to explore as well as several points of interest. **Coggeshall Grange Barn** (NT) ((01376) 562226, just under a kilometer (about half a mile) from the town center, is Europe's oldest standing timber-framed barn. Built in the twelfth century and restored in the 1980s, the barn houses a collection of farm conveyances. Open Tuesday, Thursday, and Sunday from April to October; admission fee. The Essex Way, a long-distance footpath passes by here.

Another National Trust property in Coggeshall, **Paycocke's** (NT) ((01376) 561305, West Street, is an extraordinarily well-preserved sixteenth-century wool merchant's house with intricate wood paneling and carving. There's a display of Coggeshall lace in the house, and a cottage garden. Same opening hours as the Grange Barn, for which it is possible to purchase a joint ticket. Coggeshall's **market** day is Thursday.

OUTDOOR ACTIVITIES

Ask for "Colchester's Countryside" brochure at the Tourist Information Centre. It details **walks** and events in the city and surrounding country parks. There are beautiful walks at Marks Hall Estate & Arboretum, a five-minute drive from Coggeshall.

Rent **bicycles** at Anglian Cycle Hire ((01206) 563377, Unit 7, Peartree Road. Reserve in advance.

WHERE TO STAY

The fifteenth-century **White Hart Hotel** ((01376) 561654 FAX (01376) 561789, Market End, Coggeshall CO6 1NH, still has some of its original brick, stone and timber work. There are 18 well-appointed bedrooms, each with bath; expensive. The restaurant serves international cuisine. Meals are also served in the beamed bar.

The centrally located **George Hotel** ((01206) 578494 FAX (01206) 761732, 116 High Street, Colchester CO1 1JD, is a fifteenth-century former coaching inn with individually decorated bedrooms. The restaurant (moderate) has a wide-ranging menu, and light meals are served in the lounge; inexpensive to expensive.

Occupying a Georgian building three kilometers (two miles) from the North train station is the seasonal **Colchester Youth Hostel** ((01206) 867982 FAX (01206) 868628, East Bay House, 18 East Bay, Colchester CO1 2UE; rock-bottom.

WHERE TO EAT

Baumann's Brasserie ((01376) 561453, 4-6 Stoneham Street in Coggeshall, is a lively place to enjoy Modern British fare, including daily fish specials and light lunches; moderate.

In Colchester, another winning brasserie is the **Warehouse** ((01206) 765656, 12 Chapel Street North, which uses organic produce when cooking up their delightful meals. The atmosphere is friendly and the wine list interesting; moderate.

For economical eats you might try the **Siege House** ((01206) 867121, 75 East Street, serving kebabs and pasta; or **Toto's** ((01206) 762000, 5-7 Museum Street, for pizza.

HOW TO GET THERE

Colchester is 97 km (60 miles) from London. The London–Ipswich **train** (departing London Liverpool Street) stops at Colchester North station, just under a kilometer (about a half mile) north of town. There is also train service to Colchester from Cambridge (14 per day; 90 minutes). **Coach** service runs from London Victoria (three per day; 90 minutes), as well as Cambridge (two per day;

90 minutes). The bus station is in the center of town near the Tourist Information Centre.

THE DEDHAM VALE

ESSEX — On the Suffolk–Essex border, the Dedham Vale is classic English farming country divided by hedgerows and wildflower meadows and watered by the slow-moving River Stour. This is the land of pastoral scenes made famous through the works of one of England's great landscape painters, John Constable, born here in 1776. Despite the summer invasion of visitors to this part of "Constable Country," the area is still relatively unspoiled, with quiet lanes and many timber-framed or thatched houses.

Art and Craft Centre, High Street, exhibits local handiwork, and there are stained glass and candle-making studios on site.

WHERE TO STAY AND EAT

There is luxury accommodation in Dedham at **Maison Talbooth** ((01206) 322367 FAX (01206) 322752 E-MAIL mtrecception@talbooth.co.uk, Stratford Road, Dedham CO7 6HN, a small, attractive, Georgian hotel. Afternoon tea is served in the drawing room. Breakfast is brought to your room; very expensive. The hotel offers guests transportation to their restaurant, **Le Talbooth Restaurant** ((01206) 323150, where Mod Brit fare

The sixteenth-century **Bridge Cottage** (NT) ((01206) 298260, at Flatford, has an exhibition of Constable's work. He depicted the cottage in several of his paintings. There is a tea garden here as well as an information center and boat rentals. This is an ideal spot to kick off a **walk** across pretty National Trust property; ask the staff at the cottage for routes. Other places associated with Constable, such as **Flatford Mill** (a reconstruction), **Valley Farm**, and **Willy Lott's House** (made famous in Constable's *Haywain*) are operated by the Field Studies Council ((01206) 298260, which sponsors art courses and arranges tours of the properties for groups.

From Flatford there is a riverside footpath to beautiful **Dedham** village at the head of the vale. There are some fine old buildings here, especially the fifteenth-century pinnacled **Church of St. Mary**, which appears in many Constable paintings. The

is served in the pleasant, beamed dining room with views of the river. Closed Sunday dinner during the winter; expensive.

The **Shepherd & Dog** ((01206) 272711, Moor Road, Langham, just west of Dedham, is a well-patronized village pub with daily blackboard specials including fish, steaks, savory pies and curries. An open fire warms the pub in winters and the garden is open for dining in fine weather; inexpensive.

HOW TO GET THERE

Several companies operate **bus** services from Colchester to East Bergholt, one and a half kilometers (about a mile) from Flatford.

The country's oldest recorded town, Colchester was Roman Britain's original capital before London captured the title.

HARWICH

ESSEX — The rivers Orwell and Stour converge and empty into the North Sea at Harwich. This town of 15,000 inhabitants is notable mainly as a transit point for travelers going to and from Northern Europe. The **Tourist Information Centre** ((01255) 506139 is at Parkeston Quay. For **B&B** handy to the ferry terminal there is **Una House** (/FAX (01255) 551390, part of a Victorian terrace with three rooms; inexpensive. There are express **train** services from London Liverpool Street to Harwich, a trip of just over an hour. For **ferry** services see GETTING AROUND, page 325 in TRAVELERS' TIPS.

SAFFRON WALDEN AND THAXTED

ESSEX — In the northwest corner of Essex, Saffron Walden and Thaxted are the county's most attractive and engaging small towns. Outdistancing either of these beauty spots in popularity is the famous stately mansion, Audley End, not far from Saffron Walden.

Look for the **Tourist Information Centre** ((01799) 510444 FAX (01799) 510445 in Market Square, Saffron Walden. In Thaxted, stop by the Cottage, Clarance House, Watling Street, open Thursday to Sunday.

Named after the saffron plants that were once cultivated here, Saffron Walden has many fine half-timbered and color-washed buildings and antiques shops. On the common is England's largest surviving **turf maze**, with a one-and-a-half-kilometer (mile-long) pathway. The **church**, one of the county's largest, is quite grand. Throughout the town, look for the elaborate "pargeting" (carved plasterwork) for which Saffron Walden is noted.

Situated about eight kilometers (five miles) southeast of Saffron Walden on the B184, Thaxted developed during the fifteenth century as a center of trade. The Guildhall dates from 1400, and there are a number of half-timbered houses also of ancient vintage. The **church** dates from the fourteenth century and has a lofty, 55-m (180-ft) spire. One of Thaxted's famous views is the row of eighteenth-century **almshouses** in the churchyard, topped with "gingerbread" and thatch. There is a **museum of rural life** at the early-nineteenth-century working windmill. Open weekends from Easter to September; admission fee. **Morris dancers** perform at the Swan Hotel (below) throughout the year.

One and a half kilometers (one mile) west of Saffron Walden is the great Jacobean estate, **Audley End House and Gardens** (EH) ((01799) 522399. Built by the first Earl of Suffolk and Lord Treasurer Thomas Howard in 1614, it was at the time the largest house in England. Howard's pluck in building such a palace prompted James I to quip that

the house was too big for a king but not for a Lord Treasurer. The turning of the eighteenth century, however, saw the building considerably diminished when the family had about two-thirds of it demolished to make it more manageable. In the 1760s Robert Adams created the interiors. The rooms, containing an exceptional collection of paintings, have been meticulously restored to Adams' original designs. Also in the eighteenth century, Capability Brown landscaped the great park. Open Wednesday to Sunday, in October for guided tours only (admission fees are charged for the house only or for the house and grounds). Audley End **railway** station is one and a half kilometers (just over a mile) from the house.

WHERE TO STAY AND EAT

The **Swan Hotel** ((01371) 830321 FAX (01371) 831186, The Bull Ring, Thaxted CM6 2PL, is an old coaching inn set amongst the Tudor houses of Thaxted village. The bar, which serves meals, has an open fire, and the restaurant features local produce. There are 21 bedrooms, all with bath; moderate.

One and a half kilometers (a mile) north of Saffron Walden, **Rowley Hill Lodge** ((01799) 525975 FAX (01799) 516622 E-MAIL eh@clara.net Little Walden, Saffron Walden CB10 1UZ, is a welcoming 1830s guest house with two comfortably furnished bedrooms and restful views; high end of inexpensive price range.

Rockells Farm ((01763) 838053 FAX (01763) 837001, Duddenhoe End, Saffron Walden CB11 4UY, offers B&B in a Georgian farmhouse set on an working farm with garden and large fishing lake, as well as footpaths for exploring the farm. All rooms have bath; inexpensive.

The **Saffron Walden Youth Hostel** ((01799) 523117 FAX (01799) 520840, 1 Myddylton Place, Saffron Walden CB10 1BB, is in the town center in a 600-year-old oak-beamed malt house; rock-bottom.

HOW TO GET THERE

Saffron Walden is 73 km (45 miles) north of London. The nearest **train** station is at Audley End, four kilometers (two and a half miles) from town. The closest railway station to Thaxted is at Bishop's Stortford. Biss Brothers Coaches ((01279) 681155 operates **bus** services between Cambridge and London via Saffron Walden.

TOP: Audley End House, built in 1614, was once the largest house in England. The park was designed in the eighteenth century by Capability Brown. BOTTOM: Half-timbered buildings line the streets of Thaxted.

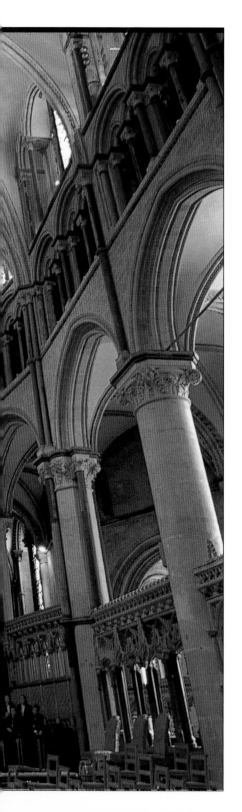

Kent
and
Sussex

CANTERBURY
GENERAL INFORMATION

THOUGH THE MOST DENSELY POPULATED PART OF England, the counties of Kent and Sussex retain great tracts of picturesque countryside and extensive stretches of interesting coastline. Along that famous shore, Kent boasts one of the country's seminal landmarks, the White Cliffs of Dover, which rise along the channel coast at England's closest point to mainland Europe. While not many people come to Southern England to work on their tan, it's fun to join the Brits-at-the-beach, and the best place to do this is at Brighton, which makes up for its pebbly seashore with unrestrained charm and a robust cultural life.

While Kent and Sussex have miles of shoreline, the greatest appeal of England's southeast is the interior touring country of the weald and downland. Once heavily forested, today the weald is a fertile, prosperous land of green fields and hop farms, where stately homes, regal castles and sumptuous gardens offer a lifetime of exploration. Along Kent's North Downs, Canterbury has evolved from a mediaeval pilgrimage center to a twenty-first-century tourist mecca with its World Heritage Site and Continental flavor. In Sussex, Rye is another of the region's historical jewels, its streets lined with ancient buildings and antiques shops.

Kent and Sussex are excellent walking country, perfect for gentle lowland rambles. There are thousands of miles of public rights of way and hundreds of miles of recreational routes in the southeast, including national trails such as the North Downs Way. Other long-distance footpaths are the 133-km (82-mile) Wealdway, from Gravesend to Eastbourne, crossing open heath, downland and river valley; the 264-km (163-mile) Saxon Shore Way, which follows the original ancient shoreline (now well inland in places) through Kent and East Sussex; and the recently opened 146-km (90-mile) High Weald Landscape Trail, traversing hop farms, woodlands, orchards and villages of Kent. Footpaths in the southeast are generally easily accessible and well-signed.

Finally, any visitor to the Southeast interested in combining a trip to France or Belgium will be pleased to know that Paris is a mere two hours by train from Ashford, Kent, and Brussels is less than that.

CANTERBURY

EAST KENT — A Continental atmosphere pervades the ancient pilgrimage city of Canterbury. A pedestrian-only old town, its cobbled alleyways are full of sidewalk cafés and it's as easy to find crêpes as it is fish & chips. One of England's most important tourist destinations, Canterbury gets very crowded and is therefore best visited off season.

At first glance Canterbury's lively streets resemble a carnival, but with patience you'll discover a city of culture. There are a good number of bookstores, many of them hosting author events.

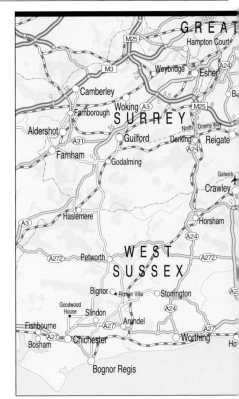

A wide variety of museums offer something for every interest. Canterbury's main drawcard, of course, is the Norman-style cathedral, seat of the heads of the Church of England since the time of Saint Augustine.

It was AD 597 when Saint Augustine arrived in Canterbury, sent by the Pope to convert the Anglo-Saxons to Christianity. Soon after the founding of the abbey at Canterbury, the town became the country's major ecclesiastical center, and in 1077 the Norman Archbishop Lanfranc ordered the construction of a new cathedral, built on the ruins of the old Anglo-Saxon edifice. The twelfth-century murder of Archbishop Thomas Becket in the cathedral set off a centuries-long trail of pilgrims and later inspired Chaucer's *Canterbury Tales*.

GENERAL INFORMATION

The **Tourist Information Centre (** (01227) 766567 or (01227) 451026 (lodging) FAX (01227) 459840 is located at 34 St. Margaret's Street. **Guided walks** depart from the center, Monday to Saturday at 11:30 AM and 2 PM in summer; winter at 2 PM only. There are also "ghostly tours" **(** (07976) 915643 on Friday and Saturday nights at 8 PM starting from Cleary's Irish Bar, St. Margaret's Street; fee charged.

There is **Internet access** at Methven's bookstore, 28 High Street. **Market day** is Wednesday.

192
Kent and Sussex

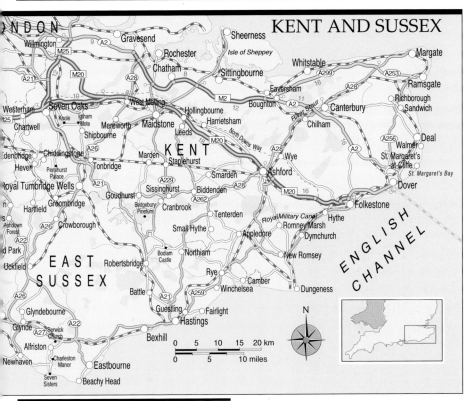

KENT AND SUSSEX

WHAT TO SEE AND DO

The old city has some fine buildings, most notably on Palace Street, Burgate, Buttermarket Square, and St. Peter's Street. Take a stroll along these ancient ways before heading for the main attractions.

Britain's most important Christian landmark, **Canterbury Cathedral** is a World Heritage Site (along with St. Augustine's Abbey and St. Martin's Church, below). This complete Norman cathedral has a treasure house of stories, ably told by cathedral guides. The most famous tale is that of the martyrdom of Thomas Becket, Archbishop of Canterbury who was murdered in the cathedral in 1170 by the knights of Henry II as a result of a struggle between church and king for control of the country. Following Becket's canonization in 1173, Canterbury became one of Europe's most important places of pilgrimage, immortalized in Geoffrey Chaucer's (*circa* 1345–1400) *Canterbury Tales*, a collection of ribald stories told by a group of pilgrims traveling from London to Canterbury.

There has been a cathedral on this site since the sixth century. The present structure dates from 1100, when it was rebuilt in Norman style after a fire. The elaborately decorated choir was rebuilt in 1174, again after a fire, and was the first

major construction in what was later to be called Gothic style. More additions ensued until the reformation, when the shrine of St. Thomas was destroyed. On the south side of Trinity Chapel, look for the tomb and achievements of the Black Prince, Edward Prince of Wales. In the Romanesque crypt, the Chapel of Saint Gabriel is not to be missed. Two-meter-thick (seven-foot) walls here are covered in beautiful murals, and supporting the ceiling are Saxon stone columns carved with fantastical creatures.

After the cathedral closes, the precincts remain open until 9 PM. Since large groups are banned during this period, the area subsides into tranquillity. The cathedral is closed to visitors on Sunday.

Just under one kilometer (about a half mile) outside the city walls to the east, are the ruins of **St. Augustine's Abbey** (EH) ((01850) 293822, Longport, marking the birthplace of Christianity in Britain, where St. Augustine founded his sixth-century abbey. St. Augustine is buried here. There is a new museum and free audio tour. Open daily, year-round; admission fee. Adjacent to the ruins, **St. Martin's Church**, on North Holmes Road, is Britain's oldest church in continual use. It was originally established by Christian Romans and Roman brickwork can still be found in the walls. The chancel and nave date to the late sixth century.

Museums

Canterbury has several worthwhile museums. Chief among them is the **Canterbury Heritage Museum** ((01227) 452747, Stour Street, set in a fine mediaeval building with a marvelous oak roof. The museum tells the 2,000-year story of the city from the Roman era up to the present day. Closed Sunday from November to May; admission fee. Delve further into ancient history at the **Canterbury Roman Museum** ((01227) 785575, Butchery Lane, an underground museum constructed within the remains of a Roman townhouse. It's conceived as an "archaeological quest" and there are lots of hands-on activities. Closed Sunday except June to October; admission fee. The **Royal Museum and Art Gallery**

fee. The **Chaucer Centre** on St. Peter's Street also has a good shop and occasional exhibits.

OUTDOOR ACTIVITIES

You can **cycle** into the North Downs from Canterbury if you don't mind some steep climbs. Routes through Kent are described in *Kent for Cycling*, a free brochure produced by the Kent County Council ((0345) 696996. Rent bicycles at **Downland Cycles** ((01227) 479643, Canterbury West Station. The same company organizes self-guided cycle tours ((01303) 844289 E-MAIL paul @downland-cycles.freeserve.co.uk, with route maps and accommodation, and baggage transfer.

((01227) 452747, High Street, houses more Roman remains discovered when digging foundations for a shopping center. Also featured are decorative arts and temporary art exhibitions. Closed Sunday except in July and August; admission fee.

At **West Gate & Museum** ((01227) 452747, St. Peter's Street at St. Dunstan's Street, which houses a collection of Civil War armory, children can do brass rubbing or try on replica armor. There are good views of the city from the gate house. Closed 12:30 PM to 1:30 PM and all day Sunday; admission fee.

Finally, a back-to-the-fourteenth-century journey is in store at the **Canterbury Tales** ((01227) 454888, St. Margaret's Street. This "mediaeval adventure" takes you into the midst of Chaucer's world, bringing to life five of his amusing tales. There is a shop here and evening ghost tours (phone for information). Open daily year-round; entrance

Starting at Farnham, the **North Downs Way** passes through Canterbury on its way from the Surrey Hills to the Kent Coast. Part of the route traces the ancient Pilgrims' Way, which took mediaeval travelers to Canterbury. The **Stour Valley Walk** follows the meandering river through the Kent countryside for 83 km (51 miles) passing through Canterbury and ending at Pegwell Bay, just north of Sandwich.

The Canterbury River Navigation Company ((01227) 762466, Westgate Bridge Steps, St. Dunstan's Street, offers **punt trips** along the River Stour from May to September between 10 AM to 6 PM.

WHERE TO STAY

Canterbury hotels and guest houses are numerous. Still, you should book well ahead in summer months, even for the youth hostel.

A late Georgian terrace with seven well-appointed bedrooms with baths, **Magnolia House** (/FAX (01227) 765121 E-MAIL magnolia_house _canterbury@yahoo.com, 36 St. Dunstan's Terrace, Canterbury CT2 8AX, has a walled garden and is only a 10-minute walk from the center; moderate to expensive.

Atmospheric and convenient, the **Cathedral Gate Hotel** ((01227) 464381 FAX (01227) 462800 E-MAIL cgate@cgate.demon.co.uk, 36 Burgate, Canterbury CT1 3RY, is an ancient pilgrims' hostelry with 25 rooms (12 with bath). This 1438 building backs right out on the cathedral and precincts. The cheaper rooms are minute. There is a dining room (guests only) where meals are served on request; rock-bottom to moderate.

The Victorian **Ebury Hotel** ((01227) 768433 FAX (01227) 459187 E-MAIL info@ebury-hotel .co.uk, 65–67 New Dover Road, Canterbury CT1 3DX, is located east of the city walls. The comfortable bedrooms have baths, and there is a **restaurant** (moderate), an indoor heated pool and spa; moderate.

Off St. Dunstan's Street, Roper Road is semi-industrial area, but the B&Bs here are handy as they are a 10-minute walk to the center. **Alexandra House** ((01227) 767011 FAX (01227) 786617, 1 Roper Road, Canterbury CT2 7EH, has seven bedrooms, four with bath. There is a private car park; high end of the inexpensive price range. Next door is **Casa Alicante B&B** (/FAX (01227) 766227, 4 Roper Road, Canterbury CT2 7EH, offering six bedrooms with bath; prices across the inexpensive range.

The **Castle Court B&B** (/FAX (01227) 463441, 8 Castle Street, Canterbury CT1 2QF, in the city center, is a listed Georgian guest house with nine rooms (five with bath) and a patio garden as well as a restaurant; inexpensive.

A Victorian close to the city center, **Ann's House** ((01227) 768767 FAX (01227) 768172, 63 London Road, Canterbury CT2 8JZ, has 18 bedrooms, some with four-posters, most with bath. Early breakfast is available; inexpensive.

Canterbury Youth Hostel ((01227) 462911 FAX (01227) 470752 E-MAIL canterbury@yha.org.uk, Ellerslie, 54 New Dover Road, Canterbury CT1 3DT, is a Victorian villa one and a half kilometers (a little over a mile) from the center, as well as being a stop along the North Downs Way; rock-bottom.

WHERE TO EAT

There are plenty of casual places to dine in Canterbury, many with more than a hint of the continent. Plunge into Canterbury's French connection at **La Bonne Cuisine** ((01227) 450551, Canterbury Hotel, 71 New Dover Road, where the staff are French and the cuisine classic; moderate.

Walk down Castle Street — a jumble of bicycles, berets and baguettes — and you could be in France. **Flap Jacques** ((01227) 781000, 71 Castle Street, looks like a tiny English pub, but the menu has other ideas. There are Breton crêpes (made from buckwheat) among other fare from Brittany for lunch as well as a long dinner menu; moderate. Most nights bring live music and a lively atmosphere; moderate to inexpensive.

Argot ((01227) 767555, 7 St. Margaret's Street, is an American-style wine bar. The stylish dining area is set with white linens, but burgers predominate on the menu and families are made welcome. Another good place for families is **Pizza Express** ((01227) 766938, on Best Lane, a branch of the

national chain, where some tables have river views; moderate.

Beau's ((01227) 464285, 59 Palace Street, is an airy French café with crêpes à l'anglaise; inexpensive.

The **Goodchild Bakery** ((01227) 780333, 10 The Butchery, makes fresh sandwiches and bakery-style pizza. Order for take out or eat in the upstairs café; inexpensive.

HOW TO GET THERE

Canterbury is 89 km (55 miles) southeast of London. **Trains** leave London from Charing Cross and Victoria stations for one of Canterbury's two train stations. Canterbury East (Station Road East) is on the London-Dover Priory line, and Canterbury

OPPOSITE: Norman-style Canterbury Cathedral. ABOVE: The ruins of St. Augustine's Abbey, the birthplace of christianity in Britain.

West (Station Road West) is on the line that goes south to the coast. National Express has an hourly **coach** service to Canterbury from London's Victoria Station. The bus station is on St. George's Lane. There are seven daily coach runs to Canterbury from Dover.

AROUND CANTERBURY

EAST KENT — Six and a half kilometers (four miles) southwest of Canterbury on the A252 is the mediaeval village of **Chilham**. The near-perfect village square, with its timber-framed houses and castle gate, is marred only by the car park at its center. There's a pub here, and several antiques shops, as well as an excellent gift and souvenir shop, Tudor Lodge ((01227) 730596. Just down the road there are cider-making, crafts and free-range pigs at **Badgers Hill Farm & Cidery** ((01227) 730573, New Cut Road. You can pick apples here from August to October.

From Chilham it's possible to join the **Stour Valley Walk** which runs through rolling landscape with panoramic views of the East Kent countryside. A good day's goal is the 11-km (seven-mile) section from Chilham to Wye. There are regular bus services between Wye and Chilham if you want to take the bus back to where you started. The village of **Wye** gives easy access to footpaths on the **Wye Downs** n.b. one of the best places to walk in Kent, with views of Thames Estuary and the Channel, but not too steep.

To the north of Canterbury, **Faversham** sits at the tip of a creek running into the Swale, the channel that divides the Isle of Sheppey from the mainland of Kent. This picturesque town makes for pleasant exploring, with its many half-timbered buildings and octagonal-pillared sixteenth-century market court. The Tourist Information Centre ((01795) 534542 is at the Fleur de Lis Heritage Center, 13 Preston Street.

WHERE TO STAY AND EAT

Given how crowded Canterbury is, if you have transportation you'd be wise to stay outside the city in a pretty Kent village inn or rural farmhouse, or even in an oast-house such as **Thruxted Oast** ((01227) 730080, Mystole, Chartham CT4 7BX, a restored hop kiln in the village center, offering B&B in three plush rooms; expensive.

Just outside Faversham, **White Horse Inn** ((01227) 751343 FAX (01227) 751090, The Street, Boughton ME13 9AX, is a fifteenth-century coaching inn with 15 rooms, a bar with local ales and a restaurant; high end of inexpensive price range.

In the same area, **Owens Court Farm** ((01227) 752247, Selling, Faversham ME13 9QN, is a hop farm and orchard offering B&B year-round, except during September harvest; inexpensive.

Chilham has the fifteenth-century **Woolpack Inn** ((01227) 730208 or (01227) 730351 FAX (01227) 731053, High Street, Chilham, Canterbury CT4 8DL, where all of the bedrooms have bath. Half-board rates are available for stays of two or more nights; upper end of inexpensive range. Inglenook fireplaces warm the beamed restaurant, where regional specialties and local real ales are served (inexpensive).

At Wye the **New Flying Horse Inn** ((01233) 812297 FAX (01233) 813487, Upper Bridge Street, Wye, Ashford TN25 5AN, is a seventeenth-century former coaching inn. There are 10 bedrooms with bath, including one single. Half board is available for stays of two or more nights; inexpensive.

The **Dove** ((01227) 751360, Plumpudding Lane, is a country pub in Dargate with heaps of charm and heavenly food; moderate. At Hernhill, the **Red Lion** ((01227) 751207, is an attractive Tudor inn neighboring the church; inexpensive.

THE KENT WEALD

KENT — Originally a raised tract of forest about 65 km (40 miles) wide, the Kent Weald remains the most heavily wooded area in England. Hallmarks of the landscape are its narrow lanes bounded by hedgerows, timber-framed houses and oast-houses — round hop kilns topped by white cones that turn in the wind. The ancient practice of "gavelkind", dividing inheritance equally among sons, is unique to Kent and gave rise to the patchy nature of the landscape. There are far more farmhouses in this area than anywhere else in England, most of them in a particular style, known as the "Wealden house" shown particularly well in the beautiful village of Smarden, along the River Beult. They were built in large numbers during the fifteenth and early sixteenth century, with the second story always jutting out above the ground floor.

Secret Garden Cycles ((01732) 367233 E-MAIL sgcycles.demon.co.uk, in Tonbridge, rents wheels, repairs cycles and offers tours.

ROYAL TUNBRIDGE WELLS

What to See and Do
Tunbridge Wells is a "new" Georgian spa town built during the same rage for fashionable watering holes that gave birth to Bath. This brick and timber town is at its best along the colonnaded walks of the **Pantiles**. A contented hour could be spent here, exploring shops of various stripes including some antiques dealers. It's possible to taste the waters at **Chalybeate Springs** from November to March; fee charged. Also on the Pantiles is the well-stocked **Tourist Information Centre** ((01892) 515675 FAX (01892) 534660 at The Old Fish Market.

To the east of Tunbridge Wells is the superb **Scotney Castle Garden** (NT) ((01892) 891081, in Lamberhurst. This valley garden is richly cultivated with rhododendron, azaleas and rare trees. The green slopes offer striking views over the ruins of the fourteenth-century moated castle. The gardens are open March to October; castle May to September; closed Monday and Tuesday; admission fee. The Tunbridge Wells Heritage Hopper ((01892) 515675 provides bus service to Scotney Castle from Tunbridge Wells on weekends and Bank Holiday Mondays from April to September.

It may take some keen orienteering, but it's worth seeking out All Saints Church ((01732) 352992 at **Tudeley** just east of Tonbridge (north of Tunbridge Wells). This humble Saxon country church was endowed in the 1960s with a complete set of stained glass windows by Marc Chagall. The windows memorialize a young church member, Sarah d'Avigdor-Goldsmid, who drowned in a sailing accident. She's depicted in the altar window. Tudeley is on the B2017. Open year-round from 9 AM to dusk; free admission.

Some of the best **walking country** of the Kent Weald is found in the escarpment to the northwest of Tunbridge Wells, around Penshurst, Chiddingstone and Chiddingstone Hoath. In this high country, **Penshurst Palace** ((01892) 870307, the ancestral home of Viscount de L'Isle, is the major attraction. In the four-hectare (10-acre) Tudor garden and parkland there is color from spring to autumn. It's also possible to visit the palace to marvel at the mediaeval barons' hall with its 18-m-high (60-ft) chestnut-beamed ceiling and state rooms stuffed with furniture, tapestries, portraits and armor.

There is a playground, a toy museum, and nature trails, as well as a restaurant, plant center and shop. Open daily from April to September, weekends only in March and October; admission fee. On B2176, north of Tonbridge.

Just west of Tonbridge is the unspoiled village of **Chiddingstone** with cobbled streets flanked by Tudor houses and buildings owned by the National Trust. Here you can marvel at the Chiding Stone, a massive and mysterious carved boulder on the edge of the village, and visit Chiddingstone Castle ((01892) 870347, a seventeenth-century house reconstructed as a mock castle in the nineteenth century. Opening hours vary; admission fee.

West of Tunbridge Wells is the village of **Groombridge**, where the Walks are a row of eighteenth-century cottages flanking one side of the pretty triangular village green. They are wonderful examples of the typical Kentish architecture: tall chimneys, red and blue brick, weatherboarding and hung tiles. **Groombridge Place** ((01892) 863999 is a seventeenth-century moated manor, with dramatic formal gardens, as well as some kids' attractions such as the raptor center and "Enchanted Forest." Open daily April to October; admission fee.

Outdoor Activities
Waymarked trails wind through **Bedgebury Pinetum** ((01580) 211044, near Goudhurst, through a forest of tall conifers. The park has over 1,500 varieties of conifers on 120 hectares (300 acres) around a series of landscaped lakes ringed by azaleas and rhododendrons. Open year-round; admission fee. The visitor center is closed weekdays in January and February. There's also a BHS-approved **riding** center ((01580) 212296 at Bedgebury. Nearby, **Bewl Water** ((01892) 890661, in Lamberhurst, is the southeast's largest lake, with boating, fishing, picnicking, bicycle rental and trails. It gets very busy on bank holidays. There's a 23-km (14-mile) path that hugs the edge of the reservoir. Open 9 AM to sunset year-round.

Where to Stay
The **Hotel du Vin** ((01892) 526445 FAX (01892) 5122044 E-MAIL reception@tunbridgewells .hotelduvin.co.uk, Crescent Road, Tunbridge Wells TN1 2LY, has handsomely decorated bedrooms in a Georgian townhouse; expensive. Good wines complement the fare in the moderately-priced French bistro-style restaurant.

A mediaeval, gabled inn, the **Star & Eagle** ((01580) 211512 FAX (01580) 211416, High Street, Goudhurst TN17 1AL, has nine atmospheric, beamed bedrooms with Jacobean furnishings. Most rooms have views of the churchyard, hop farms or orchards;

Two of the luminous Marc Chagall windows at All Saints Church, Tudeley.

moderate to inexpensive. In the open-plan, beamed bar (moderate) with log fire, varied and creative fare is offered.

For inexpensive lodging there is **Tanner House** ((01622) 831214, Goudhurst Road, Marden, Tonbridge TN12 9ND, a Tudor farmhouse offering three comfortable rooms with showers; inexpensive.

Where to Eat

Once the home of Victorian novelist William Makepeace Thackeray, **Thackeray's House** ((01892) 511921, 85 London Road, Royal Tunbridge Wells, is now a culinary treat. Fresh ingredients form the base for an imaginative menu

How to Get There

Tunbridge Wells is 67 km (41 miles) southeast of London. The town is on the London–Hastings line for which there frequent **train** departures during the day from London Charing Cross. National Express operates a single **coach** route timed for commuters, departing from Tunbridge Wells each morning and returning from London Victoria each evening. The ride takes an hour and a half.

TENTERDEN

KENT, EAST SUSSEX — Tenterden has masses of handy shops along its wide High Street. If you like staying in town, Tenterden would make a fine base

cooked with flair. The mini-bouillabaisse is a specialty, and the dessert card features chocolate Armagnac loaf with coffee sauce; expensive. Downstairs there is a wine bar bistro with simpler fare. Closed Monday, no dinner Sunday, Bistro closed Sunday and Monday.

Honours Mill ((01732) 866757, 87 High Street, Edenbridge, is an eighteenth-century water mill admirably converted to a small restaurant where adventurous adaptations of French classics are served under low beams; expensive.

Penshurst has two very good public houses. On Coldharbour Road, the **Bottle House** ((01892) 870306, Smarts Hill, is a fifteenth-century pub with decent food, brisk service, and huge portions; inexpensive. Fancier fare is offered at the **Spotted Dog** ((01892) 870253, a tiled house atop Smarts Hill with top-of-the-Weald views over Penshurst Palace from the terrace; moderate.

for exploring the weald. West of the town, a soft sylvan landscape is dotted with oast-houses, fields of yellow rape, and lambs frolicking in spring.

A small, but helpful **Tourist Information Centre** ((01580) 763572, is located in the Town Hall on High Street.

What to See and Do

A stroll down Tenterden's **High Street** reveals many shops and dwellings with their original façades, dating from Elizabethan to Georgian times.

Take your explorations further afield with a ride from Tenterden to Bodiam Castle (below) on the **Kent & East Sussex Railway** ((01580) 765155 or (01580) 762943 (recorded information). Costumed stewards staff this vintage steam railway with its Victorian engines and coach cars. You can pay once and hop on and off all day. On Sundays, there is dining aboard with lunch, afternoon tea and dinner featuring English cooking. Closed January and February; admission fee.

Just south of Tenterden, set on the edge of broad farm fields, **Smallhythe Place** (NT) ((01580) 762334 was the home of Dame Ellen Terry (1895–1928), the celebrated Victorian actress. The gorgeously preserved half-timbered house is full of Terry's personal mementos as well as her collection of souvenirs of other great actors of her time (Garrick, Bernhardt, Duse, and others). Behind the house the Barn Theatre, a memorial to Terry, continues to produce a few shows each summer. Smallhythe is located three kilometers (two miles) south of Tenterden on the B2082.

To the north is the village of **Biddenden**. Houses along the High Street date from the fifteenth century and were originally the homes of Flemish weavers. The parish church dates in part from the thirteenth century. Continuing west along the A262 soon brings you to the entrance to **Sissinghurst Castle Garden** (NT) ((01580) 710700 or (01580) 710701. These magnificent gardens were the creation of the writer Vita Sackville-West and her husband Sir Harold Nicholson. The gardens were developed around the remains of an Elizabethan mansion with its separate red brick tower. Consisting of a series of small, enclosed "rooms," the garden is both intimate and romantic with spectacular color throughout the growing season. Vita's study, in the tower, and the Long Library are open to visitors as well. Closed weekday mornings, all day Monday and from October to March; admission fee (see also MAKE A DATE WITH THE "DAFFS," page 14 in TOP SPOTS).

Built in 1385, as a fortress and home, **Bodiam Castle** (NT) ((01580) 830436, near Robertsbridge, is one of Britain's most picturesque strongholds. From its waterlily-covered moat to the castellated ramparts, Bodiam looks like a page from a fairytale book. You might think twice about paying the entrance fee since, though the exterior is nearly intact, the interior lies in ruin. There is a small museum at the ticket office. Closed Monday from November to December; separate fees for parking and for entering the castle. The **Wharf Tea Shop** by the car park does nice lunches (fish cakes, rarebit) with views of the marsh and farmland along the River Rother. You'll find restrooms here, rather than up at the museum-ticket office. There are some interesting ways to get to Bodiam Castle. In summer a 45-minute **boat trip** ((01797) 280363 to the castle departs from Newenden. The Kent & East Sussex Railway (above) runs from Tenterden.

To the east, **Northiam** is a pretty village of old houses clustered around an attractive green. The main attraction here is **Great Dixter** ((01797) 252878, an imposing half-timbered house with beautiful formal garden. Open Tuesday to Sunday from May to October; admission fee.

Where to Stay

There is a variety of stately Victorian farmhouses, country manors, and ancient inns to choose from in this picturesque country. If you're looking for accommodation around Biddenden, ask for a brochure listing "B&Bs Around Biddenden" at the Sissinghurst ticket office.

Set in 25 hectares (62 acres) of verdant gardens and grounds, **Eastwell Manor** ((01233) 213000 FAX (01233) 635530 E-MAIL eastwell@btinternet .com, Boughton Lees, Ashford TN25 4HR, has comfortable public areas with exposed stone walls, open fires, and wood paneling. The generously-proportioned bedrooms complement the remarkable architecture of this ancient estate; very expensive. This hotel has long been known for its excellent restaurant with menus that change with the seasons.

Said to have been the home of Admiral Nelson's illegitimate daughter Horatia, the seventeenth-century **Brattle House** ((01580) 763565, Watermill Bridges, Tenterden TN30 6UL, has three bedrooms and wonderful food in its candlelit dining room; moderate (no children).

Gracious **Sissinghurst Castle Farm** ((01580) 712885, Sissinghurst, Cranbrook TN17 2AB, has five sunny and spacious rooms, some with bath. This Victorian farmhouse is right on the grounds of Sissinghurst Castle, and guests have access to the surrounding parkland when the garden is closed; upper end of inexpensive price range.

You'll find friendly staff and commodious rooms at the fourteenth-century **Chequers** ((01233) 770217, Smarden, Ashford TN27 8QA, in the midst of this photogenic Wealden village. The five rooms, three with bath, are nicely decorated with lace curtains and antiques; inexpensive. Downstairs in the gastropub (moderate to inexpensive), you may hear occasional cheers from the kitchen (the chef's a football fan), but the ruckus doesn't adversely affect the very good food. If the prawn curry soup is on the menu, try it. Dining is in the small open-plan bar with log fire or in the courtyard by the duck pond.

The **Lemon Tree** ((01580) 762060, 52–56 High Street, Tenterden TN30 6AU, is a surprise. Rooms are much nicer than you'd think given the casual restaurant on the ground floor. The beamed bedrooms are tastefully decorated and well-equipped. Guests receive a discount for dining in the restaurant; inexpensive.

Where to Eat

There are plenty of places to eat in and around Tenterden. Occupying a homey white clapboard cottage in Sissinghurst village, **Rankins** ((01580) 713964, The Street, has a loyal following for its

Sissinghurst Castle Garden was laid out by the writer Vita Sackville-West and her husband Sir Harold Nicholson.

superb Modern British fare. Short, changing menus follow the seasons. Desserts are lovely. Children are welcome by prior arrangement; expensive.

The **Three Chimneys** ((01580) 291472, just outside Biddenden, is an excellent fifteenth-century public house, laden with atmosphere. Dine in one of the nooks in the front or in the spacious back looking out on the garden. The food is superb and plentiful. Unless you're ravenous, one of the starters serves as a meal; moderate. The pub's name is derived not from its chimneys (there aren't three of them), but from an old crossroads here called Les Trois Chemins.

In Cranbrook, the **Windmill** ((01580) 713119, Waterloo Road, has to be one of the friendliest pubs around, due largely to its gregarious keeper. Good traditional food is served; inexpensive.

How to Get There

Tenterden is about 97 km (60 miles) southeast of London and 19 km (12 miles)

southwest of Ashford, a major railway junction as well as an intermediary stop on the high-speed Eurostar train between London and Paris. There are several express **trains** each hour from London Victoria, Charing Cross and Cannon Street stations to Ashford. See also GETTING TO SOUTHERN ENGLAND, page 322 in TRAVELERS' TIPS. For Sissinghurst, the closest train station is at Staplehurst, about six and a half kilometers (four miles) north of the village.

CASTLES, MANSIONS AND GARDENS

KENT — The countryside surrounding the commuter towns of Sevenoaks and Maidstone is studded with stately homes, castles and gardens. You'll find plenty of assistance with arranging your visit at the **Tourist Information Centre** ((01732) 450305 FAX (01732) 461959 in Burkhurst Lane, Sevenoaks; or at Maidstone ((01622) 602169 FAX (01622) 673581 on Mill Street at The Gatehouse, The Old Palace Gardens.

WHAT TO SEE AND DO

The jewel in Kent's crown, **Leeds Castle** ((01622) 765400, Maidstone, was royal residence to six of England's mediaeval queens and home to Henry VIII. While the interior is not wildly impressive (only a handful of rooms are open to the public), the setting is splendid. The moated stronghold rises out of a 200-hectare (500-acre) park with meandering paths to the castle through the duckery and woodland garden, lush with flowers and exotic water fowl. Beyond the castle there is an enjoyable aviary, maze and grotto, as well as a vineyard, and greenhouses. You'll not go hungry here as there are three places to dine, and several shops. There is a year-round calendar of special events; call for a brochure. Open daily; admission fee.

To visit Leeds as a day trip from London, try Green Line ((020) 8688-7261 E-MAIL enquire @greenline.co.uk whose coaches depart Victoria from their Bulleid Way stop at 9:35 AM, Monday to Friday year-round (except public holidays), returning from Leeds Castle at 4 PM. Journey time is around an hour and 45 minutes.

The fare includes the price of entry. National Express offers a similar deal.

Just east of Sevenoaks, **Knole** (NT) ((01732) 450608 was the ancestral home of the Sackville family. Built in 1456, this splendid manor house was the inspiration for Virginia Woolf's fanciful portrait of Vita Sackville-West in her novel *Orlando*. Within the vast mansion's 365 rooms are collections of portraits, silver, tapestry and seventeenth-century Royal Stuart furniture. Surrounding the mansion is a deer park with a network of footpaths, and there is a restaurant and shop on the premises. Open Wednesday to Saturday from April to October. Garden open May to September and the first Wednesday of each month throughout the year; admission fee.

Still further east, **Ightham Mote** (NT) ((01732) 810378, Ivy Hatch, is a splendid moated manor dating from the fourteenth century. Highlights are the painted Tudor chapel, the billiard room and the dog kennel. Beautiful gardens and woodland walks surround the manor. There is a tea room

Leeds Castle, ethereal residence to six queens.

and shop. Open daily (except Tuesday and Saturday) from April to October; admission fee. Ightham Mote is 10 km (six miles) east of Sevenoaks.

Another moated castle, **Hever Castle and Gardens** ((01732) 865224, Edenbridge, dates from the thirteenth century. It was the scene of Henry Tudor's courtship of Anne Boleyn, who eventually became his second wife and gave birth to the future Queen Elizabeth I. The exterior of this castle is largely unchanged from the days when Anne Boleyn lived here as a child. The interior, however, was extensively renovated by the Astors in the beginning of the twentieth century. Furniture, paintings and art objects, including two "Books of Hours" inscribed by Anne Boleyn, form part of the

unfinished. There is a restaurant and shop. Open Wednesday to Sunday from April to October, and Tuesdays to Sunday in July and August; separate entry fees are charged for the house and gardens.

The Chartwell Explorer ((0345) 696996 runs between Sevenoaks train and bus stations on weekends and on some weekdays during the high season to Chartwell, Knole, and other Kent attractions. Combined rail, bus and entry tickets are also available from Connex stations ((0345) 696996.

WHERE TO STAY

Though it's possible to find lodging in the larger towns, surrounding villages offer more enjoyable

collections. A series of themed gardens — Italian, rose, Tudor, and others — set a colorful backdrop. Open daily March to November; admission fee. Located off the B2026 between Sevenoaks and East Grinstead. There is a train station at Hever village on the Uckfield line, dropping off about one and a half kilometers (a mile) from the castle.

Set in rolling, wooded country three kilometers (two miles) south of Westerham, **Chartwell** (NT) ((01732) 866368, was for 40 years the home of Sir Winston Churchill. The house is now a monument to Britain's distinguished prime minister, maintained just as the great man left it. The rooms are set up as if still lived in, though some have been altered to contain a host of Churchilliana with details of his life from cradle to grave. Extensive gardens give beautiful views of Wealden countryside. At the back of the garden is this Renaissance man's painting studio with many of his unframed paintings, some

and convenient bases for exploring the area. Set in the pretty village of West Malling, **Scott-House** ((01732) 841380 FAX (01732) 870025, High Street, West Malling ME19 6QH, is a Queen Anne house with many of its original features and an unusual entrance via the host's antiques and interior design shop. There are three thoughtfully decorated bedrooms with bath. Children aged 12 and older are welcome; moderate.

Built in the late nineteenth century, the **Chaser Inn** ((01732) 810360 FAX (01732) 810360, Stumble Hill, Shipbourne TN11 9PE, is a country inn offering individually decorated rooms with bath; moderate. The porticoed front overlooks the village green, and there is good food in two bars and the restaurant with its vaulted ceiling. This inn makes a good base for exploring Knole and Ightham Mote as well as the vineyards and hop farms roundabout.

An attractive Kent oast-house, **Langley Oast** ((01622) 863523 FAX (01622) 863523, Langley Park, Langley, Maidstone ME17 3NQ, has three generously-proportioned bedrooms, one of which occupies a part of the round oast tower. The sunny breakfast room looks out on the garden; inexpensive to moderate.

Eden Farm ((01732) 843110 FAX (01732) 843110, Eden Farm Lane, West Malling ME19 6HL, has four bedrooms (with bath), whose modern decor contrasts interestingly with the eighteenth-century farm buildings. Breakfast is a friendly affair, served around a large table; inexpensive.

A charming, white clapboard house, **Barn Cottage** ((01732) 883384 E-MAIL suzi.filleul@tesco.net,

Seven mile Lane, Borough Green, Sevenoaks TN15 8QY, has three nicely furnished bedrooms and a pretty garden. Breakfast is served in the conservatory; inexpensive.

WHERE TO EAT

In addition to the Chaser (above) in Shipbourne, there are more good pubs in the vicinity of Sevenoaks and Maidstone. Hollingbourne has the **Dirty Habit** ((01622) 880880, Upper Street, a seventeenth-century inn on the ancient Pilgrims' Way, whose name recalls the practice of monks stopping to wash their garments. This free house serves interesting fare in the beamed bar, including fresh seafood; moderate to inexpensive. Nearby, **Ringlestone** ((01622) 859900, Ringlestone Hamlet, near Harrietsham, is another atmospheric inn with brink-and-flint walls, heavy beams, inglenook fireplaces and antique

furniture. This inn is popular for its hot lunch buffets and its savory pies, some of which feature fresh game; moderate to inexpensive. They have three bedrooms. The **Plough** ((01732) 810268, High Cross Road, Ivy Hatch, is a seafood lover's pub close to Ightham Mote. Reservations advised; moderate to inexpensive.

THE CINQUE PORTS

KENT, EAST SUSSEX — A string of former port towns, the original Cinque Ports — Hastings, Romney, Hythe, Dover and Sandwich — were established during the reign of Edward the Confessor. Rye and Winchelsea joined the alliance in the thirteenth century. These towns pledged to defend the kingdom in exchange for dispensations that made them essentially self-governing.

The shifting shingle of the Channel Coast has landlocked some of these towns, but they still hold a wealth of historical interest, from the not-so-white chalk cliffs of Dover to "1066 Country," where a turning-point of English history is memorialized at Hastings and Battle.

DOVER, DEAL AND SANDWICH

The beach was a desert of heaps of sea and stones tumbling wildly about, and the sea did what it liked, and what it liked was destruction.

— Charles Dickens, *A Tale of Two Cities*

EAST KENT — Britain's closest point to continental Europe, Dover is flanked by high creamy chalk cliffs upon which stand the castle and citadel. It's an undeniably dramatic setting, but if you're looking for "bluebirds over the white cliffs of Dover" you'll probably be disappointed. Still, while far from charming, Dover does have several points of interest. Further up the coast, Deal and Sandwich appeal to history buffs.

Dover's **Tourist Information Centre** ((01304) 205108 FAX (01304) 225498 is on Townwall Street. Sandwich's seasonal Tourist Information Centre ((01304) 613565 FAX (01304) 613565 is in the Guildhall. The Deal Tourist Information Centre ((01304) 369576 is in the Town Hall on High Street.

The White Cliffs Countryside Commission (contact the Dover Youth Hostel, under WHERE TO STAY, below) arranges guided **walking tours** of Dover ending congenially at a local pub.

What to See and Do

The new **Gateway to the White Cliffs Centre** (NT) ((01304) 202756, at Langdon Cliffs, has outstanding views of the cliffs and coast as well as interesting displays on the human and natural history of this

Hever Castle — OPPOSITE: The thirteenth-century façade remains unchanged. ABOVE: A fountain in the castle's Italian garden.

legendary formation. The visitor center offers access to this protected area of coast and downland for walkers. Its possible also to tour the lighthouse at South Foreland. To get to the center follow the National Trust signs from the roundabout one and a half kilometers (one mile) northeast of Dover at Junction A2/A258. Open daily from March to October; admission fee for the lighthouse and there is a fee for parking.

Another fine place to enjoy splendid scenery is **St. Margaret's-at-Cliffe**, four kilometers (two and a half miles) north of Dover. This pretty village has B&Bs and pubs, and down a steep road is **St. Margaret's Bay**, where you can enjoy the white cliffs in relative tranquillity. See also, OUTDOOR ACTIVITIES, below.

The twelfth-century **Dover Castle** (EH) ((01304) 201628, Castle Hill, gets high marks from visitors of all ages. There's a recreation of Tudor life in the keep; the Secret Wartime Tunnels and a World War II dramatization; an underground hospital, and more. In the castle grounds are two buildings that predate the castle: the church of St.-Mary-in-Castro, a restored late Saxon (*circa* 1000) building and the Roman *pharos* (lighthouse), built in AD 43 (although the top half was restored during the Middle Ages). There are shops and a restaurant. Open daily year-round; admission fee.

Elsewhere in Dover, the **Roman Painted House**, New Street, is a well-preserved Roman hotel. Closed Monday and November to March; admission fee. The **Old Town Gaol** ((01304) 242766, High Street, gives you a glimpse of life behind bars in Victorian England. Closed Monday and Tuesday; admission fee. The **Grand Shaft** ((01304) 201200, South Military Road, is a spiral stone staircase connecting the Victorian army barracks on the cliffs with the town below. Open Tuesday to Sunday afternoon during July and August; admission fee.

Most of Deal is modern, but Middle Street, which parallels the Promenade, has some interesting old houses and some narrow lanes radiating off it. The main attraction is **Deal Castle** (EH) ((01304) 372762, southwest of the town center, built in 1539 by Henry VIII and the largest of his coastal defenses. It was built in the shape of a Tudor rose. Open daily April through October, Wednesday to Sunday the rest of the year; the admission fee includes an audio tour. To the south is **Walmer Castle & Gardens** (EH) ((01304) 364288, another of Henry VIII's coastal fortresses. It later became the official residence of the Lord Warden of the Cinque Ports. Closed Monday and Tuesday in winter, weekdays in January and February; admission fee.

Eight kilometers (five miles) north of Deal, Sandwich is a small, attractive town surrounded by open fields. Its mediaeval center is organized around a tiny central square where the guildhall still has its sixteenth-century façade and many Tudor features inside. The remains of a Roman

castle, **Richborough Roman Fort** (EH) ((01304) 612013 does a good job of evoking first-century Britain with traces of walls and foundations and a small museum. Richborough was the Romans' most important supply port. Closed Monday and Tuesday from November to March and all weekdays from December to February; admission includes an audio tour.

Outdoor Activities

The **North Downs Way** runs from Dover through Canterbury and west towards Maidstone. From Dover you can join the **Saxon Shore Way** (264 km or 163 miles), which follows the shoreline of Saxon times, diving inland to follow the Royal Military Canal and connecting with the 1066 Country Walk at Hastings in East Sussex. It is a 13-km (eight-mile) hike to Deal from Dover, and you can take the train back from Deal to Dover Priory.

A shorter ramble (about five and a half kilometers or three and a half miles) is the walk from Dover Castle to St. Margaret's-at-Cliffe, passing the Roman lighthouse. Below St. Margaret's-at-Cliffe, St. Margaret's Bay has a decent **swimming** beach. Sit in your car and watch the sea as the Britons do, or pile out and make a pebble castle, run in the surf or have a bitter at the Coastguard.

Where to Stay

A Jacobean-era farmhouse, **Wallet's Court** ((01304) 852424 FAX (01304) 853430 E-MAIL wallettscourt @compuserve.com, West Cliffe, St. Margaret's-at-Cliffe CT15 6EW, has been sympathetically converted into a welcoming and comfortable country hotel. The 10 rooms, two in the converted stable, offer every comfort, and there is a pool and spa; moderate. Very good country fare with Mod Brit flair is served in the beamed dining room. The menu changes monthly (expensive).

If you need to be close to the ferry for a quick morning getaway, there is **No. 1 Guest house** ((01304) 202007 FAX (01304) 214078 E-MAIL res @number1guesthouse.co.uk, 1 Castle Street, Dover CT16 1QH, a neat-as-a-pin four-room B&B in a Georgian townhouse serving in-room breakfast; inexpensive.

Dover Youth Hostel ((01304) 201314 FAX (01304) 202236 E-MAIL dover@yha.org.uk, 306 London Road, Dover CT17 0SY, occupies two centrally located townhouses with mostly eight-bed dorms; rock-bottom.

Where to Eat

Do try to work in a meal at Wallet's Court (above). Also at St. Margaret's (handily located across from the parish church), the **Cliffe Tavern** ((01304) 852400 FAX (01304) 852749, High Street, is a sixteenth-century clapboard building with two congenial bars and a walled garden. The inn also has bedrooms (inexpensive).

On the seafront at Deal, **Dunkerleys** ((01304) 375016, 19 Beach Street, specializes in expertly prepared seafood; moderate. On the same street, the **King's Head** ((01304) 368194, 9 Beach Street, is a flower-decked eighteenth-century inn (with adjoining guest house), where the menu features locally caught cod and plaice; inexpensive.

How to Get There

Dover is 125 km (77 miles) east of London. There is frequent **train** service from London Victoria or Charing Cross to Dover throughout the daytime. National Express operates hourly **coach** service to Dover stopping at the station on Dover's Pencester Road and at the Ferry Port, with additional

age ditches along which mute swans and sheep share fertile pasture. Towards the shore, the marsh turns to a wide shingle, a treasure trove for rock-hounds and birders.

Hythe has a seasonal **Tourist Information Centre** ((01303) 267799, in the En Route Building, Red Lion Square.

What to See and Do

The most satisfying parts of the marsh are inland. The **Royal Military Canal**, whose long arc effectively seals off the marsh from the rest of the county, is an easygoing place for walks. Built in the early 1800s to defend against the threat of Napoleonic invasion, the Royal Military Canal, running from Hythe to

services to the Dover Hoverport. National Express operates three coaches daily to Deal, a three-hour trip. **Ferries** connect Dover to Oostende, Holland, and Calais, France. See GETTING THERE, page 322 in TRAVELERS' TIPS.

ROMNEY MARSH

God to be in Romney Marsh […]
For just an hour of storm and shower.

— Ford Maddox Ford

EAST SUSSEX — Smugglers once escaped detection in the barren flats of Romney Marsh. Today, it's a good place to escape the summer weekend crowds. This unspoiled corner of Kent, though hardly undiscovered, is much less visited than the downs and coast. A haven for wildlife and waterfowl, Romney is a drained marsh crisscrossed by drain-

Cliff End near Hastings, today forms a section of the Saxon Shore Way long-distance footpath. Martello towers added during World War II still dot parts of the canal. The National Trust owns a five-kilometer (three-mile) section of the canal between the villages of Appledore and Warehorne. This is probably the best section to get a taste of canal-side walking.

Along the canal, **Appledore** is an attractive village with some antiques shops, including the popular High Class Junk, The Street. Take a look inside the church where there is a tapestry telling the intriguing story of the village from 1188 to the twentieth century. The Appledore Tea Room ((01233) 758272, 8 The Street, serves wonderful homemade cakes in a pretty beamed room.

A cherished marsh activity is **church-hopping**. Thirteen mediaeval churches remain here, often set in lonely spots and surrounded by wetlands.

Dover antidote: the white cliffs at St. Margaret's Bay.

The church at Old Romney (St. Clement's), for example, has interesting painted box pews, done because the parish couldn't afford fine wood.

Along the coast **Dymchurch** bills itself as "a children's paradise." Bright fun fairs line the beaches here. **Hythe** is a suburb of Folkestone and the northern terminus of the *Romney, Hythe & Dymchurch Railway*. As a resort it's more restrained than Dymchurch and the Old Town has some interesting bits.

The world's smallest public railway, the *Romney, Hythe & Dymchurch* ((01797) 362353 runs 22 km (13.5 miles) from Hythe to Dungeness lighthouse via Dymchurch and New Romney. One-third size locomotives tow the comfy carriages,

and there are gift shops at all the stations. The train operates weekends in March and October, daily from Easter to end September. Hythe Station is close to M20 Junction 11. New Romney Station is just off A259.

Sheep graze the bizarre landscape of **Dungeness**. The brooding mass of the nuclear power plant lends an ominous overtone to this region; nevertheless, it harbors the largest seabird colony in the southeast. The RSPB Nature Reserve Visitor Centre, on the headland, is a good place to start your explorations.

Romney Marsh is an ideal place for easy **cycling** since it is flat and the roads are relatively quiet. You can rent wheels at Romney Marsh Cycle Tours ((01308) 875296.

Where to Stay and Eat

Romney Marsh is within easy striking distance of Rye and Tenterden; see listings under these towns, page 208 and 199, for additional accommodation and dining listings.

Folkestone is a proud Victorian town of stately red brick houses where you'll find **Harbourside Bed and Breakfast Hotel** ((01303) 256528 or (0468) 123884 FAX (01303) 241299, 13–14 Wear Bay Road, Folkestone CT19 6AT. There are six rooms (with bath) and heaps of amenities in this Victorian

house. Lunch and evening meals are served; inexpensive to moderate (no children).

South of Folkestone, **Sandgate Hotel and Restaurant La Terrasse** ((01303) 220444 FAX (01303) 220496, The Esplanade, Sandgate, Folkestone CT20 3DY, has 14 comfortable bedrooms, some with sea-view balconies; moderate. The restaurant (expensive to moderate), noted for its very good French cuisine, looks out over Sandgate's pebble beach.

Just outside Appledore, **Park Farm Barn** (/FAX (01233) 758159, Appledore TN26 2AR, is a converted barn with three rooms and cheerful hosts; inexpensive.

How to Get There

Ferries run from Boulogne, France, to Folkestone. The Eurotunnel Shuttle — for automobiles and cyclists coming form from Calais, France — also arrives a few miles inland of Folkestone (see GETTING THERE, page 322 in TRAVELERS' TIPS). National Express operates frequent **coach** service to Folkestone's Bouverie Square bus station from London Victoria.

RYE AND WINCHELSEA

Rye itself was two miles off [...] It glowed too richly for England; it was too pretty, too all-of-a-piece. English towns do not, under normal circumstances, float on pure light and ripple brightly in the sky.

— Jonathan Raban, *Coasting*

EAST SUSSEX — In Rye's steep cobbled streets, antique- and craft-hunters browse shops for teapots and woolen sweaters. From the glowing windows of restaurants and inns, diners enjoy an array of good food unmatched in any other small English town. But the main allure of this Cinque Port town, once an island at high tide, is the opportunity to see an almost-intact ancient town of Tudor, Stuart and Georgian houses.

To the west, Winchelsea, another of the Cinque Port towns, has three of its original town gates. This "new" Winchelsea was built on a grid pattern in the late thirteenth century after the mediaeval town was destroyed by the sea in 1287. During the sixteenth century the inlet silted up, destroying the ports, leaving both Winchelsea and Rye far from the sea.

The **Tourist Information Centre** ((01797) 226696 FAX (01797) 223460 is located at The Heritage Centre on Strand Quay. You can rent an **audio walking tour** here and see a model of the town **sound-and-light show**, for which there is a small admission fee.

Rye Festival takes place in early September with music, children's events, art exhibitions and workshops, tours and guided walks; details from the Tourist Information Centre or write to Rye Festival, PO Box 33, Rye TN31 7YB.

What to See and Do

Rye is probably best known for photogenic **Mermaid Street**, a steep cobbled lane lined by well-preserved fifteenth- to seventeenth-century houses. Halfway up the street, the crusty old Mermaid Inn (see WHERE TO STAY, below) was a smugglers' den during the 1700s.

For an overview of the history of Rye start with **Rye Castle Museum** ((01797) 226728, housed in one of the town's historic monuments, Ypres Tower (pronounced *wi*-pers), part of the thirteenth-century town fort. A new extension of the museum is located in a restored building at 3 East Street. The exhibition at Ypres Tower walks you through the history of Rye with equal doses of smuggling and law enforcement. On East Street there's an old fire engine, Rye pottery, costumes from different periods in Rye's long history, model ships, and more. Closed weekdays in winter; admission fee.

Below the tower, **Gun Garden** has panoramic views of the River Brede, where Rye Harbour once was. Ypres Castle pub (see under WHERE TO EAT) is a handy place for lunch with the same great views from its terrace.

From 1898 until his death in 1916, Henry James lived at **Lamb House** (NT) ((01892) 890651, in West Street. The house is now open to the public and contains memorabilia of the American writer. James wrote *The Wings of the Dove, The Ambassadors* and *The Golden Bowl* here. Open Wednesday and Saturday afternoon from April to October; admission fee.

A few steps from Lamb House, the street opens onto the serene close of the mid-twelfth-century **Church of St. Mary the Virgin**, noted for its sixteenth-century clock, said to be the oldest functioning church tower clock in England. The painted clock face is flanked by two "quarter boys" who strike the bell on the quarter hours. The tower (open from 10 AM until dusk; admission fee) offers views over the town and countryside.

The **Rye Art Gallery** ((01797) 222433 or (01797) 223218, with entrances off East Street and High Street, has worthwhile changing exhibitions featuring the region's artists and craftspeople. It also hosts international traveling exhibitions. Open daily; free admission.

One of Rye's newer attractions is the **Treasury of Mechanical Music** ((01797) 223345, 20 Cinque Ports Street, where hundreds of music boxes, antique organs, pianos, and other antique music-makers are demonstrated. Closed Tuesdays in winter; admission fee.

Winchelsea is a tranquil hilltop town centered around the parish church of **St. Thomas the Martyr** — set amidst the remains of a larger church, partly destroyed and partly unfinished. Only the fourteenth-century chancel remains, forming the present parish church with its unusual square layout, set with brilliant twentieth-century stained-glass windows by Douglas Strachan. J.M.W. Turner and John Everett Millais came to Winchelsea to paint these romantic ruins in the nineteenth century.

Outdoor Activities

Rye Harbour Nature Reserve, two and a half kilometers (one and a half miles) from town, has miles of walking tracks, some paved. This is a good place for spotting birds, and there are several blinds set up for that purpose on the reserve. Look up for lapwings, kestrels, redshanks and partridges. Look down for razor shells and brown hares.

Five kilometers (three miles) from the town center, **Camber Sands** has perhaps the best beach in the area. Windsurfing is popular here, too, with rentals available at Rye Windsurfing ((01797) 225238. **Winchelsea Beach** is a desolate miles-long shingle, studded with weathered breakwaters that keep the beach from washing into the Channel. It's a paradise for rock-hounds.

From Rye you can join the **1066 Country Walk**, which stretches 50 km (31 miles) from Pevensey to Battle. It's a 24-km (15-mile) hike from Rye to Battle.

Rent **cycles** at Cyclonic Cycle Hire ((01797) 223121, Market Road, Rye or from the Surf Shack ((01797) 225746, also on Market Road.

Where to Stay

While the halls of the **Mermaid Inn** ((01797) 223065, Mermaid Street, are low-beamed and narrow, the bedrooms of this mid-sized Elizabethan inn are amply proportioned with vaulted ceilings and interesting features like built-in armoires or views over the gentle countryside. The inn was built in 1420 out of ship timbers and stone dredged from local battle sights. Very expensive.

Another of Rye's historic buildings, **Jeake's House** ((01797) 222828 FAX (01797) 222623 E-MAIL jeakeshouse@btinternet.com, Mermaid Street, Rye TN31 7ET, dates from the sixteenth-century. There are 12 bedrooms, nine with bath. With its long-standing reputation for good service, as well as its prime location, this may be one of the most popular small hotels in England, so book well in advance; moderate.

The **Old Vicarage** ((01797) 222119 FAX (01797) 227466, 66 Church Square, Rye TN31 7HFA, a listed Georgian house with a pretty, enclosed garden, has a picturesque setting, its rose-colored frontage right on the close of St. Mary's Church. The five bedrooms are decorated with Laura Ashley fabrics; moderate. Children aged eight and over are welcome.

Below Winchelsea's ancient gates, the **Strand House** ((01797) 226276 FAX (01797) 224806 E-MAIL strandhouse@winchelsea.freeserve.co.uk, The Strand, Winchelsea TN36 4JT, is a pleasant old hostelry which probably predates the "new" town of Winchelsea. The bedrooms with sloping floors

A jumble of watercraft surrounds ancient Rye.

and "duck-or-grouse" doorways are each completely unique. One of the rooms has a "priest hole," where a Catholic priest could hide from the persecutors of the Protestant Reformation. Downstairs the sitting room is warmed by an inglenook fire, and a pretty terraced garden rises in back of the property; moderate to inexpensive. The Bridge, across the street, is handy for dinner.

Right next to the nature reserve at Rye Harbour, is another **Old Vicarage (** (01797) 222088, Rye Harbour, Rye TN31 7TT. This tile-hung Victorian is a good spot for anyone who seeking serenity. There are two rooms with shared bath. Common areas feature antique furniture and open fires; inexpensive.

Monday. No lunch. Reservations advised on weekends; moderate.

Ypres Castle ((01797) 223248, Gun Garden, near thirteenth-century Ypres Tower, is a warm and friendly eighteenth-century free house serving local fish and seafood, and many wines by the glass. The lawn terrace has river views; moderate to inexpensive.

Down at Rye Harbour, the **Inkerman Arms (** (01797) 222464 is a pleasant pub with local ales on tap, a long wine menu, and traditional fare including game and cider pie, as well as a daily vegetarian choice.

For tasty snacks, the **Old Tuck Shoppe**, Market Street, has delicious organic breads (including cute

Where to Eat

For such a small town, Rye is flush with good restaurants. And when you want something light there are tea rooms around every bend.

At the atmospheric **Mermaid Inn** (above) you might choose a starter such as terrine of pheasant and venison with redcurrant marmalade, and follow up with *panaché* of fresh seafood on crisp rice noodles with lobster and tarragon sauce; expensive.

A family-run restaurant, the timber-framed **Flushing Inn (** (01797) 223292, 4 Market Street, specializes in local fish and seafood served in the cozy wood-paneled dining room, warmed by log fires. Finish your meal with homemade green fig and coffee ice cream; expensive. There are also a couple of comfortable bedrooms (call for rates).

Landgate Bistro ((01797) 222829, 5-6 Landgate, is one of Rye's best tables, with seasonal game, local fish and seafood on the menu. Closed Sunday and

hedgehog-shaped bread loafs) and pastries as well as pizza by the slab, which they'll heat for a little extra.

How to Get There

Rye is 97 km (60 miles) southeast of London. There is frequent **train** service from London Charing Cross or Cannon Street to Rye with a change at Ashford or at Hastings.

HASTINGS AND BATTLE

EAST SUSSEX — You'd think it was 1066 in Hastings again on a summer weekend when hordes of families flailing lollipop shields and ice cream swords invade the streets and beaches. To the north, the small town of Battle, built on the site of the fateful military engagement of 1066, the Battle of Hastings, seems a haven of tranquillity. The remains of

Battle Abbey stand on a rise at the head of High Street, and the town itself has scores of old buildings, some dating back to the thirteenth and fourteenth century.

Hastings Tourist Information Centre ((01424) 781111 FAX (01424) 781133 is at 4 Robertson Terrace; while the Battle Tourist Information Centre ((01424) 773721 FAX (01424) 773436 is at 88 High Street.

Battle has a spectacular **Bonfire Night**, the annual celebration of the Gunpowder Plot, on November 5.

What to See and Do

In Hastings, head for the **Old Town**, which is interesting in a dismal way. From here you can walk to the **fishing beach** and look at Hastings' famous tall black **net huts** and fish stalls, surrounded by a car park. There is a funicular at each end of the fishing beach (partially closed at the time of research) which takes passengers up to the Norman ruins of **Hastings Castle** ((01424) 422964, above the cliffs where an audio-visual presentation evokes the Battle of Hastings; admission fee.

Four years after his victory at Battle, as penance for the bloodshed he caused, William I ordered the construction of **Battle Abbey** (EH) ((01424) 773792, High Street. The abbey no longer survives, but in the center of Battle, the gatehouse remains. It's said that William had the abbey's high altar erected on the spot where Harold was killed. There is a one-and-a-half-kilometer-long (one-mile) audio tour around the battlefield explaining the events. Open daily year-round; admission fee. More 1066 remembrances can be found at **Battle Museum**, High Street, which has a reproduction of the Bayeux tapestry, depicting events of the engagement. Closed Sunday mornings and from October to Easter; admission fee. **St. Mary's** is the parish church at Battle. It dates in part from the fourteenth and fifteenth centuries, sympathetically restored in the mid-1800s.

Where to Stay

Netherfield Place ((01424) 774455 FAX (01424) 774024, Netherfield, near Battle TN33 9PP, is a Georgian-style hotel, with 14 attractive rooms, in 12 ha (30 acres) of grounds and gardens. The public areas are warmed by log fires and decorated with fresh flowers. Leisure facilities include two tennis courts, croquet and a putting green; expensive. The kitchen prepares Modern British food using the hotel's own garden produce wherever possible, served in the wood-paneled restaurant (expensive) overlooking the garden.

Set on grounds encompassing a woods for walking, a lake, tennis court, and gardens, **Little Hemingfold Farmhouse** ((01424) 774338, Hastings Road, Battle TN33 0TT, has 13 bedrooms, most with bath. In the farmhouse log fires warm the common areas, and good food is served in the dining room using homegrown ingredients; moderate.

An Edwardian farmhouse located about 20 minutes' walk from Battle Abbey, **Farthings Farm** ((01424) 773107, Catsfield, Battle TN33 9BA, is located along the 1066 Country long-distance footpath. The three bedrooms, two with bath, are charmingly decorated; high end of the inexpensive range.

To the east, **Fairlight Cottage** ((01424) 812545, Fairlight, Hastings, TN35 4AG, has three rooms, set in fine countryside with views toward Rye Harbour and opportunities for cliff walks. Evening meals are available by prior arrangement; inexpensive.

Six and a half kilometers (four miles) east of town, **Hastings Youth Hostel** ((01424) 812373 FAX (01424) 814273, Guestling Hall, Rye Road, Guestling, Hastings TN35 4LP, is a Victorian country house with one hectare (three acres) of land and a small lake; rock-bottom.

Where to Eat

A saving grace in Hastings are its many **chippies** down by the fishing beach. Ask at one of the fishmongers which fish & chips stall serves the freshest catch of the day.

The adjoining resort of St. Leonards has an excellent restaurant in **Röser's** ((01424) 712218, 64 Eversfield Place, across from the pier. Don't let the twee decor fool you; the French cuisine is seriously delicious; expensive.

Harris ((01424) 437221, 58 High Street, is a casual, place serving mainly Spanish fare; moderate.

In the area of Fairlight, **Crossways** ((01424) 812356, Pett Level Road (corner of Waites Lane), Fairlight, provides international cuisine; moderate.

How to Get There

Hastings is 105 km (65 miles) southeast of London, and Battle is eight kilometers (five miles) northeast of Hastings. There is frequent direct **train** service from London Charing Cross to Battle and Hastings. The trip takes an hour and 45 minutes (less to Battle). National Express operates **coach** services twice daily from London Victoria to Hastings's bus station on Queen's Parade. It's a ride of three hours.

ASHDOWN FOREST

WEST SUSSEX — A designated Area of Outstanding Natural Beauty, Ashdown Forest is the home of A.A. Milne's (1882–1956) Winnie-the-Pooh. It was this rolling gorse-and-heath countryside that inspired Milne's stories for his son Christopher Robin, and upon which Ernest H. Shepard based his illustrations. The area provides ample scope for woodland walks as well as visits to surrounding gardens and stately homes.

The ruins of Battle Abbey, site of the pivotal Battle of Hastings.

WHAT TO SEE AND DO

At the top of the Ashdown Forest, a five-kilometer (three-mile) circular walk from the Gills Lap car park passes the "enchanted place" — Roo's Sandypit, the Hundred acre Wood, Eeyore's Gloomy Place ("rather boggy and sad"), and other familiar landmarks from this children's classic. The Ashdown Forest Information Centre ((01342) 823583, located one and a half kilometers (one mile) east of Wych Cross on the Hartfield road, has leaflets and maps of the forest trail for sale. It's open weekday afternoons and all day on weekends from April to the end of September.

On the edge of the forest, Hartfield village has **Pooh Corner** ((01892) 770453, High Street, a gift and souvenir shop specializing in all things Pooh. The shop sometimes stocks free leaflets and forest maps, useful when the forest information center is not open. In the center of Hartfield, the **Parish Church of St. Mary the Virgin** has a nature trail posted at the timbered lych gate. It's an intriguing exploration of the world of graveyard lichens.

Three kilometers (two miles) south of East Grinstead, **Standen** (NT) ((01342) 323029 is a remarkable monument to the Arts & Crafts movement of the late nineteenth to early twentieth century. The house, a nineteenth-century addition attached to a traditional Wealden farmhouse, was designed from top to bottom by Philip Webb, a friend and associate of William Morris. Everything from the carved staircase banisters to the punched metal fingerplates on the doors was designed by Webb. Throughout the house, tapestries, woven spreads and wallpapers from the workshops of William Morris adorn the rooms. In keeping with the themes of the movement, a natural-style, 4.8-hectare (12-acre) garden spreads out from the house. There are delightful woodland walks as far as Weir Wood Reservoir. On the grounds is a pleasant cafeteria in the restored barn. Open Wednesday to Sunday afternoon from mid-March to October. It's located off the B2110.

Wakehurst Place ((01444) 894066, near Haywards Heath, is a branch of Kew Gardens (see page 110), a 200-hectare (500-acre) estate, one quarter of which is cultivated gardens with plants from around the world and the remainder woodland. As at Kew, these Royal Botanic Gardens are primarily for scientific and experimental work, but are open to the public daily throughout the year; admission fee. The mansion (not open to the public) was built in 1590.

The trees are the star attraction at **Sheffield Park Garden** (NT) ((01825) 790231. Rows of massive sequoias and an 80-year-old eucalyptus are just a few of the *grandes dames* of this garden. Throughout the garden are romantic views, such as the vista from Middle Lake beyond the waterfall to the neo-Gothic Sheffield Park House (not open to the public). The Heart of Sussex Link ((01825) 790231 links Hayward Heath Station with Sheffield Park on Sundays and Bank Holiday Mondays from April to September.

A delightful way to arrive at Sheffield Park Garden is the **Bluebell Line** ((01825) 723777, a 15-km (nine-mile) train trip that runs through Horsted Keynes to Kingscote, where there are bus connections to East Grinstead and mainline trains. The scenery is at its finest in mid-May when woodland are carpeted with bluebells.

WHERE TO STAY

Many accommodations around Ashdown Forest are within easy to reach of Gatwick, making them good candidates for early departures or late arrivals. The solemnly elegant interiors of **Ashdown Park Hotel** ((01342) 824988 FAX (01342) 826206 E-MAIL reservations@ashdownpark.co.uk, Wych Cross, Forest Row RH18 5JR, contrast sharply with the hotel's exuberant gardens. There are 107 bedrooms; those in the west wing have more character, with leaded windows and grander dimensions. The rooms are not deeply luxurious, but certainly comfy. Staff are pleasant and professional; very expensive to luxury. The hotel has an indoor heated pool and Jacuzzi, and the restaurant (expensive) serves classic fare overlooking the lake and parkland.

The woodsy village of High Hurstwood has some friendly B&Bs. **Old Mill Farm** (/FAX (01825) 732279, Chillies Lane, High Hurstwood, near Uckfield TN22 4AD, is a converted weatherboard barn with three bedrooms in a modern extension. Breakfast is in the beamed old house overlooking the farmyard where you can sometimes spot half-tame pheasants. Down the road is **The Cottage** ((01825) 732804 FAX (01825) 732804, Chillies Lane High, Hurstwood, Uckfield TN22 4AA, with three homey rooms, one with bath. Breakfast is served in the conservatory looking out on the pretty garden and valley; inexpensive.

At Standen, the National Trust has refurbished the **Servants' Wing** as a comfortable apartment in the spirit of the Arts and Crafts Movement. The apartment sleeps four, three night minimum stay; inexpensive. Contact the National Trust Holiday Cottage Booking Office ((01225) 791199 FAX (01225) 792267, PO Box 536, Melksham, Wiltshire SN12 8SX.

WHERE TO EAT

The **Anchor Inn** ((01892) 770424, Church Street, is a traditional fourteenth-century public house in Hartfield serving fish and steaks; moderate to inexpensive. On the A26 (Uckfield Road), the **Crow & Gate** ((01892) 603461, Crowborough, is a modern, food-oriented pub with an eclectic menu; inexpensive.

In the heart of the forest, on the B2026, **Duddleswell Tea Rooms** (no phone), Duddleswell, near Uckfield, is a geriatric haven with a log fire and a good selection of comfort food and cream teas. The buck rarebit (toast with cheese sauce and poached egg) is especially soothing; inexpensive.

LEWES AND GLYNDEBOURNE

EAST SUSSEX — Set on a steep hill above the River Ouse (pronounced ooze), the county administrative center of Lewes has a busy High Street and a lively pedestrian-only area around the old river port. There are some interesting buildings throughout town, including some with characteristic red and black "mathematical tiles," for example the Friends Meeting House on Friars Walk. Besides the busy shopping areas, Lewes's "twittens" (Saxon alleyways) are fun to explore.

Glyndebourne is the site of the **Glyndebourne Opera Festival**, one of England's most significant cultural events, which takes place annually from mid-May to late August. Lewes has long had a reputation for putting on the country's most impressive **Bonfire Nights** on Guy Fawke's night, 5 November.

GENERAL INFORMATION

The **Tourist Information Centre** ((01273) 483448 is located at 187 High Street. It stocks brochures on **self-guided walks** around Lewes and into the surrounding countryside.

All day on weekends and weekdays after 6 PM, there is **free parking** off High Street across from the Pelham Arms at the East Sussex County Council car park.

WHAT TO SEE AND DO

The ruins of **Lewes Castle** (EH) ((01273) 486290, all but invisible behind the high street shops, loom impressively as you turn into Castle Gate. The castle was put up by William de Warenne after the Battle of Hastings to reinforce his control of the area. Admission to the castle includes visits to the Barbican House Museum with its archaeological finds, and the Lewes Living History Model; an audio tour is available for an additional fee. The entrance is directly off 169 High Street. A combined admission ticket with Anne of Cleves House (below) is available. Open daily year-round. From the castle green you can view the **battleground** where Henry III fought Simon de Montfort in the 1264 Battle of Lewes.

An Elizabethan manor (1572) built of Caen stone taken from the ruins of Lewes Priory (below), **The Grange**, Southover Road, was the boyhood home of diarist John Evelyn. It's now the District Registry Office. You can visit the attractive **walled gardens** for an interesting view of the town stacked up the hill; closed Saturday, free admission.

A sixteenth-century timber-framed Wealden hall-house, **Anne of Cleves House and Museum** (EH) ((01273) 474610, 52 Southover High Street, is the setting for a museum of folk history and decorative arts. A Tudor-style garden surrounds the house. Open daily from March to November except Sunday morning, Tuesday, Thursday and Saturday in winter; admission fee. Departing from the museum are guided tours of the ruins of **Lewes Priory** ((01273) 475649, at 2:30 PM from the end of April through September; admission fee.

A number of **antiques shops** line High Street and Cliffe High Street, as well as several interesting **bookstores**. Dive into the Fifteenth Century Bookstore, 100 High Street, for secondhand books. Look for the London milestone set in the shop's timber frame. High-quality **crafts** are exhibited and sold at the Old Needlemakers Factory, Market Lane; closed Sunday. There is a small café ((01273) 486258 here, serving simple snacks.

Three kilometers (two miles) east of Lewes, the 1,200-seat **Glyndebourne Opera** is the spectacular venue for the annual Glyndebourne Festival. Tickets range in price from £10 to £110 and are available from Glyndebourne Festival Opera Box Office ((01273) 813813, Lewes, East Sussex BN8 5UU; book well in advance. **Glynde Place** ((01273) 858224 is an Elizabethan manor house with eighteenth-century interiors, open to the public; opening hours are limited. Call for details; an admission fee is charged.

WHERE TO STAY

Horsted Place ((01825) 750581 FAX (01825) 750459 E-MAIL hotel@horstedplace.co.uk, Little Horsted, East Sussex TN22 5TS, 10 km (six miles) north of Lewes, is a gorgeous Gothic Revivalist country house hotel with 20 elegantly-appointed bedrooms. Some rooms have private exits to the fabulous gardens and grounds planted with rare and ancient trees and flowering shrubs. Bedrooms and common areas are skillfully decorated in restful color schemes and every window affords views of the gardens. Despite its elegance the hotel remains unpretentious, and staff are helpful. The dining room provides an intimate setting for *haute cuisine*, and leisure facilities include an indoor pool, golf privileges, a tennis court, and croquet; expensive. The hotel offers excellent-value short breaks.

In Lewes, the sixteenth-century **White Hart Hotel** ((01273) 476694 FAX (01273) 476695, 55 High Street, Lewes BN7 1XE, has a lot going for it if you don't mind the tired decor in the bedrooms — some in the old inn and some in a modern annex. It's right in the center of town and the restaurant and terrace have terrific views of the chalk cliffs of the Ouse Valley. The Tudor bar has an open log fire and there is an indoor swimming pool, sauna, and gym; moderate to expensive.

If you want to be close to Glyndebourne, consider **Old Whyly** ((01825) 840216, Halland Road, East Hoathly, Lewes BN8 6EL. There are three bedrooms in this seventeenth-century manor house decorated with antiques and art objects. A garden, tennis courts and swimming pool complete the amenities and picnic baskets can be provided; expensive.

Three kilometers (a couple of miles) north of Lewes, **Ousedale House** ((01273) 478680, Offham, Lewes BN7 3QF, has three bedrooms in a Victorian house with views, large garden and woodland; high end of inexpensive price range.

WHERE TO EAT

The **Brasserie** ((01273) 487209, Riverside, Cliffe Bridge, is set on the upper floor of the bustling Riverside Market. Sunny and friendly, it does savory pies (chicken and leak, salmon and broccoli), soups and more. The seats by the window look out over the River Ouse. Last orders taken at 5 PM. There are inexpensive snack shops and sidewalk tables downstairs in the **market** as well.

Seasons Vegetarian Café ((01273) 473968, 199 High Street, is a cellar tea room and restaurant, neat and homey with cushioned benches and buzzy atmosphere. On the menu: bean burgers, cashew loaf, and green salads; inexpensive.

Robson's of Lewes Coffee Shop ((01273) 480654, 22A High Street, has a pretty dining area with bow windows looking out on a tiny garden. Fresh sandwiches and soups, quiche and sweets are available for take out as well; inexpensive.

HOW TO GET THERE

Lewes is 81 km (50 miles) south of London. **Trains** leave London Victoria every 40 minutes for the one-hour trip to Lewes. There are also good rail connections from Eastbourne and Brighton. South Coast **buses** ((01273) 474747 run to Lewes from Brighton.

ALFRISTON

EAST SUSSEX — One of Britain's most charming villages, Alfriston is ideally located for taking advantage of the wide array of attractions in this pretty corner of East Sussex. Parking is limited in Alfriston, so arrive early in the day during the high season.

WHAT TO SEE AND DO

Tucked away from the village main street, Alfriston's green, the **Tye**, is an island of tranquillity. Set alongside the Tye, the **Clergy House** (NT) ((01323)

870001, is a fourteenth-century timber-framed and thatched Wealden house. A mediaeval hall and exhibition give an idea of rural Sussex life in the aftermath of the Black Death. A cottage garden with once-common native flowers surrounds the house. Open daily April through October except Tuesday and Friday; admission fee.

Also on The Tye, the **parish church** with its impressive shingle spire has been called the "Cathedral of the Downs." The church dates mostly from the fourteenth century and the well-proportioned interior is worth a look.

At **Middle Farm** ((01273) 811411, on the A27 between Lewes and Eastbourne, you can mingle with the chickens and exotic fowl, including a hilarious New Zealand shell duck with Elvis-style pompadour. In spring, it's possible to pet wobbly-legged lambs and all through the year watch the guinea pigs tunneling busily from shed to farmyard. A gift shop sells souvenirs, games and superb animal masks. Taste and buy dozens of varieties of the local beverage in the cider shop, including the farm's own hand-pressed apple cider and perry (fermented pear juice). Another shop sells cheeses and produce, and the tea room offers a "cuppa."

Looking as if a genius child got loose with a box of oil paints, **Charleston Farmhouse** ((01273) 811265 is a must-see monument to the art of the Bloomsbury Group. This Tudor-and-Georgian farmhouse set in a rambling garden was the country home of Duncan Grant and Vanessa Bell, the Sussex outpost of a literary-artistic-intellectual movement of the early twentieth century. Every room in the house, every surface, every scrap of fabric was painted or designed by Bell and Duncan, their children, or one of their milieu. In addition to muraled walls, floors, furniture, stenciled wallpapers, one-of-a-kind fabrics and hand-thrown ceramic chandeliers, works of art — representing a who's-who of post-Impressionist painters — hang from the walls. Almost as exciting as the house is the adjacent shop, which sells replicas of Bloomsbury decorative arts as well as the works of artists-in-residence working in the Bloomsbury tradition. Open afternoons Wednesday to Sunday and bank holidays from Easter to October; admission fee. There are longer, more detailed tours each Friday. Teas are served on Saturday. Children eight and older are welcome. The house is located at the foot of the South Downs, just south of the A27 between Lewes and Eastbourne.

More of the works of Grant and Bell adorn the walls of **Berwick Church** (Saint Michael's All Saints) where the couple painted colorful murals during World War II, later added to by Vanessa's son Quentin and daughter Angelica. Many of the group's entourage posed for the Biblical characters who appear in the tableaux. Angelica sat for the Virgin Mary. Though much of the painting is candidly Christian, there is a set of delightfully secular paintings on the pulpit. Originally painted by Vanessa, some of the panels were destroyed by vandalism in 1962; they were later redone by Angelica and Duncan.

Anonymous artwork of monumental scale can be seen toward Eastbourne, just off the A27, where the **Long Man of Wilmington** lounges on a hillside. This 70-m-tall (230-ft) figure, outlined in white blocks, is depicted holding two long staffs. The date of origin is unknown; estimates range from the early eighteenth century to the Bronze Age. You can trot around the downs here and even up the Man himself.

aeval woodwork; expensive. In the restaurant the menu is Mod Brit with a hint of the East. Begin with, perhaps, seafood mousse accompanied by cucumber noodles and lemon chili dressing, followed by wild mushroom stilton tartlet with roquette leaves and tomato garlic *concassé*; reasonable. For lunch there is steak-and-Guinness pie, sandwiches, salads and jacket potatoes.

A Victorian on the edge of Alfriston, **Riverdale House (** (01323) 871038, Seaford Road, Alfriston, Polegate BN26 5TR, has six bedrooms with views of the beautiful Cuckmere Valley; inexpensive.

One and a half kilometers (one mile) or so south of town is the **YHA Alfriston (** (01323) 442667 FAX (01323) 870615, Frog Firle, Alfriston, Polegate

OUTDOOR ACTIVITIES

Pretty footpaths meander through the downland and water meadows of **Frog Firle Farm** (NT). Start from the car park signposted at High and Over, south of Alfriston on the B2108 (Alfriston to Seaford road). There's plenty to explore here from flower-strewn meadows to a pre-historic burial ground to another chalk figure, this one of nineteenth-century vintage. Public bridleways here are excellent, and popular for cycling and horseback riding.

WHERE TO STAY

One of the oldest inns in England, the **Star (** (01323) 870495, High Street, Alfriston, Polegate BN26 5TA, with 37 bedrooms, dates from the thirteenth century. The front, originally built as a guest house for pilgrims, still has magnificently carved medi-

BN26 5TT, set in a sixteenth-century house in a lovely rural area, an ideal base for rambling; rock-bottom.

WHERE TO EAT

Open for evening meals, **Moonrakers (** (01323) 870472, Alfriston, is a romantic place with a log fire and a good wine list. The mouth-watering menu may include a starter of broccoli timbale with walnut cream dressing and mains like medallions of lamb cooked in redcurrant and rosemary *jus*, or chicken filled with stilton and wrapped in bacon; moderate.

The **Singing Kettle**, Waterloo Square, Alfriston, serves tea and crumpets as well as toasted sandwiches in its cozy beamed tea room; inexpensive.

There are several food pubs to choose from. **Ye Olde Smuggler's Inne (** (01323) 870241, Market

Alfriston's "Cathedral of the Downs."

Cross, Alfriston, is a cozy place for a sandwich or fish & chips. In Berwick, the **Cricketer's Arms** ((01323) 870469 provides good lunches using local meat and fish; inexpensive.

How to Get There

The closest **train** stations to Alfriston are five kilometers (three miles) distant at Seaford and Berwick. Local **buses** run along the A259 coastal road through Hastings, Eastbourne, Seaford and Brighton to Alfriston. National Express **coaches** go to Eastbourne, 13 km (eight miles) out of Alfriston. RDH buses (01273) 474747 run between Lewes and Alfriston.

land, a meandering river, and chalk cliffs. Canoe instruction is available, and there are cycle paths and walking routes. The beaches though pebbly are pleasant on fine days. You can rent **bicycles** from Cuckmere Cycle Company ((01323) 870310 E-MAIL bikehire@compuserve.com, The Barn, Seven Sisters Country Park, Exceat, Seaford. Ask about their other locations including Horam (for the Cuckoo Trail), Bewl Water and Eastbourne.

On the road east toward Beachy Head, at **Seven Sisters Sheep Centre** ((01323) 423302, Gilberts Drive, East Dean, you can see lambing from mid-March to early May, shearing from June to mid-July. The rest of the year there are spinning, milking and cheese-making demonstrations and

THE SOUTH DOWNS AND THE SEA

EAST SUSSEX — The Sussex Downs meet the sea with magnificent drama at the chalk cliffs of Beachy Head and the Seven Sisters. This area to the west of the genteel resort of Eastbourne is typified by large prosperous farms and buildings of brick, flint, and wood, and chalk. It's beautiful walking country as the South Downs Way comes to a spectacular finale here. At present, this area of ploughed fields and pastureland is being considered for national park status. If this comes to pass there will undoubtedly be additional visitor facilities.

You can walk the five kilometers (three or so miles) from Alfriston (above) down the beautiful Cuckmere Valley to **Seven Sisters Country Park** ((01323) 870280, located on the A259. The park has some 280 hectares (700 acres) of grassy farm-

young animals to hold and feed. The farm shop sells cheese and yogurt. Closed weekdays, and all of mid-September to mid-March; £3.

Beachy Head has tremendous views over the headlands. These dramatic cliffs are famous for the number of people who jump to their deaths here each year. But there are healthier, not to say more sustainable, pursuits provided by the Beachy Head Countryside Centre ((01323) 737273, Beachy Head Road, Beachy Head, Eastbourne BN20 7YA. The center has hands-on exhibitions and play areas as well as interesting guided walks (fee charged) around the cliffs and beaches. You can get to Beachy Head on foot from Eastbourne along the South Downs Way, a distance of five kilometers (three miles).

Inland from Beachy Head, **Lullington Heath** is an unspoiled downland area, a National Nature Reserve. The **Cuckoo Trail** here follows the route of a former railway that ran from Polegate to Heathfield.

Its popular with walkers and cyclists; the mileposts each hide a cuckoo in their design.

The 162-km (100-mile) South Downs Way from Eastbourne to Winchester is Britain's only long-distance **bridleway**.

WHERE TO STAY AND EAT

On the outskirts of Eastbourne, the **Downland Hotel** ((01323) 732689 FAX (01323) 720321, 37 Lewes Road Eastbourne BN21 2BU, has comfortable bedrooms and a candlelit **dining room** (moderate) offering a selective menu. Children aged 10 and older are welcome; moderate (special breaks available).

Black Robin Farm ((01323) 643357, Beachy Head, Eastbourne BN20 7XX, is a farmhouse B&B in the heart of the Sussex Downs, and a good walking base; inexpensive.

BRIGHTON

EAST SUSSEX — The largest town in Sussex, Brighton is a kaleidoscope of new and nouveau, chic and shocking. Tucked into a framework of decaying Victorian splendor, this seaside town is a microcosm of the allure of Britain itself, where traditional neighbors meet the trendy. Where else can you dine on roast beef and Yorkshire pudding at a seventeenth-century pub and cross the street for some organic vegan dessert wine? Besides interesting dining, Brighton has plenty to see, from the gaudy wonders of the Royal Pavilion to the hungry sharks at the Sea Life Centre.

Brighton rose to prominence in the eighteenth century. In 1754, Dr. Richard Russell arrived in this seaside village touting the healing properties of seawater. Wealthy invalids came fast on his heals, and the village was soon transformed. In 1783, the Prince of Wales, later King George IV, visited Brighton and took to it, making the town fashionable. A building boom of Regency townhouses followed, as friends-of-the-king followed suit.

Day-trippers from London love to head for the seashore, and Brighton is the oldest, largest, and most famous of them all. Unless you love the crush of sweaty bodies, avoid summer weekends in Brighton.

The **Brighton Festival** ((01273) 292950 is the largest British arts festival outside Edinburgh. It takes place over three weeks each May.

GENERAL INFORMATION

The **Tourist Information Centre** ((01273) 323755 or (0345) 573512 (lodging) is across from the Town Hall, at 10 Bartholomew Square. One-hour **walking and bus tours** depart from the center; call for times.

Oddly enough, the only place at the time of research that offered **Internet** access in Brighton was the Brighton Backpackers Hostel (see WHERE TO STAY, below), for guests only. That should change; ask around for locations of cybercafés.

Blue Badge **guided walking tours** ((01903) 873172 taking in Regency Brighton depart each Thursday at 11 AM from the Tourist Information Centre; fee charged. **Double-decker hop-on hop-off bus tours** of Brighton depart from Palace Pier every 30 minutes between 10:45 AM and 4:45 PM; fee charged.

WHAT TO SEE AND DO

Called a "monument of the English Romantic Movement," the **Royal Pavilion** ((01273) 290900, is a Taj Mahal-like confection designed by Henry Holland in 1787 for the Prince Regent. It was further developed in 1815 by John Nash. While the exterior takes its influence from Mughal India, the interior is inspired by Chinese decorative art. The Long Gallery, Banqueting Room and the Music Room have all been recently refurbished. The **gardens** have been restored to the original John Nash layout, with serpentine paths lined with hollyhocks and inhabited by throngs of happy sunbathers and buskers. The **Queen Adelaide Tea Room**, with its balcony over the gardens, makes an agreeable spot for a break. Open daily year-round; admission charged.

Near Seaford, the South Downs Way national trail hugs the chalk cliffs dubbed the Seven Sisters.

Built in 1899, **Palace Pier** ((01273) 609361, Madeira Drive, is one of the United Kingdom's most popular tourist attractions, pulling in more than three million visitors a year. On summer weekends it pulsates with life. Old folks promenade, eat fish and chips, and nap on the blue-and-white-striped deck chairs (free!). And while the grown-ups snooze and schmooze, kids find a zillion and one ways to while away the time; from video and penny arcade games to rock candy to foot-tapping to the tunes of the Pier's own radio station. At the end of the pier an old-fashioned fun fair offers a dozen or so rides — each with an extra thrill on the up-swing: the silver sea sparkling below. The pier is open daily year-round; free.

Now in ruins, **West Pier** was one of the first resort piers in the country. Damaged in World War II, it faded into obscurity. Now a campaign is underway to restore the pier and, as part of fundraising efforts, tours are offered daily at 3 PM, Saturday at 1:30 PM and 3 PM. Call ((01273) 207610, or stop by the information booth at the head of the pier.

The **Sea Life Centre** ((01273) 604234, Marine Parade, retains a quaint Victorian aura with its iron-framed fishtanks glowing from dark hallways. Kids can pet sea anemone in the Rock Pool, or take brass rubbings of some of the aquarium inmates. Native fish such as the ferocious looking cold-water catfish are a highlight. Bypass the tedious "Adventures at 20,000 Leagues Under the Sea," and head straight for the Ocean Tunnel, a trip through the shark tank via an acrylic tube. Call ahead to find out the shark-feeding schedule. Open daily year-round; admission fee.

Brighton Marina, east of the center, has shops, waterside bars and an entertainment center with ten-pin bowling and pool tables. You can get there on Britain's first electric railway, the **Volks Electric Railway** ((01273) 292718, Madeira Drive, built in 1883. It runs along the beach from just west of the Sea Life Center; fee charged.

Four kilometers (two and a half miles) north of the seafront, **Preston Manor** ((01273) 292770 is a Georgian mansion built in 1738. Set in Preston Park, the house is decorated with period furniture and fittings, mainly Georgian but some much earlier. Closed Sunday morning and all day Monday; admission fee.

OUTDOOR ACTIVITIES

Brighton's **beach** is a steep bank of amber and gray pebbles, or "shingle," where a United Nations of sun worshippers splash and squeal. The water is cold, but it feels great on a hot day. For small children, an alternative to sea bathing is the **wading pool** by West Pier (free).

There is plenty of good **cycling** country around Brighton on the South Downs and along the scenic Sussex Coast. You can **rent bicycles** at Sunrise Cycles ((01273) 748881, at West Pier by the hour or day. The Tourist Information Centre offers advice on cycling in the region including self-guided itineraries and more places to hire bikes.

In-line skating is popular in town. Rent blades at Pulse Skating Solutions ((01273) 572098, 11 Octagon Fountain, BTHrighton Marina; or at West Pier.

Rent gear for **water sports**, from catamarans to boogie boards, at Sunhire ((01273) 323160, 185 Kings Road. Hove Lagoon is a calm place to learn windsurfing.

SHOPPING

For devoted shoppers, Brighton makes life worth living. Two main shopping areas spread through the oldest parts of town, one up-market, the other funky. The **Lanes** are a warren of narrow alleys lined by cottages, formerly the abodes of fishermen, which have been converted into expensive antiques shops and high-fashion boutiques. Look also for one-of-a-kind jewelry, as well as hats and shoes. North of the Lanes, **North Laine** is a warren of fun restaurants, pretty villas, pubs, and clubs, as well as some 300 shops selling everything from used vinyl and fluorescent club gear to African drums, and do-it-yourself T-shirts.

In addition to The Lanes and North Laine, Western Road, North Street and Churchill Square have all the **high street chains**. There are more **antique furniture shops** along Upper North Street and Portland Road as well as on Blatchington Road in Hove. And there is a **flea market** ("car boot" sale) in the Brighton Station car park on Sunday mornings.

WHERE TO STAY

The elegant Victorian **Grand Hotel** ((01273) 321188, King's Road, Brighton BN1 2FW, has 200 rooms, many with sea view. Afternoon tea is lovely in the sunny seafront conservatory furnished with white wicker chairs. The restaurant (moderate) offers another elegant setting with high ceilings, draped damask and sparkling chandeliers. The three-course luncheon is good value. This is a fully-loaded resort hotel with its own nightclub and health spa (massages, facials, sauna) and indoor pool; very expensive to luxury (three-night breaks with dinner and breakfast available).

Some of the bedrooms have sea views at **Topps** ((01273) 729334, 17 Regency Square, Brighton BN1 2FG, a Regency townhouse. A good breakfast and simple dinners are served in the cellar restaurant; moderate to expensive.

The Royal Pavillion, playhouse of the Prince Regent, was built in 1787 by Henry Holland.

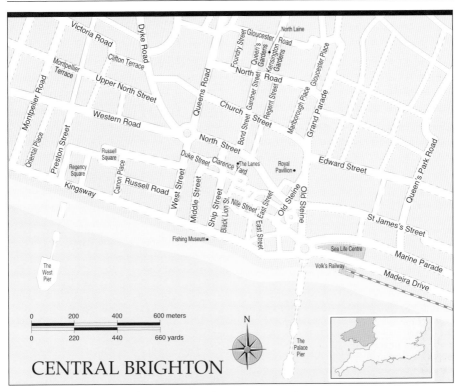

Victoria Road
Dyke Road
Gloucester Road
Foundry Street
North Laine
Clifton Terrace
Queen's Gardens
Kensington Gardens
Montpellier Terrace
Upper North Street
North Road
Gloucester Place
Marlborough Place
Grand Parade
Montpellier Road
Queens Road
Church Street
Bond Street
Gardner Street
Regent Street
Oriental Place
Preston Street
Western Road
North Street
Russell Square
Duke Street
Clarence Yard
The Lanes
Royal Pavilion
Edward Street
Queen's Park Road
Regency Square
Canon Place
Russell Road
West Street
Middle Street
Ship Street
Black Lion St.
Nile Street
East Street
Old Steine
Old Steine
Kingsway
St James's Street
Fishing Museum
Sea Life Centre
Marine Parade
The West Pier
Volk's Railway
Madeira Drive

0   200   400   600 meters
0   220   440   660 yards

N

CENTRAL BRIGHTON

The Palace Pier

The **Oriental Hotel** ((01273) 205050 FAX (1273) 821096 E-MAIL info@orientalhotel.co.uk, 9 Oriental Place, Brighton BN1 2LJ, manages to be both stylish and comfortable. Though not opulent, its space-age 1950s-a-go-go style makes you feel totally pampered. Kidney-shaped furniture adorns the "ultra lounge," and a wavy, water theme with peaceful blue tones runs through the public areas and bedrooms. Some of the 12 rooms have balconies, all are individually decorated. Breakfast includes vegetarian options. You must book months in advance for summer weekends. Room rates are inexpensive on weekdays, moderate on weekends.

A tidy, bow-windowed Regency house, the **Dove Hotel** ((01273) 779222, 18 Regency Square, Brighton BN1 2FG, has eight recently-redone bedrooms, four of which have sea view. There is a sunny breakfast room and evening meals are served by prior arrangement; moderate.

Cecil House ((01273) 325942 FAX (01273) 325222, 126 Kings Road, Brighton BN1 2FA, is an old-fashioned, bow-front guest house with 12 rooms just opposite the old West Pier. Rooms in the front have sea views which compensate for the uninspired decor. Back rooms are not recommended unless you're in a pinch. The family room (with small fridge) and balcony is good value. Otherwise, rates are at the high end of the inexpensive price range; breakfast and parking available for additional fees.

In the rock-bottom price range there is the **Brighton Youth Hostel** ((01273) 556196 FAX (01273) 509366 E-MAIL brighton@yha.org.uk, Patcham Place, London Road, Brighton BN1 8YD, six kilometers (three and a half miles) north of the center. The South Downs Way passes close by. For city-living there is the friendly, well-run **Baggies Backpackers** ((01273) 733740 E-MAIL cybercave @brightonbackpackers.com, 33 Oriental Place, Brighton BN1 2LL, just off King's Road.

WHERE TO EAT

Brighton's culinary scene is diverse but not particularly upscale — with the exception of **One Paston Place** ((01243) 606933, 1 Paston Place, just off the seafront, where Modern British features include fish and game; expensive.

Down on the water, **Alfresco** ((01273) 206523, King's Road Arches, is an Italian seafood place with a gorgeous setting next to the derelict West Pier; moderate. Another satisfying place for fish is the **Regency** ((01273) 325014, 131 Kings Road, where seafood platters, grilled swordfish, and Dover sole are served; moderate to inexpensive. **English's Oyster Bar** ((01273) 327980, 29–31 East Street, set in three fisherman's cottages in the Lanes, is an old-fashioned, high-quality seafood place, serving oysters at the bar or at your table. It's especially pleasant for lunch; moderate.

Some of Brighton's best restaurants are vegetarian. **Terre à Terre** ((01273) 729051, 71 East Street, does superb meatless dishes; moderate. **Food for Friends** ((01273) 202310, 17A–18 Prince Albert Street, The Lanes, has a vegan and vegetarian menu, including organic wines. Look for the tomato fennel mint soup, cauliflower caraway and dill quiche, or any of several creative stir fries. Breakfast is good too, with organic whole-wheat pancakes and vegetarian sausage; inexpensive.

The laid-back **Blind Lemon Alley** ((01273) 202051, 41 Middle Street, serves wraps, veggie burgers, and char-grilled tuna steak with raspberry salsa under a low ceiling with blues humming from the hi-fi. The hemp beer is only so-so; inexpensive.

Ipenema ((01273) 779474, 121 Western Road, Hove BN1, dishes up Mediterranean fare in a relaxed candlelit room (though the street outside

gets noisy). The vegetarian, fish and meat *mezes* are good options, or there are fish and lamb dishes and *tapas*; moderate to inexpensive.

At the industrial-chic **Noodle Express** ((01273) 731222, 111 Western Road, you can start with plum and garlic-glazed ribs and move on to hot lime coconut prawns on a mango salad. Mixed woks and ramen also come in many guises; inexpensive.

If you're looking for a place to lunch near the Royal Pavilion, you might try **Ha! Ha!** ((01273) 737080, 2–3 Pavilion Buildings, a trendy café-bar offering Mediterranean wraps, rich desserts, and warm chicken Caesar salad. Service is relaxed. Saturday and Sunday brunch from 10 AM to noon feature grilled smoked haddock with poached eggs; inexpensive.

The **Mock Turtle** ((01273) 327380, Pool Valley, Brighton, is a traditional English tea-shop serving home made food and sweets; inexpensive.

A tasty take-out place is **Spaghetti Junction Deli** ((01273) 737082, 60 Preston Street. Choose from beautiful salads, *foccacia* sandwiches, homemade brownies, fresh pasta and sauces and dinners to go; inexpensive.

The **Cricketers** ((01273) 329473, 15 Black Lion Street, is an attractive seventeenth-century public house complete with brass lamps, tin ceilings, and fuzzy wall paper. The courtyard was fashioned out of the former stables. On the card are roast beef and trimmings and lemon sole & chips; inexpensive.

NIGHTLIFE

"Brighton, London: What else is there?" In many minds, "London-by-the-Sea" is the only place outside the capital that could be said to *have*

Bright lights of Brighton: the Royal Pavillion.

nightlife. Brighton's reputation for a lively club culture rests on its **74 nightclubs**, such as The Honey Club ((07000) 446639, 214 King's Road Arches, which keep the town throbbing and pulsing until the early morning hours. In addition to house and garage, there is jazz, Latin, decades rock ('60s, '70s, '80s), folk and Indie to be found here every night of the week. Look for events listings in *The Latest, Impact* or *The Source.*

Brighton nightlife has another alluring quality: it's cheap. Backpacking travelers feel they get more music and madness per pound here than in London.

Finally, Brighton has a thriving gay scene, concentrated in the Kemptown area, the focal point being St. James's Street and the Old Steine. There

are shops catering to the gay community here in "Brighton's Gay Village," as well as clubs and bars.

Beyond the club scene, Brighton offers a full menu of theater, opera, dance, musicals, fringe productions, and comedy. The larger venues are the **Brighton Centre** ((0870) 900-9100, King's Road; and the **Brighton Dome** ((01273) 709709, 29 New Road. For pre- and post-West End theater there is the **Theater Royal** ((01273) 328488, New Road; and fringe theater, comedy, jazz and cabaret at **Komedia** ((01273) 647100, 44–47 Gardner Street, North Laine.

Since 1940, the **Brighton Little Theater** ((01273) 205000, Clarence Garden (opposite Western Road) has offered year-round entertainment in its 75-seat hall. An amateur company performs a mix of current and classic plays with pre- and post-show bar. Shows start at 7:45 PM. Tickets are £6 (£5 on Monday).

For art films, there is the plush **Duke of York** ((01273) 626261, Gloucester Place.

HOW TO GET THERE

Brighton is 84 km (52 miles) south of London. **Trains** depart London Victoria every half hour for the 50-minute trip to Brighton. National Express has hourly **coach** services to Brighton's Pool

Valley station from London Victoria. The ride takes two hours. There is **ferry** service from Dieppe, France, to Newhaven (15 km or nine miles from Brighton) with P&O Stena.

ARUNDEL

WEST SUSSEX — Arundel is an experiment in architectural revivalism. Though the town itself is ancient, its buildings are mostly Victorian, with the exception of parts of the castle and St. Nicholas Church. Outside of summer weekends (when it is burdened with crowds), Arundel makes a good base for exploring the countryside north along the Arun Valley and west over the South Downs. It's an **antiques** center, too, and a farmers' **market** is held the third Saturday of each month in the town center.

The **Tourist Information Centre** ((01903) 882268 FAX (01903) 882419 is at 61 High Street. There is a small museum (admission fee) here tracing the history of the town.

WHAT TO SEE AND DO

Picturesque **Arundel Castle** has been the home for centuries of the Fitzalan family, Earls of Arundel, and the Howard family, Dukes of Norfolk. The Earl of Arundel, the seventeenth Duke of Norfolk, presently lives here with his wife and five offspring. Parts of the castle and much of the grounds are open to the public. The much-restored exterior dates from the 1800s, but the Barbican (square gate) and the causeway and tower with its portcullis date from the thirteenth century. From the tower there are stupendous views of the Sussex Downs cut through by the River Arun and sea eight kilometers (five miles) distant. (Lean a little way out one of the south windows and you might catch a glimpse of the duke's helicopter, grass tennis court and wading pool.) A tour of the drawing rooms, chapel and library give you glimpses of the family's fascinating collection of furniture dating from as far back as the sixteenth century, along with paintings by Van Dyck, Joshua Reynolds, and Thomas Gainsborough. The 40-m-long (133-ft) Baron's Hall with its hammerbeam ceiling is hung with tapestries and decorated with stained glass. The Perpendicular Gothic Fitzalan Chapel, with its fifteenth-century sepulcher, is open during restoration. Arundel Castle ((01903) 883136, Mill Road, is closed Saturday mornings and from November to March; admission fee.

Continuing up the hill, Arundel's nineteenth-century cathedral is best seen from the churchyard of the much older and far more interesting **St. Nicholas Church**, built in the fourteenth century in the Perpendicular style. There are traces of mediaeval murals on the walls. Although today it is the Anglican parish church, one end of it, separated by a clear partition, is the **Fitzalan Chapel**, where Roman Catholic services are held, the Fitzalan-Howard family being Catholic.

Back in the center of the village, Arundel's hilly cobbled streets make for pleasant **strolls**, outside of the crush of high-season weekends. Down at the quay you can watch the swans battle the River Arun's powerful current, or take to the water yourself on a **riverboat cruise**. Skylark Cruises ((0378) 438166 organizes 40-minute trips up the Arun Valley, as well as a variety of longer cruises, such as a three-hour tour with a stopover at Amberley tea gardens and pub.

You can walk along the River Arun into wooded Arundel Park. There are more footpaths as well

(eight kilometers) north of Arundel. This ninth-century castle, surrounded by crenellated walls, has been transformed into a sumptuous small hotel by the resident owners. Rooms are individually decorated and feature Jacuzzis and four-poster beds; luxury price range. Dining takes place in the twelfth-century Queen's Room.

In Arundel, **Dukes Hotel** ((01903) 883847, 65 High Street, Arundel BN18 9AD, a listed 1840 building, offers accommodation in Regency-style bedrooms from suites to smallish doubles; moderate. The café (expensive to moderate) has retained its gorgeous Renaissance style wood carving and gilded ceiling. Traditional English fare is served all day.

as bird blinds at **Wildfowl and Wetlands** ((01903) 883355, Mill Road, a 24-ha (60-acre) nature preserve with lakes and marshland inhabited by thousands of ducks, swans and geese.

If you're fit for **cycling** in this hilly but gorgeous countryside, Wests Cycle Hire ((01903) 770649 can set you up; services include pick up and delivery. Around six and a half kilometers (four miles) northwest of Arundel, the **Slindon Estate** (NT) ((01243) 814484 has 32 km (20 miles) of cycling and walking trails across downland, farmland and old-growth woods. There is dormitory accommodation here for walkers and riders at Gumbar Bothy.

WHERE TO STAY AND EAT

Amberley Castle ((01798) 831992, Amberley, Arundel BN18 9ND, is a country house hotel situated in the thatched village of Amberley, five miles

The **Arundel Youth Hostel** ((01903) 882204 FAX (01903) 882776, Warningcamp, Arundel BN18 9QY, is well out of town (about two and a half kilometers or one and a half miles) in a peaceful rural setting. It makes a good base for walking and cycling. Use the large self-catering kitchen or take advantage of cheap meals served here, breakfast, boxed lunches and dinner.

Thirteen kilometers (eight miles) northeast of Arundel, **Fleur de Sel** ((01903) 742331, Manleys Hill, Storrington, has recently moved here from Haslemere (near Petworth). It remains one of the top restaurants in the region, serving the French provincial cooking of its chef and co-proprietor Michel Perraud. No dinner Sunday; expensive.

In Arundel there's **Pizza Express** ((01903) 885467, at the bottom of High Street; moderate.

OPPOSITE: Palace Pier, Brighton. ABOVE: Arundel Castle, ancestral home of the Dukes of Norfolk.

How to Get There

Arundel is 97 km (60 miles) southwest of London. The town is on the London Victoria–Portsmouth **train** line, with hourly departures during the day. Stagecoach Coastline ((01243) 783251 serves Arundel on its Chichester to Brighton **bus** line.

CHICHESTER

WEST SUSSEX — Originally a Roman settlement, the cathedral town of Chichester, though not of great distinction architecturally, is a pleasant place to explore because of its extensive no-car zone, where pedestrians can shop and stroll without the fear of vehicular homicide that haunts most British towns. It makes a good base for exploring the splendid second-century Roman villa excavations at Fishbourne and Bignor (see AROUND CHICHESTER, below). In town, the cathedral is brim full of art, from 1,000-year-old murals to contemporary sculpture, and the Pallant Gallery is another excellent art house.

There is **horse racing** ((01243) 774107 at Goodwood. The **Chichester Festival Theatre** ((01243) 781312, just outside the city walls, has an international reputation for classical and contemporary theater.

General Information

The **Tourist Information Centre** ((01243) 775888 FAX (01243) 539449 is in the pedestrian-only shopping district, at 29A South Street. For a quirky look at what makes Chichester tick visit WEB SITE homepages .tesco.net/~peteking/chichester1.html.

What to See and Do

Chichester was given a cruciform layout during its Georgian renovation, centering around the **Market Cross** which is bisected by North, South, East, and West streets.

Appraised by Daniel Defoe as "not the finest in England, but…far from being the most ordinary," **Chichester Cathedral** ((01243) 782595, West Street, dates from Norman rule; the side chapels were added in the 1200s. Enthusiastic guides are on hand to point out the cathedral's masterpieces, of which there are many. Modern works by Marc Chagall, Graham Sutherland and Phillip Jackson stand in contrast to walls of roughly cut Norman stonework and rounded arches. The cathedral's greatest treasure is perhaps the twelfth-century *bas relief* depicting Lazarus' miraculous rise of the dead. Lost for centuries, it was found under the choir stalls in 1829 during a renovation.

The same man who was responsible for much of the contemporary art that graces the cathedral

— Walter Hussey, Dean of Chichester from 1955 to 1977 — endowed the **Pallant House Gallery** ((01243) 774557, North Pallant Street, with a fine collection of contemporary art. Hussey's twentieth-century art is displayed in this beautifully restored Queen Anne townhouse with period rooms and furnishings. Featured artists include Henry Moore, Graham Sutherland, Ceri Richards, John Piper and Marc Chagall. Closed Sunday mornings and Monday; admission fee.

Set in gorgeous countryside just north of Chichester, **Goodwood House** ((01243) 755048 is the family home of the Dukes of Richmond. The state rooms have been restored to Regency designs; visiting hours are strictly limited, so call

for a schedule. **Sculpture at Goodwood** ((01243) 538449, Hat Hill Copse, offers changing exhibitions set in wooded grounds; a steep entry fee is charged. Adjacent to the house, is the race course ((01243) 774107, which also hosts monthly antique shows.

Outdoor Activities

Once a port, **Chichester Harbour** (AONB) is one of the few undeveloped shore areas in Southern England. Boat trips ((01243) 784418 around the Chichester Harbour depart from Itchenor. At the eastern entrance to the harbor, East Head (NT) is a protected sandy promontory overlooking the marshes. A walking path skirts the shoreline here.

There are more walking trails at **Kingley Vale**, Europe's largest yew forest (northwest of Chichester).

The **Centurion Way** is a short, gentle cycling route that runs west out of Chichester. For more cycling ideas, including a 324-km (200-mile) circular route beginning from Chichester, ask at the Tourist Information Centre (above). Mountain bikes and gear can be rented from **2XS (** (01243) 512552 FAX (01243) 512850 E-MAIL simonbassett .2xs@btinternet.com, Rookwood Road, West Wittering, Chichester PO20 8LT.

WHERE TO STAY

Accommodation is in short supply during theater festival periods and racing days at Goodwood, so make reservations well ahead for visits during these periods.

The Georgian-era **Suffolk House (** (01243) 778899 FAX (01243) 787282 E-MAIL info@suffolkhshotel .co.uk, 3 East Row, Chichester PO19 1PD, is a short walk from the center. The bedrooms, some of which have garden views, are well-appointed and comfortably equipped; expensive. There is a cozy bar and lounge, and English fare is served in dining room (moderate).

Ten kilometers (six miles) west of Chichester, **Kia-ora Nursery (** (01243) 572852 FAX (01243) 572852, Main Road, Nutbourne, Chichester PO18 8ET, with views of Chichester Harbour, is within walking distance of village restaurants and pubs; inexpensive.

Slightly less expensive is **Hedgehogs (** (01243) 780022, 45 Whyke Lane, Chichester PO19 2JT, just over a kilometer (about two-thirds of a mile) from the center (rock-bottom to inexpensive), where cyclist and hikers are particularly welcome. Weekly terms can be arranged.

There is institutional accommodation at the **Chichester Institute of Higher Learning (** (01243) 816070, College Lane, a manageable walk from the center; inexpensive.

WHERE TO EAT

Close to the Festival Theatre, **Comme Ça (** (01243) 788724, 67 Broyle Road, is especially pleasant on a summer evening when the dining room opens out onto garden. The French cooking emphasizes the rich flavors of Normandy, well represented in the braised wild rabbit with mushrooms, baby onions and bacon in a creamy Calvados sauce. A thoughtfully chosen wine list complements the fare. Closed Monday all day and Sunday dinner; moderate. A children's menu is available.

The **Crypt (** (01243) 537033, South Street, has an international menu of tapas, mussels, steak and pasta served by candlelight in a vaulted underground cellar. Open for lunch and dinner from; moderate to inexpensive.

Hadley's ((01243) 771631, 4 West Street, is a sunny place with a timbered interior. The lunch

menu features homemade soup of the day, or jacket potatoes and sandwiches are available. For dinner there is grilled rainbow trout served with prawns among other tummy fillers; inexpensive.

Hidden away in the Butter Market, North Street, **Splits (** (01243) 783441 does fresh sandwiches on thick slices of homemade bread. Try the curried chicken on whole-wheat; inexpensive.

HOW TO GET THERE

Chichester is 112 km (69 miles) southwest of London. **Trains** depart for Chichester from London Victoria hourly during the day for the hour-and-45-minute trip. National Express operates a daily **coach** route to Chichester; the ride takes four hours and 40 minutes.

AROUND CHICHESTER

WEST SUSSEX — Roman ruins, waterside villages and stately homes are within easy reach of Chichester. Bosham is a good alternative to staying in town.

WHAT TO SEE AND DO

Discovered in the 1960s when ditch-diggers began excavating for a proposed housing estate, **Fishbourne Roman Palace (** (01243) 785859, Salthill Road, is unique in Britain. This is both a treasure house as well as a fascinating archaeological site and education center. You can see first- and second-century Roman mosaic floors, several Saxon graves and a reconstructed Roman garden *in situ* and imagine the palace just as it was two millennia ago. Guided tours are excellent, taking in such varied subjects as first-century fashions in interior decorating and social activities of the Romans. The museum is well attuned to the interests of children, with a large explorer's area where kids can create their own tile mosaics or build a Roman arch. Closed mid-December to mid-February; admission fee.

The Roman holiday continues at **Bignor Roman Villa (** (01798) 869259, one of Britain's largest Roman remains. Discovered in 1811 near the hamlet of Bignor, these fourth- and fifth-century mosaics are more colorful and fanciful than those at Fishbourne, though not as ancient. One of the excavated rooms is maintained as a museum with displays of the finds, such as household items and coins dating from the first to the fourth century. Open daily except Monday, from March to May and in October; an admission fee is charged.

The waterside village of **Bosham** (pronounced *boz*-zum), on an inlet of Chichester Harbour, was once a busy port. Today it's a mellow hangout for artists and yachters. Its original Saxon church and

A clerical confab in the cathedral close.

manor house are depicted in the Bayeux Tapestry, as it was from here that Harold set sail in 1064 on the journey that led to his fateful encounter with William, Duke of Normandy. Stroll through the village with its many old cottages and explore the antiques shops and craft galleries (mostly along Bosham Lane). Bosham is six and a half kilometers (four miles) west of Chichester.

The **Weald & Downland Open Air Museum** ((01243) 811348 or (01243) 828485 has rescued 40 threatened historic buildings, bringing them timber-by-timber to this site, where they've been reconstructed and restored. Set on 20 hectares (50 acres) are a furnished farmhouse, barn and herb garden, working water-powered mill, sixteenth-

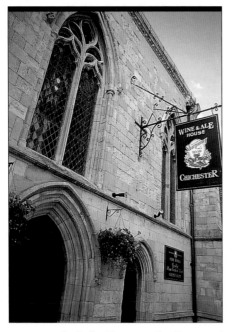

century market hall, a Victorian schoolhouse and more. Open daily March to October and weekends only from November to February; admission fee. It's in Singleton on the A286 (about eight kilometers or five miles north of Chichester).

Once the seat of the Earls of Northumberland, now in the family of the Dukes of Somerset, **Petworth House and Park** (NT) ((01798) 342207, is located 19 km (12 miles) northeast of Chichester in the village of Petworth. This late-seventeenth-century house is a mass of dazzling rooms filled with a dazzling collection of important paintings, including two works by Titian, many Dutch Old Masters, and 20 paintings by J.M.W. Turner, who had a studio here. Closed mornings as well as all day Thursday and Friday and from November to March; admission fee. The menu at the Audit Room (inexpensive) is inspired by mediaeval recipes. The deer park is open year-round; free admission. The

mediaeval village of Petworth is also worth exploring; it's noted for its antiques shops.

WHERE TO STAY

The **Spread Eagle** ((01730) 816911 FAX (01730) 815668 E-MAIL spreadeagle@hshotels.co.uk, South Street, Midhurst GU29 9NH, offers an intriguing blend of ancient and modern. The inn sets guests bang in the midst of Olde England with its sloping floors, oak beams and inglenook fireplaces, while the brand-new spa caters to twenty-first century dreams. The bedrooms are furnished with antiques and period reproductions. The spa has an indoor heated pool, sauna and steam rooms, Jacuzzi, health and beauty treatments and a fitness trainer; expensive to very expensive. In the restaurant, straightforward Modern British fare is served (expensive).

In the idyllic village of Bosham, the **Millstream** ((01243) 573234 FAX (01243) 573459 E-MAIL info @millstream-hotel.co.uk, Bosham Lane, Bosham PO18 8HL, is a handsome hotel with individually decorated bedrooms; expensive. The cocktail bar opens out onto the garden and there is also a lounge and restaurant (moderate).

The pretty Victorian, **Kenwood** ((01243) 572727 FAX (01243) 572738, Bosham, Chichester PO18 8PH (Off A259), has three spacious bedrooms. The house is set in gardens with views of the harbor, and an outdoor heated swimming pool. Breakfast is served in the conservatory, which is set up with a refrigerator and microwave for guests who want to cook up a quick meal in the evenings; inexpensive to moderate.

WHERE TO EAT

Halfway Bridge Inn ((01798) 861281, Halfway Bridge, near Petworth, is fine old a seventeenth-century inn with low timbered ceilings and oak paneling. This gastropub features local ingredients in such temptations as crab cakes with salsa, garlic-stuffed mussels for starters and Moroccan lamb stew with apricot couscous and local pheasant stuffed with pâté. A very good wine list completes diners joy; expensive.

One and a half kilometers (one mile) east of Petworth on the A283, is the **Welldiggers Arms** ((01798) 342287, Polborough Road, Petworth, a 300-year-old free house with low-beamed ceilings and log fires in the bars. The blackboard boasts local game, steaks, blackboard menu, and seafood; moderate.

The **Slurping Toad** ((01243) 539637, 38 West Street (opposite the cathedral), set in the Gothic shell of the old St. Mary's Church, serves up food by day and music by night.

Going Gothic at the Slurping Toad, Chichester, a former church.

Hampshire
and
Dorset

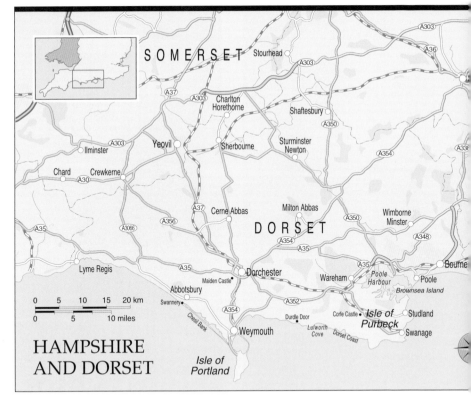

SOMERSET

DORSET

HAMPSHIRE
AND DORSET

Isle of
Portland

0 5 10 15 20 km
0 5 10 miles

ALONG WITH BERKSHIRE AND WILTSHIRE (dealt with in other chapters), the counties of Hampshire and Dorset approximate Wessex, Alfred the Great's ninth-century Saxon realm, as well as the nineteenth-century "partly real, partly dream-country" described in Thomas Hardy's darkly romantic novels and poems.

Dotted with ancient abbeys and market towns, inland Dorset preserves some of the quiet rural appeal immortalized by Hardy. Along the coast, Dorset runs the gamut from scenic to sybaritic, with the wild beauty of the Isle of Purbeck contrasting with the bright lights of Bournemouth.

At the heart of Saxon Wessex, Winchester is a delightful cathedral city clothed in ancient history and surrounded by fine scenery. Portsmouth is chaotic, but worth braving for the naval heritage area where you can board historic battleships and view an exhibition on an amazingly well-preserved sixteenth-century shipwreck. Hampshire's northeast corner merges with London's suburban buildup, and the M3 dices the county in half on its way to Southampton, yet there remain some pretty rural areas, particularly the New Forest. This former royal hunting ground today has acres of varied countryside where wild ponies roam.

From Portsmouth, Southampton or Lymington (in the New Forest) ferries make easy, 30-minute crossings to the Isle of Wight. This green, diamond-shaped isle, with its gorgeous downland and coastal views, is a paradise for walkers, especially at Tennyson Down where the poet is said to have claimed "the air is worth sixpence a pint." It's best visited off season, though, when the island's rural beauty can be enjoyed without bumping elbows with a bevy of "holiday-makers."

In Dorset the less developed areas of the coastline, especially at Studland on the tip of the Purbeck Peninsula, are superb for strolling. For long-distance hiking there is the rather unique Pilgrims' Trail, running 45 km (28 miles) from Winchester across Hampshire to Portsmouth, where through-hikers take the ferry to Cherbourg and continue on to Mont St. Michel in Normandy. The New Forest is an undaunting place for rural rambling and there are miles of off-road cycling trails through the forest.

WINCHESTER

HAMPSHIRE — The ancient capital of Saxon Wessex, Winchester is a pleasant and prosperous city, home to a magnificent 900-year-old cathedral. Winchester has a fascinating and compact old quarter, and there are opportunities for satisfying strolls in the city. Longer rambles across the surrounding countryside, along water meadows and over chalk downs, are also popular.

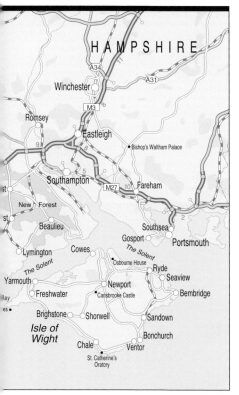

The **Tourist Information Centre** ((01962) 840500 or (01962) 867871 (lodging) FAX (01962) 841365 is in the Guildhall, The Broadway. There are **guided walks** of the mediaeval quarter leaving from the Tourist Information Centre at 10:30 AM and 2:30 PM Monday to Saturday, May to September, 2:30 only in April and October; fee charged.

Winchester has a year-round schedule of **festivals**, including a children's festival in February and the annual folk festival in April. A literature fest takes place the last two weeks in September, and Winchester's Fireworks and Torchlight Parade takes place in early November.

WHAT TO SEE AND DO

Winchester Cathedral

The vast Perpendicular Gothic nave of Winchester Cathedral ((01962) 853137 is the longest in England (169 m or 556 ft). A Saxon church on this site dedicated to St. Swithun was replaced by a Norman structure in the eleventh century, but Swithun remains the patron. Flanking the "Holy Hole," into which pilgrims once crawled to get a closer peek at St. Swithun, are a series of gorgeous Russian icons. Lots of old bones are collected in wooden chests lining the walls of the choir, including those of Emma, wife of King Canute and mother of Edward the Confessor. Besides these relics,

visitors can pay tribute at the grave of Jane Austen (1775–1817) and that of Isaac Walton (1593–1683), beloved author of *The Compleat Angler*.

A small statue in the nave memorializes William Walker, about which one of the cathedral's interesting historical threads is told. As it was built on a swamp, the cathedral required extensive restoration in the twentieth century to keep it from sinking. Much of the work had to be done underwater. For five years, Walker, a deep-sea diver, worked six hours a day in black water laying stacks of cement to shore up the tottering walls.

There are tours on the hour daily from 10 AM to 3 PM, Monday to Saturday, as well as tours of the crypt at 10:30 AM, 12:30 PM, and 2:30 PM Monday to Saturday; tower tours are offered Monday to Friday at 2:15 PM and Saturday at 11:30 AM and 2:15 PM. In summer, there are lunchtime concerts on Tuesdays at 1:10 PM. You might want to plan your visit to coincide with lunch or tea at the highly recommended Cathedral Refectory (see WHERE TO EAT, below).

More Points of Interest

With its Purbeck stone columns, pointed arches and lacy windows, the **Great Hall** ((01962) 846476 is the last remaining section of Winchester Castle, the Norman stronghold of Henry III (1216–1272). The site was originally built on shortly after William's invasion in 1066. Henry III transformed the ruins of that castle into a fortress and palace, but all excepting the Great Hall were destroyed in 1651 by Cromwell's army. Of the treasures exhibited here, the five-and-a-half-meter-wide (18-ft) **Round Table** is undoubtedly the most impressive. It's hung here so long no one can remember when it came to be here. As John Harding wrote in 1403, "The round table at Wynchester beganne/ And there it ended, and there it hangeth yet...." Believed to have been built in the mid-thirteenth century, the table is inscribed "this is the round table of Arthur with 24 of his named knights." The adjoining **Queen Eleanor's Garden** recreates a typical thirteenth-century garden; entrance to the hall and garden is free of charge.

A group of **Regimental Museums** stand in the same complex, the most interesting of which is perhaps the Gurkha Museum, Romsey Road. Closed Sunday; admission fee.

The building that houses the **Westgate Museum** ((01962) 869864, High Street, served over the years as gate, guardhouse, and debtor's prison until 1750. It was later a wine cellar, city archive, and a treasury until it became part of a pub. As its curator says, "everybody had a go at it." About 100 years ago the city restored the building, finding the original portcullis, with original 600-year-old fittings, in the process. You can see graffiti scratched into the chalk stone walls by debtors as long ago as 1597. There are facilities for doing brass rubbings (an admission fee is charged), and a rooftop with a limited view down High Street.

Founded in 1342 by William of Wykeham, the boys' school **Winchester College** ((01962) 621217, on Kingsgate Street, is the most famous of the city's many educational institutions. Guided tours are offered daily from April to September; no tours from 1 to 2 PM and on Sunday morning. In winter tours may be arranged by appointment; admission fee.

OUTDOOR ACTIVITIES

The **Water Meadow Walk** is a one-and-a-half-kilometer (one-mile) tramp from Winchester College to the Hospital of St. Cross ((01962) 851375,

appointed rooms and a walled garden; expensive to very expensive. The bistro (expensive) is noted for its freshly prepared meals and excellent wine list.

Harestock Lodge ((01962) 881870 FAX (01962) 886959, Harestock Road, Winchester SO22 6NX, is a country house hotel situated on the edge of the city, with 17 rooms; inexpensive to moderate.

Near the cathedral, the **Wykeham Arms** ((01962) 853834, 75 Kingsgate Street, Winchester SO23 9PE, is a top-notch public house with 13 comfortable rooms; moderate to expensive.

Bed-and-breakfast places are plentiful but somewhat pricey in Winchester. A five-minute walk from the center, **Cathedral View** ((01962)

St. Cross Road. If you ask for the "wayfarer's dole" at this ancient almshouse you'll be presented with a crust of bread and a cup of ale, a tradition that has been maintained since mediaeval times. Closed from 12:30 to 2 PM and on Sunday during the winter; admission fee.

At **Cheesefoot Head** (pronounced chess-ford), south of the city, there are satisfying walks around a natural amphitheater. It was here that troops got their pep talk from Eisenhower before invading Normandy.

The Tourist Information Centre also has information on **off-road cycling** in the county.

WHERE TO STAY

Hotel du Vin ((01962) 841414 FAX (01962) 822458, 14 Southgate Street, Winchester SO23 9EF, is a eighteenth-century townhouse with 23 stylishly

863802, 9A Magdalen Hill, Winchester SO23 0HJ, offers views across the city along with baths and parking; inexpensive. Also close to the center, the more moderately priced **32 Hyde Street** ((01962) 851621, Winchester SO23 7DX, is an eighteenth-century townhouse with one double and one triple room, shared bath; inexpensive.

King Alfred's University ((01962) 827322 FAX (01962) 827264 E-MAIL ecrshuds@wkac.ac.uk, Sparkford Road, Winchester SO22 4NR, offers private and shared bath and bed-only or bed and breakfast in the inexpensive range; double rooms are limited. Rooms are available January, March to April, June to September and at Christmas.

Sullivan's ((01962) 862027, 29 Stockbridge Road, Winchester, Hampshire SO22 6RW, is a good value B&B in a Victorian town cottage, with low-key decor (no sad clowns and tasseled lampshades) in four rooms, one with bath. It's a 10-minute walk

the village is the handsome Victorian Gothic **church** where you can visit the grave of Alice Liddell, the woman who as a girl was Louis Carroll's inspiration for *Alice's Adventures in Wonderland*.

Before setting off for the countryside, visit the **Tourist Information Centre** ((02380) 282269, High Street. Staff will point out some less trammeled places to walk and help you find accommodation. In the same building, the **New Forest Museum** describes the natural and human history of the forest; admission fee. The shops here and at the Tourist Information Centre are both stocked with Ordnance Survey maps and guides. For recorded information on events and guided walks call the **Forestry Commission Information Line** ((02380) 284476.

Where to Stay and Eat

For luxury in the New Forest, there is **Parkhill** ((023) 8028-2944, Beaulieu Road, Lyndhurst SO43 7FZ, a thirteenth-century hunting lodge with 20 rooms; expensive.

Tucked between the village and the forest in the hamlet of Swan Green, **Penn Cottage** ((023) 8028-2075, Swan Green, Lyndhurst SO43 7JL, is a short walk to the center of Lyndhurst. This adorable 400-year-old thatched cottage with beamed ceilings is set in a colorful garden. The two bedrooms with shared bath are quite homey and comfortable. A talkative cockatiel presides in the breakfast room and Pepper, the old dog, stands guard over the foyer; inexpensive.

Il Cervo ((023) 8028-2106, 18 High Street, Lyndhurst, provides good Neapolitan-style pizza as well as daily specials featuring seafood and steak. The lunch deal is good value at £3.95 for half a pizza and salad — while the red-and-green decor and the musak transport you to somewhere in New Jersey; inexpensive.

BROCKENHURST

Brockenhurst is the heart of wild pony territory. You may even see the adorable steeds roaming around the village — but beware, they are wild animals and shouldn't be approached or fed. Adding to the village's rusticity is a ford in the main street. If you drive into Brockenhurst from the west along the aptly named Brookley Road you'll have the fun of crossing this old-fashioned tire wash.

Where to Stay and Eat

Southwest of the village, **Chewton Glen** ((01425) 275341, Christchurch Road, New Milton BH25 6QS, is one of Southern England's renowned country house hotels, with exquisite bedrooms and a truly excellent modern French restaurant. Luxuriant gardens and grounds surround the mansion. Facilities include a nine-hole golf course, indoor and

outdoor swimming pools, indoor and outdoor tennis courts, croquet, gym and spa; luxury.

Originally a vicarage, the **Forest Park Hotel** ((01590) 622844 FAX (01590) 623948, Rhinefield Road, Brockenhurst SO42 7ZG, is a handsome old inn with all the makings for a family vacation, including riding stables and a swimming pool. Comfortable, sunny rooms — some with garden view, all have bath. The **restaurant** serves English fare; moderate.

For B&B in the area, there is the well-regarded **Evergreen** (/FAX (01590) 623411, Sway Road, Brockenhurst SO42 7RX, a 10-minute walk from the village center. Rooms have baths, and there is a pet pony.

Tucked out at the back of a fun antiques shop, **Antiquiteas Tea Room** ((01590) 622120, 37 Brookley Road, is an excellent place for tea and sweets, featuring delicious chocolate fudge cake, served with grace. Lunch is also served, especially delightful on the flowery patio.

BEAULIEU

Beautifully situated among woods and hills are the thirteenth-century ruins of the Cistercian monastery, **Beaulieu Abbey** (pronounced *bew*-lee). The fourteenth-century Palace House, once the gatehouse of the abbey, was home of the Montagu family for hundreds of years; today it houses the celebrated **National Motor Museum** ((01590) 612345, Britain's most important collection of motorized vehicles with 250 vintage cars showing the history of motoring since 1896. In the ruined Cistercian abbey, which was founded by King John in 1204, there is an exhibition of monastic life. Open daily year-round; admission fee.

Where to Stay and Eat

Three kilometers (two miles) south of Beaulieu, Bucklers Hard has one wide street flanked by pretty

Beaulieu — OPPOSITE: National Motor Museum. ABOVE: The stately Palace House.

Georgian terraces. Down by the marina there is luxurious accommodation at the **Master Builders House Hotel** ((01590) 616253 FAX (01590) 616297 E-MAIL res@themasterbuilders.co.uk, Bucklers Hard SO42 7XB, an eighteenth-century house where some of the bedrooms have river views. The hotel operates its own boat to the Isle of Wight, making it a good choice for anyone wanting a hassle-free day trip to the "little jewel;" very expensive. There is a **restaurant** and bar on the premises.

THE ISLE OF WIGHT

Look at her, snuggling into the soft underbelly of England. The little cutie. The little beauty.

— Julian Barnes, *England England*

ISLE OF WIGHT — A rural island county divided from Hampshire by the Solent Strait, the Isle of Wight is often called "Britain-in-miniature." It does seem to have a little bit (a very little bit) of everything that Britain is known for, from rolling downland to a ruined castle to seaside promenades and even a royal residence, Oxborne, at Cowes.

At just 381 sq km (147 sq miles), Wight has great appeal to families for its old-fashioned attractions, leisurely pace and sandy beaches. For natural beauty, West Wight — with its chalk cliffs and downland — outshines not only East Wight, but much of the southern big-island coast. East Wight has heaps of attractions from steam trains and toy museums to stately mansions, while "back of the Wight" villages make for quiet retreats from seaside merriment.

The National Trust ((01983) 741020 protects 1,600 hectares (4,000 acres) of the island as well as 28 km (17 miles) of coastline. They offer guided walks and garden tours throughout the year; call for details. Half of the island, including much of the coastline, is also protected as an Area of Outstanding Natural Beauty, making it a great place for walkers, cyclists, and horse riders. It's the only county thus far to have achieved the Countryside Commission's target for footpaths and bridleways.

GENERAL INFORMATION

The island's **Tourist Information Centre** ((01983) 525450 or (0500) 867979 (lodging) is at the car park on South Street in Newport. The WEB SITE www .islandbreaks.co.uk is useful for planning your trip, and you can book ferry crossings and package vacations right on the site.

Wightlink ((0990) 820202 WEB SITE www .wightlink.co.uk, runs ferries to Ventnor and from Lymington to Yarmouth. They're also the largest tour operator to the isle. **Hovertravel** ((01983) 811000 operates from Southsea and Portsmouth to Ryde (foot passengers only). **Red Funnel** ((023)

8033-4010 sails from Southampton to Cowes. The trip takes about 30 minutes.

Southern Vectis ((01983) 827005 has an extensive network of **bus** routes throughout the island, including open-top double-deckers for a thrill along the coast.

WEST WIGHT

Whether you're walking or driving, the downs of West Wight afford glorious views of green hills and sea. At the island's most westerly point, The Needles is a spectacular geological formation caused by erosion of the chalk cliffs by the foamy waters of the Solent. Yacht harbors like Yarmouth, though very busy in summer, have maintained their maritime character.

What to See and Do

Serrated chalk pinnacles rise to 30 m (100 ft) off **Needles Headland** at Wight's western tip. Overlooking the spectacular headland is Needles Old Battery (NT) ((01983) 754772, one of a number of Victorian-era defenses built against the threat of French invasion. Exhibitions include terrific cartoon illustrations by Geoff Campion of the World War II years. A tunnel leads out to a restored sea light where there are superb views of the pinnacles. (For the best vantage point, especially in the morning, walk up to the rocket test site above the Needles.) Open Sunday to Thursday from mid-March to October; admission fee. The tiny tea room has good views, too. The headland may be closed during rough weather; call to confirm. It's an uphill walk of about one and a half kilometers (a mile) from the car park at Alum Bay.

From Alum Bay it's about a one-and-a-half-kilometer (one-mile) walk up to **Tennyson Down** (NT), an excellent coastal landscape with white chalk cliffs rising to 126 m (482 ft) above sea level. You can also walk over the downs from the car parks at the top of Highdown Lane or at Freshwater Bay.

Below the Needles, a fun fair and craft shops deck the cliffs at **Alum Bay**, known for the multicolored sands found in the cliffs above the beach. You walk down to the beach or take the exhilarating chair-lift (fee charged). At the beach it's possible to collect your own colored sands; alternatively, at the fun fair there's a shop where you can purchase a glass container and sands to fill it. From the beach there are **boat trips** out to the Needles (a fee is charged).

Moving north, **Yarmouth** is a lively yacht harbor and the oldest surviving town on the island, laid out in the twelfth century. It's an agreeable place to explore on foot with its old inns and narrow streets. From Yarmouth Pier there are daily (except Wednesday and Sunday) cruises to the Needles at 2:15 PM with Dorset Pleasure Cruises ((01202) 558550. To the south, **Freshwater** is a quiet holiday center with an unusual thatched church (not always open) where there are memorials to the Tennyson family.

At Newtown, there is a nature reserve with walks around an estuary, the habitat of red squirrels and water fowl. At one end of the reserve stands the **Old Town Hall** (NT) ((01983) 531785, a late-seventeenth-century brick-and-stone building, with an exhibition of ancient documents relating to the history of this abandoned town. Hours vary; admission fee.

Where to Stay and Eat

Yarmouth gets overwhelmed during holiday season, but in the spring and fall it's a delightful place

Needles Headland, rented for stays of two or more nights. These single-story buildings, each of which has a sitting room with fireplace, and two to three bedrooms, are set on open downland with spectacular views; inexpensive. You'll need a car. Contact the National Trust Holiday Cottage Booking Office ((01225) 791199 FAX (01225) 792267, PO Box 536, Melksham, Wiltshire SN12 8SX.

The handsome old **Bugle** ((01983) 760272, The Square, Yarmouth PO41 0NS, serves Mod Brit fare (moderate) and fresh sandwiches for lunch. They have eight smallish, standard bedrooms with little of the pub's charm, but harbor views from some are outstanding; moderate. Reserve two months in advance for high season.

to haul anchor. Even in the low season, you must reserve well in advance for the **George Inn** ((01983) 760331 FAX (01983) 760425, Quay Street, Yarmouth PO41 0PE. This gracious old hotel has 17 rooms, some of which have spacious balconies or private terraces with sea views. Each room is unique; some have original pine paneling. All rooms have generous bath; luxury. The formal dining room here is the island's top **restaurant** (expensive), serving classical and modern French cuisine; there's a **bistro** (moderate) for casual dining.

Jireh House ((01983) 760513, St. James's Square, is a seventeenth-century guest house (inexpensive) with pleasant tea rooms and a **restaurant** on the ground floor. Toasties and cream teas are served during the day, and for dinner, fish and Isle of Wight lobster; moderate.

An ideal base for walking the downs are the National Trust's three **coastguard cottages** at

East Wight

Just as the coastal footpath circumnavigates the suburban sprawl of this heavily developed area of Wight, so might you chart a path to include the best of the area and avoid the worst. This part of Wight is best known as the summer stomping ground of Queen Victoria. Her Majesty's beloved "cottage," **Osborne House** (EH) ((01983) 281784 or (01983) 200022, East Cowes, has been left just as she left it at her death in 1901. Open daily April to September, winter hours by appointment only; admission fee. During **Cowes Week**, from late July to early August, yachting fever hits Cowes, headquarters of the Royal Yacht Squadron; details at the Tourist Information Centre ((01983) 291914.

The ornamental gardens of Osbourne House, Queen Victoria's summer residence.

About 16 km (ten or so miles) east along the coast, the yachting harbor of **Bembridge** is East Wight's most unspoiled spot. Just under a kilometer (half a mile) south of Bembridge on the B3395, Bembridge Windmill (NT) ((01983) 873945, High Street, dates from 1700 and is the only surviving windmill on island. There are superb views of the countryside from here. Open March to October, daily except Saturday; admission fee. Another interesting spot is the Bembridge Shipwreck Centre and Maritime Museum, filled with maritime relics.

There are satisfying walks on the southern reaches of the island. **St. Catherine's Oratory** (NT) is a mediaeval lighthouse known locally as "the

refurbished **Priory Bay** ((01983) 613146 FAX (01983) 616539, Priory Drive, Seaview, Isle Of Wight PO34 5BU, has 34 bedrooms in a cluster of interesting restored buildings including the main hotel, cottages and the poolside tithe barn; expensive. Discounts are available for stays of more than one night. The two **restaurants** serve updated Continental cuisine (moderate), and the café overlooking the bay specializes in seafood.

Already established as one of the island's best hotel-restaurants, **Seaview Hotel** ((01983) 612711, High Street, Seaview PO34 5EX, has 16 rooms (only four of which have sea views). Rooms vary widely in size, but all are comfortably and tastefully done in nautical style. The two **restaurants** (moderate)

Pepper Pot." It stands atop St. Catherine's Hill where there are sweeping views of the island. From the hill you can walk along a ridge to the Hoy Monument, returning via paths at the foot of the ridge. The hill is just under a half kilometer (one quarter mile) east of the Blackgang roundabout off the A3055. By **Hanover Point** the beach at low tide is a treasure-trove of dinosaur footprints, the richest seam of dino remains in Europe. It may be possible to book bone hunts through the Tourist Information Centre in Newport (see GENERAL INFORMATION, above).

At Bonchurch the **Undercliff** is a geological oddity formed by eroding cliffs that forms a microclimate for rare flora, both planted and natural.

Where to Stay and Eat
On 28 wooded and cultivated hectares (70 acres) between Bembridge and Seaview, the newly

here are much favored for both their stylish presentation and good cooking; moderate. Special breaks are available.

Horseshoe Bay House (/FAX (01983) 856800 E-MAIL hsbayhouse@aol.com, Shore Road, Bonchurch, Ventnor PO38 IRN, is a friendly guest house with a cliff-hanger conservatory overlooking the brine. Rooms are spacious, tastefully decorated and comfortable, and the hosts are friendly and accommodating; inexpensive.

The isle caters to backpackers with the small, seasonal, **Sandown Youth Hostel** ((01983) 402651 FAX (01983) 403565, The Firs, Fitzroy Street, Sandown, Isle of Wight PO36 8JH; rock-bottom.

Outside the hotels, **Bistro Sancerre** ((01983) 855232, in Bonchurch, is a new dining establishment overlooking the village pond. This smart restaurant serves English and Continental fare, complemented by fine wines. Seasonal opening times.

Ventnor's **Spyglass** ((01983) 852775, at the seafront, is a reliable pub with a smuggler theme. Another good pub for family dining is the **Wight Mouse** ((01983) 730431, in Chale, which has a children's menu and play area. Grown-ups like it for the live entertainment on most nights, six real ales and its 300-something whiskeys (moderate). There is also accommodation here at the Clarendon Hotel (moderate) which has its own restaurant.

BACK OF WIGHT

At the head of the River Medina, Newport is the commercial capital of Wight, a busy market town with some Georgian houses, antiques shops, and the parish Church of St. Thomas. You'll probably want to stop in at the Tourist Information Centre, here (see GENERAL INFORMATION, above).

That the Isle of Wight has been exploited for centuries is illustrated at **Newport Roman Villa** ((01983) 529720, Cypress Road, with its ruins of a third-century Roman villa, along with an enlightening museum. An historical moment of another age is preserved at **Carisbrooke Castle** ((01983) 522107 (just west of Newport), the impressive ruins of the island's only mediaeval castle. Charles I was imprisoned here from 1647 to 1648. At one of the restored mediaeval wells you can see how donkeys were used to draw water. Open daily year-round; admission fee.

To the south, **Shorwell** is a pristine village of stone and thatch, a center for good walks. On the edge of the village, Yafford Mill Farm ((01983) 740610 is a low-key attraction for families where children can ride a miniature train and visit with farm animals as well as the resident Atlantic gray seal. Open daily year-round; admission fee.

Just west are the thatched terraces of **Brighstone** village. The Brighstone Shop and Museum (NT) has an exhibition on local history, a tale of farming, life-saving, and smuggling. Open daily year-round, closed Sundays during low-season; admission fee. Brighstone's church has Norman pillars and pretty floral murals in the chancel.

North of Brighstone, **Mottistone Manor Garden** (NT) ((01983) 741302, a medley of herbaceous borders, shrubs, flowering fruit trees and sea views, is the setting for an imposing mediaeval and Elizabethan manor house. The garden is open Sunday and Tuesday from March to October; house opening is more limited; admission fee. The manor hosts a series of open air concerts in summer; call for a schedule. Beyond the formal gardens, Mottistone Estate is 263-hectares (656 acres) of downland, farmland and woods with a commendable network of footpaths.

Where to Stay and Eat

There are two moderately priced vacation **cottages** on Mottistone Estate available for stays of two or more nights. Rose Cottage, built from local stone, is a blossom-covered two-bedroom house behind the church at Mottistone village. Longstone cottage is a large brick Victorian with three spacious bedrooms, views and a garden, at the head of a valley. Contact the National Trust Holiday Cottage Booking Office ((01225) 791199 FAX (01225) 792267, PO Box 536, Melksham, Wiltshire SN12 8SX.

Just up the road from Shorwell, **Westcourt Farm** ((01983) 740233, Shorwell, Newport PO30 3LA, is fine old gabled Elizabethan farmhouse with thick stone walls, large rooms, friendly hosts and a good breakfast; inexpensive. Within walking distance of the farm is the **Crown** ((01983) 740293, Shorwell, a justifiably popular pub with outdoor dining along a babbling brook; inexpensive.

INLAND DORSET

DORSET — With virtually no heavyweight tourist attractions and no major motorways, inland Dorset is a rare gem of quiet, pastoral countryside where a few towns and villages have preserved their unique character. Possibly the county's most famous sight is the Cerne Giant, believed to be a Roman fertility figure, or perhaps just wishful thinking on the part of a latter-day hillside chalk carver.

CERNE ABBAS

Splendidly restored in the early twentieth century, the village of Cerne Abbas is watched over by the **Cerne Giant**, a chalk figure best seen from the A352 just north of the village. No one knows when or by whom this 55-m-tall (180-ft) figure was carved into the turf. Some believe he's a representation of Hercules, but he could be an even more ancient fertility symbol. He's considered a source of fertility because of his "unmistakable male attributes." If the giant and his treasures bring you to Cerne, stick around for a pleasant stroll around the village, particularly **Abbey Street** which has a number of interesting old buildings. Only the porch to **Abbot's Hall** remains of the Benedictine monastery that was founded at Cerne Abbas in the late tenth century.

MILTON ABBAS

Milton Abbas is probably the first entirely planned village in Britain. Its single wide street flanked by rows of identical thatched cottages sweeps down a green valley to a wooded lake. Above the lake stands the abbey, set in woodland, pasture and, oddly enough, a golf course.

The village was built in the eighteenth century by Lord Milton, Joseph Damer, in collaboration

The sun sets on the Needles, Alum Bay.

with the era's ever-present Capability Brown. Damer, who wanted to remove the old village of Middleton from his abbey gates, drew Brown into his schemes for a model village to be set in a dry valley above the original village site. One tenacious tenant, however, refused to move until Damer "accidentally" opened the sluice gates and flooded him out. As luck would have it the tenant was a lawyer who sued Damer for damages and won. Now all of the cottage leases contain a clause that Damer (now long departed) won't flood the lake again.

From the village you can walk the one-kilometer (half-mile) Monk's Path to the impressive **Milton Abbey,** dating from the fourteenth to fifteenth centuries and once part of a Benedictine monastery. It fell into private ownership after the Dissolution, gradually descending to the Damer family. A boys' school is housed in the adjoining mansion.

The **Hambro Arms** ((01258) 880233, Milton Abbas, Blandford Forum, Dorset DT11 0BP, has two well-appointed rooms with complementary sherry, as well as a fully stocked pay-as-you-go mini-bar. Downstairs the beamed pub serves imaginative fare by a log fire; low end of moderate.

WIMBORNE MINSTER

The small market town of Wimborne Minster was founded in AD 718, when a convent was set up here by Cuthburga, sister of King Ina of Wessex. It was sacked by the Danes in the tenth century, and the gray twin-towered church building that exists today dates from the mid-eleventh century, when the Minster was refounded by Edward the Confessor. The **Tourist Information Centre** ((01202) 886116 is located at 29 High Street.

A hotbed of nursery gardening and fruit-growing, Wimborne's **market** days are Friday to Sunday.

Wimborne centers around its well-preserved, largely Norman **Minster** (monastery church). In the narrow streets around the church are some respectable **antiques shops** and pretty Georgian houses. The **Priest's House Museum** ((01202) 882533, High Street, has rooms showing the furnishings and decor of different periods. Open Monday to Saturday from April to October; daily from June to September and for two weeks around Christmas; admission fee.

Three kilometers (two miles) north, **Kingston Lacey** (NT) ((01202) 883402, was built in the seventeenth century for the Bankes family after the destruction of Corfe Castle (below). Inside the house is a collection of paintings and Egyptian artifacts. There is a tranquil garden and marked trails, or "green lanes," dating back to Roman and Saxon times, through the vast surrounding pastures and woodland. The park and garden are open

daily from March to October; Friday to Sunday from November to December. The house is open Saturday to Wednesday from April to October; admission fee.

Where to Stay and Eat

Rural B&Bs make the most of this quiet corner of Dorset. **Beechleas** ((01202) 841684, Poole Road, Wimborne Minster BH21 1QA, is a Georgian house with nine bedrooms and open fires in the common areas. Meals feature organic produce and are served in the conservatory; expensive, Also on Poole Road, **Twynham** ((01202) 887310, 67 Poole Road, Wimborne Minster BH21 1QB, is a B&B within walking distance of the town center. There are three bedrooms sharing two baths; low end of inexpensive range.

See under MILTON ABBAS (above), DORCHESTER (below) and BOURNEMOUTH AND POOLE (below) for dining recommendations.

SHERBORNE

Built mainly of golden ham stone, Sherborne is one of Dorset's most architecturally harmonious towns, with a wealth of well-preserved mediaeval buildings in its compact center. The **Tourist Information Centre** ((01935) 815341 FAX (01935) 817210 is at 3 Tilton Court on Digby Road. **Market** days are Thursday and Saturday.

Splendid **Sherborne Abbey** was saved at the Dissolution through the efforts of the townspeople, who purchased it and made it their parish church. The abbey's most striking feature is its fifteenth-century vaulted ham stone roof.

Just east (off the A30) are Sherborne's two castles, known hereabouts as the Old and New, the former a ruin and the later a stately home open to the public. The twelfth-century **Old Castle** (EH) ((01935) 812730 is open daily from Easter to October, Wednesday to Sunday the rest of the year; admission fee. **New Castle** ((01935) 813182, was built by Sir Walter Raleigh in 1594 to replace the old castle. It's said that it was here while smoking tobacco he had brought back from Virginia that Sir Walter was doused with beer by a servant who thought he was on fire. The artificial lake between the two castles and the grounds of New Castle were designed by Capability Brown. Open Thursday and weekends from Easter to October; admission fee.

Six and a half kilometers (four miles) west of Sherborne (beyond Yeovil), **Montacute House** (NT) ((01935) 823289, in the village of Montacute, is a major stop on the stately homes trail. This is one of the country's finest Elizabethan buildings, set in 120 hectares (300 acres) of grounds and immaculately maintained gardens. Inside the great house hang 60 of the National Portrait Gallery's Tudor and Jacobean portraits. Open afternoons except Tuesdays from April to October; admission fee.

Six kilometers (four miles) north of Sherborne, **Beech Farm** ((01963) 220524, Sigwells, Charlton Horethorne, Sherborne DT9 4LN, is a dairy farm offering B&B with evening meals; inexpensive.

Pheasants ((01935) 815252, 24 Greenhill, is a local favorite for its delicious well-presented food. You might start with a beef barley soup accompanied by toasted walnut bread or smoked pheasant. There's more game on the main-course menu including venison en croute in a port wine sauce, or lemon sole in herb crust. There's a well-chosen wine list, and desserts are outstanding; expensive.

Sherborne is 211 km (130 miles) southwest of London. There is hourly **train** service from London Waterloo, a trip of just over two hours. National Express **coaches** depart London Victoria daily at around 4 PM for the four-hour trip to Sherborne.

SHAFTSBURY

By the time you get there, you'll likely have seen the view just off Shaftsbury's High Street on dozens of picture postcards. One of the best-loved vistas in the country, the cobbled **Gold Hill** is flanked by stone cottages and the buttressed abbey, diving steeply down toward the Vale of Blackmoor. There are a number of interesting craft shops here. The **abbey** lays in picturesque ruins. A museum by St. Peter's Church at the top of Gold Hill describes life through the ages in this ancient Saxon hill town.

Shaftsbury's **Tourist Information Centre** ((01747) 853514 is at 8 Bell Street.

There's casually comfortable lodging in Shaftsbury at the **Old Rectory** ((01747) 853658, St. James, Shaftsbury SP7 8HG, an eighteenth-

The 55-m (180-ft) Cerne Giant, at Cerne Abbas.

century house with three bedrooms and a log fire in the sitting room; moderate. The **restaurant**, where you can dine in the conservatory or garden, is quite pleasant.

Another fine choice for dinner lies about 13 km (eight miles) southwest of Shaftesbury, where **Plumber Manor (** (01258) 472507, Hazelbury Bryan Road, Sturminster Newton, a hotel, does very good fish dishes in the elegantly decorated dining room; expensive.

DORCHESTER

DORSET — The area around this ancient town has been occupied since prehistoric times. Later Dorchester became a Roman administrative town, and then a part of the Saxon kingdom of Wessex. Today it is the county town of Dorset, etched in readers' minds as the heart of Thomas Hardy country. The Dorchester native lived most of his life here, and the surrounding countryside inspired *Tess of the d'Urbervilles*, *Far from the Madding Crowd* and many more stories and poems. There are Hardy shrines in and around town, and the Dorset County Museum has Hardy relics. Wednesday is **market** day.

The **Tourist Information Centre (** (01305) 267992 FAX (01305) 266079 is located at Unit 11 on Antelope Walk, off Trinity Street.

WHAT TO SEE AND DO

The **Dorset County Museum (** (01305) 262735, High West Street, displays the original manuscript of *The Mayor of Casterbridge* and a reconstruction of Hardy's study. The museum also has archaeological finds from outlying prehistoric sites such as Maumbury Rings (on Weymouth Avenue), a Neolithic henge that later became a Roman amphitheater.

Just outside the town, **Hardy's Cottage** (NT) **(** (01305) 262366, Higher Bockhampton, was the birthplace of Thomas Hardy in 1840. He lived here until 1862 when he left for London to work in an architect's firm. Open daily except Friday and Saturday from March to October; admission fee. Back in town, **Max Gate** (NT) **(** (01305) 262538, Arlington Avenue, is the house that Hardy designed and occupied from 1885 until his death in 1928. It has none of the charm of the old cottage — Hardy was a better poet than draftsman — but it contains interesting objects that bring to mind Hardy's works and his many famous visitors; from T.E. Lawrence to Virginia Woolf. Open Monday, Wednesday and Saturday from March to September; admission fee. Also on the Hardy Trail is the churchyard at St. Michael's Church in **Stinsford** where the writer's heart is buried beside the grave of his wife. (His ashes lie in London's Westminster Abbey.)

About three kilometers (two miles) southwest of Dorchester is **Maiden Castle** (EH), the earth-

covered ramparts of an Iron Age fort. These earthworks are among most impressive in Britain, on such a huge scale (19 hectares or 47 acres) that legends once claimed they were built by giants.

WHERE TO STAY

The gracious **Casterbridge Hotel (** (01305) 264043 FAX (01305) 260884 E-MAIL reception@casterbridge hotel.co.uk, 49 High East Street, Dorchester DT1 1HU, is a Georgian-era building steps from the center. The 14 comfortable sunny bedrooms are tastefully appointed. Some of the rooms are in a courtyard annex and have garden terraces. There are public areas to relax in, including a bar-library where you can browse through books and brochures on the region. A bountiful breakfast is served in the conservatory; moderate.

A sixteenth-century thatched cottage that was once the local shepherd's residence, **Yalbury Cottage (** (01305) 262382 FAX (02135) 266412 E-MAIL yarlbury.cottage@virgin.net, Lower Bockhampton, Dorchester DT2 8PZ, is just east of town in the hamlet of Lower Bockhampton. Beamed ceilings and inglenook fireplaces have been preserved in the lounge and restaurant. The eight rooms overlook the garden; high end of inexpensive range.

Church Farm ((01935) 83221 FAX (01935) 83771, Stockwood, Dorchester DT 0NG, is a 72-hectare (180-acre) dairy farm offering B&B year-round in a Georgian farmhouse. All bedrooms have bath, and there is a satisfactory array of nearby pubs and restaurants to choose from for dinner; inexpensive.

WHERE TO EAT

West of town, **Le Petit Canard (** (01300) 320536, is a French restaurant twinkling with candles and fairy lights. Cooking ranges from classic to creative; expensive.

Reliably good Modern British and Continental fare have made **Mock Turtle (** (01305) 264011, 34 High Street West, one of the town's most popular restaurants. Closed Monday to Saturday lunch and Sunday dinner; moderate.

The **Potter Inn (** (01305) 260312, 19 Durngate, dishes up hot meals and sandwiches as well as homespun cakes in cozy rooms or on the sunny patio; inexpensive. On the same street, **Emma's Deli (** (01305) 259156 has picnic fixings.

HOW TO GET THERE

Dorchester is 209 km (129 miles) southwest of London. **Trains** leave London Waterloo hourly during the day for the two-and-a-half-hour trip

Heroic ruins of Corfe Castle tower over the village.

to Dorchester's two stations (South, Station Approach; West, Great Western Road). National Express also operates four **coaches** daily to Dorchester's coach station on High West Street. The ride takes four to five hours. In addition, Dorchester Coachways ℂ (020) 8668-7261 or (01305) 262992 operates coach service to Dorchester from London Victoria (Green Line terminal) daily.

THE DORSET COAST

DORSET — Along the East Dorset coast, resorts simmer with seaside entertainment, while further west the seashore is dominated by the wild natural beauty of the Isle of Purbeck, the eerie landscape of Chesil Bank and, at Abbotsbury, the largest colony of mute swans in the world. The Dorset Coast Path, part of the Southwest Coastal Path, runs the length of the shoreline from Bournemouth to Lyme Regis.

BOURNEMOUTH AND POOLE

For a genteel Victorian seaside town, Bournemouth has some gruesome associations. It is the burial place of Mary Shelley, author of *Frankenstein*. Robert Louis Stevenson wrote *The Strange Case of Dr. Jekyll and Mr. Hyde* and *Kidnapped* here.

Beyond its literary history, this sunny, pine-scented town is Dorset's largest resort, with a population of 265,000. Beaches are good here with 11 km (seven miles) of fine sand stretching from the mouth of Poole Harbour to Hengistbury Head. Most of the seafront is built up with villas and hotels, but to the west there are cliff-top parks and gardens.

Neighboring Poole has a busy quay full of yachts and yawls. There's a compact pedestrian-only center with shops and cafés, mostly with nautical themes, and a few pottery shops. From

works of Percy Bysshe Shelley, the **Shelley Rooms** ((01202) 303571, Boscombe Manor, Beechwood Avenue, focusing primarily on the poet's later works. Closed Monday; free.

Over in Poole the **Waterfront Museum** ((01202) 683138, 4 High Street, is housed partly in fifteenth-century cellars on the quay. It lays out the history of the town and port as well as the story of the founding of the Boy Scouts from the first camp on Brownsea Island in 1907. Open daily from April to June and Sept to October; admission fee.

The **Poole Pottery** ((01202) 666200, The Quay, has been producing china here for more than century. Factory tours take you through the process of forming, glazing, and firing. You can even try your hand at throwing and decorating your own pot. Closed during lunch and some weekends in winter; admission fee. There's a restaurant here overlooking the harbor.

Outdoor Activities

Sandbanks has been called "the best **beach** in Britain." You can take the chain ferry from here to Shell Bay on the Isle of Purbeck for more sandy beaches, birding and hiking (see under ISLE OF PURBECK, below).

One and a half kilometers (just over a mile) from Poole, **Brownsea Island** (NT) ((01202) 707444, is a 200-hectare (500-acre) heath and woodland sanctuary for sika deer and many species of birds. Brownsea is a haven for nature lovers too, with safe, quiet bathing beaches, nature trails, woodland walks, and wide views of the Dorset coast. There is a café and shop at the Quay. Open March to October; admission fee. Boats operate to Brownsea from Poole Quay, Bournemouth and Sandbanks.

Where to Stay

Bournemouth and Poole offer a vast selection of accommodation. One of the most distinctive is the **Mansion House** ((01202) 685666 FAX (01202) 665709 E-MAIL enquiries@themansionhouse .co.uk, Thames Street, Poole BH15 1JN, with 28 individually decorated bedrooms, and restful public areas. It's close to the seafront and the two restaurants (moderate) here are among the area's best; expensive.

The **Cottage Hotel** ((01202) 422764 FAX (01202) 381442 E-MAIL rjvhalliwell@force9.co.uk, 12 Southern Road, Southbourne, Bournemouth BH6 3SR, is located in Bournemouth's eastern suburb. This family-run hotel has seven rooms, four of which are have bath; inexpensive. Evening meals are served and half-board is available. Open March to October.

Bournemouth has two very popular hostels. The **Bournemouth (Sunnyside) Backpackers**

Poole it's possible to launch a visit to Brownsea, an nature preserve in the center of the harbor.

The Bournemouth **Tourist Information Centre** ((01202) 451700 FAX (01202) 451743 is on Westover Road; while at Poole ((01202) 673322, it's located at the Quay. There is **Internet access** in Bournemouth on Charminster Road, at CouchNet Internet Café, No. 117; or at The Cyber Place, at No. 32.

What to See and Do

In a Victorian villa, Bournemouth's **Russell-Cotes Art Gallery & Museum** ((01202) 451800, East Cliff, houses an excellent collection of Asian and Victorian fine art and artifacts as well as Modern British art. A recent extension of the buildings has added exhibits on contemporary crafts and sculpture. Open Tuesday to Sunday; free. Bournemouth also has a small museum dedicated to the life and

The shore at Bournemouth boasts 11 km (seven miles) of sand and surf.

℄/FAX (01202) 299491, 3 Frances Road, Bournemouth BH1 3RY, has 20 beds in small dorms, as well as twins and doubles. There is also **Bournemouth Boo's** ℄ (01202) 428189 FAX (01202) 428191, 31 Dalmeney Road, Bournemouth BH6 4BW, with a small co-ed dormitory. Both of these hostels are open year-round with all-day access, no curfew, a garden, and self-catering kitchen; rock-bottom.

Where to Eat

In addition to Poole's Merchant's House (above), another place for good food is **Upstairs at the Custom House** ℄ (01202) 676767, The Quay, which does Modern British and French with views of the harbor; moderate.

THE ISLE OF PURBECK

Purbeck is not an island but a wide peninsula jutting into the sea below Poole Harbour. The dark fossil-encrusted limestone known as Purbeck marble, used in so many great buildings throughout Britain, comes from this unique area of Dorset, whose coast is lined with spectacular geological features. Inland, Corfe Castle broods majestically over the green countryside, and between Corfe Castle and Studland the roadways afford fabulous views of Poole Harbour and Brownsea Island over gorse-covered heath. It all seems quite remote until you catch sight of Poole and Bournemouth sparkling across the water.

In Bournemouth there is a branch of **Café Rouge** ℄ (01202) 757472, 67–71A Seamoor Road, in Westbourne, if you want something reliably Continental. Otherwise, you might try the solid English fare at **Sophisticats** ℄ (01202) 291019, 43 Charminster Road, an owner-managed restaurant near the center of town; expensive.

A cheerful eatery in Westbourne, **Chez Fred** ℄ (01202) 761023, 10 Seamoor Road, Westbourne, does fresh fish & chips. Save room for the treacle sponge; inexpensive.

How to Get There

Bournemouth and Poole are around 178 km (110 miles) southwest of London. **Trains** depart London Waterloo throughout the day for the two-hour trip to Bournemouth. National Express has hourly **coach** service from London Victoria to Bournemouth and Poole. The ride takes about three hours.

The Southwest Coastal Path kicks off on the Isle of Purbeck for its 1,000-km (617-mile) journey around the Devon-Cornwall Peninsula.

The Isle of Purbeck **Tourist Information Centre** ℄ (01929) 552740 is at Wareham, in Holy Trinity Church, South Street.

What to See and Do

If you visit only one ruin in Southern England make it **Corfe Castle** (NT) ℄ (01929) 481294. This spectacular hilltop fortress has grand views over the Purbeck Hills. Before you climb to the castle, stop by the visitor center to glean the history of this mediaeval fortification. The ruins that you see here were not brought about by the ravages of time but were engineered purposefully during the Civil War by the Parliamentarian army after two lengthy sieges finally routed the Royalist Lady Bankes and her household. At one point the redoubtable Lady

Bankes ordered her maids and daughters to the battlements to pelt the attacking Parliamentarian soldiers with burning embers. The eventual defeat of Lady Bankes may explain why local people often claim to have seen ghosts among the ruins. Open daily year-round; admission fee. Located on the A351 Wareham–Swanage Road.

The **village of Corfe Castle** huddles around the castle gate, a delightful cluster of stone cottages set on the same high ridge as the castle. There is a well-stocked National Trust shop here and several tea rooms and B&Bs.

Outdoor Activities

The Studland Beach and Nature Reserve (NT) ((01929) 450259 is a magnificent expanse of heathland, dunes and beach, as well as a wildlife haven where thousands of wild birds roost. The beaches here are often rated amongst Britain's best. At The Knoll, the National Trust operates a year-round visitor center and café. From the car park here you can depart for brilliant coastal walks, such as the trek to Old Harry Rocks. Heading in the opposite direction from The Knoll, you can trace the beach towards Shell Bay. About halfway down this stretch of sand is a naturist beach, which extends a sunny welcome to all who care to shed their bathing costumes. A modest alternative trail loops behind the naturist enclave.

To the west, the blue cradle of **Lulworth Cove** is flanked by high cliffs. From here there is a fine cliff-top walk to **Durdle Door**, a dramatic rock arch eroded by the action of the waves.

ABBOTSBURY

A delightful village, Abbotsbury is home to the celebrated Swannery, where a colony of the regal birds live and love. If you can visit in May, you may have the thrill of holding a cygnet. In April you can see the adults mating. There are several other worthwhile attractions here, many of which appeal specifically to children. The Bakehouse (next to the Ilchester Arms) is the local **tourist information point**, stocking brochures and maps. Abbotsbury has a useful WEB SITE www.abbotsbury.co.uk/village.

What to See and Do

It's a pleasant one-kilometer (half-mile) walk from the village to **Abbotsbury Swannery** ((01305) 871858 WEB SITE www.abbotsbury-tourism.co.uk, the home of a colony of 400 to 500 mute swans, the only remaining large colony of swans in the British Isles, and the only colony that can be visited during spring nesting. There has been a swannery here since 1393. The birds are free to come and go (their wings are not clipped). It's a rare chance to wander among the birds and observe their cantankerous behavior. Open daily year-round; admission fee.

Up the road from the swannery, the huge abbey **Tithe Barn** ((01305) 871817 (the largest in England), houses a petting farm and an exhibition of replica Chinese terracotta warriors. In spring you can see lambing here. Open daily year-round; admission fee.

Rare plants flourish in Abbotsbury's **Subtropical Gardens** ((01305) 871387, where there are beautiful woodland walks as well as an aviary and play area. Open daily year-round; admission fee. Another good place to walk is to the hilltop **St. Catherine's Chapel**, built during the reign of Edward IV (fourteenth century). Access is via a footpath from the village; the church is not always open. From Abbotsbury you can walk onward to

the vast shingle beach at **Chesil Bank**, a curved 16-km-long (10-mile) bank of pebbles. Back of the shingle is Fleet Lagoon, a haven for swans and other waterfowl.

Where to Stay and Eat

There are B&Bs to choose from right in the village, as well as the **Ilchester Arms** ((01305) 871243 E-MAIL reservations@ilchesterarms.co.uk, Abbotsbury, Weymouth DT3 4JR, a seventeenth-century coaching inn with 10 comfortable rooms and beamed pub serving interesting fare by the log fire. Breakfast is in the conservatory; inexpensive.

The partially fifteenth-century **Abbey House** ((01305) 871330 FAX (01305) 871088, Church Street, Abbotsbury DT3 4JJ, stands by the ruins of the Benedictine abbey and St. Nicholas Church, with beautiful countryside views. There is a tea room which also enjoys the hilltop location; inexpensive.

LYME REGIS

Set on a broad sweep of bay, Lyme Regis is one of Britain's best-loved literary shrines. Jane Austen visited Lyme and made it the setting of a turning-point in *Persuasion*, when Louisa Musgrove

OPPOSITE: Lulworth Cove, Isle of Purbeck. ABOVE: Mute swans congregate on Fleet Lagoon.

"fell on the pavement of the Lower Cobb and was taken up lifeless!" The Cobb appears also in John Fowles's 1969 best-seller, *The French Lieutenant's Woman*, etched deeply into popular memory by the movie version in which Sarah Woodruff, played by Meryl Streep, gazes convincingly out to sea. Jumping from literature to history, Lyme is also the site of the 1685 landing of the Duke of Monmouth when he attempted unsuccessfully to overthrow James II.

You'll find a **Tourist Information Centre** ((01297) 442138 FAX (01297) 443773 near the waterfront at Guildhall Cottage on Church Street. Local guides offer two-hour **fossil walks** on the beach; details at the Tourist Information Centre.

What to See and Do
Popular opinion has settled on a jagged set of steps on the **Cobb** called Granny's Teeth as the most likely spot for Louisa Musgrove's fall. Perhaps it was to these steps that Alfred Lord Tennyson was led when he cried: "Don't talk to me of the Duke of Monmouth. Show me the steps from which Louisa Musgrove fell."

Lyme Regis Philpot Museum, Bridge Street, is well known for its excellent fossil collections as well as for its literary memorabilia. John Fowles was curator here for a decade. Open daily from April to October; admission fee. Lyme has several interesting shops selling locally quarried fossils, and a few antiques shops.

There's a small sandy **beach** at the harbor, and the **gardens** above Marine Parade are a pleasant spot for a walk or a picnic. If you have time, take the beach **walk**, a section of the Southwest Coastal

Path, west to Seaton (about 10 km or six miles); you can catch the bus back.

Just under 13 km (eight miles) north of Lyme Regis **Forde Abbey** ((01460) 221290, has 12 ha (30 acres) of beautiful gardens surrounding the family house, founded as a Cistercian abbey in 1649. Full of period furnishings and art objects, it's an interesting house with more warmth than many stately homes. Don't miss the crewel bed linens done by a talented family member in the 1930s. Another highlight is the seventeenth-century Mortlake tapestries. There is a **tea room** in the twelfth-century undercroft using produce grown on the estate, as well as a plant shop and a pottery exhibition. The garden is open daily year-round; house open Tuesday, Wednesday, Thursday and Sunday afternoons from April to October; admission fee.

Where to Stay and Eat
The eighteenth-century **Alexandra Hotel** ((01297) 442010 FAX (01297) 443229 E-MAIL enquiries @hotelalexandra.co.uk, Pound Street, Lyme Regis DT7 3HZ, has 26 attractively decorated rooms and a respected **restaurant** (moderate) with panoramic views of the bay. During winter, log fires warm the public areas, and in summer guests can enjoy a conservatory which opens out onto the garden; expensive to very expensive.

For rural lodging there is **Amherst Lodge Farm** ((01297) 442773, Uplyme, Lyme Regis DT7 3XH, with four rooms, 56 hectares (140 acres) of woodlands, fields and lakes with trout fishing; inexpensive.

In the heart of town, **Café Sol** (no phone), Coombe Street, does breakfast and lunch featuring fruit shakes and sandwiches in a sunny spot over the River Lyme; inexpensive.

The **Pilot Boat Inn** ((01297) 443157, Bridge Street, is in the town center near the seafront. They serve food all day, including vegetarian choices like vegetable samosas. Meat curries, local crab and sea bass are also on the menu; inexpensive.

Rose Cottage ((01297) 443435, 9 Broad Street, makes award-winning fudge and there is a tiny wedge of a tea room in back with good soup and toasties; inexpensive.

How to Get There
Lyme Regis is eight kilometers (five miles) southeast of Axminster, the nearest train station, served by several direct trips daily from London Waterloo. The trip takes two and a half hours. From Axminster bus service operates to Lyme.

Lyme Regis — ABOVE: The Cobb, a landmark favored by writers Jane Austen and John Fowles. OPPOSITE: Children cast their nets in tide pools.

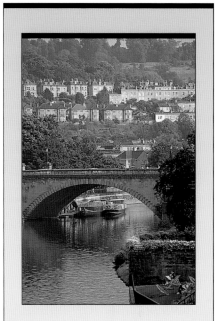

Somerset
and
Wiltshire

WHILE OUT OF REACH OF THE SUBURBAN TENTACLES of London commuterland, the counties of Somerset and Wiltshire are yet within day-tripping distance of the capital. But this idyllic corner of southwest England merits much more than a passing glance.

Somerset's Bristol Channel coast has long scenic stretches protected from development by Exmoor National Park and the National Trust. Although it is landlocked between Somerset and Dorset, Wiltshire's great chalk uplands are a rolling ocean of green hills and patchwork farms. North of the Salisbury Plain, the Wiltshire Downs are a confluence of natural beauty and mystical quirks where "crop circles" appear overnight and chalk figures and standing stones provoke continual debate.

In addition to great scenery, this area boasts some of Southern England's most famous landmarks. Both counties are known for their extensive prehistoric remains. In Somerset, the Mendip Hills and Glastonbury show evidence of Iron-Age settlement. Wiltshire is believed to have been the most heavily populated part of England during prehistoric times; its Neolithic monuments — including Stonehenge and Avebury — form a World Heritage Site and one of Britain's most important tourist attractions.

The region's biggest attraction is undoubtedly Bath. With its Georgian body and Roman heart, this honey-colored city is one of the most harmoniously designed in Britain. And there's more: Salisbury is renowned for its magnificent thirteenth-century cathedral, Wells for its cathedral and its hometown atmosphere, and Glastonbury for its romantically ruined abbey and New Age spirit.

Somerset and Wiltshire have excellent walking and riding country. The Mendips, Exmoor, and around Castle Combe are popular Somerset rambling regions. The Wiltshire Cycleway connects the dots between several of the county's major sightseeing areas, linking Salisbury with the Marlborough Downs, Amesbury (near Stonehenge), and Longleat. Wiltshire has a Walking and Cycling Hotline ((01980) 623255 for free information and advice.

BATH

SOMERSET — Built entirely of a amber limestone and surrounded on three sides by a loop in the Avon River, the city of Bath is a World Heritage Site and one of the country's most visited tourist attractions. Reconstructed Roman baths uncovered in the nineteenth century form just one fascinating layer of Bath's deep history. Bath Abbey, built on the site of a monastery where the first king of England was crowned in AD 973, is a stellar example of Perpendicular architecture. Visitors can relive Georgian pomp and circumstance with high tea at the Pump Room, and a host of interesting museums await discovery, as well as dozens of

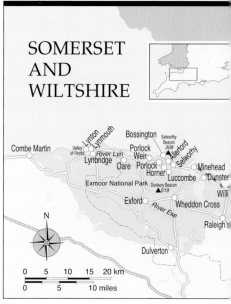

high-quality antique stores and excellent restaurants. In short, a week would not be wasted in Bath. A day is nothing like enough to sample the many offerings of this city. Take note, however, that though Bath is no longer the focal point of fashionable society as it was in eighteenth century, crowds and traffic can be overwhelming in the peak season — you'd be wise to visit outside the summer and holiday seasons.

Legend says that it was an unfortunate prince named Bladud, son of a Briton king, who first discovered the marvelous healing powers of the hot spring at Bath. Stricken with leprosy he took to the hills as a swineherd. One day the pigs, who were also afflicted, emerged cured after a brief wallow in the springs. Bladud followed suit and was cured as well; the masses ensued.

Whether Bladud existed or not, the spring was certainly a Celtic shrine. When the Romans arrived in the first century they built the original baths and a temple to Sulis-Minerva (an amalgamation of the Celtic deity Sul and the Roman goddess Minerva) naming their city Aquae Sulis. Though the baths and temple were not large, they attracted pilgrims from all over Roman Britain and across Europe.

After the retreat of the Romans in the fifth century, the baths fell into neglect and Bath's history plodded on. A monastery was founded here in 973 by King Edgar and a wealthy religious establishment along with a healthy wool trade brought prosperity to Bath once again in the Middle Ages. In the mid-sixteenth century, interest was renewed in the spring — as a healing source for infertility, leprosy, smallpox and a host of other mediaeval ailments and complaints. Pumps were installed

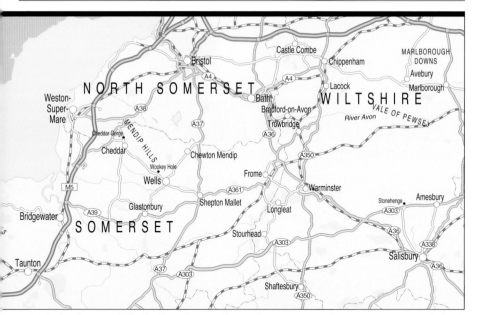

in 1663 after the visit of Charles II, so that people could drink the waters. Finally, Queen Anne gave the royal seal of approval in 1702 and the fashionable followed. See also DIP INTO GEORGIAN BATH, page 21 in TOP SPOTS.

GENERAL INFORMATION

Look for the **Tourist Information Centre** ((01225) 477101 at Abbey Chambers, in the Abbey Church Yard. You can access the **Internet** at Itchy Feet, on Bartlett Street; or at the Green Park Brassiere, Green Park Road.

Don't miss taking one of the excellent free Blue Badge **guided walking tours**, organized by Bath and Northeast Somerset Heritage Services ((01225) 477786, which start at 10:30 AM and 1:30 PM in front of the Pump Room, Abbey Church Yard. For further enlightenment, there is Bizarre Bath ((01225) 335124, a walking comedy act that takes participants on an 80-minute tour of the city and pledges "absolutely no history or culture." The tour departs nightly at 8 PM from the Huntsman Pub, North Parade Passage, near the Abbey (confirm time and starting place by calling Bizarre Bath or through the Tourist Information Centre); fee charged.

There are circular tours of Bath aboard **hop-on hop-off buses**; details at the Tourist Information Centre.

Parking in Bath can be a severe headache. Make sure your chosen lodging offers a nook for your auto. Otherwise, park overnight in one of the central garages until 8 AM, then move your car to Victoria Park or into the suburbs for the duration of your stay. You might also consider other modes of transportation (see HOW TO GET THERE, below). Several park-and-ride lots surround the city.

Bath celebrates with a **Literature Festival** in February, and the **International Music Festival** in May. For information contact Bath Festivals ((01225) 463362, 2 Church Street, Abbey Green, Bath BA1 1NL.

WHAT TO SEE AND DO

Roman Baths and Pump Room

When the Romans arrived in AD 43 they made a big fuss about Bath. Around the waters, which they considered to be both sacred and healing, they built the city they called Aquae Sulis and the Temple of Sulis Minerva.

The Roman Baths ((01225) 477785 were rediscovered during archaeological excavations in 1879. Today, the excavated baths and adjoining museum form an unparalleled look at Roman Britain. The museum contains a vast collection of artifacts, and a reconstruction gives an idea of what the baths looked like in the first century. Visitors can explore the ruins on their own or tag along with one of the well-versed guides. The **Great Bath** is open to the sky, just below street level. The 2,000-year-old mechanisms of in-flow and out-flow still fill its lead-lined pool. Part of the **East Baths** — the tepidarium and the calderium — also remain.

The Roman Baths are open daily year-round; admission fee (includes audio guide). There is a combination ticket for the Roman Baths and the Museum of Costume (below). During August and part of July the museum is open until 9:30 PM each night and illuminated by torchlight.

Looking out over the baths is the elegant Georgian Pump Room, described in the 1930s by H. V. Morton as: "the ever open door to the gouty, the rheumaticky, and the sciaticky [sic]." Today it's an ever-open door to anyone fancying a spot of tea (see WHERE TO EAT, below). Until the new spa opens, this is the only place to taste Bath's healing waters. The Pump Room remains a gorgeous tribute to Georgian sensibilities.

Abbey Church

The flamboyant front of the Abbey Church is credited to Bishop Oliver King who, during the building of the abbey, had a dream about angels climbing up and down ladders. King was not the most modest of men: Note the olive tree with a bishop's miter and crown. That's the bishop's signature (Bishop Oliver King). Built in 1490, Bath Abbey is a Gothic gem, and you mustn't miss sitting for a spell in quiet awe under the flawlessly restored (1800s) fan vaulting of creamy Bath stone. The walls are crowded with memorials: Richard "Beau" Nash (1754–1761), Bath's master of ceremonies during its eighteenth-century heyday, is remembered here, as is Isaac Pitman, the inventor of shorthand. Daytime organ concerts are offered in summer months (see NIGHTLIFE, below).

The abbey is open Monday to Friday from Easter to October; admission fee. For an additional fee, it's possible to view a collection of artifacts illustrating abbey history in the Heritage Vaults ℭ (01225) 422462. Entrance is on the south side of the abbey; year-round.

More Points of Interest

While the Roman museum tells the ancient history of Bath, the **Building of Bath Museum** ℭ (01225) 333895, The Vineyards, The Paragon, is a must for anyone who wants to understand how this Georgian boomtown came to be. Exhibits from blueprints to scale models describe the rise of Georgian Bath without sidestepping the issues of who made money and how they did it. Open February to November; admission fee.

A double feature, the **Bath Assembly Rooms** (NT) ℭ (01225) 477789, Bennett Street, house the **Museum of Costume**. The former were meeting rooms for the fashionable society of Georgian Bath, a grand backdrop for dancing, gaming and gossiping. Several Thomas Gainsborough paintings hang in the stunning Octagon Room. The Small Ballroom is surrounded by niches; a nod to Roman decoration, they were never intended to hold statues. The Main Ballroom has an orchestra balcony and wedding-cake-like Wedgwood molding. The Museum of Costume holds a rather fine collection of getups from several centuries, though the lighting is kept low to preserve the fragile fabrics and you may have to squint. Admission is free to the Assembly Rooms. Open daily year-round;

a fee is charged for the museum (including National Trust members). There is a combination ticket for the Roman Baths and the Museum of Costume.

Bath has connections with Jane Austen, who skewered the town's haute monde in *Northanger Abbey* and *Persuasion*. Before Austen, Dickens satirized the town in *The Pickwick Papers*. Many other writers spent time in Bath, including Wordsworth, Shelley, and Henry Fielding. Early editions of their works as well as an exhibition on the art of bookbinding can be seen at the **Book Museum** ℭ (01225) 466000, Manvers Street. Open year-round; admission fee.

A host of other museums and galleries round out Bath's offerings. All of the following charge admission and all are open daily year-round except where otherwise noted. The **Victoria Art Gallery** ℭ (01225) 477772, Bridge Street, houses a permanent collection of British and European art dating from the seventeenth century to the present; there are also major temporary exhibits here. The **Postal Museum** ℭ (01225) 460333, 8 Broad Street, explores the history of the British postal system; while **William Herschel House** ℭ (01225) 311342, 19 New King Street, celebrates the life of William Herschel, an amateur astronomer who made his own telescope and discovered the planet Uranus (weekends only between November and February). The Octagon Galleries at the **Royal Photographic Society Gallery** ℭ (01225) 462841, Milsom Street, is a museum of photography with an excellent book shop and café (see WHERE TO EAT, below). The **Museum of East Asian Art** ℭ (01225) 464640, 12 Bennett Street, focuses on the Georgians' love for the art of the Orient. The **Bath Industrial Heritage Centre** ℭ (01225) 318348, Julian Road, tells the story of a mineral-water manufacturing firm, Mr. Bowler's Business, with reconstructed Victorian factory rooms and workshops (weekends only from November to Easter). **No. 1 Royal Crescent** ℭ (01225) 428126, Royal Crescent, has been restored to its original John Wood design as an eighteenth-century townhouse (open February to October).

Galleries at the **Holburne Museum** ℭ (01225) 466669, Great Pulteney Street, display eighteenth-century fine and decorative arts, featuring paintings by Gainsborough and Turner, and work by contemporary British craftspeople. Watch for announcements of lectures, events and concerts. Tea house, picnicking. Open Monday to Saturday from February to December. Closed Monday from November to Easter; admission fee.

Bath has some beautiful gardens. The Botanical Gardens in **Royal Victoria Park** is a cool, quiet retreat especially on weekday mornings. In summer there are band concerts at the Parade Gardens. Open from dawn to dusk. Just outside Bath there

Bath's Georgian planners made sure the city had plenty of green space.

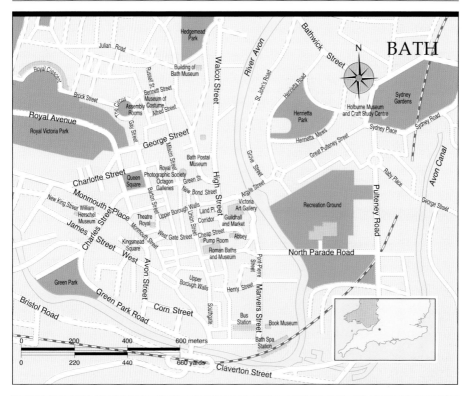

BATH

Julian Road

Hedgemead Park

Royal Crescent

Building of Bath Museum

Brock Street

Walcot Street

The Circus

Russell St

River Avon

Bathwick Street

N

Assembly Rooms

Bennett Street

Museum of Costume

Alfred Street

St John's Road

Henrietta Road

Sydney Gardens

Holburne Museum and Craft Study Centre

Royal Avenue

Royal Victoria Park

Gay Street

George Street

Henrietta Park

Sydney Place

Sydney Road

Grove Street

Henrietta Mews

Great Pulteney Street

Avon Canal

Charlotte Street

Milsom Street

Bath Postal Museum

Royal Photographic Society

Green St.

High Street

Argyle Street

Raby Place

George Street

Monmouth Place

Queen Square

Octagon Galleries

New Bond Street

Victoria Art Gallery

Recreation Ground

Pulteney Road

New King Street

William Herschel Museum

Barton Street

Upper Borough Walls

Land Pl.

Corridor

Guildhall and Market

James Street

Charles Street

Theatre Royal

Union Street

West Gate Street

Cheap Street

Abbey

Kingsmead Square

Monmouth Street

Pump Room

Roman Baths and Museum

North Parade Road

West

Avon Street

Pont-Pierre Street

Green Park

Upper Borough Walls

Henry Street

Bristol Road

Green Park Road

Corn Street

Southgate

Manvers Street

Bus Station

Book Museum

Claverton Street

Bath Spa Station

| 0 | 200 | 400 | 600 meters |
| 0 | 220 | 440 | 660 yards |

are luscious gardens at **Prior Park Landscape Garden** (NT) ((0891) 335242 (24-hour recorded information), Ralph Allen Drive, the home of Ralph Allen who made his fortune by providing the stone that built Georgian Bath. The newly restored eighteenth-century gardens and grounds feature a Palladian bridge and outstanding views of Bath. Open daily except Tuesday; admission fee. To get there from Bath you must walk one and a half kilometers (one mile) from the city center, or use public transportation. There is no parking. Call Badgerline ((01225) 464446 for transportation information.

Only five kilometers (three miles) southeast of the city, the **American Museum** ((01225) 460502,

Claverton Manor, depicts American life in the seventeenth to nineteenth centuries with a series of period rooms furnished with American artifacts and staffed by costumed guides. Open afternoons, closed all day Monday from March to November; admission fee. The tea rooms here are quite a hit.

From Pulteney Bridge, you can take a **riverboat cruise** along the River Avon, and on weekends there are boat trips along the Kennet & Avon Canal. **Punts** can be rented in nearby Bathwick. For pre-recorded information on river and canal trips in Bath call Bath Visitor ((0891) 360396 (50p per minute).

OUTDOOR ACTIVITIES

Before heading out into the Area of Outstanding Natural Beauty that surrounds Bath, take the National Trust's **circular skyline walk**, which opens

up vistas along a nine-kilometer (six-mile) promenade around the outskirts of Bath. Buy the brochure at the Tourist Information Centre.

The Avon **Cycleway** (route guide available from the Tourist Information Centre) is a way-marked circular route linking Bristol to Bath via a former rail bed. There is also satisfying cycling along the Kennet and Avon Canal. You'll need a permit for canal cycling, available from British Waterways ((01923) 201120. Rental bicycles are available at Avon Valley Cyclery ((01225) 461880, and at Lock Inn Cottage ((01225) 868068 in Bradford-on-Avon (see below).

Hot-air ballooning over the Northeast Somerset is another adventurous way to get to know the territory. Contact Bath Balloon Flights ((01225) 466888 or Heritage Balloons ((01225) 318747.

SHOPPING

Southgate Street has the high street stores, while more exclusive shops are found on Milsom Street. The Upper Town is Bath's **antiques** area. Bartlett Street Antiques Centre ((01225) 466689, 5-10 Bartlett Street, has 200 dealers under one roof and a café upstairs. Closed Sunday. Look also on George Street and Margaret's Buildings (off Brock Street). Contact the Bath and Bradford-on-Avon Antique Dealers Association ((01225) 442215, 3–4 Piccadilly, London Road Bath BA1 6PL, for a free guide to their 70 member dealers.

The **Guildhall Market**, High Street, has been a place of trade for more than 700 years. Today stall-holders continue to sell fresh flowers, and local cheeses and handmade jewelry. Gillards at No. 55–56 offers exotic and traditional loose leaf teas, including a "Jane Austen blend."

WHERE TO STAY

Lodging in Bath tends to be pricey. If you are looking for a good-value, inexpensive to moderate B&B, you might consider staying in nearby Bradford-on-Avon (see below).

The **Royal Crescent Hotel** ((01225) 823333 FAX (01225) 339401 E-MAIL reservations@royalcrescent .co.uk, 16 Royal Crescent, Bath BA1 2LS, occupies the central townhouses in John Wood's Georgian architectural masterpiece. The well-appointed bedrooms are found in various buildings around a pretty garden. There is superb formal dining (very expensive), and leisure facilities designed to duplicate the atmosphere of the Roman baths, including an indoor heated swimming pool, an outdoor heated plunge pool and a sauna; very expensive to luxury (room rate does not include breakfast).

Occupying a Georgian rectory surrounded by carefully-tended gardens, **Brompton House** ((01225) 420972 FAX (01225) 420505, St. John's

Road, Bathwick, Bath BA2 6PT, is an easy walk to the center. All rooms have baths, and parking, an important consideration in Bath, is available; mid-range to expensive.

A ten-minute walk from the center, **Leighton House (** (01225) 314769 FAX (01225) 443079, 139 Wells Road, Bath Somerset BA2 3AL, is a welcoming B&B in a detached Victorian; moderate.

A Victorian in the inexpensive price range, **Astor House (**/FAX (01225) 429134, 14 Oldfield Road, Bath BA2 3ND, has views of the city and is a short walk from the center. All rooms have bath.

Given the popularity of Bath, you might choose to stay in a tranquil area outside the city. Ten kilometers (six miles) south of Bath, **Honeycombe**

Another low-priced option is **YMCA International House (** (01225) 460471 FAX (01225) 462065 E-MAIL info@ymca.u-net.com, Broad Street Place, Bath BA1 5LH, right in the center of town. Despite the colorful lobby, be prepared for industrial-strength rooms. Prices include a continental breakfast and there are discounts for stays of two nights or more, as well as a nursery for children over five years of age. The restaurant serves cheap dinners on site. Stiff fees are charged for use of the laundry, left luggage, and just about anything else you might need. There is no parking. The dormitory rooms (rock-bottom) are a good deal, but those looking for a private room are probably better off in a B&B.

House (** (01761) 433973, St. Julians Road, Shoscombe Vale, Bath BA2 8NB, is set in the countryside with beautiful views, well-situated for trips in the city as well as country walks. One double and one twin room share a bath; inexpensive. A five-minute drive from Bath, but well outside the hustle and bustle, **Rainbow Wood Farm (**/FAX (01225) 466366, Claverton Down, Bath BA2 7AR, is a Georgian farmhouse on a 120-hectare (300-acre) working dairy farm surrounded by wooded National Trust countryside. All rooms have bath; inexpensive.

There are two hostels in Bath, both at rock-bottom prices. **Bath Youth Hostel (** (01225) 465674 FAX (01225) 482947 E-MAIL bath@yha.org.uk, Bathwick Hill, Bath BA2 6SZ, is set in wooded grounds overlooking the city. **Bath Backpackers Hostel (** (01225) 446787 FAX (01225) 446305, is at 13 Pierrepont Street, only three blocks from the train station.

Somerset and Wiltshire

WHERE TO EAT

A number of upscale eateries provide excellent dining in Bath, but there are also plenty of snack shops and bargain cafés. At the top-end, the intimate **Moody Goose (** (01225) 466688, 7A Kingsmead Square, is a downstairs restaurant specializing in French-influenced Modern English fare; very expensive. In Upper Town, the **Olive Tree (** (01225) 447928, Russell Street, at the Queensberry Hotel, provides splendid Modern British cooking, with French provincial and Italian accents, in a sleek modern setting; expensive. The **Circus (** (01225) 318918, 34 Brock Street, between the Royal Crescent and the Circus, has a cozy Old-World atmosphere and international cuisine featuring mains

OPPOSITE: The Georgian Pump Room fountain spouts Bath's famous mineral water. ABOVE: The eighteenth-century Royal Crescent.

such as roast chicken breast stuffed with banana on a coconut curry sauce; expensive. **No. 5 Bistro** ((01225) 444499, 5 Argyle Street, Pulteney Bridge, is a superb French bistro. You could start with a salad of gruyère with mandarin oranges, endives and walnuts and move on to duck in port wine sauce; expensive.

Dine in Palladian splendor at the **Pump Room** ((02115) 444477, Abbey Churchyard, which serves a continental breakfast, "Georgian Elevenses" (hot chocolate and a Sally Lunn bun), as well as high tea. Lunch and dinner feature mains such as skewered lamb; expensive. **Le Beaujolais** ((01225) 423417, 5 Chapel Row (off Queen Square), offers a changing menu featuring terrines and interna-

The **Bridge Coffee Shop** (no phone), Argyle Street, is a sweet place for an inexpensive breakfast or tea. It occupies the Pulteney Bridge toll house overlooking the weir. Over its travel gadget shop and bookstore, **Itchy Feet** ((01225) 337987, 4 Bartlett Street, has a friendly café serving sandwiches, hot meals and rich desserts like lemon cream pie. It's a congenial place to hang out, with magazines to browse and a computer to download e-mail.

Inside the Royal Photographic Society building, the **Octagon Café** ((01225) 447991, Milsom Street, is a highly recommended eatery offering "lunch for a fiver" and serving bottomless coffee until 11:30 AM. Diners get a discount on entrance to the photographic museum.

tionally influenced fare such as chicken with peanut sauce or salmon wrapped in banana leaves with *beurre blanc*. Dine in the vine-filled garden or atmospheric bar with its red-checked tablecloths; expensive.

The cute **Bathtub Bistro** ((01225) 460593, 2 Grove Street, has a tiny front room and larger dining space below with a fireplace and candlelit tables. The menu features a Greek lamb filo pie with spinach, tomato and fresh mint. There is a children's menu; moderate. The **Rain Check** ((01225) 444770, 34 Monmouth Street (behind the Theatre Royal), is Bath's best wine-bar, a smart place with grill menu and very good wines by the glass; moderate. **Iguanas** ((01225) 336666, 12 Seven Dials, Saw Close, is a good Tex-Mex place with airy decor and some interesting twists to the menu, such as enchiladas with crab and spinach or chorizo and mango; moderate.

Situated in the oldest house in Bath (circa 1482) **Sally Lunn's** ((01225) 461634, 4 North Parade Passage, calls itself "the quintessential English tea house." They've certainly had enough practice, having been at it since Sally Lunn won the hearts of Bath-goers with her sweet briochelike bun recipe in 1680. There's a museum in the basement housing the original seventeenth-century kitchen. In addition to afternoon tea, dinner is served nightly.

For more lunchtime browsing, try Kingsmead Square where cafés cluster around an ancient maple tree. A licensed branch of **Scoff's** sells organic and wholegrain breads, sandwiches and loose-leaf tea from classic blends like Darjeerling and Earl Grey to exotic Oriental infusions. Also on the square, **Sprint Pizza** is a bring-your-own-bottle place, and the **Jazz Café** has sidewalk tables and an airy dining room.

There's a pleasant little café called **Lovejoy's** ((01225) 446322, in the Bartlett Street Antiques Centre, serving toasted sandwiches, salads and hot lunches. They also do breakfast.

Ben's Cookies, in Union Passage, serves shakes made with organic ice cream and hot homemade cookies. Sit outside and listen to the music bleeding from Raw next door, watch the crowds go by and wait for the cookies to roll out of the oven.

Bath has a number of good pubs. The **Old Green Tree** ((01225) 448259, Green Street, does home cooked food, served in the oak-paneled bar. The **Pig and Fiddle** ((01225) 460868, 2 Saracen Street, is popular all week long, with a sprawl of outdoor picnic tables groaning under the elbows of a mellow crowd.

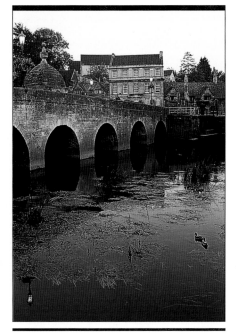

NIGHTLIFE

For what's on in Bath, consult *The Bath Chronicle,* a daily newspaper, or look for *This Month in Bath.*

The beautiful **Theatre Royal** ((01225) 448844, Barton Street, is Bath's main stage. Here you can see touring theater companies and West End previews as well as opera and ballets. Within the theater is the smaller Ustinov Studio, a new venue for comedy, experimental drama and concerts. Backstage tours are held twice weekly; call for details.

The Assembly Rooms (above) play host to **classical music** ensembles. From June to September there are lunchtime organ recitals at Bath Abbey starting at 1:05 PM; and from April to November on alternate Saturdays at 4:30 PM. Monthly summer **band concerts** ((01225) 483624, take place at the Parade Gardens in Victoria Park.

Somerset and Wiltshire

For **live music** fans, there is the casual Loft ((01255) 466467, Saw Close, off Queen Square, next to the Theatre Royal. Moles ((01225) 404445, 14 George Street, is open from 9 PM to 2 AM nightly. Friday and Saturday feature celebrity DJs, while Monday nights are devoted to local live bands. Every Tuesday brings "cheap drinks and cheesy toons."

There is jazz at Green Park Brasserie ((01225) 338565, Green Park Station, Green Park Road.

The Little Theatre Cinema ((01225) 466822 (for seat reservations), St. Michael's Place, shows **art and foreign films**.

HOW TO GET THERE

Bath is 186 km (115 miles) west of London and 21 km (13 miles) southeast of Bristol. **Trains** run hourly from London Paddington for the 90-minute trip to Bath. National Express has frequent **coach** service to Bath from London Victoria. There is also convenient coach service from Bristol to Bath.

AROUND BATH

WILTSHIRE — The North Wiltshire countryside is saturated with interesting towns and villages, beauty spots and tourist attractions. In addition to those detailed here, other areas within striking distance of Bath are Wells and the Mendip Hills, Glastonbury, Bristol, and the southern portion of the Cotswolds.

WHAT TO SEE AND DO

An attractive town built of the same mellow limestone as Bath, **Bradford-on-Avon** was a flourishing clothing-weaving center from the tenth century onward. A six-arched bridge spans the River Avon as it passes through this hillside town. The dome at one end of the bridge was once a stopping place for pilgrims on their way from Malmesbury to Glastonbury. Since it's a short train ride from Bath, Bradford makes an excellent base from which to see Bath *sans* auto; anyone who's tried to park in Bath will understand what a desirable option this is.

There is a **Tourist Information Centre** ((01225) 865797, at 34 Silver Street.

Ambling around ancient streets like the **Shambles** and **Coppice Hill** is fine entertainment in Bradford, which is a well-known center for antique hunting. The town's most remarkable antique, however, is the tiny, unadorned seventh-century Saxon **Church of St. Laurence**. This ancient house of worship was "lost" until 1856,

OPPOSITE: Cattle call at the Royal Bath and West Show. ABOVE: An ancient bridge spans the river at Bradford-on-Avon.

having been used as a cottage for many years. Some details survive such as the carved angel above the chancel arch.

About 16 km (10 miles) due north, **Castle Combe** lies tucked in a north Wiltshire valley. The old Cotswold stone houses and splendid church here have more than once won the village the title of "prettiest village in England." Often used for film sets, Castle Combe provided the backdrop for the 1967 filming of *Dr. Doolittle,* starring Rex Harrison. The bridge here crosses a swift stream that eventually joins the River Avon. It's a wonderful base for walking.

Lacock is another immaculately preserved village and film setting (*Pride and Prejudice, Moll Flanders, Emma*). The village is home to **Lacock Abbey** (NT) ((01249) 730227, where the Fox Talbot Museum of Photography commemorates photographic pioneer William Henry Fox Talbot, whose home the abbey was. The museum, thirteenth-century cloisters and grounds are open daily from February to October. The Abbey is open daily except Tuesday from March to October; admission fee.

WHERE TO STAY AND EAT

The **Sign of the Angel** ((01249) 730230, Church Street, Lacock, Chippenham SN15 LB, is a fifteenth-century house with 10 rooms. English food is served in two candlelit **restaurants**; expensive.

Fern Cottage ((01225) 859412 FAX (01225) 859018, Monkton Farleigh, Bradford-on-Avon BA15 2QJ, is a seventeenth-century stone cottage set in gardens in a little village between Bath and Bradford-on-Avon; inexpensive to moderate.

In Bradford, **Priory Steps** ((01225) 862230 FAX (01225) 866248, Newtown, Bradford-on-Avon BA15 1NQ, offers B&B within walking distance of Bradford's attractions. Set in converted weavers' cottages overlooking the town, this guest house has six bedrooms, individually furnished with antiques. Evening meals are served by prior arrangement; inexpensive.

Another B&B offering good value and rural charm, **Church Farm** ((01225) 858583 and (0589) 596929, Monkton Farleigh, Bradford-on-Avon BA15 2QJ, is a 21-hectare (52-acre) working farm with converted barn and a swimming pool. It's a good base for walking; inexpensive.

The **Seven Stars** ((01225) 722204, Winsley, is a quaint eighteenth-century coaching inn that's well known for its good food and cozy candlelit atmosphere; moderate.

HOW TO GET THERE

There are **trains** from Bath to Bradford as well as hourly buses. The trip takes about 15 minutes. To get to Lacock, you can take a short bus ride from Chippenham which is connected to London by frequent National Express **coach** services. There is also occasional bus service from Chippenham to Castle Combe.

BRISTOL

SOMERSET — Britain's number-one port during American colonial days, Bristol is now a hardworking industrial city. While it is not the magnet that nearby Bath is, Bristol has some interesting attractions. Highlights include the restored harbor, Clifton Suspension Bridge, St. Mary Redcliffe, and the SS *Great Britain.*

GENERAL INFORMATION

The **Tourist Information Centre** ((0117) 926-0767 FAX (0117) 929-7703 E-MAIL bristol@tourism .bristol.gov.uk is at St. Nicholas Church, St. Nicholas Street.

There is **Internet access** at the Intercafé, Porcupine Public House, or St. Nicholas Street at No. 30. You can also go on-line at Internet Exchange, The Mall, Cribbs Causeway; or at the Internet Café, 140 Whiteladies Road, Clifton.

There are **guided sightseeing tours** of Bristol from mid-May to mid-September. Tours generally leave from Neptune's Statue at 11 AM, and a Sunday walking tour departs from the toll station at the Suspension Bridge in Clifton at 3 PM; check at the Tourist Information Centre to confirm. **Opentop bus tours** leave daily, every half hour in summer, from near the Tourist Information Centre.

WHAT TO SEE AND DO

Bristol's maritime heritage is commemorated at the SS *Great Britain* ((0117) 926-0680, at Great Western Dock, Gas Ferry Road. This vessel, designed by Isambard Kingdom Brunel, was the first iron sea-going passenger ship, launched in 1843. It was salvaged in the 1970s and is slowly being restored. Entrance is through the **Maritime Heritage Centre**, where there are displays on the history of shipbuilding in Bristol. Open daily year-round; admission fee.

Bristol Cathedral ((0117) 926-4879, College Green, is a mix of architectural styles, but retains its Norman solidity. The sixteenth-century choir stalls are fantastically carved.

For truly outstanding ecclesiastical architecture, however, visit the church of **St. Mary Redcliffe** ((0117) 929-1487, Redcliffe Way. Queen Elizabeth I once called this "the fairest, goodliest and most famous parish church in England." With its thirteenth-century tower, this largely Perpendicular Gothic cathedral-sized church has a broad hexagonal north porch that is exquisitely carved with finely detailed human and animal figures. The church is open daily year-round; free admission.

Aerospace manufacturing is Bristol's predominant industry. This and other heavy industries are highlighted at the **Bristol Industrial Museum** ((0117) 925-1470, Prince's Wharf, where exhibitions take visitors on a journey through 300 years of manufacturing history. Closed Monday; an admission fee is charged.

In the suburbs west of the city, a suspension bridge spans **Avon Gorge**. The bridge, built between 1836 to 1864, was designed by Isambard Kingdom Brunel, who was determined to match the grandeur of the setting with a grand design. There's a large park right along the gorge and the

If you have reason to stay in downtown Bristol, you might try the family-run **Courtlands Hotel** ((0117) 942-4432 FAX (0117) 923-2432, 1 Redland Court, Bristol BS6 7EE, where each of the 58 rooms has a bath; moderate to inexpensive.

A 20-minute drive from Bristol or Bath, **Leigh Farm** ((01761) 490281 FAX (01761) 490281, Pensford, Bristol BS18 4BA, has inexpensively priced rooms with shared bath on a mezzanine landing with a large, deep tub. The farm also has self-catering units priced by the week within the rock-bottom and inexpensive ranges, depending on the size of the property and time of year.

Backpackers will find a convenient home right in the heart of the city at **Bristol Docks Youth Hostel**

National Trust's **Leigh Woods** on the opposite bank, where there are nature trails. Nearby is **Bristol Zoo** ((0117) 973-8951, one of the largest and best in the United Kingdom. It's patrolled daily by a tame elephant named Wendy. Open daily year-round; admission fee.

WHERE TO STAY

Thornbury Castle ((01454) 281182, Castle Street, Thornbury, Gloucestershire BS35 1HH, made *Conde Naste's* 50 Best Views in the World. They were writing specifically of the Queen Mary I Bedchamber, one of the Royal suites in this 18-room luxury hotel. It overlooks the Tudor garden of St. Mary's Church in the town of Thornbury a few miles north of Bristol. The room not only cosseted "Bloody" Mary, but Henry VIII and Anne Boleyn. The restaurant is excellent; very expensive to luxury.

((0117) 922-1659 FAX (0117) 927-3789, 14 Narrow Quay, Bristol BS1 4QA, which has dormitory accommodation with breakfast included at rock-bottom prices. Evening meals are served.

WHERE TO EAT

Markwicks ((0117) 926-2658, 43 Corn Street, serves top-notch Modern English and French provincial fare in the vaults of an old bank; moderate.

The **Glass Boat** ((0117) 929-0704, Welsh Back, is so-called because of its wide-paned windows looking out on the watery world of the River Avon. Permanently moored beneath Bristol Bridge, this floating restaurant is a popular spot for breakfast, where diners order anything from fresh fruits to eggs Bennie. At lunch and dinner Mod Brit

Show jumping is one of many equine sports practiced with great gusto in Southern England.

cooking, with hints from the Orient, takes over; moderate.

Bowlers ((0117) 924-5026, 40 Alfred Place, Kingsdown, does interesting organic and vegetarian cuisine; moderate.

Casa Mexicana ((0117) 924-3901, 31 Zetland Road, presents taco de pato, "crispy tortilla with shredded duck, served with jalapeno jelly and sour cream," kalhua crème brûlée for dessert; inexpensive.

NIGHTLIFE

Bristol has quite a lot to offer after dark. The **Old Duke** ((0117) 927-7137, 45 King Street, has jazz

nightly. For live music of all genres there is **Bierkeller** ((0117) 926-8514, All Saints Street. **New Trinity Community Center** ((0117) 907-7119, Trinity Road, Easton, set in a converted church, is a club as well as one of the better places in Bristol to see live bands. **Colston Hall** ((0117) 922-3686, Colston Avenue, hosts headliners, and it's also the venue for the Proms, a classical music festival that takes place in May. **Just** (no phone), Fiennes Court is Bristol's long-running gay club, while **Lakota** ((0117) 942-6208, 6 Upper York Street, boasts famous DJs (long queues to get in). Nearby, **Loco** ((0117) 942-6208, Hepburn Road, off Stokes Croft, also attracts huge crowds on weekends for its techno stylings; open 24 hours.

For **theater and ballet** there is the Hippodrome ((0117) 929-9444, St. Augustine's Parade, while the Old Vic ((0117) 926-4388, King Street, offers classic and contemporary drama.

HOW TO GET THERE

Bristol, a major transportation hub, is 194 km (120 miles) west of London. **Bristol Airport** ((01275) 474444 is about 11 km (seven miles) from the city center. Express **trains** run frequently from London Paddington to Bristol's two railway stations: Temple Meads in the city center, while Bristol

Parkway station is to the north. There is no public transportation between the two stations. Taxi fare is around £25. National Express has hourly **coach** services to the Bristol from London Victoria.

WELLS AND THE MENDIP HILLS

SOMERSET — If you come to Wells for no other reason than to see its exquisite cathedral, you won't be disappointed. This pocket-sized cathedral city takes its name from the springs that rise around its twelfth-century cathedral. The springs still feed the moat around the Bishop's Palace before trickling down the culverts along the ancient High Street.

To the north of Wells, the Mendip Hills roll toward the Bristol Channel. The characteristic silvery bluffs, deep gorges and rocky outcrops support rare flora, and the hills are dotted with ancient monuments dating from the Bronze Age, Iron Age, and the Roman and mediaeval eras. The most dramatic landscape is at Cheddar Gorge and Wookey Hole Caves, also the most crowded with coach tours. Elsewhere, though, there are pretty, unspoiled villages dotting this sheep- and dairy-farming country: Chape Allerton has a windmill and views over the gorge, and there's a cheese dairy at Chewton Mendip. Given its many caves, the Mendips are also a popular area for spelunking.

GENERAL INFORMATION

Wells has a **Tourist Information Centre** ((01749) 672552 FAX (01749) 670869 at the Town Hall on Market Place.

Le Café Bleu, 9 Heritage Courtyard, Sadler Street, has **Internet access**.

Wells **Market days** are Wednesday and Saturday; summer only.

WHAT TO SEE AND DO

Market Place in Wells, with its Georgian-fronted rows of shops, whirls busily about an eighteenth-century fountain. At the eastern end of Market Place looms the tall mediaeval gateway to the cathedral green, called Penniless Porch because beggars once sheltered here.

Wells Cathedral ((01749) 674483 was the first cathedral built in the style that was later to be named Early English Gothic. The West Front, begun in 1230, is an anthill of some 290 pieces of mediaeval sculpture seeming almost to crawl up the façade. Inside, this 800-year-old pilgrimage place has characteristic ribbed pillars and pointed arches ending in "head stops" (stone carvings at the bases of the arch), and corbels. The cathedral is much admired for its stone carvings — masons were kept busy in winter carving capitals, and their rather secular creations can be spied throughout the building (there are said to be 11 depictions of toothaches, among many other images). The chantry chapels, in Decorated and Perpendicular styles, are sights unto themselves. The great **clock** was built in 1390. When the quarter hour strikes, jousting knights ride out. Below the central tower are the striking scissor arches, added in the mid-fourteenth century to support the listing tower. The quire is the oldest part of the building, with carved mediaeval misericords and beautifully embroidered tapestries from the 1940s and 1950s. Here you can see the Jesse window to greatest effect, (so called because it depicts Jesus' ancestry) also called the "golden window" for its predominantly yellow mediaeval glass. One of the most fascinating aspects of the cathedral is the kaleidoscopic stained-glass windows in the Lady

Chapel. They're a mosaic of mediaeval glass that was found around the cathedral. The cloisters are to the south of the nave, reached up a sensuous curved stairway. North of the nave, the Chapter House is decorated with a precursor to fan vaulting; there are frequent art exhibits here. If you happen to be around for a candlelight choir concert, don't pass up the opportunity. Call the church office for details. Evensong takes place at 5:15 PM on weekdays and 3 PM on Sunday. Entrance to the cathedral is by donation; there is an additional fee to use your camera. Regular guided tours last 45 minutes.

In the Market Place once more, to the right of Penniless Porch, another gateway, the Bishop's Eye, leads into the thirteenth-century **Bishop's Palace** ((01749) 678691, still the residence of the Bishop of Bath and Wells. The oldest part of the palace is open to the public. Surrounding the moated palace are water gardens where Wells's springs rise.

Open Tuesday to Friday from April to October, daily in August; admission fee.

Flanking the north side of the cathedral is **Vicar's Close**, believed to be the most complete mediaeval street in Europe. It was built in 1348 to house the College of Vicar's Choral. The chancellor's house is now the **Wells Museum** ((01749) 673477, Cathedral Green, with its finds from the limestone caves of Mendip. Open year-round, closed Tuesday in winter; admission fee.

A few blocks west of Market Place, **St. Cuthbert's**, St. Cuthbert and Priest streets, is a Perpendicular Gothic masterpiece from the fifteenth century. The carved tie-beam roof has been richly painted to match its original colors. Open year-round; free admission.

Just east of Wells, rising almost vertically on either side of the B3135, are the gray cliffs of **Cheddar Gorge**. Spectacular, yes, but this is one of the most heavily commercialized areas of the West Country. If you decide to drive through, the best views are to be had from the north.

OUTDOOR ACTIVITIES

This is good **walking** and **cycling** country. The Tourist Information Centre is well stocked with Ordnance Survey maps and guides to routes in Somerset, rambles in the Mendips — including official guides to the Mendip Way, and pub walks in the Mendips. The Mendips are ideal for cycling, with varied scenery and quiet roads in places. To obtain leaflets detailing routes and accommodation in the region, contact the Tourism Office, Mendip District Council ((01749) 343027 or (01749) 343399 FAX (((01749) 344050, Cannards Grave Road, Shepton Mallet BA4 5BT. **Rent bicycles** at Bike City ((01749) 671711, 31 Broad Street, Wells.

An alternative to the chaos at Cheddar Gorge, **Ebbor Gorge National Nature Reserve** is another limestone ravine, but without the clamoring masses and souvenir shops. There's a pleasant nature trail here.

WHERE TO STAY

Wells has a wide choice of accommodation. Right in the center, the **Market Place Hotel** ((01749) 672616 FAX (01749) 679670 E-MAIL marketplace @heritagehotels.co.uk, Wells, Somerset BA5 2RW, has been recently spruced up but preseres many of the original features of this fourteenth-century temperance inn. The restaurant offers indoor or outdoor dining in the courtyard; expensive.

The cosy fourteenth-century **Ancient Gate House Hotel** ((01749) 672029 FAX (01749) 670319,

Wells Cathedral — OPPOSITE: Seen in the distance from the Bishop's Palace. ABOVE: Up close and tasty in the refectory.

12 Sadler Street, Wells BA5 2RR, is a privately owned hotel with rooms overlooking the west front of the cathedral and its serene precincts. Some of the nine rooms have four-poster beds. The Italian restaurant (moderate) on the first floor is very good; moderate.

If you prefer the countryside, there is **Beaconsfield Farm** ((01749) 870308, Easton, Wells BA4 1DU, a farmhouse set in one and a half hectares (four acres) of gardens and grounds with lovely views. There are three commodious bedrooms with bath, two with four-poster beds. Dinner is not served, but there are pubs nearby; inexpensive. Easton is about six and a half kilometers (four miles) west of Wells.

an interesting wine list specializing in Spanish wines and local real ales from Trowbridge; moderate.

Housed in a former stable, **Le Café Bleu** ((01749) 677772, 9 Heritage Courtyard, Sadler Street, is a funky bar-café with live music most Friday nights and dinner starting at 7:30 PM.

HOW TO GET THERE

Wells is 200 km (123 miles) southwest of London, and 34 km (21 miles) southwest of Bath. The most convenient **train** connection is at Bath. From here regional buses depart for Wells, hourly Monday through Friday; less frequently on Sunday. There are also buses from Bristol and Glastonbury.

WHERE TO EAT

For serviced dining, the Market Place and the Ancient Gate are good choices. Wells is strong on casual spots, however, including the superb wholefoods café, the **Good Earth** ((01749) 678600, 4 Priory Road, Wells. Open from 9 AM to 5:30 PM, the bounteous buffet of vegetarian dishes offers delicious homemade soups and casseroles served with a side of hearty bread swimming in garlic butter. Closed Sunday. Around the corner at 14 Queen Street is the wholefood store, **Laurelbank Dairy Co**. ((01749) 679803, where you can fill your picnic basket with gourmet cheeses, organic produce and wines.

The **Cloisters** ((01749) 674483, at the cathedral, has very good self-serve food and a pretty setting.

The **Fountain Inn** ((01749) 672317, 1 St. Thomas Street, Wells, is a traditional pub close to the cathedral. In addition to good English cooking, there is

Regional **bus** services ((01749) 673084 out of Wells go to Cheddar.

GLASTONBURY

SOMERSET — Glastonbury has long been associated with some of England's most potent legends. The town's ruined seventh-century abbey is believed by some to be the burial site of King Arthur, and the rise the town is built on to be the mystical Isle of Avalon. The earliest pilgrims came to marvel at Glastonbury's winter-flowering thorn tree, said to have been planted by a follower and contemporary of Jesus who made the first conversions to Christianity in Britain. Glastonbury Tor, legend says, is the burial site of the Holy Grail.

Today Glastonbury's magical properties continue to prosper, spawning ads in local papers for services from holistic hair dressing to feng shui and "unusual sciences." Tie-died T-shirts are an essential fashion element in Glastonbury, and a minibus takes believers on a tour of spiritual hot spots (consult the Tourist Information Centre, below, for information on local tours).

Known for its locally produced sheepskin goods (found in High Street shops), Glastonbury is equally famed for the **Glastonbury Festival**, which has been held here every summer since 1970. A farrago of theater, circus, top rock bands and ecological demonstrations, the festival raises money for Greenpeace.

GENERAL INFORMATION

You'll find the Glastonbury **Tourist Information Centre** ((01458) 832954 or (01458) 832949 (lodging) FAX (01458) 832949 at The Tribunal, 9 High Street. There is **Internet access** at Café Galatea, also on High Street. **Market day** is Tuesday in St. John's car park; summers only.

WHAT TO SEE AND DO

Glastonbury Abbey

Built over Saxon foundations between 1189 and 1220, Glastonbury Abbey was destroyed by fire during the Dissolution. Stones mark the sites of what some believe to be the island's first Christian church and the tomb of the legendary King Arthur. The most substantial remnants of this former Benedictine abbey consist of **St. Mary's Chapel** (1166), the **Abbey Church** (early thirteenth century) with remains of the "dog-tooth" decoration on the arches and windows; and the **Abbot's Kitchen** with its vaulted dome (early fourteenth century) where food was prepared for the gourmandizing abbot and his guests. It's one of the country's best-preserved mediaeval kitchens. A portly monk demonstrates sixteenth-century cookery in the Abbot's Kitchen (call the Tourist Information Centre for a schedule).

The **museum** has some fine fragments and glass artifacts; a **shop** is located at the Abbey Gatehouse. The Abbey and shop are open daily year-round; admission fee.

More Points of Interest

The view from **Glastonbury Tor**, 158 m (520 ft) above sea level, is well worth the steep hike ("tor" is Celtic for hill). Atop the mound is the last remnant of the fourteenth-century St. Michael's Church. (Look for the outline of the nave gable on the east wall of the tower.) Beyond the purple rooftops of Glastonbury, the Tor affords extensive views over Dorset, the Quantock Hills, Exmoor, and the Mendips. Access to the tor is by footpath from the end of Wellhouse Lane. Open year-round; free admission.

To the west of the Tor, the ancient Abbey Barn (circa 1350) is the centerpiece of the **Somerset Rural**

Life Museum ((01458) 831197, Chilkwell Street. The museum illustrates nineteenth- and early-twentieth-century agriculture and life in the country, tracing the life of a farm worker from birth to death. Local activities such as peat growing and cider making are highlighted. Closed Sunday and Monday; admission fee.

The Somerset Plain was once a swamp out of which rose a series of islands. In the **Lake Village Museum** ((01458) 832954, two rooms display the discoveries from an unearthed Iron Age village (circa 400 BC). The village, which was built on a platform over the swamp, was connected to islands by timber causeways, sections of which were also found. The museum is located at The Tribunal, above

the Tourist Information Centre, High Street; open daily; admission fee. The Tribunal is of interest in itself, a well-preserved mediaeval townhouse.

The **Tor Bus** takes you to the side of the Tor, running every 30 minutes throughout the day (except at lunchtime) from 9:30 AM to 5 PM, starting from the town center, near the entrance to the Abbey; fee charged. You can get off the bus to visit the Rural Life Museum.

WHERE TO STAY

Glastonbury specializes in cozy B&Bs, many of them with spectacular views. **Little Orchard** ((01458) 831620, Ashwell Lane, Glastonbury BA6 8BG, sits at the foot of Glastonbury Tor with

Glastonbury Abbey — OPPOSITE: Amid the ruins. ABOVE: A monk demonstrates sixteenth-century cooking techniques in the Abbot's Kitchen.

fine views from rooms and common areas of the
Vale of Avalon. There's a pleasant terrace in the
garden; inexpensive.

Woodlands ((01458) 832119, 52 Bove Town, Glastonbury BA6 8JE, is an interesting house built on
and added to over several centuries. The back looks
out on a garden and Glastonbury Tor; inexpensive.

A seventeenth-century riverside farmhouse,
Hartlake Farm ((01458) 835406 FAX (01458) 670373,
Hartlake, Glastonbury, Somerset BA6 9AB, has
views of the Tor and Somerset countryside. It's just
north of town beyond the Tinbridge roundabout;
inexpensive.

The **Backpackers Hostel (** (01458) 833353, at
the Market Cross, is bang in the center of town, a
magnet for seekers and slackers from across the
known universe and beyond; rock-bottom.

WHERE TO EAT

Dining is casual in Glastonbury, but there are some
interesting choices. **Café Galatea**, High Street, has
an intriguing menu, but the service can be slow.
If you can get waited on, try a salad sampler. Coffee and pastries are served in the morning and
lunch starts at noon. The evening menu offers more
substantial fare; inexpensive.

Another good eatery, also crowded at mealtimes, the **Rainbow Café (** (01458) 833896 is tucked
down an alleyway off High Street. Highlights of
the luncheon menu are a pepper-and-sweet potato flan, imaginative salads, pizza by the slice,
quiches and homemade soups; inexpensive.

For traditional fare, there is the **Blue Note Café**,
High Street, serving burgers and jacket potatoes
as well as vegetarian dishes (£4).

Burns the Bread, High Street, is the place for
sweet and savory pastries, picnic supplies and
sandwiches.

The **Miter Inn (** (01458) 831203, 27 Benedict Street,
is a friendly pub with low ceilings and broad oak
beams. The food is good and a nice variety is offered,
from stuffed plaice (£5.95) to vegetarian lasagna to
swordfish steak (£7.95); moderate to inexpensive.

HOW TO GET THERE

Glastonbury is 219 km (135 miles) southwest of
London, 41 km (25 miles) south of Bristol, and
10 km (six miles) southwest of Wells. The nearest
train station is at Taunton, where there are bus
connections to Glastonbury. One National Express
runs coach leaves London Victoria each evening
for the four-hour ride to Glastonbury.

SALISBURY

WILTSHIRE — Because of the fame of its magnificent cathedral and close, Salisbury is a ferociously
popular destination, crowded during peak sea-

son, and somewhat touristy, yet worth visiting
any time of year. Besides the cathedral, the old
town is charming, and in the lush water meadows of the River Avon one could easily spend a
day doing a great deal of nothing in the company
of willows and wildflowers, swans, geese and
the odd coot.

GENERAL INFORMATION

There is a **Tourist Information Centre (** (01722)
334956 FAX (01722) 422059, on Fish Row, as well
as a small, busy, branch at the train station on South
Western Road. During the summer months there
are **guided walking tours** leaving from the Tourist Information Centre daily at 11 AM and 6 PM;
fee charged.

Market is held Tuesday and Saturday in, where
else but, Market Square.

inspired literary works from R.D. Blackmore's *Lorna Doone* to Coleridge's "The Ancient Mariner." As for wildlife, the park has the greatest concentration of red deer in England, Cheviot goats have been recently reintroduced to the moor, and the Exmoor pony, a unique and rare breed, can be seen grazing throughout the park. Birders have plenty to do here, as coastal woodlands are nesting grounds for guillemot, razorbill, kittiwake, raven and peregrine falcons. Exmoor also has the highest concentration of sheep anywhere in the country.

It's no surprise that this rich and varied landscape is a walker's and rider's paradise. There are 1,005 km (625 miles) of **foot paths** and **bridleways**. Britain's longest national trail, the Southwest

GENERAL INFORMATION

For information in advance of your visit, contact the **Exmoor National Park Authority** ((01398) 323665 FAX (01398) 323150 WEB SITE www.exmoornationalpark.gov.uk, Exmoor House, Dulverton TA22 9HL.

There are seasonal (open April to October) **national park visitor centers** at: Combe Martin ((01271) 883319, Cross Street; Lynmouth ((01598) 752509, The Esplanade; County Gate ((01598) 741321, Countisbury; Dunster ((01643) 821835, Dunster Steep; and Dulverton ((01398) 323841, Fore Street.

Coastal Path,s begins just east of Exmoor in Minehead (see under THE GREAT OUTDOORS, page 25 in YOUR CHOICE) and follows Exmoor's 55 km (34 miles) of breathtaking coastal scenery.

Walking on Exmoor is less strenuous than in Dartmoor, and the weather is neither as harsh nor as unpredictable, though in the high moorland there are areas that are prone to mists. Before you set out on a walk, drop by a national park visitor center for help in planning your route. They'll also have printed materials, guidebooks and Ordnance Survey maps for sale.

If you'd like company, take advantage of the park authority's schedule of **guided outings**, including "safaris" to the coast, riverside pub walks, orienteering on open moorland, horseback riding, and walks focusing on the unique flora and fauna of the region. For details, contact the park authority or any of the regional park visitor centers (see below).

Look for the *Exmoor Visitor Newspaper* for year-round listings of park events and information on accommodation. It's available free at local post offices, newsstands and hotels.

LYNTON AND LYNMOUTH

"Where Exmoor meets the sea," say the tourist brochures of the twin towns of Lynton and Lynmouth. The former perched on a cliff, the latter nestled on the coast below, do occupy a prime piece of real estate. Lynmouth is especially appealing — a seaside town backed by a lush oasis of damp, pine-scented woods. With its woodland walks, B&Bs and an ancient inn, Lynmouth makes a superb place to explore the north Devon coast. Lynton, high above, is one of the park's larger population centers, with streets lined with Victorian and Edwardian buildings.

Lynton has a good **Tourist Information Centre** ((01598) 752225 FAX (01598) 752755 at the Town Hall on Lee Road; and an indispensable **National Park Visitor Centre** ((01598) 752509 is in Lynmouth on The Esplanade.

Each October brings the **Jazz Festival** to the twin towns.

A variety of **coastal cruises** can be booked at the harbor, and the park authority sometimes offers harbor cruises with ranger commentary. Book via the visitor center (above). The center sells tickets for boat trips to Lundy Island (see LUNDY ISLAND, page 283).

The local **Lyn Line Dancers** kick up their heels nightly from 8 PM to 10 PM (in season) at the harbor. They invite you to "join if you dare."

What to See and Do

Linking seaside Lynmouth with hilltop Lynton is the **Lynton–Lynmouth Cliff Railway** ((01598) 753486, a water-and-gravity-powered funicular that makes the steep trip along 274 m (900 ft) of track. Hours of operation vary with the season; fee charged.

A devastating flood in 1952 nearly wiped out Lynmouth . The **model village**, on display at the Memorial Hall, Riverside Road, Lynmouth, is 1:220 scale copy of the pre-flood Lynmouth. The builder is sometimes on hand to explain his work. Open Easter to October; free.

Exmoor's Brass Rubbing Centre (/FAX (01598) 752529, Woodside Craft Centre, Watersmeet Road, Lynmouth, is a good place to take part in this English tradition. Come early, however, as coach tours descend on the center at mid-morning. The staff are helpful and knowledgeable and there is an extensive collection of beautiful brasses, including some life-size figures (the latter by appointment only). Open daily from February to November (closed on occasional Mondays in early and late season).

Up in Lynton, there is the **Lyn & Exmoor Museum** ((01598) 752317, St. Vincent's Cottage, Market Street, with exhibits on the human and natural history of the area. Open Sunday to Friday from Easter to October (closed from 12:30 PM to 2 PM); admission fee.

Outdoor Activities

Lynton and Lynmouth are ideal for leisurely walking and exploring. Tucked into the deeply wooded combe above Lynmouth, **Watersmeet** (NT) ((01598) 753907 is the spot where Hoar Oak Water collides with the East Lyn River. An 1830s hunting and fishing lodge stands at the convergence of these two rivers. In summer, tea is served on the lawn. A shop and information center is inside. Short **walking** trails radiate from the house leading to waterfalls, viewing points, and ancient earthworks. Paid parking is available along the

roadway, from which a steep path leads down to the house.

"Rock upon reeling rock," wrote Robert Southey of the **Valley of the Rocks**, "stone piled upon stone, a huge terrific reeling mass." Created by the process of erosion, this dry dell parallels the coastline and makes for good rambling. Get directions for the trailhead in Lynton from the Tourist Information Centre.

From April to September there are **guided walks** to see Exmoor's wild Cheviot goats. Walks depart Thursday mornings from the Lynton Town Hall at 10:30 AM. For details check with the Tourist Information Centre or call ((01598) 752332.

For **horseback riding** enthusiasts, there are several stables near Lynton: Doone Valley Riding Stables ((01598) 741278, Cloud Farm, Oare, Lynton EX35 6NU; and Outovercott Riding Stables ((01598) 753341, Lynton EX35 6JR, both offer escorted rides for all levels of ability as well as self-catering cottages for riding vacations.

Where to Stay and Eat

Situated on the harbor, the **Rising Sun** ((01598) 753223, Lynmouth EX35 6EQ, is a rambling thatched-roof inn dating from the fourteenth century. Carefully restored in the 1980s, the inn has gained a reputation not only for top-notch accommodation, but also for its excellent restaurant (expensive), featuring local seafood and game.

At **Ferndale House** ((01598) 753431, Summerhouse Path, Lynmouth EX35 6EP, the comfortable bedrooms have bath. Some rooms have harbor and valley views. Breakfast is served in your room; inexpensive.

Well-located for national trail hikers (just under a kilometer or half a mile from Lynton), the **Lynton Youth Hostel** ((01598) 753237 FAX (01598) 753305, Lynbridge, Lynton EX35 6AZ, occupies a former country hotel situated in a wooded valley. A woodstove warms the living room, information is available on local walks, and meals are served; rock-bottom.

Le Bistro ((01598) 753302, Watersmeet Road, Lynmouth, is the best reasonably-priced restaurant in the area, with ragout of new vegetables in pesto sauce (£8), duckling, sea bass and other fresh fish gracing the menu. Open 6:30 PM to 10:30 PM, Monday to Saturday; moderate.

AROUND PORLOCK AND SELWORTHY

Much of the land around the Somerset villages of Porlock and Selworthy is part of the National Trust's Holnicote Estate (NT) ((01643) 862452. This 5,042-hectare (12,500-acre) area has some of the park's best scenery, including six and a half kilometers (four miles) of coastline and, inland,

An ancient clapper stone bridge spans an Exmoor waterway.

Dunkery and Selworthy have magnificent views. The cottages and farms of the Holnicote Estate are scattered in and around the villages and hamlets of Selworthy, Allerford, Bossington, Horner and Luccombe. One could make a pleasant day's drive visiting amongst these villages and hamlets. There are also 162 km (100 miles) of footpaths to explore.

At Selworthy the National Trust has a shop and **National Trust Information Centre**; open daily from March to October, weekends only in November. The shop sells leaflets on exploring the estate, including walking routes. Porlock's **Tourist Information Centre (** (01643) 863150 FAX (01643) 863014, West End, High Street, is situated in the town library and has a small exhibit on the natural history of the region. One of its booklets details four "cream tea walks" in the area. You can also get information here on accessing Exmoor via public transportation.

Escorted **backcountry horse rides** are offered by Burrowhayes Farm Riding Stables **(** (01643) 862463, West Luccombe, Porlock, Minehead TA24 8HT.

Where to Stay and Eat

Horse riders might choose to lodge at **Porlock Vale House (** (01643) 862338 FAX (01643) 863338 E-MAIL info@porlockvale.co.uk, Porlock Weir TA24 8NY, where there are riding stables and a school. The hotel, with its hunting lodge decor and oak-paneled bar, is situated in 10 hectares (25 acres) in the quaint seaside hamlet of Porlock Weir. All bedrooms have bath and views of Porlock Bay; moderate (half-board is available).

Several places on the Holnicote Estate offer inexpensive bed and breakfast: **Clements Cottage (** (01643) 703970, Tivington TA24 8SU, with three bedrooms, is a seventeenth-century cottage with views of Dunkery Beacon and Porlock Vale. **Cloutsham Farm (** (01643) 862839, Porlock TA24 8JU, a seventeenth-century hunting lodge offers B&B as well as self-catering accommodation.

In Allerford, **Cross Lane House (** (01643) 862112, Allerford, Minehead TA24 8HW, is a fifteenth-century former farmhouse set along the River Aller; rates start in the inexpensive range, less 10% if you dine here.

A thatched cottage on the Holnicote Estate, **Hillside (** (01643) 862831, Higher Allerford TA24 8HS, serves homemade bread and preserves at breakfast (inexpensive).

An eighteenth-century farmhouse on a working farm adjoining the moorland, **Hindon Farm (** (01643) 705244, Minehead TA24 8SH, is three miles (five kilometers) from Minehead and one and a half kilometers (one mile) from Selworthy. It makes a good base for walking and riding, and you can also spend time getting to know the local farm animals. Meals are served; inexpensive. Self-catering accommodation is also available on a weekly basis.

DULVERTON

The genteel town of Dulverton is Exmoor's administrative center, nestling in a steep and wooded valley on the eastern border of the park. The **National Park Information Centre (** (01398) 323841 is at the south end of Fore Street.

Dulverton's Guildhall houses the **Heritage & Arts Centre (** (01398) 324081, with displays on village history, an archive of Exmoor photographs, and special exhibitions year-round. Open March to October; free.

You can go **horseback riding** on Exmoor with Pine Lodge **(** (01398) 323559, High Chilcott Farm,

Dulverton, Somerset TA22 9QQ; or West Anstey Farm **(** (01398) 341354, Dulverton, Somerset, both of which offer hour-long rides, day rides to local inns for lunch, and self-catering cottages on the farm for riding vacations.

Higher Langridge Farm (/FAX (01398) 323999, Exebridge, Dulverton TA22 9RR, is a seventeenth-century farmhouse and working farm, located six and a half kilometers (four miles) southwest of Dulverton. In addition to the farm's beams, log fires and private bath, the area offers fine walks; inexpensive to moderate.

In the nearby town of Northcombe, there is **Northcombe Camping Barn (** (01200) 428366 a converted mill, with basic accommodation. Bring your own sleeping bag; rock-bottom (starting at around £3 per person, per night). See BACKPACKING, page 34 in YOUR CHOICE, for details on other camping barns.

DUNSTER

Dunster is an attractive ancient wool village with much to see and do, and plenty of places to have a spot of tea and a snack. There is an **Exmoor National Park Visitor Centre** ((01643) 821835, on The Steep, with printed materials on walking, as well as maps and books. Dunster has a **flea and craft market** on Monday and Friday from June 6 to September 30.

Built for the sale of Dunster cloth, the **Yarn Market**, High Street, is an eight-sided market hall dating from the seventeenth century. Also on High Street is a rebuilt nineteenth-century **merchant's**

(01643) 707650 (24-hour recorded timetable), is Britain's longest vintage railway, running through the Quantock Hills and along the coast, past Watchett Harbour and Dunster. Trains depart daily in summer months.

Where to Stay and Eat

Across from the Yarn Market, the fifteenth-century **Luttrell Arms** ((0870) 400-8110 FAX (01643) 821567, High Street, Dunster, Minehead TA24 6SG, once played host to guests of Cleeve Abbey. Bedrooms in this ancient building vary widely in size and layout but all are charming; very expensive. There is good food to be had in the two-level **restaurant** (moderate).

house. And in West street are **mediaeval woolen workers' cottages**.

The village landmark is **Dunster Castle** (NT) ((01643) 821314, which dates back to 1066. From the castle there are spectacular views over village and moor, and terraced gardens harboring many rare plant species. Open daily except Thursday and Friday from April to October. Garden and park open year-round; admission fee. Of a similar vintage, **Dunster Watermill** ((01643) 821759, Mill Lane, was mentioned in the Domesday Book (1086). It was reconstructed during the mid-eighteenth century. There are delightful walks from the castle to the river and water mill.

For more views of the village and surrounding countryside and coastline, climb **Grabbist Hill** or **Conygar Tower**.

By the former port (now a small beach) the **West Somerset Steam Railway** ((01643) 704996 or

Dollons House ((01643) 821880 FAX (01643) 822016 E-MAIL mc2@lineone.net, 10 Church Street, Dunster TA24 6SH, has three bedrooms with views of the castle or garden. Children age 16 and older are welcome; moderate.

Of Dunster's numerous tea rooms, the **Tea Shoppe** ((01643) 821304, 3 High Street, is the best. Teas, lunch and snacks. The dinner menu features Exmoor game, local products.

HOW TO GET THERE

There are **train** stations at Taunton and Barnstaple where you can rent a car, or take the **local bus** onward to Lynton–Lynmouth via Minehead. **National Express** also runs to Barnstaple.

The Exmoor pony, a unique and rare breed, can be seen grazing throughout the national park.

Devon
and
Cornwall

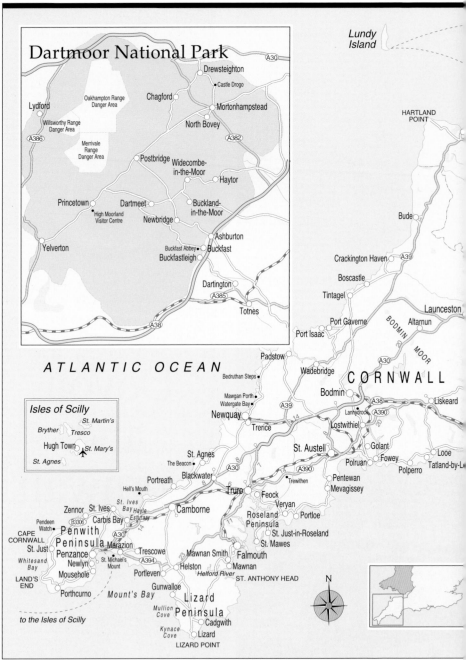

Dartmoor National Park

Lundy Island

HARTLAND POINT

Drewsteighton

Castle Drogo

Lydford

Oakhampton Range
Danger Area

Chagford

Mortonhampstead

Willsworthy Range
Danger Area

North Bovey

A386

Merrivale
Range
Danger Area

Postbridge

Widecombe-
in-the-Moor

Haytor

Princetown

Dartmeet

High Moorland
Visitor Centre

Newbridge

Buckland-
in-the-Moor

Yelverton

Ashburton

Buckfast Abbey

Buckfast

Buckfastleigh

Dartington

Totnes

Bude

Crackington Haven

A39

Boscastle

Tintagel

A385

ATLANTIC OCEAN

Padstow

Bedruthan Steps

Port Gaverne

Port Isaac

Launceston

Altarnun

BODMIN MOOR

A30

Wadebridge

CORNWALL

Mawgan Porth

Watergate Bay

Bodmin

Liskeard

A39

Newquay

Lanhydrock

A38

A390

Trerice

Lostwithiel

Isles of Scilly

Bryther

Tresco

St. Martin's

Hugh Town

St. Mary's

St. Agnes

St. Agnes

The Beacon

A30

St. Austell

Golant

Looe

Polruan

Fowey

Tatland-by-L

Polperro

Blackwater

Portreath

Trewithen

A390

Pentewan

Mevagissey

Hell's Mouth

Truro

Feock

Zennor

St. Ives

St. Ives
Bay Hayle
Estuary

Camborne

Veryan

Roseland
Peninsula

Portloe

Pendeen
Watch

Carbis Bay

B3306

Penwith

A30

St. Just-in-Roseland

CAPE
CORNWALL

St. Just

Peninsula

Marazion

St. Mawes

Penzance

Trescowe

Mawnan Smith

Falmouth

Whitesand
Bay

Newlyn

St. Michael's
Mount

A394

Helston

Mawnan

LAND'S
END

Mousehole

Portleven

Helford River

ST. ANTHONY HEAD

N

Porthcurno

Gunwalloe

Lizard

Mount's Bay

Mullion
Cove

Peninsula

to the Isles of Scilly

Cadgwith

Kynace
Cove

Lizard

LIZARD POINT

THE FAMOUSLY SCENIC COUNTRYSIDE OF THE DEVON–
CORNWALL peninsula is a rich composite of wild
moorland, rolling farmland, and dramatic coastline.

South Devon is dominated by Dartmoor National Park, a plateau of water-soaked land whose
rivers — the Dart, the Ex and the Plym — meet
the sea at Dartmouth and Exmouth, and at

Plymouth, Devon's largest population center.
While not a beauty, Plymouth is a likable city and
a good urban base for exploring the south coast's
sunny resorts — strung out from Dawlish through
to Bigbury Bay. North Devon, while it boasts a
lovely corner of Exmoor National Park (covered
in the SOMERSET AND WILTSHIRE chapter, see page
251) and more seashore holiday spots, is largely

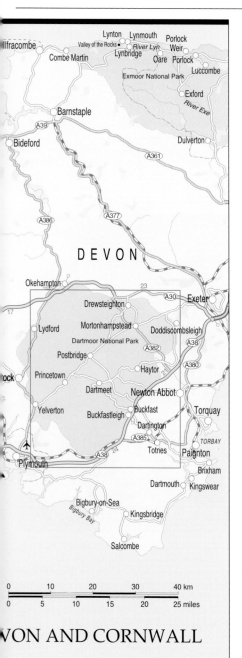

banks. And the remains of Cornwall's copper- and tin-mining industry dot the landscape with memorials to Victorian engineering.

Cornwall's two coastlines continue west in virtually unbroken splendor from the Tamar Estuary on the gentle south coast and from Bude on the rugged north, to meet in dramatic climax at the Land's End cliffs, England's most westerly point. Parts of Cornwall's south coast are almost Mediterranean in character — earning it the moniker of the "Cornish Riviera." Further west the south coast breaks up into myriad secret coves, inlets and creeks, creating peaceful anchor for sailing enthusiasts. Both coasts have stretches of silky sand beaches and turquoise waters. Arty fishing villages

— Mousehole, Newlyn, St. Ives — cling to the coast in Cornwall's "far west." It's said West Cornwall has Britain's largest concentration of artists outside of London's East End. They've come for centuries for the remarkable light and the mild climate and a landscaped composed of pre-historic standing stones and tiny farming enclosures.

Cornwall and Devon are splendid and varied walking country. The Southwest Coast Path is at its most scenic here, as it cruises along ocean cliffs, sandy beaches and through waterside villages. Cornwall is a spectacular, sometimes challenging place for cycling. One popular route is the 28-km (17-mile) Camel Trail from Bodmin Moor to Padstow. Contact the Cornwall Tourist Board ((01872) 74057 FAX (01872) 40423, Department CYC, 59 Lemon Street, Truro TR1 2SY.

Devon's Two Moors Way is a 165-km (102-mile-long) footpath that winds from Ivybridge in Dartmoor to Lynmouth in Exmoor, passing through high moorland, wooded valleys and rural scenery. The Lynton Tourist Information Center (see LYNTON AND LYNMOUTH, page 274 in WILTSHIRE AND SOMERSET) provides details of transportation links between trailheads. Bus services may be used to reach both ends of the trail. There is an official guidebook to

The harbor at Boscastle, protected by the National Trust, is one of England's great beauty spots.

VON AND CORNWALL

rich pastureland where the famous clotted cream and Devonshire cheeses are produced by local dairies.

As the West Country peninsula dips its "big toe" into the Atlantic, the placid farmland of Devon disappears in the wake of a wilder countryside. Bleak moors blanket much of the upland. Winding roads plunge deeply between vine-covered

Devon and Cornwall

the trail with maps and instructions. It can be purchased in visitor centers throughout Devon.

If you're going to do much touring in Cornwall, you'll save a bundle joining the National Trust before you go (see MEMBERSHIPS AND DISCOUNT PASSES, page 327 in TRAVELERS' TIPS). The Trust owns great swathes of coastline here — some of the duchy's most spectacular scenery.

THE NORTH DEVON COAST

DEVON — West from Exmoor, more of Southern England's finest coastal scenery extends toward the Cornish border. This Area of Outstanding Natural Beauty boasts sheer, soaring cliffs, coastal

waterfalls, and the broad expanse of Bideford (or Barnstaple) Bay. North Devon is a popular destination for coach excursions, vacationing families, and water sports enthusiasts, particularly surfers and windsurfers. The Southwest Coastal Path lays open the high cliffs for walkers.

CLOVELLY

An "English Amalfi," Clovelly rises sharply out of the sea along narrow cobbled streets and alleys. Cars are banned, but would be useless here anyway. Sledges pulled by donkeys are used to convey luggage to and from the town's two hotels. Many of the village houses are late Georgian and their careful restoration contributes to the timeless character of the village.

There is a fee to enter the hamlet, but it's well worth it. You'd pay as much to park in any other

popular seaside village. Crowds can overwhelm this tiny village in season, but out of season it is one of Southern England's most pleasurable destinations. For **information** in advance of your visit contact Clovelly Village ((01237) 431200, Clovelly, Bideford, Devon EX39 5SY.

From the car park and Clovelly's **Visitor Centre** ((01237) 431781, the famous **Up-Along Road** tumbles its cobbly wobbly way down to the quay. A treasured souvenir here is a T-shirt that says "I risked sprained ankles and heart attacks to get this T-shirt." A Land Rover service (£1.60 each way) gives rides from the Visitor Centre car park down to the quay. Charles Kingsley, author of *The Waterbabies*, spent his late childhood at Clovelly.

A visit to the **Fisherman's Cottage** with its small Kingsley exhibition is included in the price of admission to the village. From the cliff tops and especially from **Mount Pleasant** there are superb views of Bideford Bay and Lundy Island. During the summer months boats take day-trippers out to Lundy Island (see below page 283).

Where to Stay and Eat

At the head of the quay the **Red Lion** ((01237) 431237 FAX (01237) 431044, The Quay, Clovelly EX39 5TF, has 11 comfortable bedrooms (all with sea view), a wood-paneled dining room and pub. Children aged seven and older are welcome; moderate. If you'd rather stay in the countryside, there is **Hoops Inn** ((01237) 451222 FAX (01237) 451247 E-MAIL hoopsinn@webleicester.co.uk, Horns Cross, Clovelly EX39 5DL, an old thatched inn on the A39 between Bideford and Clovelly.

Bedrooms, featuring oak paneling and period furniture, are available in the old part of the inn or in the coach house. The **restaurant** serves regional cooking using Devonshire produce; moderate to expensive, with half-board and multi-day rates available.

How to Get There

Clovelly is 389 km (240 miles) southwest of London and 18 km (11 miles) southwest of Bideford. The nearest **train** station is at Barnstaple, where there is approximately hourly **bus** service to Clovelly via Bideford.

BARNSTAPLE

A county transportation hub, Barnstaple makes a logical jumping off point for North Devon and Exmoor (see in SOMERSET AND WILTSHIRE). The local **Tourist Information Centre** ((01271) 375000 is at 36 Boutport Street; closed Sunday.

Cyclists and **walkers** can retrace the furry steps of Henry Williamson's *Tarka the Otter* along North Devon's 292-km (180-mile) Tarka Trail, 34 km (21 miles) of which are open to cyclists. The trail describes a figure-eight, starting and ending in Barnstaple. Tarka Trail Cycle Hire ((01271) 324202, at the railway station in Barnstaple, rents bicycles. They're open daily from April through October with limited low season hours.

There are some first-rate farmhouse B&Bs near Barnstaple, a better choice than staying in town. Located between the sea and Exmoor National Park, **Higher Churchill Farm** ((01271) 850543, Arlington, Barnstaple EX31 4LT, serves up countryside views with their B&B. There is also a self-catering wing that sleeps four; inexpensive.

Barnstaple is 348 km (215 miles) southwest of London and 162 km (100 miles) southwest of Bristol. It is at the northwestern end of the Tarka Line (see EXETER, page 290) from Exeter. National Express has frequent **bus** service to Barnstaple from London Victoria, a five-hour trip. You can connect with bus services to many coastal points from Barnstaple.

ILFRACOMBE

North Devon's largest beach resort, Ilfracombe is a razzle-dazzle place that looks like it hasn't changed much since the turn of the last century. For all its brashness Ilfracombe does have a certain doddering authenticity. It's also the gateway to Lundy Island (see below). In contrast to the town area, the **headland** is an island of calm.

There is a **Tourist Information Centre** ((01271) 863001 at the Landmark Centre (locate the building that resembles a nuclear power plant and you've found it). The center also houses a theater and cinema complex.

The *Queen of Cornwall* ((01271) 864207 takes passengers on 90-minute **cruises** out of Ilfracombe Harbour. Two **paddlesteamers** offer a more dignified way to tour the coastline. The *Waverley* and *Balmoral* depart Ilfracombe Pier for day and afternoon trips from May through September. Ask at the Tourist Information Centre for details.

Where to Stay and Eat

Across from the former.home of Henry Williamson (1895–1977), author of *Tarka the Otter* (1927), the **Avalon Hotel** ((01271) 839325, Capstone Road, Ilfracombe EX34 9BT, is an above-average guest house with sea views. Most bedrooms have bath (inexpensive). There are discounts for stays longer than one night. For rock-bottom lodging the **Ilfracombe Youth Hostel** ((01271) 865337 FAX (01271) 862652, Ashmour House, 1 Hillsborough Terrace, Ilfracombe, Devon EX34 9NR, is part of a Georgian terrace; open seasonally.

The vine-covered terrace of the **St. James Tea Room** (no phone), St. James Place, is a pleasant place for an inexpensive snack; it's right across from the parish church. Or you can take tea amongst the garden gnomes at **Golden Bay** ((01271) 862281, 2–3 St. James Place, which also offers B&B and self-catering flats.

How to Get There

Ilfracombe is 369 km (228 miles) southwest of London, and 21 km (13 miles) north of Barnstaple. The nearest **train** station is at Barnstaple, where you can get a Red Bus ((01271) 345444 onward to Ilfracombe. National Express operates two **coaches** daily from London Victoria to Ilfracombe, a five-hour trip.

LUNDY ISLAND

Lying about 41 km (25 miles) west of Ilfracombe, Lundy Island is a marine preserve famed for.its puffin colony ("Lundy" is Norse for puffin island). Seals also thrive here as well as wild goats and deer. The island's west side is bounded by spectacular cliffs and the interior is a grassy heath, largely devoid of trees and shrubs because of the stiff Atlantic wind. Within its five-kilometer-long by one-kilometer-wide (three-mile by half-mile) area, Lundy harbors the ruins of a thirteenth-century castle, one hotel, one pub, one church and a scattering of cottages. There are no roads and no cars.

Atlantic Adventure ((01805) 622431 or (0370) 977337, offers **diving** day trips to Lundy (£25 per person) for qualified divers, or for others to explore the island and **snorkel** amongst the gray seals. The MS *Oldenburg* ((01271) 863001 organizes day **boat trips** to Lundy from Ilfracombe Pier, April to October, and from Bideford Quay year-round; fee charged.

Clovelly — LEFT: Dinghies await high tide.
RIGHT: A donkey takes a break from hauling.

The National Trust rents 24 **self-catering properties** on Lundy for short stays from April to June and from mid-September to mid-December; there is a two-night minimum. For details call or write the Lundy Shore Office ((01237) 470422, The Quay, Bideford EX39 2LY.

THE NORTH CORNWALL COAST

CORNWALL — The Bristol Channel's dark waters give way to the aquamarine surf of North Cornwall as the coastline dives southward at Hartland Point. North Cornwall has Europe's best surfing beaches, and a craggy coastline ideal for rambling and wildlife watching.

Cornwall's landscape offers frequent reminders of the past. Bronze Age standing stones dot the inland countryside. On the wild north coast are the eerie ruins of mine engine houses, icons of the once great Cornish tin and copper trade which sustained the economy here for thousands of years. Arthurian legends dating from the Middle Ages come alive at the ruins of a mysterious castle at Tintagel.

BUDE

At low tide the Bude beach seems endless. Massive chunks of streaky granite back the shore, and stone tidal pools make for good wading. There is also a tidal saltwater swimming pool right on the beach. Back of the beach the rinky-dink town is more charming than it first appears, especially during the annual **Bude Jazz Festival** when the streets and parks come alive with the sounds of New Orleans. The **Tourist Information Centre** ((01288) 354240 FAX (01288) 355769 is at The Crescent.

The early nineteenth century **Bude Canal** is now used for pleasure boating. You can learn to **kayak** here, and an obstacle course has been set up.

Where to Stay

The hotels along Summerleaze Crescent overlook the beach, but are convenient to town: **Edgecumbe** ((01288) 352451 FAX (01288) 355256 E-MAIL hotel @edgecumbe.force9.co.uk, 19 Summerleaze Crescent, Bude EX23 8HJ (inexpensive); and **Atlantic House** ((01288) 353846 FAX (01288) 356666 E-MAIL ahbude@aol.com, Summerleaze Crescent, Bude EX23 8HJ (inexpensive).

In nearby rural Crackington Haven, there are two National Trust properties offering B&B: **Lower Tresmorn** ((01840) 230667, Crackington Haven, Bude EX23 0NU, is a mediaeval farmhouse with oak beams, stone fireplaces and coastal views; inexpensive. **Trevigue Farm** (/FAX (01840) 230418, St. Gennys, Crackington Haven, Bude EX23 0LQ, is a working farm hugging the cliffs. The sixteenth-century house with flagstone floors and oak beams is furnished with antiques. Bedrooms feature Victorian oak beds; high end of inexpensive price range.

BOSCASTLE

Once an important fishing port, Boscastle's harbor still shelters a few trawlers, but its significance now is as one of Cornwall's great beauty spots. A large portion of the land in and around Boscastle harbor and village is owned by the National Trust. Wander the little streets and discover converted warehouses, gift shops, and a museum of witchcraft. Because of its popularity, parking is a problem at the height of the season; arrive early in the day or you may have to bypass Boscastle. There is an **information center** at the Old Forge shop; open April to the end of October.

A working farm within walking distance of Boscastle, **Home Farm** ((01840) 250195, Minster, Boscastle PL35 0BN, offers B&B with bath and views of the coast, village and harbor; inexpensive.

TINTAGEL

Said to be the birthplace of the legendary King Arthur, Tintagel is rich with literary and semi-historical associations. While the English Heritage ruins are unquestionably impressive — situated 90 m (300 ft) above the foaming surf — Tintagel appeals mostly to those with a keen interest in Arthurian legend.

What to See and Do

King Arthur has been associated with **Tintagel Castle** (EH) ((01840) 770328, for untold eons. Historians think that the Arthur legends have some basis in historical fact. The last major addition to the literature was Alfred Lord Tennyson's Gustave Doré-illustrated edition of *The Idylls of the King*. But the only evidence that Tintagel was the birthplace of Arthur (if in fact he existed) is Geoffrey of Monmouth's *History of the Kings of Britain*, which recorded Arthur's birth, 600 years after the event in 1139.

While the tourism board continues to spin-out Arthurian legends, archaeologists and historians shrug their shoulders. Most of the ruins at Tintagel date from the thirteenth-century house of Earl Richard, who probably built on this rocky point because of its Arthurian associations. Since 1983 — after a fire and the resulting soil erosion revealed

PORT ISAAC

A tiny bustling fishing village, Port Isaac has some of the narrowest streets in Cornwall. Situated between Tintagel and Padstow and within easy striking distance of Bodmin Moor, Port Isaac is a good base for either coastal or inland walking expeditions. The village boasts several restaurants, pubs and shops, and there is a swimming beach just under a kilometer (half a mile) away in Port Gaverne.

The National Trust lets several holiday cottages in Port Isaac, most notably the pentagonal, three-story **Birdcage**, a 200-year-old building

the foundations of 50 small rectangular buildings — it's been known to have been occupied since the Roman era, and it was at one time the stronghold of a Cornish king. Study of the remains is on-going.

The walk to the castle head is quite steep; there's a **Land Rover service** ((01840) 770060 that you can hitch a ride with for a moderate price. The castle is open daily year-round from 10 AM; admission fee.

Much of the town is taken up with souvenir hawking, but the **Old Post Office** (NT) ((01840) 770024 is worth a look. This fourteenth-century manor house is decorated with locally built oak furnishings. It is so called because one room of the house served as the letter-receiving office for the district in the nineteenth century. The room has been restored to that period. Open daily from April to October; admission fee.

that may have once been a cobbler's shop. It accommodates two (no children under 12); inexpensive, minimum three nights. Contact the National Trust Holiday Cottage Booking Office ((01225) 791199 FAX (01225) 792267, PO Box 536, Melksham, Wiltshire SN12 8SX.

PADSTOW

Another working fishing village, Padstow, set on the beautiful Camel Estuary, offers some of the best dining in the West Country. Good surfing beaches are within easy reach, and walkers can revel in spectacular scenery along cliff paths, especially from late April to early June when wildflowers proliferate. In town, there are old pubs and a good bookstore.

The beautiful Camel Estuary, Padstow.

Padstow has a **Tourist Information Centre** ((01841) 533449 FAX (01841) 532356, in the Red Brick Building on North Quay.

What to See and Do

Padstow is a perfect place to do absolutely nothing. But if you are itching for activity, take a ferry to the island of **Rock**, burial place of Sir John Betjeman (1906–1984), English poet laureate and architectural conservationist.

A castellated Elizabethan house, **Prideaux Place** ((01841) 532411 is one of the town's most interesting buildings, and still a family home. The house remains much as it was when it was built in the sixteenth century. Opening hours vary but are generally Sunday to Thursday afternoons from Easter to mid-October; admission fee.

Padstow is the jumping-off point for the **Camel Trail**, a 28-km (17-mile) bike trail that follows an old rail bed along the Camel Estuary through wooded valleys to Wadebridge, ending at Poley's Bridge high on Bodmin Moor. Padstow Cycle Hire ((01841) 533533, South Quay, rents bicycles. Booking is essential.

Where to Stay

By the waterfront, the **Cross House Hotel** ((01841) 532391 FAX (01841) 533633, Padstow, Cornwall PL28 8BG, has nine largish bedrooms with bath, as well as a garden where you can enjoy cream tea overlooking the Camel Estuary and town center; moderate to expensive. Closed January and February.

Rick Stein's three restaurants (detailed below) offer a variety of accommodation. **The Seafood Restaurant** ((01841) 532485, Riverside, Padstow PL28 8BY, has 13 bedrooms, most overlooking the harbor; moderate to very expensive. **St. Petroc's Hotel & Bistro** ((01841) 532700 FAX (01841) 532942, 4 New Street, Padstow PL28 8EA, is a small hotel situated in one of Padstow's oldest buildings. The bedrooms have bath or shower and views over the town and estuary; moderate to very expensive (with one single that goes for £40). Finally there are three B&B bedrooms with bath above the **Café** ((01841) 532777 FAX (01841) 533566, on Middle Street. Breakfast, English or Continental, is served in the coffee shop below or in the courtyard garden; moderate.

As should be obvious by now, Padstow can be pricey, so a no-frills place right in the village is a treasure. **Duke House** ((01841) 532372, advertises "no TV, no parking, no private bath" for a no-nonsense price of £15 per person for B&B and lower prices for room only.

Where to Eat

Dining at one of celebrity-chef Rick Stein's Padstow establishments is a West Country ritual. At the **Seafood Restaurant** ((01841) 532700, River-

side (by the harbor), fish comes straight off the boats into the kitchen. Rick Stein wears the toque here, but some feel that high pretensions dampen the atmosphere; very expensive. For **St. Petroc's Bistro** (see above), Stein has brought in Chef Jason Fretwell to oversee a select menu of *moules marinières, entrecôte béarnaise,* and duck *confit;* moderate. **Rick Stein's Café** (see above), offers perhaps the best value, serving good French peasant food like grilled cod with noodles and chili broth and coriander in a room with a crisply fresh design. There's nothing special about the ambiance, just good food. There is one, much coveted, outdoor table; booking is essential; moderate to inexpensive. Finally the **Delicatessen & Wine Shop**, Middle Street, offers rows of the celeb-chef's special sauces and favorite ingredients. All of these places are open for lunch and dinner. The Seafood Restaurant and the Café are closed Sunday, St. Petroc's is closed Monday.

These enterprises have spawned other good food places. On the card at the stylish **No. 6 Café** ((01841) 532093, Middle Street, are bluefin tuna and wok-fried black tiger prawns; moderate. Booking is advisable.

A less expensive option is **Pizza at Rojano's** ((01841) 532796, 9 Mill Square, where the pesto pizza has pizzazz. There are 13 other interesting pizza choices as well as pasta and salads. They also do tasty onion rings, served piled in a tower. Service is prompt and courteous. Outdoor seating is best as the small inside room tends toward anarchy. Reservations advisable; moderate to inexpensive.

NEWQUAY

A 1930s-era seaside town, Newquay (pronounced *new*-kee) is Cornwall's largest resort. Boasting the best beaches in the nation, Newquay is also the surfing capital of Great Britain. A fair slice of Newquay's visitors come for the gnarly waves, as well as the "fast food and loud pop music" with which the resort has become synonymous.

Newquay was a fishing village as far back as the Middle Ages, pulling in "pilchards by the million" until the great shoals of fish came no more. As the pilchards disappeared, the railway arrived and with it the first large influx of tourists. The pilchards were forgotten and it's been shoals of tourists and beach-goers ever since.

There is a **Tourist Information Centre** ((01637) 871345 FAX (01637) 852025 in the Municipal Offices on Marcus Hill.

What to See and Do

Newquay's golden sand beaches are backed by shining black cliffs. Take in the beach scene from North Quay Hill — colorful fishing boats, rocky headlands, towering Newquay Island, beach bums and surfer dudes. Newquay, like other Cornwall seaside spots, is prone to fog, which only adds to the atmosphere.

Adjoining the town are four **beaches**: Lusty Glaze, Tolcarne, Great Western and Towan. These beaches face more or less north and are somewhat protected by Towan Head. On the other side of the head is Fistral Beach. Facing west, Fistral is Newquay's largest beach and the only one that gets the full force of the Atlantic, making it one of the finest surfing beaches in Europe. For more details on surfing, see SPORTING SPREE, page 27 in YOUR CHOICE.

While the beaches get most of the attention at Newquay, the wonderful **Newquay Sea Life**

place good value with inexpensive rates. Weekly rates are available.

At the comfortable **Harbour Hotel (** (01637) 873040, North Quay Hill, Newquay TR1 1HF, all the bedrooms have harbor views. The **restaurant** (inexpensive) serves seafood and traditional English fare, with some imaginative choices such as a starter of melon, tomato and onion salad and a main dish of Dover sole. You can also get a slice of cottage pie.

On the road to Padstow, **Bre-Pen Farm (** (01637) 860420, Mawgan Porth TR8 4AL, lies in the midst of National Trust coastal property overlooking the bay. Bedrooms are available with bath; inexpensive rates.

Centre ((01637) 878134, Towan Promenade, is a kick. There's a walk-through tunnel as well as scores of aquariums where you can observe sharks, sea horses, and fish.

Fishing trips leave daily from Newquay harbor, ranging from all-day excursions to three-hour conger hunts. Most outfits supply tackle, bait and tuition, and you can keep your catch. There are also one-hour pleasure **boat trips**, which leave when full.

Where to Stay and Eat

If you want to stay in town, there are plenty of places, though the beachfront properties can be dowdy. Of this lot, **Hotel Tregella (** (01637) 874661, Island Crescent, Newquay TR7 1DZ, is perhaps one of the more upbeat. The hosts are friendly and the bedrooms are nicer than the lobby would lead you to believe. Views are fabulous, making this

Even if nothing else about Newquay entices you, you might come here merely to have a snack at the **Island Tea Garden** (no phone), Towan Beach. Set stunningly atop tiny New Quay Island, it is reached by a 1930s-era suspension bridge — one of the West Country's most famous vistas. Open weekdays; inexpensive.

How to Get There

Newquay is about 405 km (250 miles) from London and 52 km (32 miles) from St. Ives. British Airways has daily **flights** from Gatwick to Newquay. There are four **trains** a day from Par, which is on the main London to Penzance line. National Express operates four daily **coaches** from London Victoria to Newquay's bus station at Coach Bay.

Trerice, built in 1572, is famous for its decorated gables and ornate interiors.

AROUND NEWQUAY

About 13 km (eight miles) south of Newquay, **St. Agnes Beacon** is a heather-covered ridge connecting the coast with the village of St. Agnes. This is a former tin and copper mining area — softened and greened over the years yet still dotted with remnants of the industry and scarred by mine shafts. Gray seal and basking shark can sometimes be seen around the coastline, as well as cliff-nesting birds. The coastline here is spectacular.

There is a car park at the small cove of **Chapel Porth**, where you can access footpaths to St. Agnes Beacon and Head. All of this land, including the cove, is preserved by the National Trust and relatively undeveloped, though crowded in summer. The beach is patrolled by lifeguards. There are wonderful cliff walks from Chapel Porth in either direction along a coastline dotted with relic engine houses.

North of Newquay, the coastal route winds along stretches of cliffs interspersed with golden beaches, such as pretty **Watergate Beach**, a resort hamlet. The **Bedruthan Steps** (NT) are spectacular series of massive gnarled rocks rising to heights of 60 m (200 ft) just off the coast.

About six and a half kilometers (four miles) south of Newquay, **Trerice** (NT) ((01637) 875404 is an Elizabethan house famous for its decorated gables. Built in 1572, it has changed less over the years than many of its contemporaries. The interiors are trimmed with ornate plaster ceilings and ornamented fireplaces. Oak and walnut furnishings and tapestries adorn the great hall and bedrooms. The opening times vary; call for details; admission fee.

DARTMOOR NATIONAL PARK

DEVON — Dartmoor National Park's 1,837 sq km (700 sq miles) consist of a high boggy dome divided roughly down its center by the River Dart. Surrounding this damp plateau is a barren rock-strewn landscape with abrupt stone outcrops, called "tors." Scattered through this desolate area are prehistoric remains, Iron Age hut circles, and tin minings. Around its edges the land of Dartmoor softens into river valleys, "combes," where dozens of villages nestle.

Ninety percent of the rugged Dartmoor landscape is pastureland; much of it is accessible to picnickers, motorists and day hikers. Famous "beauty spots" such as Dartmeet and Lydford Gorge attract sightseers, where grown-ups idle the day away strolling and sunning and children play in the clear shallow waters or fish for minnows from the mossy banks. Everywhere you go on the moor are the Dartmoor ponies. Note that although some appear quite tame, you should not feed them as it develops habits that are dangerous to the ponies.

GENERAL INFORMATION

The Dartmoor Park Authority is based in Princetown at the **High Moorland Visitor Centre** ((01822) 890414 E-MAIL dnpinfo@dartnp.dartmoor-npa.gov.uk WEB SITE www.dartmoor-npa.gov.uk, Princetown, Yelverton PL20 6QF. Here you'll find a museum-discovery center with information on the park, its history and inhabitants. Keep it in mind as a refuge for a rainy day; free. For those who plan to walk the moors, the center offers a good selection of maps, guidebooks and minor hiking gear. Staff are on hand to help you plan your route and advise you of weather conditions.

Seasonal information centers operated by the park authority are located at: Hay Tor ((01364) 661520, the lower car park on the main road; Newbridge ((01364) 631303, the riverside car park; and Postbridge ((01822) 880272, on the B3212. In advance of your visit you can contact Dartmoor National Park Authority ((01822) 890414, High Moorland Visitor Centre, Princetown, Yelverton PL20 6QF.

Be sure to pick up a copy of *Dartmoor Visitor*, the free newspaper issued by the park authority, packed with information, maps, accommodation and dining listings and events calendars.

WHAT TO SEE AND DO

On the A386 about halfway between Okehampton and Tavistock, **Lydford Gorge** (NT) ((01822) 820320 is Devon's deepest ravine. There are several scenic walks here, including a five-kilometer (three-mile) loop and several shorter routes to the falls. Open daily from April to October; admission fee. Continue northeast on the A386 for Okehampton, a busy market town with the **Museum of Dartmoor Life** ((01837) 52295, West Street, and a ruined fourteenth-century castle.

On the east side of the park along the A382, the large, busy village of **Chagford** has a thatched bank and two old-timey general stores. Visit the Church of St. Michael and look for the carved roof bosses, one of which shows the symbol adopted by the Dartmoor tin miners: three rabbits. Legend says that a local lass named Mary was shot on the church steps immediately after her marriage. Some people think this legend spawned R.D. Blackmore's *Lorna Doone*, the romantic seventeenth-century tale of love and murder on Exmoor. Above the little village of Drewsteignton, **Castle Drogo** (NT) ((01647) 432629, a twentieth-century mock castle built by Sir Edwin Lutyens, lords over the River Teign. In addition to touring the house — an odd mixture of mediaeval style and twentieth-century luxury — there are terraced gardens in which to stroll, as well as nature walks, a play area for kids, and a croquet lawn. Open daily except Friday from April to October with limited winter hours; admission fee.

The village of **Moretonhampstead** started life as a Saxon town. The name derives from the Saxon "Mor Tun," meaning the settlement beside the marshy ground. You'll find hotels and guest houses and several ancient public houses here as Moretonhampstead was once on the old coaching road between Plymouth and Exeter. The Tourist Information Centre ((01647) 440043 is located in the center of town. Look for the booklet describing town trails and Moreton's own eight-kilometer (five-mile) "letterbox" trail, a Dartmoor tradition somewhat akin to a scavenger hunt.

You can't visit Devon without a traditional cream tea. The Green Restaurant, alongside St. Pancras Church at **Widecombe-in-the-Moor**, does it right, featuring their homemade scones. They also do light meals and morning coffee. Widecombe also has two good pubs (see WHERE TO STAY AND EAT, below). St. Pancras Church, known as the "Cathedral of the Moors," has an impressively high tower. The Sexton's Cottage is a National Trust and national park information center and shop.

A tiny hamlet between Widecombe and Ashburton, **Buckland-in-the-Moor** is known for its photogenic group of thatched cottages. The Church of St. Peter has a puzzle built into its clock, and visitors try their hand at deciphering the phrase, a memorial to member of a local family. On the edge of the hamlet, woodcarvers and potters ply their trade at the Roundhouse Craft Centre. In front of the craft center, the Horse Wheel Café is handy for light meals and cream teas.

Outside Buckfastleigh, the Benedictine monks of **Buckfast Abbey** ((01364) 642519 welcome visitors. The abbey is renowned for its bee-keeping, its tonic wine and its stained glass workshop. There are three shops, a restaurant, and a video and exhibition. The shops, selling products from monasteries around the world — wines, liqueurs, preserves, textiles, perfumes, and the abbey's own honey and pottery — are alone worth the journey. Open daily; free admission.

OUTDOOR ACTIVITIES

If you plan to **walk** on Dartmoor — whether its a half-hour jaunt or a multi-day hike — visit the High Moorland Visitor Centre, in Princetown (see GENERAL INFORMATION, above). Walkers should note that there is a large **firing range** operated by the Ministry of Defense in the northern part of the moor. It is used for target practice during certain periods of the year; otherwise the public has access to these areas. The areas are marked by red-and-white posts. If you wish to walk in these areas you must check firing times, which are advertised in local newspapers and posted at visitor information centers.

Guided walks, ranging from fairly strenuous hikes to easy-going strolls, are offered by the park authority. Just show up at the starting point, no need to book in advance unless otherwise noted in the *Dartmoor Visitor* (available at tourist information centers and the park authority office; see below). The National Trust also offers guided walks from Easter to the end of October. Pick up a program guide at any tourist information center or phone ((01837) 55565 or (01626) 834748.

Trailtracks Cycle Hire ((01837) 54400 or (0410) 495300 (mobile) rents **bicycles** and offers route planning, return transport, and breakdown backup for moorland cyclists. Book well in advance, particularly during the summer months.

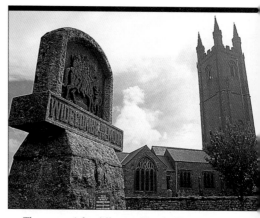

There are eight **riding stables** in Dartmoor. Among them are: Lydford House Riding Stables ((01822) 820321, Lydford; and Shilstone Rocks Riding and Trekking Centre ((01364) 621281, Widecombe-in-the-Moor.

WHERE TO STAY AND EAT

Accommodation in Dartmoor ranges from luxury hotels to self-catering cottages to camping barns (see under BACKPACKING, page 34 in YOUR CHOICE). There are scores of tea houses throughout the park, as well as many pubs. Restaurants are found in the larger hotels.

One of the West Country's finest establishments, **Gidleigh Park Hotel** ((01647) 432367 or 432225 FAX (01647) 432574 E-MAIL gidleighpark @gidleigh.co.uk, Chagford, Devon TQ13 8HH, is a luxury resort, part of the Relais & Châteaux group. This 15-room country-house hotel is set in 18 hectares (45 acres) of cultivated gardens and woodlands along the north branch of the River Teign, right in Dartmoor National Park; luxury. If you dine in the **restaurant** (very expensive) you can enjoy a stroll around the gardens and woodlands.

At Widecombe-in-the-Moor, a tablet memorializes the trip of Uncle Tom Cobbleigh to the Widecombe Fair.

An Edwardian country house hotel on the east side of Dartmoor, **Bel Alp House** ((01364) 661217, Haytor, Newton Abbot TQ13 9XX, has eight roomy bedrooms, some with views. Public areas are warmed by log fires, and there is a **restaurant** and garden; expensive.

Near Lydford Gorge, **The Castle** ((01822) 820242, Lydford, Okehampton EX20 4BH, is a Tudor inn with 10 bedrooms, most with bath. There are antique furnishings and log fires in the beamed public areas, and good food and real ales in the **restaurant**; moderate.

Higher Venton Farm ((01364) 621235, Widecombe-in-the-Moor, Newton Abbot TQ13 7TF, is a green-trimmed thatched farmhouse with ducks and

as Totnes–Buckfastleigh ((01364) 642338 (11 km or seven miles; seasonal) and, on summer Sundays, Exeter–Okehampton. Long-distance **coaches** serve Exeter, Okehampton, Plymouth and Newton Abbot and local bus services connect major towns to points within the national park.

EXETER

DEVON — Animated by its university population, the bustling, largely modern city of Exeter is the administrative center of Devon.

Founded by Romans in AD 50, Exeter became an important town under the Anglo Saxons, and eventually developed a major cloth manufactur-

chickens in the yard and an old-fashioned rooster alarm clock. The sunny bedrooms (with bath) are comfortably arranged. A hearty breakfast is served in the beamed dining room; inexpensive. There are riding stables nearby at Lydford House Hotel.

Widecombe has two pubs. The **Rugglestone Inn** ((01364) 621327, Widecombe-in-the-Moor, is a great little place just outside the village center. There's a cozy interior with log fire for murky days and a wide grassy lawn for fine ones. Light meals and snacks are served. In the village center, the **Old Inn** ((01364) 621207 is renowned locally for serving huge portions; inexpensive.

ing industry, which continued until the eighteenth century. It was also a busy port. The center was flattened during bombing in 1942, but a few old buildings survive, most notably the splendid cathedral. Substantial sections of Roman and mediaeval wall still encircle Exeter.

The **Tourist Information Centre** ((01392) 265700 FAX (01392) 265260 is at Civic Centre on Paris Street. There is **Internet access** at the buzzing Hyperactive, 1B Queen Street, Central Station.

Exeter has a daily **market**, and the **Exeter Festival** takes place from the end of June to the beginning of July.

HOW TO GET THERE

There are direct **rail** services from London to mainline stations at Exeter and Newton Abbot. A branch line links Plymouth–Gunnislake, as well

WHAT TO SEE AND DO

The towers of the **Cathedral Church of St. Mary and St. Peter** are Norman, dating from the 1100s. They were left standing when the rest of the church was demolished in 1260 to make way for the present edifice, finished around 1394, and considered England's finest example of Decorated Gothic architecture. The fourteenth-century three-tiered west front is adorned with stone figures (Kings Alfred, Canute and William I among them), and the interior has magnificent rib-vaulting. Other notable features are the minstrel's gallery, the carved bishop's throne, and the elaborate chantry chapels. Guided **tours** are offered at 11 AM and 2:30 PM weekdays, 11 AM on Saturday. An entrance donation is requested.

The area around the shaded cathedral close is the most attractive part of the city, especially **Southernhay** just east of the close with its Georgian brick terraces. Exeter's **Quay** is a lively area where restored nineteenth-century warehouses have been converted into cafés, antique galleries, and craft shops. At the Old Quay House there's a visitor center (open April to October) with an audiovisual show and displays on the history of Exeter. **Boats** can be rented for short trips along the canal.

The Benedictine **Priory of St. Nicholas at the Mint** ((01392) 265858, Mint Lane, is an eleventh-century monastery with an unusual vaulted Norman undercroft, a Tudor room, fifteenth-century kitchen, and a magnificent guest hall with seventeenth-century furnishings and displays of mediaeval stone and woodcarving. Open 3 PM to 4:30 PM Monday, Wednesday, Saturday from Easter to October; free. In addition, there are guided tours on the last Tuesday of the month.

With its ornate Elizabethan façade and fifteenth-century roof, the **Guildhall**, High Street, is believed to be the oldest municipal building in Britain. Inside are some fine portraits and a display of civic regalia; free. Also off High Street, the **Underground Passages** ((01392) 265897 (enter through Boots Arcade) are a network of tunnels built in the thirteenth century to provide the city with a constant supply of fresh drinking water. There's an introductory video followed by a guided tour of the passages. Call for opening hours; admission fee.

OUTDOOR ACTIVITIES

It's possible to **walk** along the ship canal to Exminster and beyond to the Exe Estuary where there is excellent **birding**.

A 49-km (30-mile) round-trip **cycling** tour of Dartmoor starts from Exeter running through Doddiscombleigh and Bovey to Widecombe-in-the-Moor.

WHERE TO STAY

Set in a Georgian-style house near the cathedral, **St. Olave's Court** ((01392) 217736, Mary Arches Street, Exeter EX4 3AZ, has 15 rooms, a walled garden, and good food in the candlelit restaurant; moderate.

The snug **Coachman's Rest** ((01392) 461472, London House, Broadclyst, Exeter EX5 3ET, is a restaurant situated eight kilometers (five miles) from the city center, on National Trust property, with two bedrooms; inexpensive.

There are two youth hostels in Exeter. The **Exeter Youth Hostel** ((01392) 873329 FAX (01392) 876939 E-MAIL exeter@yha.org.uk, 47 Countess Wear Road, Exeter EX2 6LR, is set in grounds close to the River Exe. There is regular bus service from here into town; rock-bottom. **Globe Backpackers** ((01392) 215521 FAX (01392) 215531 WEB SITE www.backpackers.co.uk, 71 Holloway Street, Exeter EX2 4JD, has no curfew and has web access; rock-bottom.

WHERE TO EAT

Close to the cathedral, **Lambs** ((01392) 254269, 15 Lower North Street, serves homemade English fare in an eighteenth-century house. Closed Saturday morning and all day Sunday and Monday as well as two weeks in August; moderate.

St. Martin's Café Bar ((01392) 310130, Cathedral Close, is a laid-back, airy space where food is served throughout the day; inexpensive.

There is a branch of **Café Rouge** ((01392) 211778 at 92 Queen Street.

HOW TO GET THERE

Exeter is 280 km (173 miles) west of London, and 75 km (46 miles) northeast of Plymouth. Exeter Airport ((01392) 367433 is eight kilometers (five miles) east of the city; however, there are no direct flights from London. **Trains** from London Paddington depart hourly during the day for the two-and-a-half-hour trip to Exeter's two train stations: Exeter St. David's, St. David's Hill; and Exeter Central, Queen Street. There are also hourly trains from Plymouth to Exeter. The mainline train from Barnstaple to Exeter (known as the Tarka Line) runs along the River Taw and is superbly scenic. National Express operates frequent **coach** services to Exeter's Paris Street station. The ride takes four hours.

THE SOUTH DEVON COAST

DEVON — In contrast to the north, the South Coast of Devon is more built up, with scores of bucket-and-shovel holiday centers clinging merrily to the sea. Torquay is the busiest of these seaside resorts, complete with palm trees and seaside promenades.

The Southwest Coastal Path (here called the South Devon Coast Path) runs 87 km (54 miles) through ever-changing scenery. The Coast Path Hopper is a bus route linking 41 km (25 miles) of

Exeter Cathedral.

the path from the moth of the River Avon to Start Bay, allowing you to take the bus back to your starting point after a day of coastal rambling.

TORQUAY

The largest of the "English Riviera" resort towns, Torquay forms a glamorous (some might say brash) crescent along Torbay, merging seamlessly into Paignton and Brixham. Torquay is famed as the birthplace of mystery writer Agatha Christie. Torre Abbey and the Torquay museum both have exhibitions on her life and work.

There is a **Tourist Information Centre** ℂ (01803) 297428 FAX (01803) 214885 on Vaughan Parade in Torquay. There is **Internet access** in Torquay at NetZone Internet Cafe, 6 Newton Road; or Cyberpoint, 238 Union Street, Torre, Torquay.

Built around the remains of a monastery founded in the twelfth-century, **Torre Abbey** ℂ (01803) 293593, King's Drive, is now an art gallery. Nearby, the **Torquay Museum** ℂ (01803) 293975, Babbacombe Road, deals with the natural history of the area and archaeological finds from **Kents Cavern Showcaves** ℂ (01803) 294059, which can also be visited at Isham Road, on the edge of town.

The **Paignton Zoo** ℂ (01803) 557479, St. Michael's, has some 1,300 animals in its landscaped 30 hectares (75 acres). It's possible to take a 11-km (seven-mile) scenic ride along the coast on the *Paignton & Dartmouth Steam Railway* ℂ (01803) 555872, Queens Park Station, Torbay Road, to Kingswear. There's a passenger ferry that carries on from Kingswear to Dartmouth.

Where to Stay and Eat

Convenient to the Torquay seafront and center, **Kingston House** ℂ (01803) 212760, 75 Avenue Road, Torquay TQ2 5LL, is a graceful Victorian offering six bedrooms, all with bath; inexpensive. On the outskirts of Torquay, **Fairmount House Hotel** ℂ/FAX (01803) 605446, Herbert Road, Chelston, Torquay, is set in a pleasant garden. There are eight bedrooms with bath; moderate.

The cosy **Mulberry Room** ℂ (01803) 213639, 1 Scarborough Road, Torquay, serves interesting fare using local produce, and afternoon teas feature homemade cakes. Close Monday and Tuesday; moderate.

For rock-bottom accommodation there is the **International Backpackers Hostel** ℂ/FAX (01803) 299924 WEB SITE www.backpackers.co.uk, 119 Abbey Road, Torquay TQ2 5NP; or **Riviera Backpackers** ℂ (01803) 550160 FAX (01803) 566135, 6 Manor Road, Preston Sands, Paignton. Both have all-day access, Internet and no curfew.

How to Get There

Torquay is 310 km (190 miles) southwest of London, and 14 km (23 miles) southeast of Exeter.

There are frequent **trains** departing from London Paddington, arriving at Torquay station on the sea front; the trip takes just over two hours. National Express operates seven daily **coaches** from London Victoria to Torquay's bus station on Lymington Road. The ride takes around five hours.

TOTNES

Due west of Torbay, Totnes is a market town with a flourishing arts community, though ringed by unsightly suburbs. Totnes is also the "natural-health capital of the west," with craft and antiques shops flanked by natural medicines and organic food shops. Totnes is situated upstream from Dartmouth at the highest navigable point of the River Dart. You can get here via river steamer from Dartmouth, along a beautiful stretch of the river which motorists never see.

General Information

You'll find the **Tourist Information Centre** ℂ (01803) 863168 FAX (01803) 865771 in The Plains.

The annual **Dartington International Summer School and Festival of Music** ℂ (01803) 865988, takes place in July and August at nearby Dartington Hall Estate. The six-week festival features concerts, workshops and lectures by renowned musicians and artists. Throughout the year Dartington Arts ℂ (01803) 863073, Dartington Hall, offers theater, music, films and exhibitions. Call for a free schedule. Totnes' **Orange Race**, held in July, celebrates the exploits of the famous Devonian, Sir Francis Drake.

Tuesday mornings from May to September and all day Tuesday from March to November, Totnes hosts an **Elizabethan street market** and **craft market**. The food market takes place on Friday and Saturday throughout the year.

What to See and Do

Totnes Castle (EH) ℂ (01803) 864406 is a Norman motte-and-bailey fortification with views over the town and river. Open daily from April to October; Wednesday to Sunday the rest of the year; admission fee. The mediaeval **Guildhall** ℂ (01803) 862147, Rampart Walk, and the **church** with its intricately carved screen are worth seeing as well. The Guildhall is open weekdays from April to October; free.

The heyday of Totnes is relived at the **Elizabethan Museum** ℂ (01803) 863821, Fore Street, where there is also a gallery devoted to English mathematician Charles Babbage (1791–1871) who laid the groundwork for the development of computers. Open April to October, Monday to Saturday; admission fee.

The *South Devon Railway* ℂ (01364) 642338 is a vintage steam train that operates between Buckfastleigh and Totnes along the east bank of the River Dart. Along this 11-km (seven-mile) trip, wildlife abounds — heron, swans, badgers, foxes, otters and other Devon denizens are often spotted. Trips are offered Wednesday, Saturday and Sunday in October; Tuesday, Wednesday, Saturday and Sunday in April and May; daily from late May through early October; admission fee.

Where to Stay and Eat

Cott Inn ((01803) 863777 Dartington, Totnes TQ9 6HE, just outside Totnes on the A384, has been serving up real ales since 1320. Food (moderate) in this delightful inn is well-prepared and imaginative; pork cobbler is a house specialty. Six bedrooms, all with bath (moderate).

Well Barn Farm ((01803) 812783, Torbryan, Ipplepen, Newton Abbot TQ12 5UR, a small sheep

((01803) 834224 FAX (01803) 835631 on Mayor's Avenue. **Market** days are Tuesday and Friday.

What to See and Do

The **Butterwalk** is a row of seventeenth-century timber-framed houses where **Dartmouth Museum** ((01803) 832923 features exhibits on the town's maritime history; admission fee. Down by **Bayards Cove**, eighteenth-century houses line the cobbled quay. It was here that the Pilgrim's ships, the *Speedwell* and the *Mayflower* were repaired in 1620 after a too-hasty departure from Plymouth.

Just south of town is the picturesque **Dartmouth Castle** (EH) ((01803) 833588, Castle Road, built in 1481, fortified during the Victorian era.

farm offering B&B and trout fishing. The farm adjoins managed woodland and heathland conservation areas and is eight kilometers (five miles) from Totnes; call for rates.

How to Get There

Totnes is 365 km (225 miles) southwest of London and 19 km (12 miles) northwest of Dartmouth. It is on the main London-Plymouth **train** line with frequent departures from London Paddington.

DARTMOUTH

Home to the Royal Naval College, Dartmouth is an attractive waterside town at its most picturesque around the yacht-filled harbor. From here the narrow streets of this ancient seaport wind through the town where there are some fine Elizabethan houses. You'll find the **Tourist Information Centre**

Tours of the lugubrious castle are lightened by excellent vistas across the estuarial plains. Open daily from April to October, Wednesday to Sunday the rest of the year; admission fee.

Take the **boat trip** on the River Dart with Read Cruisers ((01803) 832109, 4 Broadstone, Dartmouth; or Dart Pleasure Craft ((01803) 834488, 5 Lower Street. Dartmouth, passing the Greenway House, home of Agatha Christie.

Where to Stay and Eat

The **Royal Castle** ((01803) 833033 FAX (01803) 835445, 11 The Quay, Dartmouth TQ6 9PS, is a seventeenth-century coaching inn right on the waterfront. Some of the bedrooms have terrific views, and there is a **restaurant** and bar; expensive to very expensive.

Elizabethan façades decorate a Dartmouth street.

Next to the National Trust's Coleton Fishacre Garden, **Coleton Barton Farm** ((01803) 752795, Brownstone Road, Kingswear TQ6 0EQ, is a working farm along a coastal footpath offering inexpensive accommodation. Close to here, **Grove Lodge Farm** ((01803) 752649, Broad Road, Kingswear TQ6 0EF, is a modern house set on a working farm. It's close to the coastal path and a fine place for birding. Bedrooms all have bath and some have sea views; call for rates (no children).

Overlooking the River Dart, the **Carved Angel** ((01803) 832465 is a Dartmouth favorite for its excellent cuisine and warm atmosphere; expensive. For more casual fare, there is **Billy Budds** ((01803) 834842, 7 Foss Street, a bistro where the

Though it's a modern city, Plymouth's greatest allure remains its multi-layered history. As it commands the entrance to the English Channel, Plymouth's strategic value was recognized early on by King Edward I, who assembled a fleet of 325 ships here — the country's first navy. Over the ages the town proved an important staging area for colonization and exploration. Sir Francis Drake, the first Englishman to circumnavigate the globe, left from Plymouth on his journey of exploration and treasure hunting in 1577. The Pilgrim Fathers departed Plymouth in the seventeenth century bound for the New World. Captain James Cook's explorations of 1768 to 1780 began at Plymouth as well. Another chapter in Plymouth's history —

seafood is particularly good. Reservations are required; moderate.

How to Get There
Dartmouth is 381 km (235 miles) southwest of London and 57 km southeast (35 miles) of Exeter. **Trains** from London run to Totnes and Paignton, where one **bus** each day carries on to Dartmouth. Stagecoach ((01803) 613226 operates a **passenger ferry** between Kingswear and Dartmouth.

PLYMOUTH

DEVON — Devon's largest population center, Plymouth is a lively, modern city. It makes a good urban base for exploring South Devon, since it's within easy reach of Dartmoor and some decent beaches. A large part of the city center is a pedestrian-only shopping mall.

World War II — is responsible for the fact that even though the city launched so many important moments in history, only a few remnants of the old city remain to tell the story.

GENERAL INFORMATION

The main **Tourist Information Centre** ((01752) 264849 or (01752) 227865 (24-hours) FAX (01752) 257955 is at Island House, 9 The Barbican. You'll find a second Tourist Information Centre at the Plymouth Discovery Centre ((01752) 266030 FAX (01752) 266033, by Marsh Mills traffic circle off the A38.

Double-decker hop-on hop-off **bus tours** leave every 20 minutes from various points around the city. The tour lasts an hour and tickets are valid all day. Further details can be found at the Tourist Information Centre.

If you want to explore further afield, take a **ferry-boat trip** to St. Anthony Head (below) where you can **hike** on to Place, a fifteenth-century private home with limited opening hours (see under FOWEY, above).

You might be surprised to find one of the world's top 20 hotels on the toe of the Roseland Peninsula, but the **Hotel Tresanton** ((01326) 270055 FAX (01326) 270053, St. Mawes TR2 5DR, has earned that distinction from an international travel magazine. The whitewashed exterior builds on the village's Greek isle appearance, while the interiors employ blues and ocher, with a World Beat approach to decorating (note the didgeridoos). Fashioned out of a cluster of old houses

Prince of Wales Pier. The trip takes 25 minutes and affords excellent views of the twin forts of Pendennis and St. Mawes. The ferry departs every 30 minutes in season. By road, St. Mawes is about 19 km (12 miles) east of Falmouth.

St. Anthony Head
Known to many as the setting for the television series "Fraggle Rock," St. Anthony Head is well worth a detour for its fine views of the Fal Estuary, Lizard Peninsula, Falmouth and St. Mawes. You can explore ramparts and embattlements dating from the nineteenth century onward, and hike down to the 1834 **lighthouse**, which keeps ships clear of the notorious Manacles rocks. Open during summer.

on different levels, converted into a yacht club in the 1940's, the hotel has 26 impeccable bedrooms, some with terraces, all with sea views. The restaurant, overlooking the water, serves superb international fare using local produce and the bounty of the Cornish waters. It would be agreeable simply to laze on the terrace the day long, but if you're looking for action there are sailing and windsurfing lessons as well as a 15-m (48-ft) skippered yacht for hire for six to eight people. There is fishing for conger eel, shark and bass, and families can go shrimping or fishing for mackerel, or enjoy trips to see seals on Black Rock. Finally, an in-house cinema specializes in "foodie" movies; very expensive (discounts of 15% for long stays; half board available).

By car, St. Mawes is about a five-hour drive from London. Falmouth and St. Mawes are linked by a regular **pedestrian ferry** service from Falmouth's

The **Officers' Quarters** are in a single-story stone building which has been converted into three comfortable cottages with fireplaces and views across Falmouth Bay. Three-night minimum; inexpensive to moderate. Contact the National Trust Holiday Cottage Booking Office ((01225) 791199 FAX (01225) 792267, PO Box 536, Melksham, Wiltshire SN12 8SX.

Veryan and Portloe
The picturesque inland village of Veryan is noted for its distinctive **roundhouses** — circular, thatched, nineteenth-century cottages situated at the entrance to the village. It's said that these cottages were constructed in-the-round to ward off the evil that was thought to settle in corners, thus giving Satan nowhere to hide. (These are private

Young and old cast their lines at St. Mawes' waterfront.

homes and not open to the public.) Besides its devil-defying roundhouses, the village boasts **Veryan Galleries**, featuring the works of contemporary Cornish artists. Closed Sunday.

East of Veryan, white cottages with multi-colored shutters cling to the hills round about the picture-perfect fishing hamlet of **Portloe**. Little-changed over the last century, the hamlet supports five small boats which bring in crab and lobster, while divers hunt sea urchins in season. From the village, you can take the Southwest Coastal Path for high cliff walks and stunning scenery.

The **Lugger Hotel and Restaurant** ((01872) 501322 FAX (01872) 501691, Portloe, Truro TR2 5RD, has an ideal spot on the tiny cove at Portloe. This

The National Trust rents several **holiday cottages** — mostly farmhouses and converted farm buildings — around Veryan, three night minimum stay; inexpensive to moderate. Contact the National Trust Holiday Cottage Booking Office ((01225) 791199 FAX (01225) 792267, PO Box 536, Melksham, Wiltshire SN12 8SX.

Mevagissey
Mevagissey is a working fishing harbor and tourist temptation nestled at the base of the Pentewan Valley. Each June brings **Feast Week**, with folk music, gig racing and the traditional Flora Dance that winds through the village streets. The **Tourist Information Centre** (/FAX (01726) 842266 is at 14 Church Street.

former seventeenth-century smuggler's inn looks the part with its low ceilings, fat oak beams and a dining room and terrace overlooking the water. The menu offers a choice of *table d'hôte* or *à la carte;* seafood is a specialty. Reservations are recommended for dinner; jacket and tie required. The Lugger is open March to October. Dinner, room and breakfast packages are available as well as special interest breaks for garden lovers and walkers; moderate.

Another option in Portloe is **Cliff Garden** ((01872) 501751 FAX (01872) 501807 E-MAIL rdasent736 @aol.com, Portloe, Truro TR2 5QZ, a restored cottage with two bedrooms with bath and sea views; inexpensive rates.

In Veryan, the cliff-top **Broom Parc** ((01872) 501803 FAX (01872) 501109, Veryan TR2 5PJ, is a country house situated in this National Trust protected coastal area; inexpensive rates.

Your first stop in Mevagissey will undoubtedly be **Valley Side Piskie Gnome** where, if you're lucky, you might find the proprietor hard at work painting garden gnomes. From here Mevagissey's narrow streets melt into a jolly mass of shops vending ice lollies, postcards, water wings and fudge.

The best part of Mevagissey is its bustling harbor, where a fleet of fishing boats bring in the skate, lobster, plaice and sole that are served in local restaurants. Inland mackerel **fishing trips** out of Mevagissey can be arranged with local fishermen; ask at the harbor or inquire at the Tourist Information Centre. The Mevagissey Shark Angling Centre ((01726) 843430, West Quay, offers deep-water fishing trips for shark and conger.

By the harbor, a small **aquarium** is stocked with the denizens of the local deep. Open daily from Easter to October; admission fee.

Just one and a half kilometers (one mile) from Mevagissey is Cornwall's most famous green spot, the **Lost Gardens of Heligan** ((01726) 845100, near Pentewan. Like a fairytale heroine, the gardens of Heligan slept for 70 years, "lost" under bramble and ivy following the decline of the family estate. Now an ongoing program, Britain's largest-ever garden restoration project is creating a living museum of nineteenth-century horticultural methods. Heligan comprises 32 hectares (80 acres) of greenery, from meticulously researched period kitchen gardens to exotic fruit groves. There are nine hectares (22 acres) of jungle with tree ferns, bamboo and tropical vegetation, formal Victorian walled gardens, hothouses and landscaped ponds. A tea room and covered picnic area offer a pleasant (if busy) place for a break. There is a gift and plant shop. Open daily; admission fee.

There are some interesting accommodations and restaurants in Mevagissey, such as the **Sharksfin Hotel** ((01726) 843241 FAX (01726) 842552, The Quay, Mevagissey PL26 6QU, which occupies a former eighteenth-century pilchard "palace" right on the harbor. Bedrooms are modestly decorated with smallish windows, but the harbor views are nonetheless fascinating. To complete the maritime picture, the reception desk is carved out of a fishing boat. There is a casual waterside **restaurant** and bar; expensive.

Salamander ((01726) 842254, 4–6 Tregoney Hill, is an island of calm in this lively village. The chef-proprietor prepares a varied menu, with starters such as mushroom ragout *en croûte* and mains featuring the daily catch or, perhaps, seared duck breast with plum sauce. Finish with a rich dessert or English cheeses and chutneys; moderate.

Down near the harbor, homey **Alvorado** ((01726) 842035, Fore Street, must be the only Portuguese restaurant for many miles around. The menu dazzles diners with a long list of starters such as char-grilled Portuguese sardines or fava beans sautéed in olive oil with bacon and smoked sausage. Mains are just as extensive; char-grilled seafood kebabs are a specialty. Portuguese wines complement the fare; moderate.

The closest **train** connection for Mevagissey is at St. Austell, which is a four and a half hour trip from London.

BODMIN MOOR

CORNWALL — A rugged granite plateau similar to Dartmoor but on a smaller scale, Bodmin Moor covers 208 sq km (79 sq miles) of grand walking and cycling country. The industrial town of **Bodmin** with its humble brownstone buildings has a **Tourist Information Centre** ((01208) 76616 at Shire House on Mount Folly Square. Bodmin is the starting point for a **steam train** journey aboard the

Bodmin & Wenford Railway ((01208) 73666. The station is on the B3268 Lostwithiel road near the center of Bodmin.

Du Maurier fans will no doubt profit from a visit to **Jamaica Inn** ((01566) 86250, which the author used as the setting and name of her 1936 novel of smuggling and murder. In the same complex is **Mr. Potter's Museum of Curiosities** ((01566) 86838, brimful of Victorian stuffed animal tableaux and bric-a-brac. Open daily year-round; admission fee.

Four kilometers (two and a half miles) southeast of the town of Bodmin, **Lanhydrock House** (NT) ((01208) 73320 is a seventeenth-century manor, home of the Agar-Robartes family. Largely rebuilt after a fire in 1881 (only the gatehouse and north wing are original), it's been called the finest house in Cornwall. A horseshoe-shaped garden, famed for its magnolias, surrounds the house. The house is open daily except Monday from April to October; garden open daily from March to October; admission fee. The tea room, serving cream teas, homemade soups, pies and flans, is open through the end of October.

At the comely gray-stone village of **Altarnun**, just off the A30, is the church of St. Nona. Sometimes called the "Cathedral of the Moor," this mostly fifteenth-century building has elaborately carved pew ends. Penhallow Manor Hotel and Restaurant serves afternoon tea.

For B&B on the moor, **Treffry Farm** (/FAX (01208) 74405, Lanhydrock, Bodmin PL30 5AF, is a dairy farm, B&B in a Georgian farmhouse. The three bedrooms have baths. The farm adjoins Lanhydrock so there are scenic walks from the doorstep.

Bodmin is a stop on the London–Penzance **train** line. National Express **buses** serve the town of Bodmin with two daily departures from London Victoria.

TRURO

CORNWALL — Truro's skyline is easily identifiable by the three graceful spires of its neo-Gothic cathedral. A Georgian town with traces of its seventeenth-century architectural framework, Truro makes an agreeable base for exploring the waterside hamlets and villages of Carrick Roads, the once-great shipping lane linking Truro to Falmouth Bay.

The **Tourist Information Centre** ((01872) 274555 is in the Municipal Buildings on Boscawen Street. Local Blue Badge guides offer **heritage walks** ((01872) 271257 on Wednesday and Thursday from April to October starting at 11 AM and 2 PM. Meet at High Cross outside the cathedral; admission fee. The Tourist Information Centre can provide information on **cycling** in Cornwall. **Internet** access is at The Internet Place, 5 Frances Street; closed Sunday.

Popular Mevagissey is still a working fishing village.

WHAT TO SEE AND DO

Many visitors are surprised to learn that **Truro Cathedral**, so mediaeval in appearance, was built in the late nineteenth century. The interior is starkly beautiful, with a set of Victorian stained-glass windows that are admired throughout the country. Tea and lunch are served in the **refectory**.

Visit the **Royal Cornwall Museum** ((01872) 272205, River Street, for a crash course in the art, history, archaeology and geology of the duchy. Recent improvements have added a gallery on the natural history of Cornwall and a textile gallery, both with hands-on activities for children. Open Monday to Saturday; admission fee.

Truro is within striking distance of some fabulous gardens. Set in 200 hectare (500 acres) **Trelissick Garden** (NT) ((01872) 862090, in Feock (six and a half kilometers or four miles south of Tru-

ro), looks out over Carrick Roads, the great old shipping lanes of west Cornwall. A young garden, the heart of Trelissick is awash with rhododendrons, hydrangeas and camellias, while old-growth oak and beech woods and parkland fill the perimeter. There is a tea room as well as a shop. Open year-round; admission fee. **Trewithen House & Gardens** ((01726) 883647, on the A39 between Truro and St. Austell, is a fine early Georgian house set in woods and parkland and surrounded by camellias, rhododendrons, magnolias and rare tress and shrubs. Open March to September, Monday to Saturday; Sundays also in April and May. Finally, one of Cornwall's most intimate and delightful gardens is, **Bosvigo** ((01872) 275774, Bosvigo Lane, only a short walk from the center of Truro. This small and secluded garden of herbaceous borders is unusual in Cornwall horticultural circles because it's at its most colorful

Travelers'
Tips

TO GET THE MOST OUT OF YOUR TRIP TO SOUTHERN England you'll need plenty of practical advice, from how to get there to stretching your budget and keeping tabs on the weather.

GETTING TO SOUTHERN ENGLAND

The four main points of entry to Southern England — and the United Kingdom for that matter — are Heathrow (LHR; 24 km or 15 miles from London) and Gatwick (GTW; 44 km or 27 miles from London) airports, the port at Dover, and the Channel Tunnel. In addition to these four principle points or entry, there are major ports serving ferries from

five hours from touchdown at one airport to take-off from the other.

Southern England's **secondary airports** are London City ((020) 7646-0000; Luton ((01582) 405100; and Stansted ((01279) 680500. Information on these airports is accessible from WEB SITE www.baa.co.uk.

Ground transportation from Heathrow and Gatwick to London is detailed in HOW TO GET THERE, page 124 in LONDON.

BY TUNNEL

The 50-km-long (31-mile) Channel Tunnel connects England with France. There are two ways to travel

Continental Europe and the Channel Islands at Plymouth, Portsmouth and Harwich.

BY AIR

Heathrow ((020) 8759-4321 WEB SITE www.baa.co.uk is the busiest airport in the world, serving 60 million passengers each year, and operating an average of 1,200 flights per day. From New York alone there are 22 flights each day into Heathrow, and 36 flights a day from Paris.

Gatwick ((01293) 535353 WEB SITE www.baa .co.uk is also one of the world's busiest international airports, flying 30 million passengers each year to 280 destinations, all on a single runway!

For travel between Heathrow and Gatwick there is **Speedlink** ((020) 8668-7261 departing every 15 to 30 minutes (£16). The trip takes an hour, but those in the know say to allow four to

the Channel Tunnel: the Eurostar train for passengers, and the Eurotunnel Shuttle for automobiles, motorbikes, bicycles, buses and recreational vehicles. You cannot drive your car through the Channel Tunnel.

Eurostar is a passenger-only train service connecting London with Paris and Brussels via the Channel Tunnel. There are frequent daily departures; reservations are required. Call Eurostar direct, or contact a travel agent to book tickets. Rail Europe ((0990) 848848, books continuing TGV (*train grande vitesse*, or high-speed train) service from Lille or Paris to Lyon, Avignon, Nice, Dijon, Poitiers and Bordeaux; from Brussels, the high-speed **Thalys** continues to Amsterdam, Antwerp and Cologne.

Taking the Eurostar is slightly faster than flying between London and Paris; trips from Paris take just under three hours. And Eurostar passengers avoid the hassle and expense of travel to and from the airports from the city centers, since the Eurostar arrives at London's **Waterloo International Station**, adjoining the main Waterloo station. When Britain upgrades its train tracks, the journey will be even shorter. Some Eurostar departures make intermediary stops at Ashford (Kent), Calais, Frethun or Lille.

Eurostar **information and reservations lines** for various countries are as follows:

Belgium ((02) 555-2555 (information) or (0900) 10177 (reservations) WEB SITE www.sncb.be.
France ((08) 3635-3539 MINITEL 3615 SNCF, 3616 SNCF or 3623 SNCF WEB SITE www.sncf.fr.
Britain ((0345) 303030 or (01233) 617575 WEB SITE www.eurostar.com.
United States TOLL-FREE (800) 677-8585 WEB SITE www.raileurope.com.

Those taking a motor vehicle into Britain will board the **Eurotunnel Shuttle** ((0990) 353535 (formerly called Le Shuttle) in Calais, France, and debark in Folkestone, Kent. It is possible to purchase a ticket in advance, but it's not necessary as services through the tunnel operate on a turn-up-and-go basis, 24 hours a day, 365 days a year. There are no fixed departure times, but there are generally four trains per hour. Journey time is 35 minutes, 45 minutes for night services. There's more information as well as on-line booking at WEB SITE www.eurotunnel.co.uk.

Cyclists should make a reservation with the Eurotunnel Shuttle Cycle Service ((01303) 273300, extension 8700.

Long-distance coaches from Europe also board the Eurotunnel Shuttle then continue on to London Victoria Coach Station. **Eurolines** is the main provider of European coach services to and from London. It's the cheapest and slowest way to get there. Visit their WEB SITE www.eurolines.com for branch offices throughout Europe, or contact the United Kingdom offices at ((0990) 143219 FAX (01582) 400694 E-MAIL welcome@eurolinesuk .com, 4 Cardiff Road, Luton, Bedfordshire L41 1PP.

BY SEA

Ferries link Britain with most of the countries bordering the English Channel or the North Sea. All craft making the crossing are equipped to transport automobiles. Note that the Channel can be rough, so you may want to take precautions if you're prone to seasickness. A useful, independent, on-line guide to ferry services to and from the United Kingdom is the **Seaview Cruise and Ferry Information Service** WEB SITE www.seaview.co.uk.

Hoverspeed operates high-speed ferries between **Dover and Calais** that take 35 to 50 minutes to make the crossing. P&O Stena Lines run from Dover to Calais in 75 minutes; and Sea France connects Dover to Calais in 90 minutes.

Hoverspeed also connects Folkestone and Boulogne in 55 minutes.

If your final destination is the West Country, you might consider entering Britain through **Plymouth** via Roscoff, France (six hours) or St. Malo (nine hours). These routes are served by Brittany Ferries.

Another alternative, Brittany Ferries and P&O EF operate services to **Portsmouth** from Caen (six hours), St. Malo (five and half to seven and a half hours), Le Havre (five and a half to seven and a half hours), and Cherbourg (five to seven hours).

If you're coming from Northern Europe, you can take a DFDS Seaways ((08705) 333000 passenger and car ferry to **Harwich** (Essex).

Fares, schedules and reservations can be obtained through a travel agent. Book well in advance for North Sea and Channel crossings during the summer season. Some ferry services are seasonal.

For information on **cruises**, see TAKING A TOUR, page 62 in YOUR CHOICE.

ARRIVING (AND LEAVING)

American, Canadian or Australian citizens visiting the United Kingdom need a valid passport and a round-trip ticket; a visa is not required for visits of less than six months. Additional information on entry requirements may be obtained from the British Embassy ((202) 588-7800 WEB SITE www.britain-info.org, 3100 Massachusetts Avenue, NW, Washington, DC 20008; or from British consulates in Atlanta, Boston, Chicago, Houston, Los Angeles, New York and San Francisco.

Citizens of European Union countries must produce a valid passport or identity card.

Duty and tax free allowances are: 200 cigarettes or 50 cigars or 250 grams (about 9 ounces) of tobacco; no more than two liters of wine and one liter of alcohol; 50 ml (or 1.7 fluid ounces) of perfume; and £145.00 worth of other goods.

OPPOSITE: All aboard? Tiny train steams through the Bath and West Show. ABOVE: Dorset pastorale.

There is no restriction on the **amount of money** you can bring in and take out of the United Kingdom.

You will pay an **air passenger duty** of £20 (approximately US$32) when you purchase your plane ticket.

Until recently any **pet** brought into the United Kingdom had to spend six months in quarantine. Laws have been liberalized to some degree, and now pets can enter the United Kingdom from certain countries, without undergoing quarantine, provided they meet very stringent requirements — including outfitting Fido with his very own microchip. Visit the Ministry of Agriculture, Fisheries and Food WEB SITE www.maff.gov.uk for details on the Pet Travel Scheme.

All travelers leaving the United Kingdom pay a £5 to £10 **Airport Departure Tax**.

The British sales tax, called the **Value Added Tax** (VAT) is 17.5% and is almost always included in the price in shops, hotels and restaurants. Tourists who buy goods from participating shops (look for the red, white, and blue Tax-free Shopping decal) may apply for a VAT refund if they intend to leave Britain for a destination outside the European Union within three months of the date of purchase. Large stores generally will handle the paperwork for you, but only if you request it. If you'd like to know more, write for a brochure from South Bank VAT Centre ((020) 7202-4087, HM Customs and Excise, Dorset House, Stamford Street, London SE1 9PY.

EMBASSIES AND CONSULATES

For British High Commissions and Embassies other than those listed below, visit the **British Foreign & Commonwealth Office** WEB SITE www.fco.gov.uk.
Australia British High Commission ((02) 6270-6666 E-MAIL canberra@uk.emb.gov.au WEB SITE www.uk.emb.gov.au, Commonwealth Avenue, Yarralumla, Canberra, ACT 2600.
Canada British High Commission ((613) 237-1530 WEB SITE www.britain-in-canada.org, 80 Elgin Street, Ottawa K1P 5K7.
New Zealand British High Commission ((04) 472-6049 E-MAIL bhc.wel@xtra.co.nz WEB SITE www.brithighcomm.org.nz, 44 Hill Street, Thorndon, Wellington 1.
South Africa British High Commission ((021) 461-7220 E-MAIL britain@icon.za, 91 Parliament Street, Cape Town 8001.
United States British Embassy ((202) 588-6500 WEB SITE www.britainusa.com, 3100 Massachusetts Avenue NW, Washington, DC 20008.

The principle English-speaking embassies in London are as follows:
Australia: Australian High Commission ((020) 7379-4334, Australia House, Strand, London WC2B 4LA.

Canada: Canadian High Commission ((020) 7258-6600, (020) 7258-6316 (consular services) or (020) 7258-6356 (passports) FAX (020) 7258-6533, MacDonald House, Grosvenor Square, London W1X 0AB.
New Zealand: New Zealand High Commission ((020) 7930-8422, 80 Haymarket, London SW1Y 4TQ.
South Africa: Embassy of South Africa ((020) 7451-7299, South Africa House, Trafalgar Square, London WC2N 5DP.
United States: United States Embassy ((020) 7499-9000 FAX (020) 7495-5012 WEB SITE www.usembassy.org.uk, 24 Grosvenor Square, London W1A 1AE.

Other embassies can be found in the Central London area telephone directory.

TOURIST INFORMATION

The **British Tourist Authority** (BTA) is the national tourism office for Britain. In advance of your trip, contact or visit one of the BTA's foreign offices (below). Many of the maps and brochures available free in the foreign offices cost money in Britain, so it's best to collect what you can before you go. Alternatively, contact the British Tourist Authority ((020) 8846-9000, Thames Tower, Black's Road, London W6 9EL, or visit their comprehensive WEB SITE www.bta.org.uk.

Once you arrive in London, you can take advantage of the **Britain Visitor Centre**, 1 Lower Regent Street, Piccadilly Circus, London SW1Y 4XT England. The office is open year-round, weekdays from 9 AM to 6:30 PM, Saturday and Sunday from 10 AM to 4 PM, and does not accept telephone calls, other than accommodation inquiries ((020) 7808-3864.

British Tourist Authority Offices worldwide include the following:

Australia ((02) 9377-4400 FAX (02) 9377-4499, Level 16, Gateway, 1 Macquarie Place, Sydney NSW 2000.

Canada ((905) 405-1840 TOLL-FREE (888) 847-4885 FAX (905) 405-1835, 5915 Airport Road, Suite 120, Mississauga, Ontario L4V 1T1.

France Maison de la Grande Bretagne ((01) 4265-3921 FAX (01) 4265-3910, 19 rue des Mathurins, 75009 Paris.

Hong Kong (2882-9967 FAX 2577-1443, Room 1504, Eton Tower, 8 Hysan Avenue, Causeway Bay, Hong Kong.

Ireland ((1) 670-8000, 18–19 College Green, Dublin 2.

East of England Tourist Board ((01473) 822922 FAX (01473) 823063, Toppesfield Hall, Hadleigh, Suffolk IP7 5DN.

Heart of England Tourist Board ((01905) 761100, Larkhill Road, Worcester WR5 2EZ.

Southern Tourist Board ((023) 8062-0006 or (023) 806-0555 (24-hour help line) FAX (023) 8062-0010, 40 Chamberlayne Road, Eastleigh SO51JH.

South East England Tourist Board ((01892) 540766 FAX (01892) 511008, The Old Brew House, Warwick Park, Tunbridge Wells TN2 5TU.

West Country Tourist Board ((01392) 425426 FAX (01392) 420891 E-MAIL post@wctb.co.uk WEB SITE www.wctb.co.uk, 60 St. Davids Hill, Exeter EX4 4SY.

New Zealand ((09) 303-1446 FAX (09) 377-6965, 17th Floor, Fay Richwhite Building, 151 Queen Street, Auckland 1.

South Africa ((11) 325-0343 FAX (11) 325-0344, Lancaster Gate, Hyde Park Lane, Hyde Park 2196 (visitors); PO Box 41896, Craighall 2024 (mail).

United States ((212) 986-2200 TOLL-FREE (800) 462-2748 E-MAIL travelinfo@bta.org.uk, Seventh Floor, 551 Fifth Avenue, New York, New York 10176-0799625 and North Michigan Avenue, Suite 1510, Chicago, Illinois 60611.

In some countries, British Embassies, Consulates and High Commissions also supply tourist information.

The regional tourist boards of Southern England are another excellent source of advice and information:

London Tourist Board, Sixth Floor, Glen House, Stag Place, London SW1E 5LT.

There are hundreds of **tourist information centers** in Southern England, maintained by local authorities and staffed by local experts. Services vary depending on the popularity of the area, but many centers offer a wide range of services, from information to accommodation booking, tickets, maps, and guides. You'll find phone numbers and street addresses for tourist information centers throughout this book under GENERAL INFORMATION.

GETTING AROUND

By Train

Though it is not as affordable or convenient as one might hope, the railway, nevertheless, presents a pleasurable way to see Southern England.

OPPOSITE: After repairs London's Millennium Bridge will welcome foot traffic. ABOVE: Vintage enthusiasts.

Keep in mind that in the southeast the rail system is London-centric; you may have to keep returning to the capital to get where you're going, even if it's out of the way. Often, too, your connection in London may be at a different station, forcing you to cross town to make your train.

The various **rail passes** offered to non-Europeans can be a bargain, but it depends on how you plan to travel and how much. The Britrail Pass gives you continuos unlimited travel over the entire British Rail network, available in periods of eight days to one month. The Flexipass is good for travel on four to 15 days within the period of one month. Note that both of these passes must be purchased before arriving in the United Kingdom. They're available from Rail Europe TOLL-FREE IN THE UNITED STATES (888) 274-8724 or WEB SITE www.raileurope.com. The web site is for North American consumers, but does offer travelers from other countries a listing of local ticketing agencies. Holders of the Britrail Pass are eligible for discounts on Eurostàr. Anyone aged 16 to 25 or over 60 can apply for a Railcard, which gives you a 33% discount, valid for one year. There are also rail passes covering restricted areas of the country (the southeast, Cornwall, Devon, etc.).

Apart from passes, buying rail tickets outside the United Kingdom offers no savings. In fact figures quoted by travel agents abroad can be higher than the amount you would pay once you arrive. Once in the United Kingdom, call **National Rail Inquiries** ((0345) 484950 for information about mainline trains throughout Britain. For trains on the Continent, call ((0990) 848848. At busy times, such as national holidays, it is a good idea to reserve seats in advance.

BY BUS

Coach (or long-distance bus) travel is comfortable, flexible and reliable, and usually costs less than the train (sometimes one third to one half the price of a rail ticket); however, it can take up to twice as long. All coaches have washrooms and some have refreshment services on-board.

The main coach company is **National Express** ((0990) 010104, linking the principle cities and towns of England (as well as those of Scotland and Wales). For trips to the "home counties," those counties surrounding London, there is **Green Line** ((020) 8668-7261. In London, National Express and Green Line coaches leave from Victoria Coach Station.

It's possible to purchase coach tickets and passes in the United States from British Travel International TOLL-FREE (800) 327-6097, PO Box 299, Elkton, Virginia 22827, or on arrival in England at London Victoria Coach Station or at Heathrow or Gatwick airports.

A number of **discount schemes** can make coach travel even more attractive. Inquire about passes and discount cards when you make your reservations.

BY CAR

Though you don't need a car to enjoy Southern England, it is useful for visiting stately homes and gardens and for getting into remote areas. In major cities and towns, on the other hand, a car can be a definite liability, especially in London where traffic is dense and parking prices are exorbitant. One option, should you decide to rent a car, is to rent as you go at major rail stations. Hertz and Britrail offer the Flexipass which **combines rail travel with car rental** for side trips. For details, contact the British Tourist Authority in your country (see TOURIST INFORMATION, page 324).

Rental **rates** are expensive in Britain. You can often get a better deal by making arrangements in your home country. Most of the big international rental agents are represented in Britain, including: Alamo, Avis, Budget, Europcar (associated with Dollar in the United States), Hertz, National, and Thrifty. Consult your local yellow pages for phone numbers.

Auto Europe TOLL-FREE IN THE UNITED KINGDOM (00800) 55-555 TOLL-FREE IN THE UNITED STATES (800) 223-5555 WEB SITE www.autoeurope.com, offers discount prices and other travel services; as does **Auto Net** TOLL-FREE IN THE UNITED STATES (800) 221-3465.

If you're driving your own car, you might want to join a **motoring club** for 24-hour breakdown assistance. The major associations in the United Kingdom are the Royal Automobile Club (RAC) ((0800) 726999 WEB SITE rac.co.uk, and the Automobile Association (AA) ((01206) 255800 WEB SITE www.theaa.co.uk.

BY AIR

Given that Southern England is such a compact area, flights within the country will probably not be part of your itinerary. But, they do exist and, for those who can afford the steep prices, are an attractive alternative to the seven-hour drive to Cornwall. If you are arriving in Britain on a long-haul flight, you can sometimes add on a short internal hop to another airport for a reasonable cost. If you're planning to travel onward from the United Kingdom to other European destinations, you might consider the air passes available from British Midlands TOLL-FREE IN THE UNITED STATES (800) 788-0555 (or any major travel agent); and KLM ((0990) 074074 or TOLL-FREE IN THE UNITED STATES (800) 247-9297 (or a travel agent). Passes allow travel within a network of flight services and are available only to passengers living outside the United Kingdom and Europe or those purchasing an international flight ticket to the United Kingdom.

SPECIAL NEEDS

While England's newer attractions tend to have modifications allowing access to all, ancient monuments can present problems of access for visitors with disabilities. There are a number of useful resources in England for travelers with disabilities. A directory compiled by a wheelchair user, *All Go!* lists **hotels and restaurant** with facilities for disabled travelers. It's available by calling ((020) 7383-2335.

For the London Tourist Board's newsletter, "London for All," write to London Tourist Board & Convention Bureau, Glen House, Stage Place, Victoria, London SW1E 5LT.

Heaps of information can be obtained, also, from **Holiday Care Service** ((01293) 774535 FAX (01293) 784647 MINICOM (01293) 776943, Second Floor, Imperial Buildings, Victoria Road, Horley RH6 7PZ, a national charity which provides information and advice to disabled people trying to arrange vacations. Contact their Reservation Service for hotel or self-catering bookings at accessible establishments. They will also provide lists of accessible accommodations by area, where to rent equipment, and information on transportation for disabled visitors. Holiday Care Service also puts out the annual *Guide to Accessible Accommodation and Travel,* with a listing of 1,000 establishments inspected by Holiday Care Services in association with the British Tourist Authority, and sections on transportation, accessible tourist attractions, and suggested itineraries.

Finally, British Tourist Authority (see TOURIST INFORMATION, page 324) maintains a list of companies offering accessible tours.

MEMBERSHIPS AND DISCOUNT PASSES

Using passes and memberships can stretch your sightseeing budget. Throughout the guide, the initials "NT" or "EH" indicate that an attraction it is a National Trust or English Heritage property. For paid-up members of these organizations, entrance is free. **National Trust membership** is £28 a year (individual); details from National Trust ((020) 8315-1111, PO Box 39, Bromley BR1 1NH. **English Heritage membership** is £26 (individual); details from English Heritage Membership Department ((020) 7973-3000, PO Box 1BB, London W1A 1BB. You can visit their WEB SITES www .nationaltrust.org.uk; www.english-heritage .org.uk, for a complete list of properties. If you're interested English Heritage sites, the English Heritage Overseas Visitor Pass, which give you free entry into all EH properties for periods of one or two weeks, is a good choice.

Many travelers use the **Great British Heritage Pass**, which offers entry to 600 of Britain's abbeys, castles, gardens, mansions and palaces, including Windsor Castle, Hampton Court, Stonehenge, Warwick Castle and the Roman Baths and Pump Room at Bath. The pass is available in periods of seven days, 15 days or one month. It can be purchased outside of Britain or in the United Kingdom by holders of a foreign passport from The British Visitor Centre, Lower Regent Street, London W1; or Tourist Information Centres at airports, ports of entry, and major cities throughout England.

There are a number of discount schemes for **London**. The newest contender is the London Pass, available on line at WEB SITE www.londonpass.com or at the London Visitor Information Centre. It includes free admission to 40 points of interest, and free use of public transport. The jury is still out on whether this scheme really saves you money. **London for Less** is a slim guidebook (£12.95) that includes a discount card good for reduced rates at 45 London area attractions, as well as hotels, restaurants, shops and car rental agencies. It's available at bookstores or buy it on-line at WEB SITE www.for-less.com. The **GoSee Card** (formerly the White Card) WEB SITE www.london-gosee.com comes in periods of one, three or seven days, and includes free admission to 17 major London sights. It's available at museums and visitor centers.

Garden figures seem to flee the rain at Beaulieu Abbey, Hampshire.

ACCOMMODATION

It's a good idea to book ahead for accommodation in London. If you can reserve well in advance you'll have a better chance of securing a comfortable room in a quality establishment that doesn't overcharge.

Outside London, finding quality accommodation is a snap. There are B&Bs everywhere of every conceivable description, from simple bungalows with shared bath to luxurious converted farmhouses. Inns (pubs) often have rooms above the bar, some basic, some deluxe. And country house hotels offer rural idylls fit for a king.

Whether you should make reservations for accommodation outside London depends upon a number of factors. If you want a popular hotel or B&B during the high season, reservations will have to be made sometimes months in advance. However, if you prefer to keep your options open, even in summer, you can find satisfactory accommodation as you travel using the recommendations provided in this book as a starting point, or by taking advantage of the services of local tourist information centers where staff will be happy to reserve a place for you at your chosen destination. As a general rule, you should reserve by mid-morning for weekend nights.

Many, but not all, accommodations in England participate in the English Tourism Council's revamped and simplified **rating system**. The new system is based on overall quality rather than on a list of specific amenities as the old method was. Hotels are rated from one to five stars, and guest accommodations (i.e., guest houses, B&Bs, inns and farmhouses) are rated from ♦ to ♦♦♦♦ (one to five diamonds). You can find out all about what these ratings mean at the English Tourism Council's WEB SITE www.englishtourism.org.uk.

BED AND BREAKFAST

B&B accommodation is as varied as the personality of your hosts. National schemes for quality control mean that you are guaranteed a high level of cleanliness and certain amenities depending upon the rating (see above). While not all good B&Bs have ratings, all of the B&Bs that *are* rated can be relied upon for quality. Invariably, you'll find that your room has an electric kettle and the makings for tea, coffee and sometimes hot chocolate. As you move up the price scale, you may be treated to a bottle of mineral water, chocolates, and even cookies. Rooms without bath will generally have a tap and sink for washing up.

Farmstays have the added attraction of seeing the day-to-day goings on of a working farm. Bedrooms may be situated in the farmhouse, or in some cases, in renovated farm buildings. The

Farm Holiday Bureau ((01203) 696909 FAX (01203) 696630 WEB SITE www.farm-holidays.co.uk, maintains a list of 1,000 approved farms offering bed-and-breakfast or self-catering accommodation. A copy of their publication *Country Lodgings on a Budget* can be obtained from any British Tourist Authority overseas office (see TOURIST INFORMATION, page 324).

There are many B&B **booking agencies**. Among the longest-running is Bed and Breakfast (GB) TOLL-FREE IN THE UNITED STATES (800) 454-8704 FAX (01491) 410806 E-MAIL bookings@bedbreak .demon.co.uk WEB SITE www.bedbreak.com, with 17 years' experience. Prices start at US$33 per person in London and US$29 per person outside the capital. You can also find reams of B&B listings on the World Wide Web. Try, for example, The Great British Bed and Breakfast WEB SITE www.kgp-publishing.co.uk, which has hundreds of detailed listings.

APARTMENTS

In London, staying in an apartment can cut costs, though not all rental properties are in the inexpensive category. Staying in an apartment can be an attractive arrangement for families, since it means you won't have to rely on restaurants for every meal. **Agents** specializing in London apartment rentals include: London Connection ((801) 393-9120 TOLL-FREE (888) 393-9120 FAX (801) 393-3024 E-MAIL sales@londonconnection.com, 2342 Washington Boulevard, Ogden, Utah 84401; and Home from Home ((020) 7584-8914, 22A Gloucester Road, London, SW7 4RB.

ACCOMMODATION RATES

As **accommodation rates** change often, this guide relies on a set of price categories ranging from "rock-bottom" to "luxury." Since prices are higher in London than in the provinces, rates are grouped correspondingly. Prices listed below assume a double room, two-person occupancy during peak season, including VAT and English breakfast (except where otherwise noted in the text).
Luxury £250 and upwards
Very Expensive £130 to £249
Expensive £84 to £129
Moderate £55 to £84
Inexpensive £30 to £54
Rock-bottom less than £29

EATING OUT

Dining in Britain is no longer the ordeal it once was (see GALLOPING GOURMETS, page 57 in YOUR CHOICE). Still, quality is variable. It's best to use the recommendations provided in this book rather than taking the luck of the draw.

toilets are notoriously difficult to flush. Success usually arrives after several attempts.

Despite the contrariness of their toilets, restrooms (called "WCs," or "loos") are rarely difficult to find in England and are almost universally clean and well-stocked. If you are wondering where to find the "Loo of the Year" (three victories in a row!), you'll find it in the Church Close car park in Broadway, Worcestershire. Other super loos honored by this award — nominated by the toilet-going public for over a decade now — are those at Eurotunnel's main passenger terminal in Folkestone; Continental Ferry Port, Portsmouth; Cotswold Wildlife Park, Burford; and London's Hyde Park Corner.

away wherever you are staying (except when you are cashing traveler's checks).

Because of terrorist attacks in London in the past, security alarms go off occasionally. They're usually false alarms caused by unwitting passersby leaving bags or packages lying unattended. Always cooperate speedily, however, if you are asked to evacuate the area.

Public transportation in England is quite safe. Roads in the United Kingdom are excellent, though often overcrowded, especially in urban areas. Roadside assistance is readily available.

Drunk driving carries stiff penalties in the United Kingdom. The legal blood-alcohol limit for drivers is 80 mg per 100 milliliters.

SECURITY

According to the United States Embassy, "the United Kingdom benefits from generally low crime rates, and incidents of violent crime are rare." Tourists can reap those benefits with certain caveats. Be on guard against pickpockets and thefts of items left in parked cars. Pickpockets target tourist attractions and restaurants, as well as busy transportation points and unattended cars parked at tourist sites. As you might expect, urban areas have the highest incidence of theft. Even in remote rural areas, such as parts of Cornwall, you should always lock your car and avoid leaving valuables in plain view.

Wherever you travel, make sure your passport is safe. Unlike some other European countries, the United Kingdom does not require visitors to carry identity documents with them at all times. So leave your passport in a hotel safe or tucked securely

A final word: Nothing can prepare North Americans for the British motorist's utter disregard of pedestrians. Use extreme caution, and keep in mind the English saying: "If you break your leg crossing the road, don't come running to tell me about it!"

For police, fire or ambulance service, dial (999. This is a free call.

WHEN TO GO

The English climate is mild and temperate, with few extremes, rarely climbing above 90°F (32°C) or below freezing. There is no particular rainy season (it rains all year), but March and June are statistically the driest months. Southern England is drier, relatively speaking, than the northern

Fourteenth-century Old Wardour Castle, Wiltshire, provided the setting for Kevin Costner's *Robin Hood*.

regions. Cornwall is generally milder than the rest of the south, and the Isle of Wight is blessed with the most daylight hours.

Remember to take into account that England lies at a latitude roughly equivalent to Newfoundland. While the warm Gulf Stream keeps winters mild, daylight hours are scarce. Even in the deep south of Cornwall, January has a mere two hours of full daylight. On the flip side, England's summer months shine with daylight until 10:30 PM.

Christmas Day is not a good time to travel in England, unless you've been invited to someone's home. Just about everything is closed and Brits lock themselves up with their family to celebrate the season by the hearth. If you want a little more

breathing room when you come, remember that the largest wave of tourists washes up on Britain's shores between mid-April and mid-October, with another crest before Christmas — though the tide never truly ebbs. Stately homes and museums and some other tourist attractions in smaller towns or rural regions often close for the winter. Still, out-of-season travel in England has much to recommend it. Some of the most popular attractions are almost too mobbed to enjoy in the high season; and high prices come down, at least in January and February, when lots of other discounts should be available as well.

While in Britain you can get a **national weather forecast** by calling AA Weatherwatch ((0336) 401932 FAX (0336) 415701.

You'll want to factor in **public holidays** when planning your trip to England. Most banks and many stores, historic properties and other attractions

are closed on public holidays (though many museums open on bank holidays), and public transportation runs on a reduced schedule. However, in some cases, festivities and events surrounding holidays can add pleasure to your trip (see FESTIVE FLINGS, page 53 in YOUR CHOICE). Public holidays in England are as follows:

New Year's Day   1 January
Good Friday   Friday before Easter
Easter Monday   Monday after Easter
May Bank Holiday   First Monday in May
Spring Bank Holiday   Last Monday in May
Summer Bank Holiday   Last Monday in August
Christmas Day   25 December
Boxing Day   26 December

You might also want to take into account **school vacations**, especially if you are planning a trip to the seaside, or if you are interested in university accommodation (see page 328). The main summer vacation is from mid-July to early September. For the rest of the year, dates vary within regions, but in general there is a three-week vacation at Christmas and at Easter, plus a week in mid-October and in mid-February. Regional tourist boards (see under TOURIST INFORMATION, page 324 in this chapter) can provide details.

WHAT TO BRING

Don't plan to buy necessities in the United Kingdom; just about everything is more expensive here than in North America and many parts of mainland Europe. Bring what you need.

Apart from special occasions, evening wear is not especially formal in England. Some restaurants require "smart casual," but you will see a wide range of styles wherever you go. Some expensive restaurants have dress codes (e.g., a tie for men); they'll usually let you know this when you when you make your reservation.

For the rest, sturdy, hard-soled boots help shore up wobbly ankles for walking on cobblestones, gravel and other rough surfaces. A Swiss army knife is handy for picnicking.

PHOTOGRAPHY

Cities are perhaps the biggest challenge for photographers. How do you capture its essence in a handful of photographs? The skyline is a city's signature, and London's has become more interesting since the building of the London Eye, the gigantic space-age Ferris wheel. For ideas on vantage points (e.g., Parliament Hill in Hampstead Heath) check postcard racks, ask city tour guides, and hotel personnel or staff at the tourist office. For a night shot, a magenta filter will take the green cast out of the windows of office buildings (caused by fluorescent lighting). This filter also adds dramatic color to the night sky.

In London and elsewhere, a wide-angle lens is useful for shots of buildings, even one that borders the extreme, such as a 20 mm lens. Get a rotating "half-blue" filter to make gray British skies more appealing. 400-ISO films have improved enough over the last few years that you could consider using them exclusively, except for sunny days or at the beach.

It's not strictly necessary to carry heavy camera equipment, however. You might find yourself less fatigued and therefore more inspired carrying a compact camera with a zoom lens and a built-in flash.

GLOSSARY

For those used to American English, there are a few vocabulary differences that can be confusing. The following is a short glossary of some oft-misunderstood terms.

At the Hotel
En Suite   Private in-room bath
Engaged   Busy (telephone)
First floor   Second floor
Ground floor   First floor
Lift   Elevator
Way out   Exit

At the Restaurant
Aubergine   Eggplant
Barley wine   Extremely strong ale
Beetroot   Beets
Biscuits   Crackers
Bitter   Traditional dry ales, served warm
Broad beans   Similar to Lima beans
Chips   French fries
Cider   Alcoholic apple cider
Cockle   A type of small shellfish
Coffee, white   Coffee with cream
Courgette   Zucchini
Crisps   Potato chips
Crumpets   Light muffins
Cuppa   Cup of tea
Flan   Tart filled with fruit or custard
Fool   Pureed fruit with sugar and cream
Gammon   Lean bacon, usually boiled
Iced lolly   Popsicle
Jelly   Jell-O
Kippers   Small salted, smoked herrings
Lager   Equivalent to American beer
Licensed   Alcohol is served
Maize   Corn
Marrow   Squash
Mince   Ground beef
Pasty   Meat-filled pastry turnover
Plaice   Similar to sole
Porter   A weak stout
Public bar   Stand-up section of a pub
Real ale   Draft beer

Serviette   Table napkin
Shandy   Lemonade mixed with beer
Soda   Soda water only
Spotted Dick   Suet pudding with raisins or currants
Squash   Fruit-flavored drink
Stilton   A traditional blue cheese
Stout   Dark, heavy-bodied beer
Sultana   Raisin
Swede   Rutabaga, yellow turnip
Sweet, pudding   Dessert
Sweets   Candy
Toad-in-a-Hole   Sausage baked in batter
Treacle   Molasses
Trifle   Dessert made from sponge cake, jam,

wine, whipped cream and custard and jelly
Whiskey   Scotch Whisky

On the Road
Bobby   Policeman
Bonnet   Car hood
Boot   Car trunk
Bumper   Fender
Car hire   Car rental
Charabanc   Sight-seeing bus
Circus   Traffic circle or rotary
Coach   Long-distance bus
Dipped headlights   Low beams
Diversion   Detour
Double bend   S-curve
Dual carriage way   Divided highway
Flyover   Highway overpass

OPPOSITE: Canterbury Cathedral, Kent. ABOVE: On the soapbox, Speaker's Corner, London.

Give way   Yield
Handbrake   Parking brake
Hoarding   Billboard
Lorry   Truck
Manual gearbox   Stick shift
Motorway   Freeway
Number plate   License plate
Panda   Black and white police car
Pavement   Sidewalk
Pelican crossing   Pedestrian crossing with
flashing yellow lamp
Petrol   Gasoline
Road surface   Pavement
Roundabout   Traffic circle
Silencer   Car muffler

Sleeping policeman   Speed bump
Spanner   Wrench
Tip   Garbage dump
Verge   Road shoulder
Way out   Exit
Zebra crossing   Pedestrian crossing

Out and About
Bank holiday   Public holiday
Bank note   Paper money
Barrister   A lawyer who argues in court
Bathroom   Room with a tub or shower, but not
always a toilet
Bespoke   Custom-made
Biro   Ball-point pen
Brolly   Umbrella
Caravan   Camping trailer
Chemist shop   Drug store, pharmacy
Cloakroom   Restroom

Dear   Expensive
Drawing pin   Thumbtack
Dustbin   Trash can
Elastoplast   Band-aid
Fag   Cigarette
Flat   Apartment
Football   Soccer
Garden   Yard
Hoover   Vacuum cleaner
Ironmonger   Hardware store
Jumper   Pullover sweater
Lavatory   Bathroom
Left luggage   The baggage room
To let   For rent
Lift   Elevator
Loo   Toilet
Mackintosh, mac   Raincoat
Nappy   Diaper
Newsagent   Newsstand
Nought   In reference to numbers, zero
Off-license   Liquor store
Pillar box, Post-box   Mailbox
Plimsolls   Canvas sneakers
Pram (perambulator)   Baby carriage
Public school   Private school
Pushchair   Baby stroller
Queue   Line of people
Quid   Slang for a pound (£)
Redundant   Out of work, laid off
Ring up   To call on the telephone
Rubber   Eraser
Service flat   Rental apartment with cleaning
service
Single or return   One-way ticket or round-trip
Solicitor   A lawyer who works outside the
court room
Stalls   Orchestra seating
State School   Public school
Sticking plaster   Band-aid or adhesive tape
Subway   Pedestrian underpass
Surgery   A doctor's or dentist's office
Ta   Thanks
Tights   Pantyhose
Torch   flashlight
Trunk call   long distance
Tube   Subway
Twee   Cutesy
Underground   Subway
VAT   Value-added tax
Vest   Undershirt
Water closet, WC   Toilet
Wellingtons, wellies   Rubber boots
Windcheater   Windbreaker
Zed   The letter "Z"

WEB SITES

Britain is second only to the United States in the
sophistication and scope of its web sites. You'll find
many organizations, hotels, and tour operators

listed in this book on the World Wide Web. While some web sites are slow or obtuse, most are quite useful, allowing you to retrieve information quickly, make contact via e-mail directly from the site, receive regular updates on special deals, or even make a reservation. You'll find web sites listed throughout the book that I've found useful. The following additional sites offer essential information and pertinent services, as well as links to other web pages.

TRANSPORTATION

www.raileurope.com
Find a rail pass, plan your vacation, book on-line.

and games to choose from for very reasonable prices.
www.megalithic.co.uk
A pictorial guide to prehistoric sites in Britain.
www.regia.org
This site brings Anglo-Saxon, Norman and Mediaeval history to life.

TRAVEL IDEAS AND RESOURCES

www.thisislondon.com
The *Evening Standard* on-line has a guide to London, including articles on children's London, opinionated reviews of restaurants and cultural events, and more.

www.railtrack.co.uk
Speedy rail timetable inquiries.
http://bahn.hafas.de
Offers detailed rail schedules throughout Europe and Britain, but does not list fares for Britain. Comprehensive and easy to use.

PEOPLE AND CULTURE

www.royal.gov.uk
Everything (official) you ever wanted to know about the British monarchy.
www.number-10.gov.uk
Prime Minister Tony Blair's web site.
www.prairienet.org/britcom
British comedy.
www.informationfrombritain.com
The Foreign and Commonwealth Office's on-line publications shop. Scores of interesting titles, poster

www.britainexpress.com
An encyclopedic guide to Britain with destinations, accommodations, links, forums, and essays on obscure facets of British culture.
www.bt.com/phonenetuk
Need a phone or fax number in the United Kingdom that's not listed in this guide? Then you should go here.
www.meto.gov.uk
Wither the weather.
www.onlineweather.com
Another weather site.
www.oanda.com
On-line currency converter. Plug in your own currency against the pound and make a print-out for your wallet.

OPPOSITE: A Morris dancer entertains spectators in Devon. ABOVE: Internet café brings the world to Southampton, Hampshire.

OUTDOORS

www.countryside.gov.uk
The Countryside Agency oversees the United Kingdom's national trails. An excellent source of information on walking in England.
www.ramblers.org.uk
Another great resource for walkers. At the Ramblers Association web site you can order publications, such as their fact sheet on "Walking in Britain" or guides to scores of paths and areas.
www.greenscape.co.uk
Greenscape organize customized walking holidays and tours throughout Britain.

www.fatbirder.com
This well-organized site links up birding enthusiasts from all over the world — with comprehensive information on birding in the United Kingdom.

Recommended Reading

BAINBRIDGE, BERYL. *English Journey: Or the Road to Milton Keynes.* Carrol & Graf, 1997. A superbly written work retracing J.B. Priestley's classic travelogue (below).

BARNES, JULIAN. *Letters from London.* Vintage, 1995. This contemporary look at London is based on the author's columns for *The New Yorker.*

BRYSON, BILL. *Notes from a Small Island.* Doubleday, 1995. Hilarious and informative essays from the author's perspective as a long-time American expatriate.

DEFOE, DANIEL. *A Tour through the Whole Island of Great Britain.* 1724-6; Penguin, 1986. Dip into one of the world's first travel guidebooks for a perspective on how traveling in England has changed over the centuries.

HIBBERT, CHRISTOPHER. *The Story of England.* Phaidon, 1998. A concise illustrated overview of Britain's past.

HILLABY, JOHN. *Journey through Britain.* A blow-by-blow account of the author's end-to-end walk.

LEE, LAURIE. *Cider with Rosie.* Penguin, 1959. The author describes growing up in the Cotswolds between the wars, in prose saturated with gorgeous descriptions and fascinating anecdotes.

MORTON, H.V. *In Search of England.* 1927, out of print. A delightfully eccentric story of the author's 1920s motor tour of the island.

PRIESTLEY, J.B. *English Journey.* 1934, out of print. This curmudgeonly tale of the loss of the English countryside to encroaching industry is an English classic.

RABAN, JONATHAN. *Coasting.* Picador, 1986. In the 1980s, the author circumnavigated the coastline of Great Britain, writing this richly lyrical account of his trip.

STRONG, ROY. *The Story of Britain.* Pimlico, 1998. A comprehensive and highly readable tome with beautiful illustrations.

THEROUX, PAUL. *The Kingdom by the Sea.* Penguin, 1983. While Raban (above) was sailing the coast, this American writer walked and rode trains around Britain's shores , producing one of his best travelogues.

TOTH, SUSAN ALLEN. *My Love Affair with England* (Ballantine, 1992), *England for All Season's* (Ballantine, 1998) and *England As You Like It* (Ballantine, 1996). Carefully crafted essays on typical aspects of English life from an avowed anglophile.
The Traveller's History Series. Interlink Books. Popularly written titles are available for London (Richard Tames) as well as for the whole of England (Christopher Daniell).

Photo Credits

All photos by Nik Wheeler, except those on pages 95 and 104, taken by Alain Evrard.

The British Museum boasts bits of the Parthenon.

Travelers' Tips

Quick Reference A—Z°Guide
to Places and Topics of Interest with
Listed°Accommodation, Restaurants
and°Useful°Telephone Numbers

The symbols Ⓕ FAX Ⓣ TOLL-FREE Ⓔ E-MAIL Ⓦ WEB SITE refer to additional contact information found in the chapter listings.

A **Abbotsbury** *247*
accommodation
Abbey House ℂ (01305) 871330 Ⓕ *247*
Ilchester Arms ℂ (01305) 871243 Ⓔ *247*
attractions
Abbotsbury Swannery
ℂ (01305) 871858 Ⓦ *247*
St. Catherine's Chapel *247*
Subtropical Gardens ℂ (01305) 871387 *247*
Tithe Barn ℂ (01305) 871817 *247*
general information
tourist information point *247*
pubs
Ilchester Arms ℂ (01305) 871243 Ⓔ *247*
accommodation *36, 328*
accommodation services 40
Country House Association
ℂ (01869) 812800 *40*
Landmark Trust ℂ (01628) 825925 Ⓕ
U.S. ℂ (802) 254-6868 *39*
National Trust Holiday Cottages
ℂ (01225) 791199 *40*
Pride of Britain group ℂ (01264) 324400 *41*
apartments 328
Home from Home ℂ (020) 7584-8914 *328*
London Connection
ℂ (801) 393-9120 Ⓣ Ⓕ Ⓔ *328*
bed and breakfasts and farmstays 328
B&B booking agencies *328*
Farm Holiday Bureau
ℂ (01203) 696909 Ⓕ Ⓦ *328*
Great British Bed and Breakfast Ⓦ *328*
Benedictine monasteries 36
British Universities Accommodation
Consortium Ⓦ *36*
camping 36
Forestry Commission ℂ (0131) 334-0303 Ⓕ *36*
Tent City, London
(020) 8985-7656 Ⓕ Ⓔ Ⓦ *36*
caravans 36
homestays 62
Parish Holidays ℂ (01256) 895966 Ⓕ *62*
Servas US ℂ (212) 267-0252 Ⓕ Ⓔ Ⓦ *62*
rating systems 328
youth hostels 36
Backpackers Britain Ⓦ *36*
Youth Hostel Association
ℂ (01727) 845047 Ⓔ Ⓦ *36*
airports *See* getting to Southern England
Aldbury *145*
Alfred the Great *72, 228*
Alfriston *212, 214*
access 214
accommodation
Riverdale House ℂ (01323) 871038 *213*
Star ℂ (01323) 870495 *213*
YHA Alfriston ℂ (01323) 442667 *213*

attractions
Berwick Church *212*
Charleston Farmhouse ℂ (01273) 811265 *212*
Clergy House (NT) ℂ (01323) 870001 *212*
Frog Firle Farm (NT) *213*
Long Man of Wilmington *213*
Middle Farm ℂ (01273) 811411 *212*
parish church *212*
Tye green *212*
environs
Seven Sisters Country Park
ℂ (01323) 870280 *214*
Seven Sisters Sheep Centre ℂ (01323) 423302 *214*
general information
Cuckmere Cycle Company
ℂ (01323) 870310 Ⓔ *214*
pubs
Cricketer's Arms ℂ (01323) 870469 *214*
Star ℂ (01323) 870495 *213*
Ye Olde Smuggler's Inne ℂ (01323) 870241 *213*
restaurants
Moonrakers ℂ (01323) 870472 *213*
Singing Kettle *213*
Appledore *205, 206*
accommodation
Park Farm Barn ℂ/FAX (01233) 758159 *206*
restaurants
Appledore Tea Room ℂ (01233) 758272 *205*
shopping
High Class Junk antiques *205*
arriving in Southern England
See getting to Southern England
Arundel *220, 222*
access 222
accommodation
Amberley Castle ℂ (01798) 831992 *40, 221*
Arundel Youth Hostel ℂ (01903) 882204 Ⓕ *221*
Dukes Hotel ℂ (01903) 883847 *221*
attractions
Arundel Castle ℂ (01903) 883136 *220*
Fitzalan Chapel *221*
Slindon Estate (NT) ℂ (01243) 814484 *221*
St. Nicholas Church *220*
Wildfowl and Wetlands ℂ (01903) 883355 *221*
general information
Skylark Cruises ℂ (0378) 438166 *221*
Tourist Information Centre
ℂ (01903) 882268 Ⓕ *220*
history 220
restaurants
Fleur de Sel ℂ (01903) 742331 *221*
Pizza Express ℂ (01903) 885467 *221*
Queen's Room, Amberley Castle
ℂ (01798) 831992 *40, 221*
Ashdown Forest *209*
accommodation
Ashdown Park Hotel
ℂ (01342) 824988 Ⓕ Ⓔ *210*

The symbols Ⓕ FAX Ⓣ TOLL-FREE Ⓔ E-MAIL Ⓦ WEB SITE *refer to additional contact information found in the chapter listings.*

345

The symbols Ⓕ FAX Ⓣ TOLL-FREE Ⓔ E-MAIL Ⓦ WEB SITE *refer to additional contact information found in the chapter listings.*

347

The symbols Ⓕ FAX Ⓣ TOLL-FREE Ⓔ E-MAIL Ⓦ WEB SITE refer to additional contact information found in the chapter listings.

353

The symbols Ⓕ FAX Ⓣ TOLL-FREE Ⓔ E-MAIL Ⓦ WEB SITE *refer to additional contact information found in the chapter listings.*

355

The symbols Ⓕ FAX Ⓣ TOLL-FREE Ⓔ E-MAIL Ⓦ WEB SITE *refer to additional contact information found in the chapter listings.*

359

Polperro *298*
attractions
  coastal walk *298*
general information
  guided walks *298*
  pleasure boat trips *298*
restaurants
  Kitchen **(** (01503) 72788 *298*
  Three Pilchards **(** (01503) 72233 *298*
Poole *244, 246*
access *246*
accommodation
  Mansion House **(** (01202) 685666 Ⓕ *245*
attractions
  Poole Pottery **(** (01202) 666200 *245*
  Waterfront Museum **(** (01202) 683138 *245*
environs
  Brownsea Island (NT) **(** (01202) 707444 *245*
restaurants
  Upstairs at the Custom House
    ((01202) 676767 *246*
Porlock *275*
accommodation
  Clements Cottage **(** (01643) 703970 *276*
  Cloutsham Farm **(** (01643) 862839 *276*
  Porlock Vale House **(** (01643) 862338 Ⓕ Ⓔ *276*
general information
  Burrowhayes Farm Riding Stables
    ((01643) 862463 *276*
  Tourist Information Centre
    ((01643) 863150 Ⓕ *276*
Port Isaac *285*
accommodation
  Birdcage *285*
Porthcurno *33, 317*
attractions
  Minack Theatre **(** (01736) 810181 *33, 317*
  Museum of Submarine Telegraphy
    ((01736) 810966 *317*
Portloe *See* Veryan
Portsmouth *228, 231, 232, 233*
access *233*
accommodation
  Elms Guest House **(** (023) 9282-3924 Ⓕ Ⓔ *233*
  Fortitude Cottage **(** (023) 9282-3748 *232*
  Portsmouth and Southsea Backpackers
    Hostel **(** /FAX (023) 9283-2495 *233*
  Portsmouth Youth Hostel
    ((023) 9237-5661 Ⓕ Ⓔ *233*
  Sally Port **(** (023) 9282-1860 *232*
attractions
  Admiral Nelson's HMS Victory, Flagship
    Portsmouth *232*
  Charles Dickens' Birthplace Museum
    ((023) 9282-7261 *232*
  Clarence Pier *232*
  D-Day Museum **(** (023) 9282-7261 *232*
  Flagship Portsmouth **(** (023) 9283-9766
    or 24-hour information
    ((023) 9286-1512 Ⓦ *231, 232*
  Mary Rose Ship Hall and Museum *232*
  Royal Naval Museum, Flagship
    Portsmouth *231*
  Sea Life Centre **(** (023) 9273-4461 *232*
  Southsea Castle *232*
festivals and special events
  Lord Mayor's Show (May) 1 *231*
  Portsmouth and Southsea Show
    (August) *231*

general information
  bus and boat tours *231*
  Tourist Information Centre
    ((023) 9282-6722 Ⓕ *231*
restaurants
  Bistro Montparnasse
    ((023) 9281-6754 *233*
  Rosie's Vineyard **(** (023) 9275-5944 *233*
  Sally Port **(** (023) 9282-1860 *232*
  Snookies **(** (023) 9282-5821 *233*
  Wine Vaults **(** (023) 9286-4712 *233*
postal services *331*
public holidays *334*
Purbeck, Isle of *228, 244, 246, 247*
attractions
  Corfe Castle (NT) **(** (01929) 481294 *246*
  Lulworth Cove Lulworth Cove *247*
  Studland Beach and Nature Reserve (NT)
    ((01929) 450259 *247*
  village of Corfe Castle *247*
general information
  Tourist Information Centre
    ((01929) 552740 *246*
Purbeck Peninsula *228*

Q **Queen Elizabeth I** *69, 75, 76, 132, 141, 143,
     184, 202, 260*
     Queen Elizabeth II *60, 69, 79, 98, 128*
     Queen Victoria *77, 100, 237*

R **Rack Isle** *151*
   religion *75, 76*
   restaurants *328*
     restaurant prices *329*
   Richmond Park ((020) 8948-3209 *110*
   Ringlestone Hamlet
   accommodation
     Ringlestone **(** (01622) 859900 *203*
   pubs
     Ringlestone **(** (01622) 859900 *203*
   River Avon *22, 259, 260, 261, 266, 272, 292*
   Rogers, Richard *88*
   Rolling Stones, The *79*
   Roman conquest *72*
   Romans *72, 82, 141*
   Romney Marsh *205, 206*
   attractions
     churches *205*
     Royal Military Canal *205*
   general information
     Romney Marsh Cycle Tours
       ((01308) 875296 *206*
     Tourist Information Centre
       ((01303) 267799 *205*
   Roseland Peninsula *300, 301, 302, 303*
   access *300*
   accommodation
     National Trust Holiday Cottage Booking
       Office **(** (01225) 791199 Ⓕ *300*
     Officers' Quarters, St. Anthony Head *301*
     Roseland Holiday Cottages
       ((01872) 580480 *300*
   general information
     King Harry Ferry **(** (01872) 863312 *300*
   rugby *30*
   Rye *206, 207, 208*
   access *208*
   accommodation
     Jeake's House **(** (01797) 222828 Ⓕ Ⓔ *207*

The symbols Ⓕ FAX Ⓣ TOLL-FREE Ⓔ E-MAIL Ⓦ WEB SITE *refer to additional contact information found in the chapter listings.*

363

The symbols Ⓕ *FAX* Ⓣ *TOLL-FREE* Ⓔ *E-MAIL* Ⓦ *WEB SITE refer to additional contact information found in the chapter listings.*

365

The symbols Ⓕ FAX, Ⓣ TOLL-FREE, Ⓔ E-MAIL, Ⓦ WEB-SITE refer to additional contact information found in the chapter listings.

368

The symbols ⓕ FAX ⓣ TOLL-FREE ⓔ E-MAIL ⓦ WEB SITE refer to additional contact information found in the chapter listings.

367